ALSO BY SELINA HASTINGS

Nancy Mitford
Evelyn Waugh
Rosamond Lehmann
The Secret Lives of Somerset Maugham
The Red Earl

SYBILLE BEDFORD

SYBILLE BEDFORD

— A LIFE —

Selina Hastings

ALFRED A. KNOPF New York
2021

THIS IS A BORZOI BOOK
PUBLISHED BY ALFRED A. KNOPF

Copyright © 2020 by Selina Hastings

All rights reserved. Published in the United States by Alfred A. Knopf,
a division of Penguin Random House LLC, New York. Originally published
in Great Britain by Chatto & Windus, an imprint of Vintage,
a division of Penguin Random House Ltd, London, in 2020.

www.aaknopf.com

Knopf, Borzoi Books, and the colophon are
registered trademarks of Penguin Random House LLC.

Library of Congress Cataloging-in-Publication Data
Names: Hastings, Selina, author.
Title: Sybille Bedford : a life / Selina Hastings.
Description: London ; New York : Chatto & Windus, 2020. |
Includes bibliographical references and index. |
Identifiers: LCCN 2020019903 (print) | LCCN 2020019904 (ebook) |
ISBN 9781101947913 (hardcover) | ISBN 9781101947920 (ebook)
Subjects: LCSH: Bedford, Sybille, 1911–2006. | Authors, English—20th century—
Biography. | Women authors, English—20th century—Biography.
Classification: LCC PR6052.E3112 Z68 2020 (print) |
LCC PR6052.E3112 (ebook) | DDC 823/.914—dc23
LC record available at https://lccn.loc.gov/2020019903
LC ebook record available at https://lccn.loc.gov/2020019904

Jacket photograph by Lord Snowdon / Trunk Archive
Jacket design by Chip Kidd

Manufactured in the United States of America
First United States Edition

FRONTISPIECE: Aldous Huxley, Sybille Bedford (center),
and Eva Hermann on the beach, Sanary-sur-Mer, ca. 1931

To Julie Kavanagh
with gratitude and love

CONTENTS

PREFACE

"I wish I'd written more books and spent less time being in love," Sybille Bedford said once in an interview. "It's very difficult doing both at the same time." Certainly, from adolescence until well into old age, there was rarely a period when Sybille was not in love, some of her relationships long-lasting and profound, others little more than temporary infatuations. With one exception her affairs were with women, her remarkable talent for friendship ensuring that she always remained on good terms with her lovers, as is clear from the enormous volume of correspondence which fortunately still survives. Over many decades Sybille wrote hundreds of letters detailing not only her affairs but also her travels, her domestic life, her passion for good food and wine, the people she knew, the houses she lived in, and—crucially—the enervating struggles she experienced with her work. For her ambition had always been to write.

In her twenties, and under the influence of her friend and mentor Aldous Huxley, whose fiction in those early days she uncritically admired, she completed three novels, none of which was ever published. "I think as far as writing was concerned," she was later to say, Aldous "was rather a hindrance because I admired him as a writer . . . and I wanted to write like him, which of course didn't work at all." Indeed it was not until 1956, when Sybille was in her forties, that a novel of hers first appeared. *A Legacy* was widely acclaimed on both sides of the Atlantic—Evelyn Waugh was among many who enthusiastically praised it—and from then on her position as a distinguished member of the literary profession was established.

Sybille grew up in Germany during the early years of the twentieth century, her childhood both intellectually inspirational and at the same time emotionally deprived. The most influential figure in her life was her mother, who while regarding her with benign indifference also provided much of the motivation for Sybille's later career as a writer. Elisabeth ("Lisa") Bernhardt, clever, beautiful and irrepressibly self-centred, was widely read in English, French and German; convinced that she was possessed of a remarkable literary talent, she intended one day to produce a work that would win her acclaim throughout the cultural salons of Europe. Although such a masterpiece never materialised, nonetheless it was Lisa who from Sybille's earliest years encouraged her to read, and inspired in her the immutable desire to become a writer. Years later, Sybille said of her, "My mother wanted to be a writer. Like me she suffered from sloth and distractions . . . but I grew up in such an atmosphere of books and writers that it was like a vocation."

Throughout Sybille's long life there were indeed numerous distractions, her often turbulent private life, her acute interest in so many aspects of the world around her, frequently preventing her from concentrating on her work. From earliest childhood into old age she was constantly on the move, uprooting over the years from one location to another, from Germany to France, England, Italy and the United States. Restless and energetic, she was full of curiosity and loved to explore, writing articles about her travels in Portugal and Switzerland, Denmark and Yugoslavia, Italy and France, as well as an enchantingly idiosyncratic book about the months she spent in Mexico immediately after the war. In her early years, she was adventurous and brave, enjoying long journeys driving alone across Europe, but as time passed and the insecurities implanted in childhood began to surface, she grew increasingly apprehensive and afraid. In later life Sybille made sure she never travelled without a companion, habitually suffering from acute anxiety, terrified that the train would be late, the taxi fail to arrive, the plane fall from the sky.

In both Europe and America, Sybille was to become part of an extensive network of writers and intellectuals, most of them women, many lesbian like herself, who decade after decade recorded in their copious correspondence the details of their daily lives, their affairs with each other, the jealous scenes, betrayals and passionate infatuations. Many, like Sybille, were married, and although on the whole discreet when in the wider world, unlike their male counterparts they had little reason to conceal their predilections. While in Britain for most of the twentieth century male homosexual practice was illegal, women were free to do as they pleased, and despite the occasional moral outburst—Edgar Wallace in the *Daily Mail* referring to lesbianism as "a vicious cult," the *Sunday Express* demanding the suppression of Radclyffe Hall's novel, *The Well of Loneliness*—the subject attracted little interest in society as a whole.

Sybille, nonetheless, had a strong desire for discretion, a profound reluctance, except when with her inner circle, to reveal the nature of her private life. When at one point she was offered an introduction to a distinguished literary agent in Paris, a woman who lived with an English girlfriend, she instantly turned it down. "I will not <u>choose</u> a Lesbian agent. I can't bear this girlery and cliquerie. One's tastes are private. It's bad enough (in some ways) to be oneself." When in her seventies she was asked to address the Oxford University Gay Society, a large "NO" was scrawled across the invitation. Interestingly, although she had numerous infatuations and affairs, the first as a young girl, the last when in her nineties, in only one of her novels does she write of a physical relationship between women.

Writing, her identity as a writer, was always of supreme importance to Sybille, although she constantly berated herself for not working harder, for failing to produce more. "[I'm] always putting off everything . . . wanting to write, and then, for long, long wasted periods, not writing," she complained. A gifted linguist, fluent in three languages, Sybille decided early on to write in English: "the English language is one of most marvellous instruments there is," as she stated more than once. Yet part of the powerful attraction of her prose comes from a profoundly European sensibility, the worlds she creates elusive yet concise, familiar yet intriguingly different. Her range was wide. Over time she produced two books and several articles on legal process, a subject that had always fascinated her, covering some of the most famous cases of the era, among them the trial of Bodkin Adams, of Jack Ruby, the *Lady Chatterley* trial, and also the Auschwitz trial, during which twenty-two former guards at the camp faced accusations of murder. As well as her book on Mexico, *A Visit to Don Otavio*, she wrote vivid and highly personal accounts of her travels in Europe; she undertook one biography, of her friend, Aldous Huxley; and at the very end of her life completed a personal memoir, *Quicksands*.

Yet the most widely read and admired of Sybille's works have always been two of her four novels, the first, *A Legacy*, published in 1956, and the last, *Jigsaw*, which appeared over three decades later, in 1989. Both narratives are deeply rooted in her family history and in her own early years, drawing on the extraordinary and often harrowing events of her peripatetic childhood and youth, memories which were to remain embedded deeply within her and to provide her with inspiration for the rest of her life.

SYBILLE BEDFORD

ONE

LISA AND "*LE BEAU MAX*"

Although Sybille Bedford wrote always in English, in fact she was German. Born in Berlin on 16 March 1911, Sybille was the child of a hopelessly incompatible couple. Her father was an eccentric Bavarian baron, passive and remote, who much preferred the company of animals to people, while her mother, daughter of a wealthy merchant from Hamburg, was energetic, fiercely intelligent and very beautiful, always avid for masculine attention. Maximilian von Schoenebeck and Elisabeth ("Lisa") Bernhardt met in Berlin; Schoenebeck, recently widowed and in search of a new wife, proposed, and Lisa, recovering from a failed affair, unwisely accepted. They were married in April 1910, and less than a year later their only child was born. For both parents Sybille's arrival was regarded as a serious disappointment, for Maximilian because he had hoped for a son, and for Lisa because it barred the way out from a marriage she was by now desperate to escape.

Sybille's memories of her early childhood were of an almost idyllic period, living with her parents in a fine country house with garden and orchard, days spent playing in a sunny nursery or outside romping with a large pack of good-natured dogs. It was not long, however, before she began to sense the tensions that existed between her parents, and over time to learn of the dramas, and in her father's case, the scandals and tragedies of his earlier life. The age difference between her parents was considerable, Maximilian forty-six when he married, Lisa twenty years younger, and although Lisa knew something of her husband's history there were certain episodes of which he never spoke, one scandal in particular only discovered by his horrified daughter in her extreme old age.

The Schoenebecks, Roman Catholic and members of the minor aristocracy, were originally from Westphalia, but since the early nineteenth century had been settled at Neuburg am Rhein, close to the border with France in what was then the Kingdom of Bavaria. A family of local bureaucrats and officials, they had been ennobled in 1825, granted the title of *Freiherr*, or baron. By inclination the family had looked always towards France, and when among themselves preferred to speak French rather than German. As the century progressed they did their best to ignore the increasing power of Prussia, which they regarded as a barbarous menace, appalled when in 1871, after the defeat of France in the Franco-Prussian War, the unification of Germany was ratified at Versailles and Wilhelm I of Prussia declared the German emperor.

Sybille's father was the second of five boys. His father, Daniel August von Schoenebeck, was a district judge in the city of Karlsruhe, only a few kilometres from the family's small estate at Neuburg. His mother, Ida Johanna Himbsel, was the daughter of a famous engineer, Ulrich Himbsel, who built one of the earliest railways, from Munich to Starnberg, and established the first steamship service on the Starnberger See.

Maximilian was born on 22 July 1863. His was by all accounts a happy childhood. At Neuburg the family inhabited a pleasant manor house set in a sheltered valley and surrounded by farmland. Max's boyhood memories were of a rural idyll, of apricots ripening on the wall, of dogs and ducks and horses, "and the smell of seasons . . . of winter honey, walnuts and March wool, of the pig killed at Michaelmas and Easter, and the hams baked whole inside a loaf of bread." Daniel August, Max's father, was good-natured, easy-going and allowed his sons to do very much as they pleased. He was also a notable gourmet, author of a slim brochure entitled *Quelques Remarques sur la Théorie du Braisage des Mets* ("Some Remarks on the Theory of Braising"), dedicated to the great French chef Carême. As might be expected, the family cuisine was of an unusually high standard, with plentiful supplies of fruit and vegetables, mutton and beef from the home farm, freshwater fish, and during the shooting season generous supplies of game.

Maximilian was a handsome boy, tall and dark-haired, with a gentle, dreamy nature. He and his four brothers were tutored at home before being sent for a short period to a Jesuit seminary. Uninterested in either books or music, Max preferred his own company to that of others; he loved animals, and kept not only dogs and cats but geese and a tame raven. As a very young man he discovered a passion for antique furniture and *objets d'art,* and true to family tradition he developed a profound love for France and in particular for French wines and cuisine. Under his father's tutelage he learned how to cook, creating exquisite little dishes over a small spirit lamp purchased for the purpose. As he grew older and began to travel Max indulged in a rather less harmless pursuit, gambling, a hobby extensively pursued in the casinos of Paris and Monte Carlo. Although he had few close men friends, Max had a weakness for beautiful women, whom he effortlessly beguiled with his elegance, good looks and courteous manner; when in their company he appeared happy and animated, and during his twenties and thirties he had many liaisons, which he conducted with refinement and politesse, frequently infatuated, never in love.

Solitary by nature, indifferent to current affairs and lacking in any kind of professional ambition, Max was nonetheless obliged to earn his living. His father's estate was not large, there were five sons to support, and thus as a young man Max found himself following two of his brothers into the army. By temperament wholly unsuited to such a career, he nonetheless remained with the military until well into middle age, during which time he was severely damaged by two appalling experiences. One escalated into a notorious scandal, widely reported both in Germany and abroad, while the other remained almost completely buried until many years after his death.

Despite the Schoenebecks' entrenched hostility to Prussia, it was a Prussian cavalry regiment, the 9th Hannover Dragoon Guards, that Max aged twenty joined as a second lieutenant in 1883. At the period when Max enlisted, the Hannover Dragoons were stationed at Metz on the French border, and a photograph taken at this period shows Max standing very upright, immaculate in his uniform, yet despite the gold braid and bristling, bushy moustache, he has a look of apprehension in his eyes, the expression of a man who is lost.

Unlike his brothers, Max had no wish to make the army a full-time career, electing instead to join the reserves. In peacetime, reserve officers were required to spend only twelve months with their regiment every three years, and later every four or five years. After his service with the Dragoon Guards, Max transferred to the 10th Magdeburg Hussars, then to the 3rd Baden Dragoons, from which he finally retired in 1909 at the age of forty-six with an army pension and the rank of major.

The long intervals between periods of military duty Max spent mainly abroad. In 1886, when he was twenty-three, his father died, leaving him a modest legacy, which at first appeared sufficient to support his somewhat aimless peregrinations. This rather withdrawn young man, given to periods of depression, "an innocent eccentric," as his daughter later described him, spent months at a time in Spain, lived for a while on Corsica, and rented remote villas in unfashionable parts of the Côte d'Azur. He soon assembled a menagerie that included a lemur and a family of chimpanzees which he treated almost as his children. He loved to draw and to paint, and indulged his long-standing passion for collecting porcelain and antique furniture, spending hours wandering through antiques shops in little towns, talking to dealers and buying quantities of ancient bric-a-brac. By now a sophisticated gourmet, he took pleasure in exploring the local markets, examining with great concentration the displays of fruit and vegetables, fresh fish, game and country cheeses. Unfortunately, however, this agreeable existence was not to last. Impractical and naive, wholly ignorant of the value of money, Max soon found he had spent almost his entire inheritance, leaving him with no choice but to find a rich wife.

Baron Maximilian von Schoenebeck, "*le beau Max*," soon became a familiar figure in fashionable Paris restaurants as well as at the gaming tables of Nice, Menton, Cannes and Monte Carlo, where he regularly lost large sums at baccarat and roulette. France was always the country he loved above any other, and it was in the French demi-monde where he felt most at home. Of his many mistresses Max asked only that they be chic, placid in temperament and well mannered; intelligence was never a requirement. Generous with presents and unfailingly polite, he always maintained amicable relations with the old mistress even as he was beginning negotiations with the new.

In 1893 Max, now aged thirty, was again on leave from the army, currently in pursuit of an English heiress. This was a period when relations between France and Germany were dangerously strained, with intense resentment on the part of France over the German annexation of Alsace-Lorraine, while the Germans had been seriously alarmed by the recent Franco-Russian rapprochement. A new military attaché, Colonel Maximilian von Schwartzkoppen, had been sent to Paris from Berlin, and under his regime an extensive intelligence network had been established. Numerous purloined letters, military documents and maps of French fortifications were regularly delivered to Schwartzkoppen's office, supplied both by French and German agents, including civil servants and members of both countries' armed forces. Max was one of the serving officers involved, and his activities were shortly to lead him into serious trouble.

While in Paris at the end of the summer, Max was befriended by a French journalist, M. P. Durville. Durville was an expert on military affairs, having served in the French army and survived the terrible siege of Metz in 1870, which had left him with a profound loathing for Germans and Germany. Now, during this period of increasingly strained relations between the two countries, he was on the alert for any sign of espionage and double-dealing, and during his conversations with Schoenebeck began to see an irresistible opportunity. As Max began to confide his anxieties—his desperate need of money to finance the wooing of his wealthy heiress—Durville appeared sympathetic, promoting himself as pro-German and promising to do what he could to help. Before long Durville had persuaded Max to take part in a fake operation, passing on to German intelligence detailed maps and drawings of French fortifications near the eastern frontier. It was arranged that Max should collect these documents from Durville's office on 7 November. Six days later he was arrested and brought to trial the following month. Found guilty, Max was sentenced to five years, later reduced to three, in the Conciergerie, the infamous dungeon on the Île-de-la-Cité, where during the Reign of Terror Marie Antoinette, among thousands of others, had been incarcerated.

As Max was neither a high-ranking officer nor a notable society figure the story attracted little attention at the time. A year later, however, with the sudden explosive impact of the Dreyfus case—Dreyfus also accused, wrongly as it turned out, of spying for the Germans—Max's treachery briefly became front-page news. The Paris paper *La Presse* triumphantly headlined the story "*Un Espion Allemand en Correctionnelle. Comment Schoenebeck a été arrêté—Révélations sensationnelles*" ("A German spy in court. How Schoenebeck was arrested—Sensational revelations"), running a lengthy interview with Durville, who provided a detailed account of Schoenebeck's duplicity.

Fortunately, the case made little impact in Germany. Apart from his immediate family, and of course the German military, few were aware of Schoenebeck's fate. In later life he himself never spoke of it, and Sybille knew nothing about it until at the age of eighty-seven she was contacted by a historian in Freiburg who had been researching the story. The information shocked and appalled her. "Your letter has distressed me very much," she wrote. "My father a prisoner of France? Three years in the Conciergerie? To me, it comes like a delayed bombshell." No one in the family had ever mentioned such an event, she continued. "The idea that my father should have been as much as suspected of having spied against France, is very painful to me . . . My father, as I see him, as I remember him, <u>loved</u> France, was, as I became, an extreme Francophile."

At first she was mystified, but gradually certain memories from her distant childhood began to surface. One day, Sybille recalled, Max had been showing her some drawings he had made. "We leafed through an old sketchbook of his—which may have contained a sketch of barred windows and sketches of a turreted building: 'That was when I was in the Conciergerie.' Or words to that effect. No comment. No show of feeling. No narrative. To me, it felt gloomy if romantic, and as real or unreal as his other tales . . . I just took them in as a child will: tales in books, tales of life."

Immediately after his release from prison Max left for Germany, where his return was welcomed by his regiment. Far from a disgrace, his sentence was regarded simply as an unfortunate consequence of his honourable activities in the service of his country, and shortly after his return to the Dragoons he was rewarded with promotion to first lieutenant. In July 1898 he retired from active service, after which he moved to Berlin. Three months later he was married.

Berlin at the turn of the century was a rapidly spreading metropolis, with a population growing at a greater rate than anywhere else in Europe. From Prussian capital to the capital of the German Empire, Berlin had expanded into a great modern city, flourishing, in Sybille's words, on "a tide of big money, big enterprise, big building, big ideas." Now there was an extensive network of broad streets, with handsome department stores, modern theatres and fashionable restaurants. There was a transport system with not only horse-drawn trams but an elevated railway, the Ringbahn, and throughout the city a number of spacious public gardens—the Tiergarten, the Charlottenburg gardens, the Bellevuepark. There was a thriving financial and industrial centre, with new offices, public buildings and apartment blocks rising in almost every district. Most impressive was the wide and magnificent avenue of Unter den Linden, down which the resplendently uniformed Kaiser could often be seen riding at the head of a glitteringly accoutred troop of guards.

One of the fastest-growing sections of society in Berlin was Jewish, with a population four times larger than anywhere else in the country. Due to the current period of prosperity much of the previously pervasive atmosphere of anti-Semitism had subsided. This wealthy and rapidly expanding Jewish community included a large number of assimilationist families, either with no religious faith or who were converts to Christianity, many of them regarded as an influential if slightly ambiguous elite, "*ni Gotha, ni ghetto*" ("neither from the *Gotha* [the directory of European princely and ducal families] nor from the ghetto"). There was a strong Jewish presence not only in banking and commerce but also in journalism, publishing, medicine and the law; and it was during this period that many of the most affluent Jewish families began marrying into the Christian aristocracy and the *haute bourgeoisie*.

For Maximilian von Schoenebeck, thirty-five and financially insecure, the prospect of such a match appeared irresistible. Soon after arriving in Berlin he met and quickly became engaged to Melanie Herz, the twenty-seven-year-old daughter of Hermann Herz, a prosperous

Jewish industrialist. The Herzes inhabited an imposing three-storey mansion on Voss Strasse, close to the Potsdamer Platz and backing onto the Imperial Chancellery. Wealthy manufacturers, part of a vanguard of assimilated Jewish businessmen, they were closely connected to some of the big banking families, to the Mendelssohns, Schwabachs and Bleichröders. One of their most notable forebears was the celebrated Henriette Herz, who in her Berlin salon had entertained such cultural celebrities as Goethe and Mirabeau, Schiller and Mme. de Genlis. This glamorous cultural background, however, held little significance for the next generation, who inhabited an altogether different environment. As Sybille was to describe them, the Herzes "had no interests, tastes or thoughts beyond their family and the comfort of their persons. While members of what might have been their world were dining to the sounds of Schubert and of Haydn, endowing research and adding Corot landscapes to their Bouchers and the Delacroix . . . [the Herzes] were adding bell-pulls and thickening the upholstery."

Hermann Herz's father had originally made his fortune running an oil mill at Wittenberg on the banks of the Elbe, a business that had rapidly expanded, by the 1860s becoming a global industrial concern and diversifying in a number of directions. Not long after Max married into the family, the Herzes' already substantial fortune exponentially increased with the development of a specialist detergent, "Schwarze Wäsche," or "Black Wash." The firm had been working for years on the difficult problem of effectively laundering black cloth, until finally, and with almost miraculous good timing, the new product was launched in January 1901, only days before the death of Queen Victoria. With the consequent massive demand for mourning that resulted, "Schwarze Wäsche" became a phenomenal bestseller.

Unlike many Jewish families of their social standing, the Herzes had not become Christian; in fact they had little religious faith of any kind, and certainly no objection to their daughter's engagement to Baron Schoenebeck, readily agreeing to her conversion to Catholicism. Melanie was provided with a handsome dowry, and the two were married in Berlin on 17 October 1898.

After the wedding the couple left Berlin to live in Spain, in a rented villa with a large garden near Granada. Here Max continued to follow the life he had led since boyhood, buying antique furniture and spending much of his time with his beloved menagerie. Within only a few months, Melanie became pregnant, and on 19 July 1899 gave birth to a daughter, Maximiliane Henriette Ida. Six years later Melanie died of tuberculosis, leaving Max alone, with a small child on his hands. Unable to cope, he returned briefly to Berlin, where he left the little girl in the care of her Herz grandparents, while he returned, no doubt with relief, to a peripatetic and often solitary existence abroad, supported by a generous income provided by the Herzes. For the next couple of years he was able to continue much as before, alternating between rural solitude and the pleasures of the town, indulging in numerous affairs and heedlessly gambling away his annual income. It was three years after Melanie's death that Max met the woman who was to become his second wife.

Lisa Bernhardt, charming, beautiful and rich, seemed to have all the qualities Max required. Recently Lisa had broken off an affair with a married man, whose wife had reportedly threatened suicide after discovering her husband's infidelity. In need of distraction and accustomed to male admiration, Lisa encouraged the advances of this charming *homme du monde*, who was instantly infatuated. Attracted as much by her elegance and sophistication as by her considerable fortune, Max lost little time in proposing, and Lisa, bruised by the failure of her recent relationship, accepted.

Born on 24 October 1883, twenty years younger than Schoenebeck, Lisa was the daughter of a wealthy businessman from Hamburg. Her father, Max Bernhardt, half Spanish and a prominent member of the Jewish community, had made a fortune with a substantial business importing goods from India. His wife, Anna Levy, was the daughter of a successful lawyer, with a considerable income of her own. The Bernhardts travelled widely, with Anna, in the early years at least, accompanying her husband on his journeys not only in Europe but to the Americas, India, Sumatra and Japan. Unfortunately the marriage was wretchedly unhappy since Bernhardt, a womaniser and compulsive spendthrift, had repeatedly to be rescued from financial crises by his wife. The couple had two children, a son and a daughter, but before long Anna came to loathe her husband and his irresponsible, hedonistic way of life. An affair with a dancer was the final straw, and in 1905, when Lisa was twenty-two, the couple divorced, after which Anna continued to live in Hamburg, in the fashionable district of Fontenay near the banks of the Alster.

Lisa, who after the divorce never saw her father again, was adored by her mother. Anna had done everything she could during Lisa's childhood to nurture her exceptional intelligence, encouraging her to read widely, making sure she was fluent both in English and French. Before their divorce, Lisa had frequently accompanied her parents on their travels in Europe, her mother taking her to visit the galleries and museums which she herself had come to know so well. A ravishing young woman, Lisa was of medium height, with a curvaceous figure, golden skin and a head of thick chestnut-coloured hair; she was lively and clever, impatient of stupidity and inclined to be opinionated, thoroughly enjoying vigorous debate in the company of those she considered her intellectual equals. From girlhood she had attracted male admiration, indeed quickly came to expect it, and by her early twenties had enjoyed a number of affairs. She had also received several proposals of marriage, including one from the millionaire banker Henry Ladenberg, all of which she turned down.

Lisa was twenty-five when she met Max von Schoenebeck. Initially intrigued by the handsome baron and amused by his eccentricities, she viewed the prospect of marriage with favour. But before long Max's lengthy silences, his complete lack of interest in literature, history and politics, convinced her she would be making a mistake. In December 1908, however, a few months after their first meeting and just as Lisa was on the point of breaking off the engagement, a scandal erupted which traumatised Max, and indeed the entire Schoenebeck family.

Of his four brothers Max had always felt closest to Gustav, a full-time career soldier in the Prussian army, who was then stationed at Allenstein, a garrison in the east of the country, near the Russian border. Here in December 1908 Max was spending a comfortable Christmas with Gustav and his wife, Antonia, whose substantial dowry had provided the couple with a far higher standard of living than that affordable on army pay. Gustav, like his brother indifferent to social life, spent most of his time either on exercises with his battalion or hunting, leaving his very pretty, very flirtatious wife to amuse herself with his fellow officers. For almost a year Antonia had been conducting an affair with a Captain Goeben, who had quickly became obsessed by her, determined somehow to do away with her husband. Early on the morning of 27 December, Max entered his brother's room to find him lifeless, lying on his bed bleeding from a gunshot wound in his forehead. Accused of the murder, Goeben confessed and was sentenced to death, but cut his throat shortly before he was due to be hanged.

Inevitably, the story became the subject of much salacious gossip and was widely reported, both in Germany and abroad. It was endowed with far greater significance, however, when taken up by the campaigning journalist, Maximilian Harden, in his weekly publication *Die Zukunft.*

Harden, a ferocious critic of the Kaiser, had recently been prominent in publicising what became known as the "Eulenburg affair," exposing homosexual conduct and widespread immorality at the highest level of the army and of the imperial court. Now with the Allenstein case Harden was able to fuel his argument. The article received enormous publicity and the Schoenebeck name quickly became notorious, leaving Max devastated not only by the murder of his brother but also by the shame and unwelcome exposure the case had brought on the family. Harden "wrote a searing leader under the heading of our family name," Sybille later recorded. "The scandal was remarkable for the variety of ill-natured emotions it aroused; it even excited more anti-Semitism, my father's first marriage to a deceased Jewish heiress was dragged in and the poor Herzes with it." She was never to forgive Harden for the damage he caused, later portraying him in her novel *A Legacy* as Quintus Narden, "a muckraker who writes with heavy irony of a noble family's failings, tells the truth but never the whole truth."

When Lisa saw how painfully the scandal had affected Max she felt unable to abandon him. After nearly a year of mourning, plans were made for the wedding, with Lisa, who had been baptised Protestant at birth, received into the Catholic Church. On 23 April 1910, she and Max were married in the Ludwigskirche in Berlin.

Impatient as ever to leave Germany, Max took his new wife to Spain, to Ronda in Andalusia, where they settled into a pleasant whitewashed villa with a shady patio and large, overgrown garden. For Max this was an ideal location: here he contentedly passed the time painting, communicating with his birds and animals, and disappearing at regular intervals to Granada and Seville, from where he would return accompanied by packing cases full of elaborately carved furniture, pictures, porcelain and ancient statuary. But for Lisa the experience was stifling. Ronda, hemmed in by mountains, was bitterly cold in winter, in summer full of dust and flies, with little to disturb the silence of the narrow, shuttered streets. They knew almost no one and it was unthinkable for a gentlewoman to go out on her own. Lisa, full of energy, craving admiration and intellectual stimulus, longed for a sophisticated social life; with her husband she had almost nothing in common; he rarely picked up a book, except for the occasional volume of *Sherlock Holmes*, cared little for company, and was capable of maintaining a broody silence for hours at a time. It was not long before Lisa made up her mind to leave him, but before she had the opportunity to raise the subject she discovered she was pregnant—her escape route, at least for the immediate future, effectively cut off.

Max, who had been disappointed that his first child was a girl, was delighted by the prospect of an heir, even if it meant abandoning his beloved Spain to return to Germany for the birth. It was arranged that for the next few months the Schoenebecks would stay in Berlin, in a comfortable apartment on Lietzenburger Strasse in Charlottenburg, a prosperous district to the west of the city centre.

Although Max never cared for city life, at least this brief period gave him the opportunity to become better acquainted with the daughter from his first marriage. Maximiliane, now eleven years old, had been living with her Herz grandparents in Voss Strasse, a luxurious if somewhat suffocating environment for an only child. Her grandparents were affectionate and kind, but also restrictive, with every minute of her day controlled by rules and timetables. She had seen her father on only a few occasions, during his infrequent visits to Berlin, but now for the first time she was allowed to accompany him on outings, and without the presence of nursemaid or governess. Max for his part quickly grew fond of this lively child, with her thick dark hair, large eyes and pretty face, always known, for her rather feline features, as "Katzi."

Fortunately, when Lisa was introduced to Katzi she took to her at once, amused by her frivolity and high spirits.

On 16 March 1911, Lisa gave birth to a girl. When Max, waiting for news, was informed he had fathered not a son but another daughter he immediately left the room, slamming the door behind him. The first member of the family to see the baby, barely an hour old, was Lisa's mother, Anna Bernhardt, who had recently arrived from Hamburg. *"Sie sicht so schlau aus"* ("She looks so clever"), said the doctor who delivered the child, before returning his attention to Lisa, whom he was reviving with injections and cups of strong coffee. Several days later the baby was christened Sybilla (always known as "Sybille") Aleid Elsa, and for the next few weeks, while Lisa recovered her strength, the Schoenebecks remained in Berlin, Max courteously concealing as best he could his impatience to leave the city.

The plan was not to return to Spain but to stay in Germany, to settle in the south-west of the country, not far from the region where Max had spent his childhood, and as near as possible to his beloved France. To this end, and by means of Lisa's substantial income, a property had been purchased at Feldkirch, a small village in the grand duchy of Baden. It was in Feldkirch that the Schoenebecks were to settle, and Feldkirch that was to provide Sybille with one of the most fertile sources of inspiration for her fiction.

TWO

BARONIN BILLI

The property on which the Schoenebecks now settled was in the Breisach, in the south-west of the country. A gentle, rural region of fertile fields, orchards and low vine-clad hills, studded with small farms and villages, it is situated close to the edge of the Black Forest. Feldkirch is a small village in the midst of an area of rich arable land, with the ancient cathedral city of Freiburg lying fifteen kilometres to the east, while to the west, within easy walking distance, is the Rhine and the border with France. The climate is inclined to extremes, with bitterly cold winters, during which the region for months lies deep in snow, while the summers are hot, the high temperatures occasionally relieved by a cooling "*haar*," a sea mist blown in from the Mediterranean.

The schloss, purchased in 1911 with Lisa's money, stood on the edge of the village, a handsome three-storey manor house, with large shuttered windows and a steeply pitched tiled roof, surmounted by an ornamental clock tower. Originally built in the mid-sixteenth century by a Catholic family, the Wessenbergs, it had been almost completely destroyed during the Thirty Years' War, and reconstructed from its foundations during the 1680s. A massive, heavily carved front door faced the sandy road leading through the village. At the back was a walled garden, shaded by lofty chestnut trees; at the far end was an area of rough grass referred to as "the park," and beyond it a view of pasture and distant hills; there were stables, a well-tended vegetable garden, beehives, and an orchard planted with apple and plum trees. Near the front entrance was an old tithe barn which stood beside the broad main street of the village, a long, curved road lined on either side by a row of small but solid houses with steeply sloping roofs. There was also a smithy, a post office, a schoolhouse and shop, as well as a fine Romanesque church, St. Martin's, and an inn, the Gasthaus zum Kreuz, much frequented by the local farmers.

Although not large, the schloss was airy and full of light. On the ground floor was a baronial hall, and on the first floor, up a broad stone staircase, were a couple of spacious drawing rooms, heated by glazed china stoves and furnished with Lisa's collection of paintings and pretty French furniture. On the second floor were Max's bedroom and dressing room, Lisa's large, balconied Louis XV bedroom, one only slightly smaller for Katzi, and Sybille's day and night nurseries; the maids' rooms were under the roof on the top floor. The library and smoking room contained Max's substantial collection, much of which overflowed into the rest of the house: a dense conglomeration of ancient pewter, silver and bronze, of keys and candlesticks, porcelain and faience, of altar vessels and religious statuary, of tables and chairs, desks and commodes, sofas, a sedan chair, looking-glasses, medieval chests, fragments of tapestry and stained glass. "We lived inside a museum," Sybille wrote, "one that no one came to see." The house was efficiently run by a team of domestic servants: as well as Sybille's English nanny, there was Katzi's French governess, a *femme de chambre* for Lisa, a French butler, a cook, two maids from the village, a coachman, a stable boy, gardener, and an Italian odd-job man who looked after the electrical plant.

For Sybille, these early years at Feldkirch were in many respects an Arcadia, inspiring her imagination and remaining forever embedded in her memory. Throughout her life she was to look back fondly on this period. "What was best about it for me," she later recalled, "were the stables, the vista of lawn and old trees, the grapevine on the south wall . . . from which we vinified a small barrel each year . . . the apple orchard with a score of varieties for eating and strong cider, the kitchen garden growing strawberries and asparagus on sandy soil, sent off in the early morning to the markets of Breisach, Freiburg and Basel."

Sybille, known in her early days as "Billi," was an appealing little girl, not dark, like her parents, but blonde with blue eyes, in colouring resembling Anna Bernhardt, her maternal grandmother. "We are the only two blue-eyed blondes in all the family!!" as Anna told her with satisfaction. "We both look so utterly Nordish." Sybille had a large nursery plentifully supplied with toys, including a train set which she loved, but most of all she enjoyed spending time outside, organising her own little wooden house in the garden, trotting round the lawn on a small pony, romping with her father's large, good-natured dogs, her mother's spaniels, Katzi's fox terrier. It was Katzi, her half-sister, now in her teens, who was her favourite companion, and who, Sybille recalled, "gave me love and the fundamental early disciplines—'Don't tell lies,' 'Have you washed your hands?,' *'No, you can't have it.'* "

Yet although in many respects an idyllic existence, beneath the surface there was profound unease. When still very small Sybille was told by her mother that she had not been wanted: her arrival, Lisa explained, had been considered a disaster by both parents, by her father who had hoped for a son, while Lisa herself had felt trapped by the birth, obliged to stay in a marriage she was impatient to leave. In the course of time Max was to grow fond of his daughter, if never capable of demonstrating much affection, while Lisa remained wholly lacking in maternal instinct. "I never had any maternal love," Sybille recalled. "My mother was not interested in children, not at all. She once said to me: 'You were very sweet as a baby, but you're going to be very, very dull for a very long time—perhaps ten or fifteen years. We'll speak then, when you've made yourself a mind.' Of course I thought that was quite normal."

No less distressing was the growing estrangement between Sybille's parents. To the few neighbours whom they occasionally entertained—Count Kaagenegg, Baron Neveux, the Gleichensteins, the Landenbergs—the couple gave an impression of unity: Maximilian always exquisitely dressed, so calm and courteous, while Lisa animated the occasion with her charm and high spirits, laughing and talking her way through dinner indoors or in summer sitting at tea under one of the big trees in the garden. But in truth husband and wife had little in common. "My father could not stand clever women," Sybille wrote. "My mother had been too beautiful for him to notice that she was one and when he did notice it was too late." Lisa had been equally misled, believing Max's "cover of eccentricity" to be the mark of an interesting and intellectual mind.

The reality was different. Max was content to spend hours a day sitting smoking in his library, reading saleroom catalogues while listening to popular operatic arias hissing from an ancient gramophone with a giant horn. When in company he appeared calm and in control, yet inwardly was prey to countless fears and insecurities, his calm "the immobility of someone asleep and yet at bay." Lisa, on the other hand, sociable by nature, was restless and longed to escape. She had never been popular in the region, seen as an unwelcome outsider by the villagers, and offending the neighbours by her outspoken opinions and obvious disdain for rural society. Lisa craved male admiration and intelligent company; she was hungry for stimulating discussion, eager to talk about new novels and writers, impatient to see the latest plays and exhibitions. Like her mother she was an art lover, and had lately discovered the French impressionists, a genre far removed from Max's rusty medievalism; recently one of her admirers had given her a painting by Paul Klee, which immediately became her most treasured possession, travelling with her wherever she went. Frustrated by her husband's passivity, she was growing increasingly dissatisfied with the agrarian backwater in which her marriage had landed her.

One of the few enthusiasms the couple shared was for good food, but even here they failed to find much common ground. Max, brought up on the cuisine of the great French chefs, was a true connoisseur, a dedicated perfectionist, his sensitive palate alert to every nuance of texture and flavour. Lisa, in her husband's view, clung too closely to a more robust Germanic tradition. She liked her meat—venison, partridge, hare—plainly roasted, and relished the local home-cured bacon, sausage, loin of pork, as well as the coarse rye bread and plum and cherry tarts. At Feldkirch, the cook, "female and north German . . . was on the mistress's side," Sybille recalled, "and so food, the one thing my parents had counted on for pleasant daily safety, turned out to be what they quarrelled about tenaciously and often. I can still hear the altercations about my mother's having ordered cauliflower covered in white sauce."

It was not long before Lisa, bored and frustrated, began spending long periods away from Feldkirch, sometimes, when obliged by circumstances, taking her daughter with her. On one occasion, when Sybille was not yet three, she and her nanny accompanied her mother on a visit to Copenhagen, where they stayed in a hotel. The purpose of the expedition was for Lisa to keep an assignation with her current lover, the distinguished writer Peter Nansen. Known as the Danish Maupassant, Nansen, then in his fifties, was a notorious womaniser, with Lisa only one in a long sequence of mistresses; she, however, convinced herself their affair had been important to both, and for many years kept his photograph always by her. One day, during the nanny's afternoon off, Lisa had been obliged to take her daughter with her when visiting Nansen, parking the pram in the entrance hall of his apartment. As Sybille remembered it, "I was in some kind of a narrow space and my mother wearing an enormous hat and veil was bending over me . . . 'Please be good, please keep quiet, he hates to have a baby in the hall. Please just go to sleep.' I did. For the whole blessed afternoon."

In August 1914, only a couple of years after the family had settled in Baden, their peaceful existence was disrupted by the outbreak of war. Both the Schoenebecks were passionately opposed to war. Max, who despite, or perhaps because of, having served in the Prussian army, had always loathed the Kaiser and his flamboyant militarism; the present hostilities, he was convinced, were "a dangerous folly bringing ruin to all concerned and best not to be thought about." Lisa, as a committed pacifist, took a more universal view, believing that no war could be justified, that fighting led to nothing but cruelty, hatred and a brutal waste of life. To her small daughter she took trouble to explain in the simplest terms that war was barbaric, that it meant killing and maiming, and that no nation should ever declare war on another, however just the cause.

Max, worried by the nearness of Feldkirch to the French border, wanted to leave immediately. His plan was to go to Berlin and take refuge with the Herzes, a scheme instantly dismissed by Lisa, who insisted they would be much better off where they were. And for a while life in the village continued much as before, with few shortages or signs of disruption. Inevitably, however, the atmosphere began to change: convoys of wounded were seen returning from the front to be cared for in field hospitals in Freiburg, and as increasing numbers of men were called up, a spirit of defiant patriotism became the norm. It was soon clear that the village no longer maintained the attitude of unquestioning respect towards the family at the schloss, and before long hostile comment began to spread about the Schoenebecks' pacifism; it was considered unpatriotic, too, that among themselves they continued to speak in French and English, the two enemy languages. "One day," Sybille recalled, "a stone was flung over the park wall when nanny and my half-sister and I were playing. It hit me on the forehead, just a gash but there was a lot of blood and I howled. I still have the scar, a small one, under an eyebrow."

In the spring of 1915, the decision was made to close the schloss and leave Feldkirch. Max had recently been recalled to the army, and was put in charge of the officers' prison camp at Karlsruhe—where he was delighted to find himself in the company of French- and Englishmen— while his wife and daughters set off for Berlin. Sybille was barely four years old, and yet for the rest of her life she remembered that long, slow journey from west to east. With most available forms of transport requisitioned for the movement of troops, it was difficult for civilians to travel, but eventually tickets were bought, books and clothing packed into trunks and the house closed for the duration. Beginning at Freiburg, the journey was to take several days, at times seeming almost interminable as they moved haltingly across the country in a series of overcrowded trains, sometimes stopping for hours to refuel in gloomy, steel-vaulted stations. For months there had been fierce fighting on both fronts, in France and Belgium in the west, Galicia and Poland in the east, resulting in the daily conveyance of thousands of wounded throughout the country. It was the sight of this battered army that made such an impression on Sybille: "soldiers on the platforms, in the corridors, looking in through windows, soldiers being helped into the compartment— soldiers on crutches, soldiers with head bandages, soldiers with great casts about their chests." Finally the Schoenebecks arrived in Berlin and made their way to the Herz mansion on Voss Strasse.

Interestingly, Sybille in her writing says nothing about the harsh conditions suffered by Berliners throughout the war. And yet by the time she and her mother arrived in the capital the evidence was unavoidable: the streets full of uniformed soldiers, many wounded and begging; there were rigorous restrictions on lighting and heating, a scarcity of fuel, and most serious of all, severe food shortages, largely due to the lethal efficacy of the British naval blockade, which had been in place since August 1914. Bread and flour rationing had been introduced within months, both fruit and vegetables quickly grew scarce and a law was passed forbidding the consumption of meat on certain days of the week. Inevitably, such restrictions were hardest on the poor, but for those, like the Herzes, who could afford to pay there was a well-organised black market in which, for up to four and five times the pre-war prices, meat, fish, eggs, sugar, butter, milk and cheese continued to be available.

The house on Voss Strasse and its inhabitants provided the inspiration for some of the most memorable passages in *A Legacy*. Sybille and her mother were to spend many months in that suffocating, opulent environment, where the routine was rigid and unchanging, with little connection to the world outside. The members of that "Judaeo-Agnostic household," as Sybille described it, "sunk in upholstery and their own corpulence . . . lived contentedly in a luxurious cocoon, an existence that was wholly centred on their own domestic comfort . . . [They] never went to the theatre, looked at pictures or listened to music; they cared nothing for books . . . They took no exercise and practised no sport . . . They did not go to shops. Things were sent to them on approval, and people came to them for fittings." The household was ruled by Frau Herz, Katzi's grandmother, a stout old lady who spent most of the day contentedly sunk into a large armchair. Elaborately dressed, she was "swaddled in stuffs and folds and flesh, stuck with brooches of rather grey diamonds, topped by an arrangement of rough grey hair . . . She wore a dog collar of pearls, a watch on a ribbon from her neck and a bunch of keys at her waist." Almost her sole duty was the planning of menus, and for this the cook came upstairs to see her for half an hour every morning.

At Voss Strasse, despite stringent rationing, the meals continued much as before, lengthy, substantial and very, very rich. Every morning there was a big cooked breakfast, served to the ladies in their bedrooms, to the gentlemen downstairs; and so that no one should suffer pangs of hunger while waiting for luncheon, a second breakfast was provided mid-morning, with cold venison, potted meats, foie gras, eggs in cream, chicken and pressed tongue, all accompanied by glasses of sherry and port. Occasionally, if there were an odd number at table, Sybille was brought down to sit next to her step-grandmother, where, raised up on a couple of cushions, she watched with fascination as course succeeded course: cream of chicken, crayfish in aspic, vol-au-vents, calf's tongue in Madeira, chartreuse of pigeon, mousseline of artichokes, Nesselrode pudding full of chestnuts and cream. "Everyone spoke freely in his or her own way and so I imbibed quite a deal of German-Jewish family life."

Sybille was cared for by a nanny while in Berlin, with an elderly tutor arriving twice a week to give her lessons. During this period she saw even less of her parents than she had at Feldkirch. Her father appeared only occasionally, amiable but remote, soon retreating into his customary state of languid indolence, exquisitely polite but inwardly detached from his surroundings. For Max the Herz opulence was vulgar, and while staying in Voss Strasse, "he held himself aloof like a prisoner of honour at the victor's banquet." Lisa, too, found the environment distasteful, and spent most of the day either away from the house, pursuing projects of her own, or else reading in her room upstairs, appearing only for dinner in the evening. Eventually, claiming she needed her independence, she rented a large flat in Hohenzollern Strasse belonging to Theo von Brockhusen, an artist and a former member of the expressionist group known as "die Brücke." It was here in 1917 that Brockhusen painted a portrait of Sybille at six years old, but it disappeared, assumed lost during the war.

Although none of the Herzes showed any particular interest in Sybille, they were well disposed and materially she was indulged, her upstairs nursery well supplied with toys, including a rocking horse, a miniature railway, a puppet theatre and a toy stable. Every day she was taken for a walk, usually to the nearby Tiergarten, "the rather dismal public park," with its boring straight paths and lawns surrounded by railings. Infinitely preferable was the Siegesallee, the broad, tree-lined boulevard that ran through the park and on to the Königsplatz. Along its entire length on either side stood a series of vast and magnificent marble statues of the Prussian kings and warriors of the past, designed as the Kaiser's grandiose monument to his country's glory. His critics derided the Siegesallee, dubbed "Puppenallee," or "Dolls' Avenue," and regarded it as a ludicrous example of imperial folly. But to Sybille these towering heroic images, nobly gesturing, splendid in their armour and elaborate robes, were thrilling. "I would stand before each Margrave of Brandenburg or King of Prussia upon his pedestal and study his countenance and dates and that of his spouse and counsellors . . . My favourites were an epicene youth leaning upon his shield, Heinrich the Child, and a mysterious personage covered in chain mail, Waldemar the Bear."

As before at Feldkirch, the most important person in Sybille's life was her half-sister, Katzi: it was Katzi, "warm, generous, pleasure-loving," whom she adored and on whom she relied the most. But Katzi was growing up, eager for fun, new clothes and a lively social life. She had been caught more than once out on the town flirting with handsome young officers over coffee and cakes, and in order to teach her a lesson had been sent for several months to a convent, where, predictably, she was miserable. On her return to Voss Strasse, it was Lisa who became her ally. Lisa was charmed by her stepdaughter's high spirits and sympathetic to her keen interest in the opposite sex. Indeed for both women male admiration was central to their existence, and on this, despite the difference in age, they quickly colluded like a couple of sisters. "Men were attracted to them; rarely to both, though it happened," Sybille recalled. Lisa had many friends in the theatre, one of whom, a drama critic, "took my mother to rehearsals of Ibsen and Shaw . . . then walked my sister in the public gardens treating her as . . . a very attractive, very alive young creature. There was not a niggle of jealousy." It was Lisa, too, who although tone deaf herself, supported Katzi in her plans for a musical career, arranging an audition for her with the lieder singer Therese Behr, wife of the pianist Artur Schnabel. But Katzi's ambitions were for grand opera, not lieder, so that particular project came to nothing.

Fortunately for Sybille she was soon to be rescued from her somewhat solitary existence. By the beginning of 1918 Lisa had become immersed in a new affair, which made her even more impatient than usual with her maternal responsibilities. Thus it was decided that her daughter should go to Hamburg, where she could stay with Anna Bernhardt, Lisa's mother.

Blonde, blue-eyed and very pretty, Anna had been partly deaf since childhood, which sometimes led to difficulties in her social life, but she was intellectual and remarkably well read in German, French and English. Having lived alone since her divorce thirteen years earlier, Anna was delighted to care for the child, determined to do everything she could to make her happy and encourage her obvious intelligence. Sybille quickly settled into the comfortable house on Oberstrasse and became devoted to her kind and generous grandmother. A tutor was engaged, there were daily lessons in physical exercise, and Sybille soon made friends with a number of neighbourhood children. She also spent time with another member of the family, Anna's Spanish mother-in-law, "a very small, very wrinkled, old woman . . . who never left the house . . . She hobbled about passages tatting lace, carrying a plate of pudding to her upstairs drawing room. In spite of my shrinking from age . . . she and I drank our chocolate and ate sweets together entirely in the manner of equals."

When after a period of several months Anna was instructed to bring Sybille back to Berlin the child was distraught. She had grown deeply attached to her grandmother and found the prospect of leaving her painful in the extreme. To add to her wretchedness, she discovered on returning to Voss Strasse that Katzi was away, staying with the family of a young man to whom, briefly, she had become engaged. Years later Anna recalled the scene as she prepared to say goodbye. Her granddaughter had been hysterical: "You cried: 'Katzi is gone, and now you go away, oh I won't live any longer!' And at the station you cried so desperately that people came to hug and cheer you."

The Armistice was declared on 11 November 1918, two days after the abdication of the Kaiser and the establishment of the German Republic. By this time living conditions had deteriorated dramatically, even for such families as the Herzes. The head of the family, Katzi's grandfather, had died at the beginning of the war, and now it was discovered that almost no money remained. The consequence of this revelation was not only the immediate introduction of stringent economies in household expenditure but also the end of Maximilian's generous allowance, arranged on his marriage to Melanie and continued ever since.

Shortly before the Armistice, and with the end of the war clearly in sight, Maximilian and Katzi had left to return to Baden. Lisa meanwhile went with her daughter for a few days to Boltenhagen, a resort on the Baltic coast, where during the past couple of summers she had taken both Sybille and Katzi on holiday from Berlin. Their journey home was unfortunately timed, coinciding with the outbreak of what became known as the November Revolution, an uprising begun by sailors of the Imperial Navy which quickly spread across the country. Mother and daughter were caught up in the revolt at Schwerin, in the Duchy of Mecklenburg, where they were ordered off the train and herded into a hotel on the main square. "Here the sailors with their banners and slogans were mutinying all right," Sybille recalled. "There was shooting and much noise . . . The windows giving on to that square were broad and high. Most of us were crouching on the floor. Not so my mother: she stood up to look. The sailors, she said firmly, were right to mutiny—it was time, the Kaiser's regime was rotten . . . The shooting must have stopped by nightfall. Whoever was in charge did not judge it safe for us to leave. The bedrooms were full up, so we all slept on the floor. After daybreak, another train, another journey . . ."

Eventually Lisa and Sybille reached Feldkirch. On the surface little had changed: the village had been left unharmed, the farms were still functioning, although there was a notable shortage of young men. At the schloss there were fewer servants: no coachman, no butler, and a couple of local girls taking the place of the trained parlourmaids previously employed. The stables were empty, as all the horses had been requisitioned, and there were no other animals—no pigs, no sheep, no chickens or ducks; the garden was a tangle of nettles and ivy and fallen trees. Fortunately, however, the interior of the house was found to be intact, its "contents undisturbed, dusted, my father's collection in museum-order, and thus for a brief spell of time, on a diminishing scale, a *vie de château* resumed."

Yet although the house itself remained largely unaltered, some major changes were about to occur in the Schoenebecks' family life. The first, taking place only weeks after Sybille's arrival home, was Katzi's permanent departure following her wedding on 24 December 1918. Katzi at only nineteen had married a man much older than herself, Hans Erich Borgmann, a wealthy alderman, who immediately took his young wife back to his home town of Wiesbaden. Katzi's sudden departure was extremely painful for Sybille: her sister had been her only ally, and now she was gone. Left alone with her parents, the little girl felt painfully isolated: she had no friend, no one to play with, no one in whom she could confide.

As before, neither of her parents had much time for her. Maximilian spent most of the day in his library, or in the park with a newly acquired menagerie, which included several large dogs and a couple of donkeys, Fanny and Flora, on which Sybille, without much enthusiasm, learned to ride. Lisa, bored by her husband, bored by the country, was impatient with her daughter, whose childish inadequacies, as she saw them, frequently exasperated her. Sybille, who feared her sharp tongue and dreaded being alone with her, was relieved when Lisa disappeared to spend time with one of her lovers. "[My mother] did not suffer little fools gladly. That I was her own made not a scrap of difference. When I was slow, she called me slow, when I was quick she called me a parrot. Compassionate in her principles, she was high-handed even harsh in her daily dealings." In middle age, looking back at her childhood, Sybille wrote, "[the] truth is that I have never grown up, and did not do so because I always missed having a real mother and father: parents in fact, a family."

By the age of eight Sybille had received no formal education at all. "My father hadn't thought about it, my mother vaguely held that any child of hers would somehow pick it up." It was not until an acquaintance expressed shock at this state of affairs that it was decided that something must be done, and arrangements were hastily made for her to attend school at the Ursuline convent in Freiburg.

The convent of the Society of the Sisters of St. Ursula of the Blessed Virgin, known as the Schwarzen Klosters ("Black Abbey"), is a large, solid, five-storey building with a handsome church attached; constructed in the early eighteenth century, its purpose had always been to provide schooling for girls. Sybille entered as a day girl, bewildered suddenly to find herself in a maze of endless rooms and corridors, peopled by black-clad nuns and swarming with girls, all older and in appearance far more sophisticated than herself. At first Sybille was petrified by the nuns, by their large crucifixes, their veils and habits, although she soon found them to be kind and only "gently dictatorial." As a new girl she was placed on a bench at the back of the class, where rather to her surprise she forgot her fear and found herself immediately engaged, quickly winning the approval of the teachers by enthusiasti-cally joining in the discussions. "[I was] entranced by the magic of a verbal lesson . . . Surprise and approval were in the air. I drank it up. So far, so good. Then came a recess. Another nun took charge. She banged a gavel and in a strong voice called '*Diktat*'—pens and copy books were presented right and left like small arms . . . I froze."

Although at an early age she had taught herself to read, Sybille had not learned to write. The nuns were astonished: a child of her age unable to write! Never had there been such a case before. "They swarmed around me, black cloth billowing about unseen feet—humming to each other in distress . . . What would they do? Teach me to write. From scratch. Well, they tried. At once. Day after day I was whisked off into a discreet little study on an upper floor." Unfortunately the process was only partly successful, and for the rest of her life Sybille's handwrit-ing remained virtually illegible, "hard to read for me, impenetrable for anyone else." Over the years it was to remain a constant source of com-plaint from her numerous correspondents, who variously described it as indecipherable, a cat's scrawl, an Egyptian hieroglyph. "I can never read your writing (alas, what I have missed)," lamented one old friend, while another in a frenzy of frustration exclaimed, "Your handwriting is calculated to defy the most expert cryptographers!"

For reasons she never discovered, Sybille's attendance at the con-vent lasted only a few weeks. "It just came to an end . . . I had not been withdrawn, I had not been expelled, I was just back home." Lisa, unconcerned, made some vague suggestion of hiring a governess, an idea irritably dismissed by Max, who instead decided his daughter should complete her education at the village school.

And so this was arranged, with Sybille, now nine years old, attend-ing classes every weekday from 1 p.m. until 4 p.m. The schoolhouse was a fairly new building, with a ground-floor classroom in which about thirty children sat with their slates, the youngest in front, the seniors, the eleven-year-olds, at the back. In recognition of her aristocratic status, Sybille, addressed as "Baronin Billi," was given a desk to herself—the other pupils shared a desk between four—and positioned a little apart from the rest of the class. There was one teacher, "a youngish man in a town suit," who divided his attention between the varied age groups, giving dictation as well as reading and singing lessons and making sure the catechism was learned by heart. Lessons were conducted in educated German, *Hochdeutsch*, although between themselves the children, Sybille included, always spoke in the local dialect, *Alemannisch*. Sybille soon made friends among her fellow pupils, much preferring the company of boys to girls. With her new companions she enjoyed taking part in boisterous games, often in her room at the schloss, and in fine weather roaming the fields, Sybille in dungarees or in a favourite Red Indian outfit, a present from her mother. She joined her little gang in helping with the harvest, stacking logs, or "getting on a farmhorse when no one was looking," often ending the day in one of the village houses for a meal of cold bacon, bread and cider.

Sybille had been at the school only a short while before her life at home changed dramatically. Relations between her parents had long been wretchedly unhappy, alternating between periods of glacial silence and increasingly bitter quarrels ending in violent shouting matches. Then one day Lisa declared she was leaving for Berlin, taking Sybille with her. For a brief period mother and daughter stayed at a *pension* in the centre of the city, Sybille knowing nothing of the purpose of the visit, until Lisa suddenly announced that her father would shortly be coming to take her back to Feldkirch. When Maximilian arrived, Lisa remained upstairs, refusing to see him, and thus the miserable marriage came to an end.

Max, although angry and humiliated by what he regarded as his wife's unforgiveable behaviour, agreed to divorce Lisa, a process eventually finalised at the regional court in Freiburg on 22 April 1922, twelve years almost to the day after the couple had married in Berlin. Four months later Lisa gave birth to a son, by yet another of her many lovers, but the baby died after only a few weeks.

When Lisa went, so did her income. Now Max was left with almost nothing except for the schloss—which although purchased with Lisa's money she had allowed him to keep—and his military pension. Retired from the army shortly before the war with the rank of major, Max had been awarded the statutory pension, which previously had been of little consequence; now, however, its inadequacy was distressingly apparent and Max immediately applied for a retrospective promotion to lieutenant-colonel; his request was refused.

Suddenly impoverished, Max was obliged to dismiss all the servants, and most rooms in the house were closed, with living quarters confined to the top floor. Here Max had his bedroom and dressing room, Sybille slept in Katzi's old room and the morning room was used for dining, with a makeshift kitchen installed in what had been the governess's bedroom. A village woman, Lina Hauser, was brought in to do all the domestic work, sleeping in a tiny room off the corridor and joining the Schoenebecks for meals. Lina—"a shy, stiff peasant," kind, simple, deeply religious—was devoted to Max and worked tirelessly and without complaint. It was Lina who did all the housework, the washing and ironing, the cooking (described as "execrable" by Sybille), as well as chopping firewood, lighting stoves, feeding the poultry, picking fruit, and working in the kitchen garden. Here she was helped by Sybille, who also joined her in mucking out the donkeys' stables and making the dogs' dinners in the makeshift kitchen. Lina, Sybille recalled, "treated me (affectionately) as her kitchenmaid-cum-stable boy . . . To her I was both an underservant and the employer's daughter."

"Overnight," Sybille wrote, "we were the new poor." Yet their situation was hardly unique: by 1921 the whole country was in the grip of a raging inflation, largely due to the massive reparations, hundreds of billions of gold marks, demanded from Germany by the Allied powers. The mark, which in August 1914 had been valued at 4.19 to the U.S. dollar, in December 1922 was valued at 7,589 to the dollar, and by November the following year at 2.5 trillion to the dollar, effectively reducing to penury a large part of the population. "The scale of its catastrophic course then is no longer within our imaginations," wrote Sybille nearly eighty years later. "What had bought a house the year before, a piano last month, a pound of butter last week, bought a newspaper in the morning but no longer on that afternoon." Unlike many, the Schoenebecks were fortunate in that at Feldkirch they were able to live off the land, and at least they had enough to eat and were able to keep the house running. "We turned ourselves into a no-cash economy. Produce and barter." Felled timber and cider made from apples from the orchard were exchanged for bread, butter, milk, salt and candles; potatoes were grown on part of the ploughed-up lawn, while poultry, pigs and a couple of sheep were kept in the little park. Occasionally a small parcel would arrive with packets of tea or peppercorns sent by Katzi from Wiesbaden, which as part of the prosperous French zone suffered fewer restrictions than the rest of the country.

In contrast to his wife, Maximilian was well liked in Feldkirch: unfailingly polite, he took trouble to engage with the villagers, listening to what they had to say, ready to discuss topics of local interest and concern. Now, although leading a life of almost hermetic retirement, he continued to show his customary courtesy, always asking after wives and children of the local farmers, sharing a glass of wine with the men after their bartering had been concluded. There was, however, only one member of the community invited inside the house: the parish priest, for whom every six months or so Max himself, with a certain amount of sighing and complaint, prepared an elaborate dinner.

Attending Mass at the parish church was one of the few activities which Sybille and her father undertook together. As owners of the schloss, the Schoenebecks had their own pew, near to the altar and at a distance from the rest of the congregation; in recognition of their status they entered the church not through the main door, like everyone else, but through the sacristy. From the beginning Sybille was fascinated by the theatricality of the ritual, by the priest in his embroidered vestments, the acolytes with their censers, the organ music, the prayers, the chanting of the litany. Soon she had learned the litany by heart, boasting that she could recite it from beginning to end without once looking at her missal. Before long the challenge was taken up and she was put to the test. "One evening in May I found myself kneeling in conspicuous isolation, missal shut beside me, chanting in the right blend of *Hochdeutsch* and patois line after line punctuated by the thunderous response behind me. '*Du Engel des Herrn.*' '*Bet f'r oonsh!*' (Patois for '*Bete für uns.*') '*Du heilige Jungfrau.*' '*Bet f'r oonsh!*' '*Du elfenbeinerner Turm.*'

'*Bet f'r oonsh!*' . . . It lasted for the best part of five minutes and it was intoxicating." Shortly before her tenth birthday, Sybille, with other young girls from the village, began preparing for her first Communion. By this time she had become so enthralled with the whole performance that she asked if she might serve as an altar boy; her father, somewhat to her surprise, was agreeable and so was the priest, but when her request was referred to the bishop he turned it down.

It was from this moment that Sybille's disillusionment with Catholicism began. Over the coming months, although she continued to accompany her father on Sundays, she began to turn against the Church, to dismiss what she was being taught to believe. When she was told by some of the villagers that her parents, because of their divorce, would go to hell, she became even more obdurate in her objections. "I made my first Communion in a state of smug rebellion," she wrote. "I did not like what I was being made to hear—mortal sin, hellfire, finicky Church commandments. So I took against religion, simple as that: disliked it, didn't believe it, didn't want to."

As the weeks passed, Sybille became increasingly aware of a painful sense of isolation; when not at school or engaged in housework, she was often left to herself, reading, riding her bicycle or knocking tennis balls against the wash-house wall. Domestic life was busy but it was also bleak. Lina, brisk and efficient, was no substitute for Lisa, while Maximilian, sunk in gloom, remained impenetrable and out of reach, the pessimism and intense anxieties to which he was always prone now weighing more heavily than ever. "One could never tell, he used to say, what one might find upon returning from a journey . . . My father loved me very much," Sybille recalled, "but he couldn't show it." The only occasions when she experienced any real connection with him were in the evening after the day's work was done. Sometimes there was a game of roulette, and often over dinner Max would reminisce about his past, his country childhood, his periods abroad in France and Spain, gambling in Monte Carlo, his beloved menagerie, even his career in the army—although with no mention of any scandal.

For Maximilian one of his few pleasures was his fine cellar. All his life he had been a connoisseur, with a sophisticated palate and an expert knowledge of the great vintages and chateaux, over the years accumulating a substantial collection, part of which still remained. Now every evening his daughter was sent to fetch a bottle for the following day. The brick-lined cellar was deep belowground, down a steep and narrow flight of steps, the dark, subterranean vaults a terrifying place for Sybille, who, candle in hand, felt she was entering a sinister kingdom peopled by ghosts. When she had safely returned, she handed the bottle to her father, who put it aside to settle. Once seated at table he took up the wine decanted the day before, pouring a careful half-glass for his daughter and for Lina, before tasting it himself with great concentration. Sybille watched him carefully, imitating his every gesture and expression. "I sniff mine, take a mouthful slowly, twirling the wine in the glass, as he has told me to do . . . He has taught me to pronounce the names on the labels and to look at the pictures of the chateaux, he has been to them, has met the owners . . . Next day I am allowed to cut the seal and, unless the wine is very old, draw the cork, wipe the neck inside and out. The decanting is done by my father, my hands are not strong enough yet to do it properly." For Sybille these sessions were important, remembered as the only real communication she ever had with her father. Perhaps predictably, his love of wine inspired a lifetime's passion, a subject about which she was to become extremely knowledgeable and which she was to pursue with dedication throughout the years to come.

Yet in every other area Sybille felt she remained at an impossible distance from her parent. She was aware of his unhappiness, his increasingly fragile health—he had grown very thin, with a bronchial cough that sounded throughout the night—and yet she felt unable to love him or show compassion. Much of the day Max sat smoking and staring into space; his fury with Lisa remained unabated and he spent hours brooding in an angry silence. There was an aura of defeat about him. As the weeks passed, his daughter found it increasingly difficult to cope; at first she was impatient and annoyed, then overwhelmed by depression, by an acute sense of desolation which seemed to come from nowhere. Craving warmth and affection, she longed for her sister, for Katzi, the one person who demonstrably loved her and who seemed to understand her. Sybille decided to run away.

Katzi was living in Wiesbaden, where her husband, Hans Erich

Borgmann, was *Beigeordneter*, or deputy mayor. The journey, of over 300 kilometres, would be complicated and so her plans were made with care. Money was no problem, thanks to a generous tip Sybille had received from one of Lisa's lovers, to which she now added some notes discreetly removed from her father's wallet. The main difficulty was how to leave the house without anyone hearing her go. The gates were locked at night, the front door bolted, the ground-floor windows barred; the scullery door, however, had a modern lock, easily opened, and thus very early one June morning Sybille crept silently downstairs, out by the back door and climbed over the garden wall. "I then proceeded to walk, not run, at a good pace . . . I carried a purse and a book, a book about Red Indians, and nothing else . . . When after an hour or so I got to the railway station I went straight in and asked for a single ticket, half fare, fourth class . . . I first took a local to Freiburg then changed to another slow train to Karlsruhe . . . [where] I changed again . . . I read my book; I felt no hunger, and I felt quite calm."

Once arrived in Wiesbaden, Sybille asked directions to the Borgmanns' house. Here she found her brother-in-law at home and the whole place in an uproar. Her absence had been discovered not long after she had left; Max, frantic with worry, immediately contacted the police and telegraphed to the Borgmanns. Katzi had been out playing tennis and on her return was shocked to be told what had happened; she was visibly distressed, warmly embracing the runaway while at the same time explaining to her the fearful turmoil, emotional and practical, that her disappearance had caused. Within a couple of days Max himself arrived, looking so shaken that the Borgmanns insisted he stay for a while to recuperate. "My father did not reproach me, asked no questions," Sybille recalled. "With me—we were seldom alone—he showed little beyond an aloof sadness." The missing money was never mentioned, Max's sole reproach to his daughter, "Billi—you left the house unlocked, open to enemies and thieves."

The few weeks spent with the Borgmanns were purely pleasurable. Unlike the rest of the country, Wiesbaden was flourishing; the Rhineland had been occupied by France since 1918, and as a consequence of the substantial French presence in the town trade restrictions had been abolished, and there was plenty of food in the shops and little unemployment. Borgmann himself was, like his wife, a Francophile; he spoke excellent French and was almost as sophisticated a connoisseur of French food and wine as his father-in-law. The house on Parkstrasse was comfortable and well run, the table excellent, and almost every evening there was a lavish soirée, usually with a recital given by both singers and instrumentalists. As deputy mayor of Wiesbaden, Borgmann was responsible for the running of the state opera and ballet; a serious music-lover, he had many musician friends, who attended his parties, as did a sophisticated circle of well-to-do White Russian émigrés and French army officers. As hostess, Katzi charmed them all with her prettiness, vivacity and chic.

For Maximilian, Parkstrasse provided an essential period of recuperation. It was also in a sense a return to his way of life as a bachelor: here he was able to idle away his days smoking French cigarettes, visiting the casino, enjoying the company of charming women and an excellent standard of French cuisine. For Sybille the experience came as a revelation, "the most stimulating period of my life so far." She was dazzled by her new environment and the unaccustomed freedoms she was granted. Now thirteen, she was allowed to stay up for the evening concerts, enthralled by the music of Bach, Brahms, Mozart, Stravinsky; she was taken to the opera, to watch the fireworks, and taught to play tennis at the local club. She came to like Borgmann, accompanying him to the races most afternoons, and she was intensely happy to be reunited with her sister, even if Katzi had little time to spare: as sociable as ever, she spent much of the morning in bed or with her dressmaker before going out to meet friends in town. Katzi had had a daughter, whom she treated with affection, although, as Sybille carefully noted, "not the quality of the affection she had given to me spontaneously from birth." The child had been born at the end of the first year of her marriage, by which time Katzi was already out of love with her much older husband; before long she began embarking on a number of affairs with men her own age, very much as she had while still a girl in Berlin.

The weeks passed quickly and soon arrangements were made for the Schoenebecks' return to Feldkirch. Sybille was appalled when she learned they were leaving, but there was nothing she could do, and almost before she realised what was happening she found herself with her father on the train to Freiburg. When they arrived at the schloss, Lina welcomed her with tears and reproaches: "How could you have done this to him?" Although she had been miserable yet again to part from Katzi, Sybille soon resigned herself to the inevitable, settling back into the familiar regime, "hard-working days filled with bucolic tasks carried out cheerfully and not badly, accepting contentment." From time to time, and to her great joy, Katzi herself made an appearance, arriving in a big chauffeur-driven Panhard and always bringing with her some delicious pâté or chocolate. Ostensibly she came to spend time with her father, but in fact these visits were essentially a pretext, a chance for her to go off for a few days with her current lover.

Whereas before at Feldkirch it had been possible to survive by hard work and some simple bartering, now suddenly it was not. In order to keep his little household going, Max was obliged to start selling part of his beloved collection. From time to time he would disappear into his library to select one or two small but valuable items, for him a painful process, although his demeanour gave little away. Early the following morning, the two donkeys would be harnessed to the carriage, and Max, his slender figure immaculately dressed in hat and tailored greatcoat, gloves in one hand, Gladstone bag in the other, was driven by one of the local farmers to the station. In the evening, having conducted his business in Freiburg or Basel, he returned. Nothing was said about the events of the day, but from his bag would be taken little treats for Lina and his daughter—chocolate, gingerbread, salted almonds. A few weeks would pass and then the exercise would be repeated. And so it went on—until suddenly everything changed.

Since Lisa's departure, she had kept in touch with her daughter by letter. Now Lisa suddenly decided that she wanted Sybille to come and live with her for at least a year. As she was legally within her rights, Max had no choice but to consent. Timetables were consulted, clothes packed, and an escort engaged to accompany Sybille on the journey.

At the end of November 1925, not many weeks before Sybille was due to leave, Maximilian suddenly fell ill with appendicitis and was taken to hospital in Freiburg. The operation was successful, but soon afterwards he suffered an attack of bronchial asthma, and on 4 December, at the age of only sixty-two, he died. "My strange, defeated, formal father vanished," wrote Sybille. "This was indeed the point of no return: my father's lightning death."

Katzi and Borgmann, who had arrived a few days earlier, had taken Sybille with them to stay at a hotel in town. After the funeral Borgmann gave several formal dinners for local dignitaries and then the three of them returned to Wiesbaden. From here shortly afterwards Sybille set out to meet her mother. She was never to set foot in the schloss, her childhood home, again.

THREE

FROM ICY ENGLAND TO THE WARMTH OF THE MEDITERRANEAN

Following the harrowing few weeks surrounding her father's death, leaving Feldkirch and parting from her beloved Katzi, Sybille might well have felt apprehensive about the future. Now aged fourteen, she was about to embark on a new life, in a different country, in the care of a mother whom she barely knew and who had never demonstrated much affection for her. Instead, as the train moved south out of Germany, through the Austrian Alps and towards the Italian frontier, she felt her spirits rise and she found herself filled with an intoxicating sense of freedom. "[I] experienced a state of sheer joy, a fulfilment of a longing that lies dormant in many of us whose birth has been into the rain." Once over the Brenner Pass the train stopped at the border and the chaperone departed, her place taken by a young woman, Doris von Schönthan, a recent acquaintance of Lisa's whom she had hired at the last moment to accompany her daughter. The two of them were to travel to Merano in the South Tyrol, where mother and daughter would be reunited.

For Sybille, Doris von Schönthan, from an impoverished but aristocratic Prussian family, was of an entirely new species, a member of the jazz-age generation of the Weimar Republic. Idealistic, full of hope and ambition, Doris was determined to make a career while at the same time enjoying herself to the limit. Her talk was of nightclubs and parties, of young poets and painters, of communism, expressionism and avant-garde film. Doris herself had applied for a job with a film company, talking excitedly of her prospects in a world of which Sybille knew nothing—"Needless to say I had never been to a cinema." The journey passed quickly, and once arrived in Merano the two of them found a message from Lisa telling them to wait at the hotel where she would join them in a few days' time. Comfortably settled, they were delighted to have the chance of exploring the town, window-shopping, strolling through the immaculate public gardens, and after dinner setting out on moonlit walks, Doris alight with her ambitious plans for the future.

Sybille was enthralled by her new companion, grateful to her for providing a buffer against her unpredictable parent. When her mother eventually arrived she seemed curiously abstracted; when questioned, she was evasive, saying only that the future was always uncertain. After a couple of days Lisa decided to move to Cortina, taking Sybille and Doris with her, but soon after they arrived she announced she again must leave, and vanished without explanation. A day or two later Doris, too, departed, having finally been offered the job with the film company for which she had been hoping. Thus Sybille, recently turned fifteen, was left entirely alone to wait for her mother's return.

Yet far from feeling abandoned, Sybille felt pleased with her new independence. Hotel life she found most agreeable: she had a comfortable room in which Lisa had left a large number of books, all Tauchnitz editions of English language literature; the staff were kind, and she enjoyed sitting by herself in the dining room. "Waiters, young and old, were charming to children, especially so to a child who liked to eat." At a corner table for one, hands washed, her short fair hair carefully brushed, a book open by her plate, she studied the menu with care, always including in her order a small carafe of wine—inevitably judged inferior to the contents of the cellar at Feldkirch. Her only problem was the inquisitiveness of her fellow guests, who, suspecting scandal, were constantly trying to probe for details about her mother's activities. "They knew perfectly well she was off with somebody she shouldn't have been with, and they kept saying: 'A little girl like you, alone, won't you come to our table?' " Nevertheless when one week, then two, passed with no word from Lisa, Sybille began to feel anxious. Fortunately, after a few more days her mother returned, "not unduly disconcerted to find me by myself," and finally explained the situation.

Since leaving Max, Lisa had led a peripatetic existence. Not long after her divorce she had received a proposal from a wealthy German painter, Otto von Wätjen, previously the husband of the artist Marie Laurencin. Lisa had agreed to marry him, but at the last moment had changed her mind, much taken by a young man she had met by chance during a concert at a private house, a recital by the pianist Artur Schnabel. Neither she nor the young man was musical, and the two came together after each separately succeeded in escaping the performance, discreetly leaving the salon to take refuge on a balcony overlooking the garden.

Norberto Marchesani, always known as "Nori," a young Italian of outstanding beauty, had instantly fallen in love with Lisa. One of a large family, Nori had been brought up on a farm at Bolzano; his father was a university professor, he himself was on the point of completing a degree in architecture. Within a very short time, Nori had proposed to Lisa, and she, charmed and flattered, was at first inclined to laugh it off, but soon found herself completely smitten. The obstacles in front of them were considerable: Lisa had to break off her engagement to Wätjen, while Nori was faced with trying to placate his family, who were appalled that he was intending to marry not only a divorced woman, but one who was Jewish by birth and nearly fifteen years his senior. A further problem was that Nori had no money, while Lisa's income had severely diminished as a consequence of the German inflation. "I was never quite clear about my mother's finances," Sybille admitted. "From having been well off she appeared to have reached a point where she had to be very careful (this was not in her nature)." Eventually everything was settled, and Lisa and Nori were quietly married in September 1925, three months before the death of Maximilian.

Now alone with her daughter, Lisa for the first time talked frankly on a personal level, describing her various dilemmas, confessing how guilty she had felt about breaking her engagement to Wätjen, but also how profoundly she had come to love Nori. Although still youthful in appearance, she was worried by the difference in their ages, she forty-two, Nori in his late twenties; yet he was so devoted, so tolerant and good-natured that she could not believe it would ever make for any difficulty between them. Never had Sybille felt so close to her mother, never before had Lisa talked to her as an equal. " 'Billi—can you understand that one can miss one human being . . . to the point of . . . well, extinction of all else?' 'Yes,' I said . . . For the first time I felt the sting of compassion . . . It was as if some ice had been broken between us."

Soon afterwards Lisa decided to move south, she and Sybille travelling by train to Rome, then on to Naples. Not long after the start of the journey they were joined by Nori. "Our compartment door opened and in stepped a young man more handsome than I could have imagined him to be. He kissed my mother's hand." This was Sybille's first encounter with her stepfather and she took to him immediately. Tall and slender, with a head of glossy brown hair—he "looked as though he had stepped out of a Renaissance canvas," Sybille wrote later—Nori was elegantly dressed and exquisitely well mannered; as quickly became clear, he was also gentle and kind, with a boyish sense of humour and a winning smile. From the beginning Nori sympathised with Sybille's situation, his understanding laying the foundations of a friendship that was to be important to both. Sybille for her part was charmed by Nori, touched by the fact that he was prepared to listen and take her seriously, as well as tease and make her laugh; his manner was lightly paternalistic while at the same time he treated her as the near contemporary she was. The fact that in age he was almost exactly halfway between mother and daughter enabled him in a sense to act as interpreter and intermediary for both.

After Naples, the three of them moved at a leisurely pace to Sorrento, and then for a time to Sicily, before returning to the mainland. Lisa was an energetic guide, taking her two companions to see the famous sites she had first visited as a child with her mother, Anna Bernhardt—Capri, Pompeii, Positano, Paestum, Ravello. For Sybille this was an enthralling experience, not only the exploration of the country but also the fact that every day "we ate the food of the Italian south . . . *melanzane*, thick-cut pasta, calamari, *frittura di pesce* . . . peaches, figs, *mozzarella di bufala* dripping with freshness."

It was while they were in Sicily that her mother told Sybille that she had decided to send her to England to complete her schooling. No doubt wishing for some time alone with Nori, Lisa was also genuinely anxious that her daughter should be properly educated. Since they had grown so much closer over the past few months, Lisa had come to recognise in Sybille not only her own passion for reading but her ambition to become a writer. In Lisa's view, if Sybille wanted to write, she should "stop rattling about like a polyglot parrot . . . [she] should go to England. To a first-rate boarding-school." Recently Lisa had met an English couple, Christopher and Berry Perkins, who had three children of their own, and who she was sure would agree to take her daughter as a paying guest and oversee her education. And so it was arranged. Nori escorted Sybille from Palermo to Naples, from where, and entirely on her own, she was to take the train to Paris and then on to London. "[I was] given a bag to wear under my clothes with lire, French francs and a large crisp white paper which was a five-pound note."

At Victoria Station Sybille was met by Berry Perkins, an amiable woman in early middle age, who took her to spend the night in the Green Park Hotel on Piccadilly. Next morning they set off for Peterborough in Northamptonshire where the Perkinses were temporarily living.

Both Perkinses were painters, Christopher having trained at the Slade, where Dora Carrington, Mark Gertler and Stanley Spencer had been among his fellow students. By the mid-1920s his work was becoming known, although a recent exhibition in London had not been a success, and soon afterwards he and his family had been obliged to move in with his parents. His father, a retired manufacturer of agricultural machinery, lived in considerable comfort in a large house with his wife and a number of relations. This new environment was unlike anything previously experienced by Sybille, who never forgot what she described as "the banality" of her introduction to English life: "parlourmaids, icy bedrooms, sodden vegetables . . . pony traps, Boots' lending library . . . four punctual sit-down meals a day, no wine in sight . . . no horses, no motor car, a (nice) pony and trap, stacks of bicycles." Christopher and Berry she liked, although she had little in common with either; but Christopher was kind and even-tempered, Berry "a light-hearted, self-deprecatory woman, ready to put up cheerfully, if not always effectively, with what circumstances threw at her."

Before long Christopher managed to secure a teaching job in London, and the family moved to an apartment in Hampstead. Sybille saw little of the three children, who were away at school most of the time, while she, dressed in a handed-down blazer and gymslip, was sent to take lessons with a local tutor, a man who fortunately turned out to be an inspirational teacher. "Being taught, learning, was all I had imagined it might be. Most mornings I walked to his Hampstead study for a couple of hours, some of the afternoons I worked . . . Reading was pleasure given dignity by being called work . . . The tutor steered me away from much that had been already impregnated by my mother, such as the nineteenth-century French and Russian novelists and poets, I became inducted to the Victorians, to Fielding, to Dryden and Pope, to Gibbon."

Unfortunately this rewarding arrangement was short-lived as yet again the Perkinses were obliged by their perilous finances to move, first to Winchelsea on the south coast, then returning for a while to London, followed by a few weeks in Peterborough—and so it went on. While in London other teachers were found, some good, others less so, and increasingly, instead of attending lessons, Sybille spent more and more time reading and writing on her own. Crucially it was during this period that she began to realise where her future lay. "My attachment to England was instinctive, a bid for, if not roots, a kind of self-preservation. From early on I had the absolute if shadowy conviction that I would become a writer and nothing else; I held on to the English language as the rope to save me from drifting awash in the fluidities of multilingualism that surrounded me."

Under the Perkinses' liberal regime, Sybille was free to spend her spare time very much as she chose. During one of their longest periods in London, the Perkinses rented a flat in Belsize Park, and on most days, after a morning spent with her books, Sybille took a bus into the West End. Here she started to explore the different areas of the city, the fashionable shopping streets of Bond Street and Savile Row, the grandeur of Whitehall and St. Paul's, the Georgian terraces of Bloomsbury; with keen interest she read the menus posted in the windows of Soho restaurants, and was intrigued by the sight of bewigged barristers standing talking outside the law courts in the Strand. One day for the first time she entered the National Gallery and was struck by two artists in particular, El Greco and Piero della Francesca, whose impact "raised a curtain I had not known was there." From then on she became a frequent visitor not only to the National Gallery but to the Wallace Collection and the Tate.

At the end of every school term Sybille returned to Italy, where Lisa had planned to settle permanently. Now, however, the atmosphere was becoming uneasy, with the country fast turning into a police state. In 1924 Giacomo Matteotti, the socialist politician and critic of Mussolini, had been murdered. Since then the situation had grown ever more threatening, with Mussolini and his Fascist party effectively creating a dictatorship. Neither Nori nor Lisa had made any attempt to hide their socialist sympathies. "They had not belonged to any visible resistance to Il Fascismo, yet it was obvious that they were not for . . . refusing to join what one was expected to join, posting compromising material to a foreign address, circulating copies of the London *Times*." And so in the spring of 1926, "almost from one week to the next," the decision was made to leave Italy and settle in France.

Before the move took place, however, there were some complicated matters to be settled. Since her father's death, no legal guardian had yet been appointed for Sybille, her mother considered ineligible as she now held an Italian passport and was no longer resident in Germany. For weeks documents had been arriving in the post from the court in Baden, the sight of the buff envelopes causing Sybille acute anxiety. At her suggestion Katzi's husband, Hans Borgmann, was asked to assume the role of legal guardian, to which he agreed; but then Katzi suddenly left him for another man and he backed out, leaving Sybille with no option but to be declared a ward of court.

Further problems then arose over the Feldkirch property: this Maximilian had left to be equally divided between his two daughters, but only on condition that the estate remained within the family and his collection preserved in perpetuity. This was clearly impossible, and so the lengthy process was begun of revoking the will so that everything could in due course be auctioned off—a sale which did not take place until a further two years had passed. Consequently Sybille was left with no income of her own, until finally Lisa's trustees came to the rescue, agreeing to maintain her for the time being.

It was in the early spring of 1926 that the family left Italy for good. Curiously, in her written accounts, both fictional and factual, Sybille maintained she was not present, that only later she learned the details of the long journey by train and its somewhat haphazard ending in a small port on the Mediterranean coast. But in fact she was there, as her arrival in France on 12 April with her mother and stepfather was recorded by the Sûreté nationale, which at that period was keeping a careful watch on traffic entering the country over the Italian border.

Lisa's original intention had been to stay for a while in Biarritz, where she had friends, before deciding where to settle. This plan was abandoned, however, while they were still en route. The train journey seemed endless, with lengthy delays while crossing the border, the three of them crammed into a carriage full of suitcases, coats, a picnic basket, boxes of books and Lisa's three little black-and-white Japanese spaniels. Once in France the stops became increasingly frequent, and it was nearly midnight when they reached the station where they were to board the express to take them on to their final destination. But "by the time we got to the station the express had gone," Sybille recalled, "and as my mother didn't want to sit up all night in the train we got out." Fortunately they were directed to a bus standing by, into which the three of them climbed with their luggage and dogs, and after a short rattling ride were deposited within sight of a hotel, which despite the late hour still had its lights on and rooms available.

Next morning they woke to find themselves in a small fishing port, Sanary-sur-Mer, halfway between Toulon and Marseilles. Their hotel, the Hôtel de la Tour, built on to what had been a medieval watchtower, stood at one end of a pretty harbour full of dinghies and fishing boats. The harbour was lined with palm trees, and away from the water, on the other side of the road, was a row of cafés, bars and little shops. The town appeared peaceful and charming and the decision was taken to remain, at least for a while. A house was found, the Villa Ker Mini, "a hot, ill-stuck-together bungalow," situated on the edge of a narrow bay, ten minutes' walk from the centre. Here they could stay while Nori and Lisa began the search for more suitable accommodation.

In fact for the next nearly fifteen years Sanary became Sybille's home, but much more than that: the town itself, the country behind it, the sea and rocky shore, and above all its cast of remarkable characters were to provide not only the setting and inspiration for her finest novel but also an important emotional focus that was to remain with her for ever. Indeed no other period in her long life affected her as profoundly as the years spent in that idyllic region in the south of France, nowhere that she identified with so closely. The sea and the landscape, the friends she made there, the emotional impact of her love affairs, were part of a world to which in her memory and imagination she constantly returned. "The accommodating tolerance of the French *manière de vivre* gave one a large sense of living rationally, sensuously, *well*, of pleasure on many levels: now and before us and for years to come, as no other place in Europe, no other place in the world, France between the wars made one this present of the illusion of freedom."

Meanwhile the family began to settle into a more organised existence. The bungalow was given up and another house found, unprepossessing but comfortable enough, on the chemin du Diable, a narrow street near the centre of town. Sanary itself was very different from the fashionable Riviera, far removed socially and culturally from the luxurious villas and large hotels of Nice and Cannes. Sanary was a modest but thriving community mainly comprised of fishermen and shopkeepers, with a lawyer's office, a pharmacist, two doctors, a couple of retired naval officers, and a few writers and painters living in modern villas situated on the outskirts of town. In the square, the place de Sanary, was the Mairie and the parish church of St. Nazaire. Along the cobbled streets were a number of bars and cafés, and small shops with beaded curtains over their doorways; during the week there was a busy market with stalls displaying meats and cheeses, locally grown fruit, flowers and vegetables, while the fishermen sold their daily catches on the quayside. A little distance beyond was a sandy beach with a few bathing huts, and stretching uphill behind the town an ancient Mediterranean landscape of scrub and terraced hills, vineyards, cypress, ilex and olive groves.

Almost from the beginning Sybille was enchanted by Sanary. She loved the simple Mediterranean cuisine, the swimming, the hot summers. "The great constant was the climate, the inflexible summer climate of the Mediterranean coast. It embraced, contained, our existence;

the ever-present sun and sea, the scented air, the strident sounds of tree-frog and cicada were the element we moved in." And crucially, it was here for the first time that she began to know and understand her mother.

In later life Sybille admitted that although she profoundly admired her mother she was never able to love her. Lisa was too self-centred, too volatile, and almost proud of the fact that she was wholly lacking in maternal instinct. Now that her daughter was growing up, however, Lisa began to look on her as a rewarding companion, someone to whom she could talk almost as an equal, who listened eagerly as she expounded her liberal idealism, her moral and political philosophies. Most inspiring for Sybille was her mother's passionate love of reading, her wide knowledge of French, English and German literature. As Lisa's ambition was to become a writer herself, for years she had talked of ideas for books which she had never had the time or patience to produce. She "was very well educated and she instilled into me the idea that it was a very grand thing to be a writer . . . I suppose I always had a passion for writing, but being brought up to talk about Dostoevsky at breakfast was a great advantage. I owe her an enormous amount."

Indeed even more than her beauty and charm, it was Lisa's conversation that drew people to her, the wit and ebullience of her talk, which was "never relentless, quite interruptible, full of self-mockery . . . [and] often very, very funny." During this early period of their life in Sanary, Sybille for the first time saw her mother serene and happy, her contentment endowing her with a natural grace and radiance that proved magnetically attractive. Although Lisa never cared much about what she wore, often flinging on the nearest garment to hand—rumpled trousers, an old linen shirt—her beauty was as striking as ever, aesthetically as remarkable as that of her handsome young husband.

For Nori was nearly always at her side, providing the love and emotional support which in her earlier marriage she had never known. Nori adored Lisa, loved her "gently, dearly, protectively, beyond the dazzle and the attraction, with the wholehearted devotion of one human being to another." Although with most women he was naturally flirtatious in a gently teasing manner, there was no question but that it was his wife who was the centre of his existence. Watchful and protective, he was always at hand to solve her problems, calm her anxieties, find the keys she had lost, the purse mislaid, gently reassuring her with his affectionate banter. "She would smile sweetly at him: all was as it should be . . . their difference in age did not seem to be a factor—not to her, not to him, and this was also the face they presented with complete naturalness to the world, and the world appeared to accept."

With Sybille, too, Nori was kind and completely at ease, delicately navigating this somewhat unusual relationship, part fatherly, part fraternal. It was he who smoothed the path, made it possible for mother and daughter to grow closer, for Lisa at last to recognise her relationship to her only child. It was not all perfect, of course. As at Feldkirch, Lisa was given to violent outbursts of temper: even a minor annoyance could set her off and she would explode with rage, leaving Sybille shaken and depressed while Lisa herself, apparently unaffected, recovered within minutes. As at Feldkirch, too, the servants disliked her: the two maids who came in by the day dreaded her bad moods, and if there were a problem, broken china or a malfunctioning stove, they always went to Nori, not Lisa, to report it.

Yet on the whole the atmosphere within the family was one of calm and cheerfulness. The Marchesanis soon settled into their new way of life; they began to make friends, find congenial company among their neighbours. When Sybille was not in her room reading she could often be found with a group of young companions swimming and playing on the beach. (Over dinner one evening a friend of Lisa, the German poet and playwright Ernst Toller, said to her, "Funny kind of girl you've got here, comes in from making sandcastles then reads André Gide.") To increase their inadequate finances, Nori, a trained architect, set himself up in business as a builder and decorator. Soon he started finding houses for summer visitors, which he would then renovate and repair, and in this he was assisted by Lisa. "My mother had a knack of making any room look charming . . . and [Nori] was immensely handy with anything he touched; together they supplied taste and imagination." All in all that first summer in Sanary was a period of tranquillity, with little indication of the devastating sequence of events that were ultimately to unfold.

Sybille continued living in London during the school term, returning to Sanary for the holidays. She also, in September 1927, went to Berlin to see her sister, Katzi, who had recently remarried. Katzi's second husband, Hans Gunther von Dincklage, was a German diplomat of notable intelligence and charm. Tall, blond, blue-eyed, Dincklage, always known to his friends as "Spatz" ("Sparrow"), was strikingly handsome, a playboy with an unquenchable appetite for social life that matched Katzi's own. Yet there was more to him than that: after a distinguished wartime career as a cavalry officer, Spatz had been employed by the *Abwehr*, posted to both Warsaw and Paris, working undercover to collect strategic information for the German military. Now with his wife he was shortly to move to Sanary, a location of some significance for one of his profession, not least on account of its proximity to the French naval base at Toulon. As Sybille wrote later, her sister's second marriage was in time to become "a disaster of lifelong consequences."

At first, however, all seemed to be well. Since their father's death, it was Katzi who had been dealing with the lawyers commissioned to arrange the sale of the Feldkirch estate. This was finally put up for auction—the house and park and Maximilian's entire collection—over three days in May 1928, the sale producing a satisfactory sum, enough to provide both daughters with a modest but sufficient income for the foreseeable future. A legal guardian was appointed for Sybille, an ex-Cabinet minister whom Lisa had known during her marriage to Max. But for Sybille, while relieved that her father's complex legacy was at last resolved, her most immediate pleasure was in her ownership of her father's gold cigarette case and lighter. At seventeen, slightly plump, with her fair hair cut boyishly short, dressed in a plain jacket and skirt, Sybille adopted with relish the role of *cavaliere servente*. "I carried the case filled with sixpence worth of Craven A, flashing it around in solemn hospitality . . . [springing] up to offer a light to any woman as soon as she put cigarette to mouth."

It was in this same year, while Sybille was lodging with the Perkinses in Belsize Park that, somewhat to her surprise, she was visited by her mother. Unknown to her daughter, Lisa had been conducting a secret liaison with an Englishman, and had come to London to see him. Although happy in her marriage, Lisa always craved male admiration, a craving that grew more powerful with age as she sought reassurance that her sexual magnetism remained undimmed. While on a visit to Paris she had met the art critic, and notorious womaniser, Clive Bell, husband of Virginia's Woolf's sister, Vanessa. The two of them had had a brief affair, and now after Bell's return to London Lisa was anxious not to lose her new admirer, who she also hoped might assist her in launching a literary career of her own. Bell had recently published his *Civilization: An Essay*, and Lisa offered to write about it for a German magazine; in return she asked him to help her find works in English that she could translate into German—"*Il faut m'aider un peu dans ma car-rière littéraire, n'est-ce pas?*" ("You should help me in my literary career, no?").

Described by Virginia Woolf as "the Don Juan of Bloomsbury," Bell was initially taken with Lisa, talking excitedly about his "beautiful Germanness." Before long, however, and no doubt alarmed by Lisa's neediness, Bell's interest waned as he turned his attention to a pretty young actress, and Lisa was reduced to writing him plaintive letters which, it seems, were left unanswered. "*Pourquoi pas de ne répondre à ma lettre? Ca vous embêtait d'écrire? . . . Pourquoi? . . . Je suis seule . . . J'ai tellement envie de vous revoir . . .*" ("Why don't you answer my letter? Is it a bother for you to write? . . . Why? . . . I'm alone . . . I so much want to see you again . . ."). Despite this somewhat lowering experience, Lisa's spirits had sufficiently recovered by the time she returned to Sanary for her to boast that the distinguished art critic Clive Bell had asked her to marry him.

Meanwhile Sybille was coming to the end of her time with the Per-kinses: in the autumn of 1928 Christopher was offered a teaching post in New Zealand and the family planned to leave England the follow-ing January. In order to supplement her income Sybille decided to try teaching German, advertising her services in *The Times*, but the results were disappointing, with only a couple of pupils applying, and the immediate future began to seem worryingly insecure. Fortunately it was at this point that Sybille made a couple of new acquaintances, who would completely transform her London life. Through a friend of Lisa, Sybille had been given an introduction to two German sisters, Toni and Kate Silbermann, both in their late thirties, Jewish émigrés, whose well-to-do family had been impoverished by the post-war inflation. While living precariously in Berlin Toni had met and married an Englishman with whom she had moved to London, where soon afterwards she was joined by her sister Kate.

Toni's husband, Percy Muir, a couple of years younger than his wife, was a highly regarded antiquarian book dealer. He was currently working at Dulau's bookshop in Bond Street, where both sisters were employed as occasional assistants. Kate, who had adopted her sister's married name, first made contact with Sybille, inviting her to tea at her small flat in Marylebone. Kate was no beauty, her face long and sallow, her eyes small, her brown hair dull and crinkly, and yet she had an irresistible appeal. Clever and amusing, she enchanted her guest with talk about her past in Germany, her love of music and theatre, her passion for reading. As Sybille left, Kate gave her a copy of a novel, *Antic Hay* by Aldous Huxley, an author of whom Sybille at that stage of her life knew nothing. The book made an extraordinary impact, and after reading it, Sybille "got hold of everything else by Aldous Huxley . . . [his books] seemed to bring me everything I would then have liked to know and think."

Soon after this first encounter Sybille was introduced to Toni and Percy, who lived in a tiny mews flat behind one of the Nash terraces in Regent's Park. Toni was exquisitely beautiful, witty and a mesmerising talker, but unlike her sister restless and discontented, her constant querulous complaints on the whole blandly ignored by her calm, good-natured husband. The sisters were extremely close, and Sybille was fascinated by both, although it was Kate whom at this stage she came to know better. With plenty of time at her disposal, Kate saw Sybille almost daily; Sybille took a room in a lodging house a couple of doors down from Kate in Gloucester Place, and together the two of them visited galleries and museums, lunched in cheap restaurants, attended an occasional matinee in the West End. Kate was never available on weekday evenings, but Sybille was often invited to supper with Percy and Toni, and at weekends accompanied all three on trips to the country, to Cornwall, to Suffolk, and then to a cottage Percy rented in Essex. "And so began what became a pattern in my life: friendships, attachments to a group, a couple, a family not my own . . . The autumn in London was a kind of turning point. I had not been unhappy before; now I was consciously, buoyantly happy, looking forward to something new, something good every day."

The cottage at Great Bardfield was a particular source of pleasure. Roomy and comfortable, it had a pretty garden with an orchard, and it was here that Sybille came to know Percy Muir, as the two of them tinkered happily with Percy's Morris Cowley in the garage. Percy, an expert on nineteenth-century manuscripts and modern first editions, was about to leave Dulau's to join the distinguished rare-book dealer Elkin Mathews. A quiet, thoughtful man with a subtle sense of humour, he could be excellent company, relishing intelligent talk, politely concealing his boredom when the conversation turned to gossip and feminine frivolities. Many of his closest friends were writers, among them Ian Fleming and also A. J. A. Symons, who rented a house in Finchingfield, the next village to Great Bardfield. "AJ," as he was known, was a sociable, garrulous man, a collector and bibliographer, founder of the First Edition Club and later of the Wine & Food Society. A writer by profession, although hardly an industrious one, AJ's best-known work, *The Quest for Corvo*, would be published in 1934. Insecure financially, he privately indulged in some dubious business practices to fund his extravagant way of life, but locally he was well liked. He and his wife entertained generously; and, from the moment the Muirs first arrived, invited them almost every weekend to luncheons and dinners, in which as a matter of course Sybille was included. She was dazzled by Symons and by his articulate, literate friends, "whose horizons embraced France, Italy, Greece and beyond. At the end of a short bicycle ride in Essex I had arrived at a side-stream of the English literary world. I had found my first Garsington."

Equally impressive was AJ's expertise as oenophile and gourmet. His standards were high, and much time was devoted to planning menus, attending wine tastings and keeping his own cellar well stocked. Before dinner at Finchingfield guests were taken down to the dark, brick-lined basement for a candlelit tour of the cellars, vividly recalling to Sybille her childhood experience of her father's cellars at Feldkirch. Once seated at table, AJ would expound at length on the contents of his glass, reverently holding it up to his nose and extolling its qualities before inviting his friends to do the same, a process which exasperated some, but which deeply impressed the youngest member of the company.

While in London one day Kate asked Sybille if she knew anything about legal process, and if she would be interested in attending a trial. Immediately intrigued, Sybille shortly afterwards accompanied Kate to the Royal Courts of Justice in the Strand. Here they sat up in the public gallery above the court, the case in progress a libel suit brought by a popular band-leader. Sybille was spellbound, fascinated by the learning and eloquence of the judge and counsel, by the brilliant theatricality of the performance. From that moment, "I was hooked for life. By the English legal system, by the supreme importance of a Rule of Law and the ways it was applied . . . Everything captivated: the voices, the casuistries of the arguments, the rigidities and the drama of that formalised man's world." In later years Sybille often said she wished she had been able to train as a barrister, a career impossible in those days for a woman; she was, however, to pursue her passion for the law, in time becoming highly respected as a writer on the subject, reporting in both Europe and America on some of the most famous trials of the twentieth century.

So enthralled was she by this first experience that Kate immediately arranged for her to attend again. On this occasion Sybille went on her own, and through the favour of a judge's clerk known to Kate was allowed to sit in a far more privileged position, down in the well of the court. Absorbed in this new experience, it was only later she began to wonder how it was that Kate, who appeared to have no friends at all, certainly no connection to the law, was so familiar with this very specialist environment.

The mystery was soon explained. Early one morning as Sybille was leaving her lodgings, a few yards in front of her she saw Kate walking home down Gloucester Place wearing a long chiffon evening dress under her coat. Over dinner that weekend Sybille finally learned about Kate's other life. For several years she had been the mistress of a High Court judge, Henry McCardie, widely respected in his profession. Although unmarried, McCardie was careful to conceal the fact that he had a mistress, knowledge that would seriously have damaged his career, as Kate well understood. Thus every weekday evening she travelled by Underground from Baker Street to Westminster, always elegantly attired, to spend the night with McCardie, returning home the following morning to resume her normal daily routine.

With the beginning of summer, Sybille, now eighteen, again left London to return to her mother and stepfather in Sanary. The Marchesanis were currently living at La Tranquille, a villa situated a little way outside the town. Nori's plan was eventually to restore and redecorate the property before letting it, but meanwhile it provided a convenient, if not particularly comfortable, base for the family to stay. For Sybille the summer of 1929 was the beginning of an intense, if ephemeral, period of happiness, a period free of anxiety, of days spent swimming, reading, making new friends, eating well, and absorbing the sensuous atmosphere of the Mediterranean. "From May to October there was no rain, only night-dew, thus nothing changed: the earth was monochrome, the sea reverberated the sky. Morning after morning we woke to clear light, coolness modulating through the hours into the still, unwavering heat of noon, the small evening breezes, the warm night luminous from sky and phosphorescent sea. How permanent they felt, these even summers, how reassuring . . ."

As well as decorator and architect, Nori had recently started working as an art dealer, a venture in which he had been energetically supported by Lisa. With her love and knowledge of painting, and her various acquaintances in the art world, she had encouraged her husband in this promising new project, helping him make contact with local painters and providing introductions to artists and galleries further afield. Before long Nori was travelling regularly to Paris and Amsterdam, returning full of enthusiasm for his new business.

During his frequent absences Sybille was able to spend significant periods alone with her mother. Now approaching fifty, Lisa was still a beautiful woman; men admired her, flirted with her, yet there was detectable an undercurrent of anxiety, a hunger for reassurance as she looked for the flattery and attention which in earlier years she had accepted as her due. One incident which Sybille remembered with acute discomfort was when Lisa turned to her unexpectedly to ask, " 'Have I changed?' . . . Her beauty had been an intrinsic attribute . . . Now it seemed not so . . . I did what her question imposed, and I did it a fraction too late, I looked at her. I saw what unasked I might not have seen: intimations of wear . . . What was gone? A glow? She was older." Lisa said nothing but Sybille was painfully aware that her hesitation had been noted.

On the whole, however, Lisa seemed content, satisfied with her marriage, at least for the present. While Nori was away she and her daughter enjoyed an agreeable companionship. The mornings were spent in their separate rooms, Lisa reading and writing in bed with her beloved spaniels sprawled around her, Sybille absorbedly making her way through the works of Balzac, Zola, George Sand, the Goncourts. At midday the two of them walked into town, did a little shopping, before settling outside with an aperitif at one of the bars in the main square. They returned to the villa for lunch, cooked by the *femme de ménage*, and afterwards there was more reading, and Sybille often went to the beach to meet friends and to swim—"salt water, rock pools, open bays, pellucid depths, breakers and spray . . . It was then that I did my dreaming." If there were no plans for the evening Sybille, equipped with napkin, bowl and torch, set off at dusk to collect their dinner, a ready-prepared dish from one of the restaurants. This Lisa ate off a tray, while her daughter insisted on sitting upright at a table covered in a cloth and properly laid, complete with baguette and bottle of wine. Lisa "had tried to laugh me out of what she called my clubmanly dinners, I said that not bothering to sit up to eat was an appalling feminine habit. We agreed to disagree." Looking back, Sybille recalled this period as a time of welcome serenity: "a mother and her daughter, a pair of sisters, a woman and girl—ensconced happily, very happily, in our wind-blown villa, like two explorers in their base camp. Such a time never came again."

Since their arrival in Sanary, the Marchesanis had made a number of friends. During the summer Sybille found herself involved in a constant round of social engagements, sometimes with Nori and Lisa, sometimes with companions of her own age with whom she played games on the beach, or in the evening danced to a couple of accordions in the square. With her parents she was regularly included in card games at the Café de la Marine, in games of boules in the afternoon, in lengthy Sunday luncheons at the houses of various neighbours. Lisa enjoyed such society, talking incessantly as ever, about literature, politics, history, while Mlle. Marchesani, as Sybille was known, listened intently to her mother's disquisitions. When given the chance she readily joined in, although it was sometimes difficult, especially for new acquaintance, to make out what she was saying: her voice was low and she had a curious habit of mumbling, an odd stuttering in her speech that rendered it frustratingly indistinct. Over the years there were many who complained of these inaudible mutters, delivered almost as though she were talking to herself, a criticism which she acknowledged—up to a point. "[I did have] a slight stammer . . . [but] never quite knew whether it was involuntary or put on."

Among the more colourful characters in Sanary society were the painter Moïse ("Kiki") Kisling and his wife, Renée. Kiki, born in Poland but since the age of nineteen living in France, a friend of Picasso and Matisse, had known Lisa in earlier days in Paris. Sociable and ebullient, full of energy and good humour, Kiki, now in his early thirties, was a small, bear-like man, while his wife was tall and muscular, deeply bronzed, her short fair hair bleached almost white by the sun. While Kiki dressed in neatly ironed shirts and blue cotton trousers, Renée favoured strong, plain colours, a string of heavy shells around her neck, shell and ivory bracelets on her powerful arms. Although husband and wife led somewhat separate lives—Kiki, an energetic womaniser, was often away fulfilling portrait commissions—they were tolerant of each other, and devoted parents to their two little boys, who were particularly adored by their mother. In Sybille's view, when she came to know them, Jean and Guy were a pair of savages, shrieking as they leapt in and out of the sea, running round the table during meals outdoors, and when in the house casually peeing on the carpet.

From their first meeting Sybille was fascinated by Renée, a "great handsome monster . . . [with] large prominent blue eyes . . . a nose like a parrot's beak . . . [and] a smile of serene, archaic sweetness." Within a short while Sybille became included in the Kislings' family life, with Renée keeping a motherly eye on her, not hesitating to criticise or scold when necessary. She was a superb cook, and Sybille loved to watch her at work, acting as her *sous-chef* in the kitchen. A powerful swimmer, Renée kept her own fishing boat, on which in the early mornings Sybille sometimes accompanied her. They "would go out on the dawn sea, still, flat and grey, far out beyond the sight of land: fish, then swim off the boat and swim again, and return before high noon. That was magical." Tough, generous and quick-tempered, Renée did exactly as she pleased, indifferent to others' opinion, showing no compunction in openly indulging her strong sexual appetite with both men and women. "*Si on est ami*," she used to say, "*il n'a aucune différence si on fait l'amour avec*" ("If you are friends, it's all alright to make love together"). Indeed Sybille was one of several female friends with whom Renée had a physical relationship, taking her upstairs to bed one night and making love to her "in a manner compounded of protectiveness, sensuality and great ease."

For Sybille this was almost certainly an initiation, a profoundly moving experience and one which she never forgot. From a young age Sybille had been attracted to her own sex, developing powerful crushes in early adolescence on a number of her mother's women friends. With Renée, she had taken a first step into an adult world, drawn into a warm, maternal friendship that seamlessly expanded into one of tender eroticism.

An occasion to which Sybille during the summer always looked forward was the film show on Sunday nights. The shabby little two-tier cinema, housed in a converted garage, was a popular venue, the ground floor packed with noisy young men and their girlfriends drinking and smoking, while upstairs respectable tradesmen sat with their wives. Sybille and Lisa often attended together, both of them enjoying the outing. "The screen was bad, the piano lively . . . [the films] were good. Movies: black and white, silent. American mostly . . . Chaplin, Douglas Fairbanks, Buster Keaton, Harold Lloyd." One evening while waiting for the show to begin, they noticed a couple of strangers walk in. "They were slim like cats' shadows, matched in size, quietly, gracefully moving side by side . . . Stylish and aloof, they seemed apparitions stepped from the vanguard of some coming world . . . To me, they were the most beautiful pair of human beings I had ever seen."

Pierre and Jacqueline Mimerel, both of whom were to make a significant impact on Sybille's life, were newly arrived in Sanary, currently living in a rented villa on the western side of the bay. In their early thirties, the couple were cultured and sophisticated, obviously well-to-do, recently arrived from Paris to start a new life in the south for the sake of Pierre's somewhat fragile health. Until recently Pierre had been working for the firm of Bernard Grasset, publisher of, among others, Proust, Maurois, Mauriac and Henry de Montherlant; before long, however, the results of his traumatic wartime experiences—the loss of three brothers, he himself fighting in the trenches aged only sixteen— proved seriously damaging and he was advised to leave Paris for good.

The Mimerels quickly became part of that small group of Sanary society to which the Marchesanis belonged. On the surface the two couples liked each other well enough, although there were some significant areas of incompatibility. Politically, Pierre was on the far right, which Lisa found distasteful, while he disapproved of what he saw as her extreme leftist stance, as he did that of the Kislings and others of their political persuasion. Socially, however, the pair proved agreeable company, Pierre courteous, intelligent and well read, while Jacqueline could be delightful, much admired for her vivacity and chic. Both were tall, slender and elegantly dressed, bringing with them an aura of metropolitan glamour to this small seaside community.

For Sybille the arrival of the Mimerels was to effect a transformation. Not only was she spellbound by their style and sophistication but she soon found herself inextricably bound up with both on a number of levels. With Pierre, as well as an interest in French history and literature, she discovered a shared passion for cars. Nori, a keen motorist himself, had begun teaching Sybille to drive, taking her out in a small, second-hand Peugeot he had recently acquired. One hot afternoon while the two of them were stalled on the quayside, with Sybille laboriously trying to shift gear, Jacqueline suddenly appeared. She quickly suggested that Sybille learn in one of their own much more modern vehicles; not only that, but the mechanic they employed would act as instructor, an offer that was eagerly accepted. "I was car-mad . . . speed-mad as well . . . I snatched at the chance of driving any wheels on offer." Sybille passed her test at the first attempt, after which to her intense delight she often found herself motoring about the countryside with Pierre, spending happy hours with him in his garage, tinkering with the engines of his impressive collection, the pride of which was a De Dion-Bouton of 1911.

For the rest of her life Sybille remained devoted to Pierre, loving him for his kindness and calm temperament, looking on him as her father figure: *"je suis fier d'être ton père"* ("I am proud to be your father"), he told her more than once. Despite his right-wing politics, Sybille admired his wisdom and learning, as she did his irony and wit. Pierre's "daily life was animated by laughter . . . being with him entailed constant teases, often at one's own expense."

With Pierre's wife Sybille's relationship was very different. With Jacqueline she fell helplessly in love: indeed almost from the moment they met, Sybille was smitten by this tall, slender, dark-haired beauty. Jacqueline was witty and intelligent, although, unlike her husband, in no sense an intellectual; "her springboard was triviality and one-upmanship . . . a hunger . . . to be effective, to make a great splash." Jacqueline craved admiration, needed to be the centre of attention, although it was male attention she was after, rather than the yearning of an eighteen-year-old girl. Sybille's adoration irritated her yet at the same time it gave her a satisfying sense of power; when in company Jacqueline was charming to Sybille, ruffling her hair, treating her like a clever child; but when they were alone she often made her impatience clear, was brisk, cutting, dismissive, although she could also switch with disconcerting speed to provocative and flirtatious, teasing Sybille by comparing their relationship to that of the young Octavian and the Marschallin in *Der Rosenkavalier*.

Looking back many years later Sybille recalled her love for Jacqueline mostly in terms of anguish. Her obsession was overwhelming, she thought of Jacqueline every waking moment, longing for her presence, counting the minutes between one meeting and the next. "In the mornings I would hang about the *place* waiting for her to appear, rush to her car, open the door before it had stopped, kiss her hand . . . snatch at anything portable . . . Then I'd follow her to Chez Benech, the *crémerie*, the fruit stalls. When my presence bored her—often—she showed it . . . I knew I was being teased. I knew I was making a fool of myself. It changed nothing . . . [I was] lost in love."

Meanwhile Sybille's life at home continued much as before. Nori's business was prospering: as well as his building work, he had begun to sell Provençal furniture, driving out into the country with Lisa, who enjoyed such expeditions, looking for the antique tables, chairs and chests of drawers certain to appeal to the sophisticated society which in increasing numbers were now renting houses on the coast. The Marchesanis' own standard of living had markedly improved: the villa in which they were currently staying, La Tranquille, had been made roomy and comfortable and they had a cook and maid to look after them. On evenings at home, the three of them played paper games, which Sybille loved, and games of cards, including patience, at which Nori was expert. "I still see him, that slim young man with his long beautiful hands, bring out the two small packs of pretty cards and lay them out on the dining table . . . He had a good repertory and taught me some of it; I have often found Miss Milligan or Nine-Up a soothing resource."

During this period Sybille and Nori grew closer than ever, tacitly bonding over their shared responsibility to keep watch over Lisa. They enjoyed their mornings together, as Lisa, a bad sleeper, always heavily doped with Veronal, rarely appeared before midday. Sometimes the two of them would drive into town, or out into the country, or simply stay at home doing odd jobs and talking. Nori had recently bought a type-writer, which thrilled Sybille, who saw it as a solution to the illegibility of her handwriting. Nori taught her how to use it, and they would com-pete to see who could type the fastest. Yet despite the generally peaceful atmosphere both were aware of the dangerous unpredictability of Lisa's moods, both instantly alert to any sudden change in atmosphere. It was Lisa who was the dominant member of the household, Lisa who had to be the centre of attention. "Without being really selfish or eccentric [Lisa] behaved as though she owned her entourage, and of course above friends and daughter, one owned one's husband." When describing the relationship she had with her stepfather at this period, Sybille compared it to that of two brothers, "serving—in different ranks—in the same regiment." Once when Nori returned to the house after a few days away to find everything in order, he embraced Sybille gratefully. "He touched my shoulder. 'You have looked after her.' It was like changing the guard."

At the beginning of the summer of 1929, Lisa decided to go on her own to Switzerland for a cure: the mountain air, she believed, would do her good. The family was on the point of leaving La Tranquille, which Nori had sold to an old friend of Lisa, from Germany, Hilda von Gunther, whom Sybille fondly remembered from her childhood at Feldkirch. The move to their new house would take place while Lisa was away, and on one of the last evenings at the now almost empty villa

Nori decided to give a party: the interior would be transformed into a ship and everyone was asked to come dressed as sailors.

Sybille loved the idea, thrilled when Nori disguised her as a pirate in a striped top and cotton trousers—she had never worn trousers before—colouring her face dark brown, with sideburns and thick black eyebrows drawn in charcoal. They hung Chinese lanterns from the ceiling, Nori mixed huge bowls of punch, and there was a small band on the terrace. The evening was an immense success. "We all danced, regardless of age or sex. I felt carried away, ecstatic, outside myself." The only disappointment, a considerable one, was that neither of the Mimerels had appeared. Then suddenly at midnight, down from the rafters came swinging two buccaneers, "Levantine pirates, their stylish captain in wig and kerchief . . . his slim lieutenant bristling with daggers and cutlass in belt"—Pierre and Jacqueline in person. Sybille was ecstatic: nothing could have prepared her for such an intoxicating surprise, nothing, she felt, could exceed her rapture at such a miraculous turn of events.

The next morning, sleepless and still high on the euphoria of the night before, she and Nori decided to drive to Saint-Tropez for lunch. They were accompanied by a brother and sister, Cécile and Frédéric, contemporaries of Sybille's, whose parents were good friends of the Marchesanis. Cécile had long had a crush on Nori, while Frédéric, who regarded most girls of around his age as potential targets, had for some time had his eye on Sybille. Arriving in Saint-Tropez, they ran into a couple of Nori's clients, who invited them aboard their yacht for cocktails and a late lunch; this lasted until early evening when the whole party decided to go ashore for drinks and dinner, followed by dancing at a local nightclub. It was 4 a.m. by the time they left, too late to drive home, especially as the car was discovered to have a flat tyre. Luckily, after wandering the streets for a while a small backstreet hotel was found with two rooms available. Nori and Cécile took one, Sybille and Frédéric the other. "We got out of our clothes . . . and into the bed. Frédéric began making love to me . . . [He] was very sure of himself—this was evidently not a new experience for him. I did my best not to let him suspect that it was that for me. It didn't hurt very much, nothing to fuss about; mildly disagreeable all in all."

For Sybille the incident was of little importance. She had experienced one previous heterosexual encounter, with a cousin of Nori's who had made a pass at her one day when the two of them were out on a walk. He had sat down with her under a tree, Sybille assumed to have a cigarette. "There ensued, at once and in complete silence, what I had read about as heavy petting. I was too surprised to be taken aback and almost at once surprised again by entirely unexpected and delicious sensations. When we stood up . . . [we] resumed our walk as though absolutely nothing had occurred." In personal terms neither Nori's cousin nor Frédéric meant anything to her, an indifference which Frédéric would shortly come to resent.

By the time Lisa returned to Sanary the move to the new house had been completed. Les Cyprès, by far the most comfortable of their houses so far, was situated about a mile from the centre, to the west towards the more populous town of Bandol. It was an old house, "ochre-washed, one-storeyed, a simple facade of long windows with the faded-blue wooden shutters of the region, standing on the highest of three terraced levels flanked on each side by a row of cypresses . . . Inside it was cool, the floors plain, polished deep-red tiles, the rooms . . . well-proportioned, the walls whitewashed, the woodwork in light colours." Sybille loved Les Cyprès, and looked forward to spending the rest of the summer there.

Meanwhile her passion for Jacqueline continued to obsess her, and each day she went into town, wandering about in the hope of seeing her. Late one morning, when the *place* was crowded with shoppers, she caught up with Jacqueline just as she was climbing into her car to drive home. In a moment of desperation Sybille for the first time confessed that she loved her. " 'May I tell you something?' 'Would it amuse me?' 'It well might.' . . . 'In that case do tell me.' I looked at her. Straight. With complete concentration. Then I uttered the three fatal words . . . 'You've chosen an odd time of day for making your dramatic announcement,' " Jacqueline said drily before driving off, leaving Sybille feeling miserable and humiliated and as deeply in love as ever.

At the end of August, when the summer season was nearly over, Pierre came up with the idea of a tennis tournament. Both he and Jacqueline were experts, having played in the past with such stars as Jean Borotra, René Lacoste and Suzanne Lenglen. A date was fixed in the first week of September, the tournament, lasting several days, to take place on the tennis courts at the Grand Hôtel des Bains in Bandol, where a number of notable players were staying. The whole occasion proved a great success, and towards the end of the week an elaborate dinner was held at the hotel, at which both the Mimerels and Marchesanis were present. At the end of the evening, as Nori was backing the car out of the hotel yard the boy Frédéric ran up to them, and in Sybille's words, "jumped onto the running board . . . shouting into the open car window, '*Vous avez mal gardé votre fille, Madame! Elle court après les femmes . . .*' " ("You haven't taken good care of your daughter, Madame! She runs after women . . ."). Nori quickly drove off, and nothing was said. "Arrived at Les Cyprès, we bade each other a good night."

Worse was to follow. The next day was the last of the tournament, during which Sybille, by extraordinary chance and to her profound dismay, was matched against Simonne Mathieu, the new French number one. Jacqueline, outraged, considered this ridiculous, and demanded Sybille be withdrawn, but she was overruled by Pierre. Surprisingly, once on court Sybille's nervousness disappeared and she played well, so that although inevitably she lost, her defeat was far from shameful. That evening a reception was held at the hotel where Jacqueline was to present the prizes. It was a formal occasion, the men in black tie, Sybille, much against her will, wearing a pale blue taffeta evening dress bought for her by Lisa. Towards the end of the proceedings, Sybille's name was called out and she walked up to the platform to receive a runners-up award from Jacqueline, who, obviously furious, gave it to her but without looking at her or even shaking her hand. "As I walked back, a few baffled people attempted applause." It was a humiliating experience, and once they were home Lisa exploded, enraged that her daughter's behaviour had now become public knowledge. She must leave immediately, Lisa said; it was out of the question to remain in Sanary any longer. And two days later Sybille set out on the return journey to London, made miserable by her mother's words. "You are not afflicted by a great love, you are afflicted by a crush . . . And don't go about thinking of yourself as a doomed Baudelairean pervert burdened by the love that dare not speak its name . . . Come back when you are in a more reasonable mood."

Ironically, it was Jacqueline who in later years came most to regret the unhappy nature of their relationship. Decades later, after the two of them had come across each other again, she wrote to Sybille, *"j'ai beaucoup de regrets et de remords d'avoir été si cruelle, parfois, pour l'enfant que tu étais. J'étais moi-même trop jeune, peut-être, pour comprendre, comme je l'ai compris plus tard, la beauté irremplaçable de ces sentiments si purs, si neufs, si totaux d'une adolescente . . . Tu n'as, je crois, jamais compris l'émotion que je ressentais et le très émouvant et délicieux souvenir que je garde"* ("I feel so much regret and remorse at having been so cruel to the child you then were. I myself was too young, perhaps, to understand, as I understood later, the irreplaceable beauty of those emotions of yours, so pure, so new, so completely those of a young person . . . You have never, I think, understood the emotion I felt and the very moving and delicious memory that I retain"). As for Sybille, when at the age of seventy she was asked by a friend who had been the greatest loves of her life, she named Jacqueline as one, but with a telling proviso: "In terms of pain, desperation, 'carried away,' deep sense of loss: Yes. In terms of fulfilment, life affection: No."

FOUR

THE DELIGHTS AND DANGERS
OF SANARY-SUR-MER

For Sybille the transition from summer in Sanary to the shabby bed-sitting room in Gloucester Place was inevitably depressing. Haunted by her unrequited love for Jacqueline and its humiliating exposure, she yet did her best to put it behind her, relieved that none of her London friends knew anything about it. In order to increase her inadequate income, she again started to teach, offering lessons in French and German, her pupils mainly young men preparing for the diplomatic service or for business abroad. Thanks to Percy Muir, she also found work translating booksellers' and auctioneers' catalogues, less well paid than teaching but welcome nonetheless. Her only problem was with her atrocious handwriting: without Nori's typewriter she was obliged to write in capitals in order to make her transcriptions legible.

As before Sybille's social life revolved around the Muirs, although to her disappointment the weekends in the country had come to an end. During her absence, relations between Toni and Percy had seriously deteriorated, Percy having fallen in love with a young woman whom he had met at the Symonses' house in Essex. From the moment Toni discovered the affair the Muirs' marriage was over: not only did Toni refuse to discuss the matter with her husband, but she immediately moved out of their flat, taking her sister with her to an apartment in Highgate. Kate meanwhile continued her evening journeys into the West End to see her judge, who to her delight had recently suggested that for the first time the two of them should go on holiday together. With Sybille's help rooms had been booked at a hotel in Sanary for a fortnight in the summer.

When in due course the two of them arrived in the south of France, Sybille went to meet them at the Hôtel de la Plage. Henry McCardie turned out to be delightful, impressing Sybille not only with accounts of the various trials he had participated in but also with his knowledge of wine, evident in the expert analysis of the fine burgundy he had ordered for their luncheon. Unfortunately the affair with Kate was not to last. For some years McCardie had been a secretive and compulsive gambler, and in 1933 he was suddenly to lose almost everything he owned. Unable to face the consequences, he shot himself one evening while alone in his apartment. Kate was devastated, and from then on retreated further and further into herself; although the friendship with Sybille continued until the end of her life, it was Toni who arranged everything, who became the spokeswoman for them both.

During the period of Sybille's adolescence in England, the friendship and support of the Muir sisters had been of crucial importance. In the years to come, however, she was to see them only infrequently, although she continued to keep in touch. In those early days she had spent more time with Kate, but it was with Toni that she was to form the closer relationship, writing to her regularly, regarding her as the confidante to whom, almost more than anyone else, she could reveal her private life and feelings. While Sybille retained a genuine fondness for the sisters, she was aware, too, of an eccentricity and sadness about them that continued to intrigue her. For over half a century their strange story lay dormant in her imagination—before it was retrieved and vividly brought to life as a substantial component of *Jigsaw*, the last of her four published works of fiction.

When Sybille returned to France at the end of June 1930, she was nineteen, a short, sturdy figure, her blonde hair cut short like a boy's. During the months of her exile in London she had longed to return, longed for the world of which she had come to feel part. "[I had] come to feel that Sanary <u>was</u> the true South, and that Sanary and the French were for me. I had fallen for it and for all that it had offered already. Here was my home, here I was going to live . . . and here, the gods willing, I was going to write my books." She felt intensely happy to be once more in these familiar surroundings, and at first all seemed to be well, the house in immaculate condition, both Lisa and Nori quietly pleased to see her. Very quickly, however, she sensed a tension between them, that Nori in particular seemed on edge; she noticed, too, that Lisa had aged, had grown thinner, her face more lined. There was an uncomfortable atmosphere between husband and wife, the cause of which Lisa lost little time in explaining to her daughter.

Unexpectedly one day Doris von Schönthan, the young woman who had acted as escort when Sybille first left Germany, had arrived in Sanary for a few weeks' holiday. Lisa had been delighted to see her, welcoming her to the house, enjoying long conversations about actors, poets, writers, the changing political climate, particularly the rise of the right wing and the fragility of the Weimar Republic. It was not long, however, before she noticed a powerful attraction developing between Doris and her husband, which inevitably sparked a series of explosive rows. On this occasion her husband was unable to reassure her: Nori admitted that he and Doris had fallen in love, and although he promised to end the affair eventually this would not happen overnight.

For Lisa the situation was intolerable. In all her relations with men, it was she who needed to be in control. "She was too beautiful, too talented, too amusing," Sybille recalled. "Everybody adored her, and she constantly went from one man to another, and when it happened to her she just couldn't take it." For almost the first time her rages made no difference, her raw, resentful moods had no effect. She felt desperate, furious with Nori, and at the same time terrified of losing him, of being left to live alone. Unable to sleep even with increased doses of Veronal, she consulted the local pharmacist, who gave her the name of a doctor known for his liberal prescribing. Dr. Joyeu, referred to behind his back as "Docteur Lugubre," was as "gaunt as a starving horse, yellow-faced with darkly ringed, sunken eyes and a few strands of flat black hair." Obligingly he produced a syringe and gave Lisa an injection which had an immediate, almost magical effect: within minutes she was feeling calm and happy. The doctor wrote her a prescription and told her she might inject herself once, at the most twice, a day. Delighted, Lisa returned home, handing a little box containing a glass syringe, a thin steel file, and some tiny ampoules to Nori, instructing him that it was he who must administer the injections as she could never do it for herself.

This was all explained to Sybille shortly after her arrival, by which time Lisa had already increased her dosage. Predictably that "wonderful feeling," as she described it, was lasting for shorter and shorter periods, with her moods in between growing progressively darker, her gaiety and good humour succeeded by profound depression, by a spiteful despondency and frequent outbursts of rage. Lisa showed Sybille the equipment. "You had better learn how to do it," she told her. "Because I have to have it three times a day now. Sometimes four." "What is this magic substance?" Sybille asked. "Morphine," her mother replied.

The following month some friends of Lisa's came to stay for a couple of nights, the rumbustious South African poet Roy Campbell and his English wife, Mary. Campbell was a heavy drinker, and after an alcoholic luncheon he suddenly demanded to be taken to see his old friend, Aldous Huxley, who had recently moved to Sanary. Sybille was astonished: since first being introduced to Huxley's work by Kate Muir she had become an avid admirer, reading his novels with intense enthusiasm. Now the idea of actually meeting the great man himself was overwhelming. "I was not prepared, I did not think of, an encounter with the writer in the flesh."

With Nori at the wheel, the Campbells and Sybille drove over to La Gorguette, an area to the west of town where close to the beach the Huxleys' new property was situated. A few months previously Aldous Huxley, his Belgian wife, Maria, and nine-year-old son had left Paris, where they had been living for the past couple of years, for the south of France, in order to be with their old friend, D. H. Lawrence, during the last weeks of his life. After Lawrence's death they had decided to remain in the region and had bought a house, an unprepossessing little villa which they had had enlarged and renovated; on the two stone gateposts at the entrance the local mason had painted in bright green letters what he had understood to be the spelling of their name, "Villa Huley." With Roy Campbell leading the way, the four visitors walked through the open front door to find Aldous, in khaki shorts and sandals, "sitting on a red-tiled floor, grasshopper legs neatly disposed, amidst piles of books he was trying to cram into a rotating cage . . . Aldous smiled sweetly and said, 'Roy! How nice of you to come!,' then turned to us, raising high both hands, 'There is no <u>horror</u> greater than the <u>First</u> Day in the <u>New Home</u>.' "

Sybille was immediately fascinated by this strikingly handsome man. Then in his late thirties, Aldous was very tall, slender, bespectacled, with a keen, sensitive face and a head of thickly dishevelled dark hair. After a few minutes Maria came into the room, delicate and tiny, a pale-faced beauty with dark blue eyes and auburn hair, dressed in white trousers and a linen shirt, a string of coral beads round her neck. She made them warmly welcome before disappearing to supervise the making of tea. While the Campbells talked to Aldous, Nori, instantly aware of how much these new neighbours would appeal to Lisa, left in the car to fetch her. He soon returned, and everyone settled round a table beneath an arbour in the garden. Lisa, who appeared calm and fresh-faced, immediately began an intense dialogue with Aldous about books and politics. When the maid brought out a tray of tea and placed it on the table, Lisa, "going on with what she had been saying and without taking her eyes off Aldous, reached across the table, seized the pot and drew it to herself . . . However, she did not pour out . . . My mother, hand on teapot, went on talking. Maria now made a discreet move to regain possession. My mother grasped the pot more firmly, drew it closer to herself and, still without losing the thread of her conversation, opened the lid, peered inside and quickly dropped the lid again . . . Our cups stayed empty."

That evening, after the Marchesanis and Campbells had returned home, a car drew up, a big, beautiful red Bugatti, and out of it stepped Maria carrying a bunch of tuberoses for Lisa and a small home-made loaf.

From that day onward the Huxleys became key figures in Sybille's life. She looked up to and worshipped them both, and they for their part were to become not only friends, but in a sense her guardians, too. "The Huxleys took me on. When I said Aldous was the best man I ever met, so was his wife. They were both extraordinary people and it was a very, very good marriage, I think." Indeed it was. Aldous was the epitome of the cerebral intellectual; a highly disciplined, hard-working writer and philosopher, he lived most of the time in a world far removed from most people's daily experience. Bookish and scholarly, he possessed an intense curiosity about the world that rarely descended to the mundanity of ordinary human existence. He would talk brilliantly in his "culture-saturated purr," holding his listeners enthralled; then, disconcertingly, as though unaware of their presence, would often lapse into a long, thoughtful silence, silences, that as the poet Edith Sitwell described them, "seemed to stretch for miles, extinguishing life, when they occurred, as a snuffer extinguishes a candle." Kind and generous by nature, unfailingly courteous, Aldous was remote and emotionally detached, indifferent and benign, maintaining an impenetrable barrier between himself and the rest of humanity. Two tragedies in his early life—the death of his mother when he was fourteen, a brother's suicide a few years later—had made him withdraw "into an inaccessible inner shell"; as one acquaintance phrased it, "Nature has erected on the edge of his emotional garden a board: 'trespassers—against the will of the owner—are apt to be prosecuted.' "

Possessed of an exceptionally intuitive intelligence, Maria was her husband's facilitator, and he depended on her for almost everything. It was she who protected his privacy, cared for him, and read to him. As a boy Aldous's eyesight had been seriously damaged, consequently leaving him unable to read without strong spectacles, and so Maria typed his manuscripts, and minutely organised every hour of the day to suit his working routine. She ran the house, looked after their son Matthew, undertook all the shopping and cooking, instructed the maids, and organised their social life, inviting to luncheons and dinners those friends whom Aldous wished to see while fending off others who bored him. He relied on her to tell him all the gossip of the town, to provide the bridge between his private self and the world outside. As Sybille soon discovered, many friends looked on Maria as a confidante, a sympathetic shoulder to cry on, "offering gossip, pouring out our troubles, our stories, answering anything she might ask (and my goodness, she did ask, but of her own quick interest and to pass on to Aldous), to be scolded, comforted and teased." Although fragile in appearance, Maria had enormous energy, and was often in the garden at first light, planting and pruning her vines and figs, digging over the carefully tended beds of vegetables. One of her greatest pleasures was driving her red Bugatti at sometimes reckless speed along the narrow coastal roads, a dashing and glamorous figure, slender and beautiful, with her magnolia complexion and enormous dark eyes.

From the time of that memorable first meeting, Sybille began to spend more and more time with the Huxleys. She adored them both, Aldous for his exceptional intellect and moral authority, Maria for her beauty and kindness, as well as for her forceful character and remarkable intelligence. Maria "was very outspoken, she was very critical; in fact she could be quite didactic . . . One was not allowed to get away with things . . . And how she could puncture pretension. By teasing or laughing . . . If Aldous girded himself to rebuke or educate, he generally did it by letter; which of course was so much worse for the recipient." Despite Aldous's disciplined working routine, the Huxleys enjoyed an active social life. As one of Maria's sisters put it, Maria *"était toujours heureuse d'avoir autour d'elle des êtres qui pouvaient distraire Aldous"* ("was always happy to have around her people who could distract Aldous"). Guests came to stay, friends to luncheon and dinner, they themselves frequently dined out with neighbours, among them the Marchesanis. Best of all for Sybille were "the hilarious Huxley picnics, on beach and cliff and windswept plateau, nocturnal picnics with Aldous's planter's punch to drink, Maria's eccentric food—she was fastidiously anti-food . . . fried rose leaves, fried zucchini and rabbit, quince jelly to eat, games to play. These and music at night—Aldous's Beethoven records listened to in hammocks in the garden under the stars and leaves."

It was not long after her first meeting with the Marchesanis that Maria began to realise the difficult situation in which Sybille was entrapped. Within a very short time she became not only friend and confidante, but also someone who could provide an important refuge from the stressful environment at Les Cyprès.

The strain on Lisa of Nori's continuing affair was growing increasingly intense. Doris, his girlfriend, had left Sanary, and was now moving from one hotel to another along the Riviera, where Nori visited her at regular intervals, often remaining away for several days at a time. His absences reduced Lisa to periods of profound depression punctuated by explosions of anger, meanwhile growing ever more dependent on her daily doses of morphine. With Nori away, it was Sybille who was obliged not only to collect the prescriptions from the sinister Dr. Joyeu but also to give her mother the injections. Nori had carefully instructed her in the procedure: sterilise the syringe in boiling water, file open the little glass ampoule, fill the syringe, then swab Lisa's arm before inserting the needle. For a while afterwards Lisa enjoyed a few hours of content-ment, but as the days, then weeks, passed these periods of tranquillity grew shorter and soon she was demanding injections throughout the day. "We were ignorant of all that is now common knowledge . . . We did not know the meaning of addiction. Nor its signs."

Understandably, Sybille escaped from her mother's company when-ever she could to the Villa Huley, where she was soon introduced to a new and highly literate society. It was through Aldous and Maria that she met Cyril Connolly and his young American wife, Jean Bakewell, who had recently arrived and were living in a rented villa on the out-skirts of town. Connolly had a somewhat difficult relationship with the Huxleys: he hero-worshipped Aldous, the main reason he had come to Sanary, but the Huxleys saw Cyril as a self-indulgent time-waster, and they disapproved of his chaotic way of life, his exotic and inconti-nent pets. "Eating your dinner with your fingers reading before the fire meant leaving grape skins and the skeletons of sardines between the pages. The ferrets stank; the lemur hopped upon the table and curled his exquisite little black hand around your brandy glass." Sybille was intrigued by Connolly and enjoyed his stimulating, astringent com-pany. "He was nice to me (mildly) . . . I didn't know that people were afraid of him, of his silences, his rudeness. I was too obscure for Cyril to be beastly to."

Among other English writers encountered with the Huxleys were those two erudite Bloomsbury figures, Raymond Mortimer and Edward Sackville-West, both regular guests at Villa Huley. Although in theory Aldous was unsympathetic to male homosexuality, to "the buggers," as in true Bloomsbury tradition he always referred to them, he had many bugger friends, Raymond and Eddy among them. Raymond, "spinster-ish and in his little brown way, intensely vital," had been at Balliol with

Aldous, subsequently establishing himself as a noted essayist and critic, while Eddy, a few years younger, had been a pupil of Aldous's during his early career as a schoolmaster at Eton. Sybille took to them both, particularly to Eddy, who had been a colleague of Percy Muir's at the Bond Street bookshop. Percy used to talk amusingly about Eddy, whom he admired while also finding him profoundly irritating. "I disliked this very superior, willowy young man, with his long wavy hair . . . his cordless, rimless monocle, his languid Oxford-accented speech, and his general Bloomsburyism," Percy wrote in his memoir. "It was bad enough to have an impertinent whippersnapper unseat a valuable book from its hallowed position; to find he was right was altogether too much."

It was also with the Huxleys that Sybille was introduced to the celebrated American novelist Edith Wharton, memorably described by Aldous as "a formidable lady who lives in a mist of footmen, bibelots, bad good-taste and rich food in a castle overlooking Hyères." When asked to lunch on one occasion the Huxleys took Sybille with them, an experience she found daunting, interpreting her hostess's habitually condescending manner as specifically hostile towards herself. Shortly afterwards the Huxleys returned Mrs. Wharton's hospitality by inviting her to one of their famously eccentric picnics. "Never shall I forget the sight of Mrs. Wharton, rotund, corseted, flushed and beautifully dressed . . . being led by Aldous up a goat-track on a rock face to the nonchalantly chosen picnic ground."

There were others among the Huxleys' friends whom Sybille came to know, among them an American couple, both writers, William Seabrook and his mistress, Marjorie Worthington. Seabrook's large house was almost opposite the Villa Huley, and the two couples saw each other frequently. Maria was particularly fond of Marjorie, a shy young woman who obviously adored her "Wolf," as she referred to him. According to the much relished local gossip, Seabrook was a man of sadistic inclination: a small building next to the house was hung with iron rings where he enjoyed chaining up naked young women—ankle shackled to wrist was a favourite posture. "A number of disagreeable and sensational stories were going round about his sexual savageries, yet he never hinted at these practices to the Huxleys." They knew about them, nevertheless. "Sanary," Aldous wrote to one of his correspondents, is "in a flutter of excitement to know Mr. Seabrook, because the rumour has gone round the village that he beats his lady friend . . ."

Despite his private practices, Willie Seabrook was a generous host and Sybille enjoyed his lavish, lively parties, although she remained wary of the man himself, "a very strange man indeed . . . beset with inner problems." Marjorie recorded in her diary her first meeting with Sybille one evening when dining with the Huxleys. "A young German girl, very blonde and red-cheeked, wearing a dinner jacket and a monocle . . . introduced to us as La Baronne something or other . . . hearty, sense of humour, spoke Eng. with British accent." In a novel published a few years later Marjorie portrayed Sybille as "Ilsa von Stembeck, a young German girl, who dressed, from preference and not fashion, in mannish slacks and shirts."

The Huxleys were due to go to London in September 1930, planning to stay there until the end of the year. One of the last occasions on which Sybille saw them that summer was in August, at a soirée given by Pierre and Jacqueline Mimerel to celebrate the completion of their impressive new villa, La Pacifique. It was a glamorous event, attended by most of Sanary's international society, the Huxleys, the Marchesanis, as well as some fashionable Parisians, including Charles de Noailles and the novelist Drieu La Rochelle and his wife, and also several English friends of Aldous and Maria. The greatest pleasure for Sybille was the presence of her sister. Katzi's husband, now based in Paris as a special attaché at the German Embassy, had rented a villa for the summer, and the two of them were much sought after during the busy social season, Katzi as pretty and frivolous as ever, Dincklage, "her sun prince," handsome, clever and flirtatious. At the party Katzi attracted much attention in a ravishing white evening dress, while her sister by contrast wore a cut-down black dinner jacket of Aldous's and a plain black skirt. Sybille and her mother had arrived late, Lisa making a tempestuous scene and refusing to leave the house, then suddenly changing her mind, throwing on a shabby lace dress, with a lopsided mantilla covering her hair. They both enjoyed the evening nevertheless. After dinner there was an act by two famous cabaret stars, Félix Mayol and Maurice Chevalier, their performance setting "the audience alight . . . Aldous and my mother, lured from their separate inner worlds, gave themselves to its small magic."

Sybille dreaded the Huxleys' departure, and taking leave of Maria was particularly painful. From Aldous, however, there was no show of emotion, simply some practical directions to specific volumes of Greek philosophy in his study with a kindly recommendation that she read them before his return.

Shortly after the Huxleys left, so did Nori, this time on a tour of Spain with Doris which was to last for several weeks. Before his departure, he gave Sybille further detailed instructions on how to cope with Lisa while he was away; he also promised to send regular telegrams with his location so that she could contact him in an emergency.

With Nori gone, Sybille found herself yet again alone with her mother. As before, Lisa moved through periods of drug-induced euphoria followed by intervals of serenity during which she earnestly promised to give up what she referred to as her "*paradis artificiels.*" As these paradisal effects dissipated, however, she grew violently angry, railing against Nori's cruelty and betrayal, her outbursts giving way to moods of black depression which could last for hours. When elated, Lisa insisted on Sybille driving her along the coast to shop extravagantly and dine in expensive restaurants, which Sybille knew they could not afford. She would terrify her daughter by suddenly demanding an injection   right now, this instant, they must find a lavatory or pull in by the side of the road as she was unable to wait another second. At this stage of her mother's addiction, there was no mistaking the cause of her unnatural appearance, "the staggery walk, the glitter in the eyes, the erratic make-up." Behind her back Lisa was mockingly referred to as "Madame Morphesani"; anecdotes were told of how she would appear at lunch or dinner in a lively mood, then suddenly slump, grey-faced and silent, clutching at her daughter, with whom she would disappear for a few minutes, returning vivacious as ever, as if nothing had happened. It was, said one observer, like seeing Coppélius from *The Tales of Hoffmann* winding up his puppet-doll.

Then suddenly an already desperate situation was made worse when without warning the local pharmacy told Sybille they could no longer accept Dr. Joyeu's prescriptions, that legally such dosages were beyond the limit. To keep her mother supplied, Sybille was now obliged to go ever further afield, to Bandol, La Ciotat, Toulon, Le Lavandou, "to find yet another pharmacy still willing or ignorant enough to cash the prescription I tried so nonchalantly to tender . . . There was no intention of cutting down . . . I did what I had been advised: take these prescriptions as far afield as you can, and *never, ever* to the same place twice." Inevitably her resentment of her mother's behaviour, of the unending emotional stress it imposed, affected Sybille's feelings for Lisa. "I did feel pity, though not enough . . . I was exasperated, frightened, seldom kind . . . I longed for escape."

A form of escape materialised at the end of the year with the return of the Huxleys. Immediately recognising the gravity of the situation, Maria took charge, insisting that Lisa must be persuaded to enter a clinic for professional treatment of her now very serious condition. Gently but authoritatively Maria began talking to her, and eventually Lisa agreed to see a highly regarded specialist in Nice. When the day came Sybille and Nori, who was once more at home, accompanied Lisa to Nice on the train. The consultant "was brutal and direct . . . never had he had a case of such rapid addiction . . . Need for an institutional cure was urgent." Arrangements were quickly made, a room booked at a private clinic for a stay of several weeks, during which no contact with the world outside would be permitted. Aware that the Marchesanis' finances had been seriously depleted by Lisa's extravagance, the Huxleys insisted on paying for everything.

When after several weeks Lisa came home the change was immediately apparent: she was calmer, more confident, more even-tempered, and although very thin, her lovely face noticeably more lined, she seemed ready to return to a semblance of normality. Undoubtedly relieved by the improvement in her mother's condition, Sybille was struck by her altered appearance, her face "etched with a tragic refinement . . . with lines and features grown more Jewish now than Latin." Before long Lisa felt well enough to go out and see friends, and only with Nori did she refuse to abandon hostilities, constantly attacking him, complaining bitterly of the way he had treated her.

Sybille's position with the Huxleys, her role almost as an honorary member of the family, was by this time well established. It was now, however, that her relationship with Maria started to shift, emotionally, to evolve at a much deeper level. From the beginning Sybille had looked on the older woman as friend and mentor, an almost maternal figure, on whom she depended and whom she wholeheartedly admired. Now the two of them became lovers—a sexual bonding that was to continue intermittently for a number of years. And at about the same time Aldous added Lisa to his long list of sexual conquests.

The Huxleys' marriage had always been unconventional. Aldous was extremely susceptible to beautiful women, although apart from Maria he felt little emotional engagement with any of them. In analysing this aspect of his character one of his girlfriends remarked, "I doubt that Aldous is capable of love (personal love) and I think the recognition of this lack in him has made him so unusually kind." As for Maria, not only did she tolerate her husband's liaisons, she encouraged and enabled them, regarding them as a necessary distraction from his work. Aldous enjoyed making love but he had no interest in courtship ("He would have grudged the time—it was dinner and bed, or nothing"), and thus it was Maria who arranged the meetings, purchased the presents, and frequently befriended the women themselves. "In a subtle way she prepared the ground, created opportunities, an atmosphere . . . It was a measure of how certain they were . . . of the great niceness that there was between them."

And Maria, too, enjoyed extramarital affairs, always with women, which came as a surprise to some: as one acquaintance put it, "her feminine appearance left her masculine side well hidden." For a number of years during the 1920s Maria had conducted an affair with Mary Hutchinson, a friend of Virginia Woolf and one-time mistress of Lisa's admirer, Clive Bell; as Mary at the same period was also a lover of Aldous's, the result was a happy *ménage à trois*, regarded as richly rewarding by all three. Now with Sybille, Maria opened up a sexual dimension to their friendship which was to remain important to both. In reflecting upon their lovemaking some years later Maria wrote to her, "I recall delicious softness, gentle warmth and flowing curves . . . Thank you for all the pillars of your hidden treasures. I accept them gratefully . . . It seems we were always in tune."

As to Aldous, there would have been little trace of his affair with

Lisa had he not chosen to describe it in easily identifiable detail in one of his novels. In *Eyeless in Gaza*, published in 1936, Aldous, with his cool, clinical eye, had bestowed on the character of Mary Amberley Lisa's temperament and appearance. Mrs. Amberley is known for her charm, intelligence and sexuality—her "graceful indolence, so wildly exciting because of that white round throat stretched back like a victim's, those proffered breasts, lifted and taut beneath the lace"—but equally apparent is her emotional neediness, her desire for attention, and perhaps most tellingly her terror of the physical signs of ageing. In one scene her lover watches as she walks upstairs: "The first half of the flight she negotiated at a normal pace, talking as she went; then, as though she had suddenly remembered that slowness on stairs is a sign of middle age, she suddenly started running—no, *scampering* . . . when they returned to the drawing room, no tomboy of sixteen could have thrown herself more recklessly into the sofa or tucked up her legs with a more kittenish movement."

With her mother in a relatively stable condition, Sybille continued to enjoy herself. It was at dinner at the Villa Huley one evening in June 1931 that she met a young woman with whom she was to form a lifelong friendship. Eva Herrmann, American, thirty years old and very beautiful, was a gifted artist who had come to Sanary with a commission to draw a pencil portrait of Aldous for a New York magazine. For Sybille the impact of meeting this pale, delicate, dark-haired young woman, "with a lovely, secret Etruscan face," was powerful and immediate. Although Eva was shy, she soon relaxed under the influence of Maria's kindly manner, responding to Sybille's obvious sympathy and interest. Sybille for her part knew at once that this was the start of an important relationship, and so, it quickly became clear, did Eva. Over the next few days they saw each other whenever possible, meeting at the Hôtel de la Plage, where Eva was staying; and when after a few days Eva eventually left Sanary to go to Italy, Sybille drove her to the station. As the train drew out, Eva leant out of the window: "Our friendship is for life," she said; and so it turned out to be.

Born in Munich in 1901, Eva was one of five children, the daughter of Frank Herrmann, a wealthy German-American painter. Husband and wife, both Jewish, divorced in 1910, and in 1919 Frank took Eva to live in New York. Two years later Eva left the United States to enrol in an art course in Berlin, and it was while in Germany that she began an affair with the young communist writer Johannes Robert Becher, under whose influence she herself became a communist sympathiser. By 1924 Eva had established herself as a talented caricaturist, and after her return to New York the following year won a series of commissions from several newspapers and magazines. In 1929 her success was formally recognised when the *New Yorker* published *On Parade*, a volume of forty-two of her drawings of famous authors. While living in New York Eva had become friends with Klaus and Erika Mann, children of the revered German novelist Thomas Mann, and it was with the Mann siblings that Eva had arrived in the south of France, the purpose of her journey a commission to draw Aldous Huxley, whose phenomenally successful novel, *Brave New World*, had recently been published. After a week in Sanary Eva left for Italy to visit her father, returning a few days later to Bandol where she joined Klaus and Erika at the Grand Hôtel des Bains.

Only during the first weeks of their long friendship were Sybille and Eva lovers, Sybille discreetly joining Eva every night in her hotel bedroom, returning to Sanary at dawn. When at the end of the month Eva again took her departure, this time for Russia, Sybille went by car to meet her for twenty-four hours in Venice, after which, driving at reckless speed, she caught up with Eva's train for three highly charged minutes before it left the station in Verona. Sybille then returned to Sanary, where she collapsed, falling asleep while still seated behind the wheel; here she was discovered by her current *amitié amoureuse*, Christa von Bodenhausen, in whose apartment she had been staying.

Christa von Bodenhausen, an attractive young woman in her early twenties, was part of a growing population of German émigrés settling in and around Sanary during the 1930s, although Christa, like Katzi's husband, Dincklage, was one of the few who were not Jewish. It was after the Reichstag election of September 1930, and the dramatic rise in power of the Nazi Party, that the first expatriates had begun to arrive, attracted by the peaceful atmosphere and beautiful coastline of the south of France. At this early period there was little sense of immediate danger, rather a desire to exchange an unstable way of life for a more secure and tranquil alternative. France was an obvious choice: a democratic country sharing a border with Germany, with its Mediterranean coast offering a warm climate and a cheaper cost of living than in Paris.

Among the earliest of the new arrivals were Julius and Annemarie Meier-Graefe, he an eminent art critic now in his sixties, she, his third wife, always known as "Bush," a lively, flirtatious young woman over thirty years his junior. When Sybille was introduced to Bush, "I kissed her hand . . . I still knew enough to follow, on this occasion, the custom of the German and Austrian upper classes which was that an unmarried woman kisses the hand of a married one." Sybille was enchanted by both husband and wife, relishing the leisurely al fresco dinners on their shady terrace, the wide-ranging conversations about painters and writers and life in pre-war Berlin. Meier-Graefe, who in the past had been a lover of Lisa's, was "a life enhancer if ever there was one, a viveur, at the same time oddly delicate, moody, sharp, very difficult." Bush, with whom Sybille was to enjoy an enduring friendship, was by contrast "gay and giggly . . . running the house hospitably, typing the books, managing at the same time to get on with her own painting."

Over the next few years Meier-Graefe was to provide crucial support in helping others of his countrymen leave Germany and settle in the region. Most of these early exiles were relatively well off, able to rent comfortable villas and afford a leisurely way of life. Yet despite bringing an increased prosperity to the neighbourhood, the newcomers were not always welcome: memories of the last war were still uncomfortably vivid, and in many local communities there was an innate xenophobia that lay only just below the surface. "Swarmed upon by actual living Germans, distaste and instinctive fear rose readily to the surface. '*Un Boche, c'est toujours un Boche,*' could be heard when a cleaning woman had been reprimanded or paid late." Even among Sybille and her friends there was a somewhat judgemental attitude. "Rather a dismal crew," as Aldous described the exiles, complaining that "Swarms of literary Germans infest the countryside like locusts." Maria, who with her Belgian family had herself been a refugee in the First World War, was also somewhat equivocal in her reaction. As an émigré, in her view, "one behaved with dignity, pliancy, showed gratitude, whereas the present refugees, the more visible ones, were throwing their weight about." Inevitably her attitude influenced Sybille. "Maria remained distant, disapproving. I was ambivalent in my likes and dislikes. Together, Maria and I collected anecdotes, told Aldous, laughed."

In the spring of 1932 Sybille, now twenty-one, went to Germany, her first return to her native country in nearly seven years. The main purpose of the expedition was to disentangle her somewhat complicated financial affairs, and, if possible, to arrange for her bank account to be moved to France. Passionate as ever about cars and motoring, Sybille had recently bought a cheap little open-top Ford, in which with considerable courage she set off alone from Sanary, driving for several days across France and over the German border. After arriving in Baden she went first to Feldkirch, not to the schloss, but to the village to call on her father's old maid, Lina Hauser. From there she met the Huxleys and Raymond Mortimer in Berlin, where the four of them spent several days exploring the city, a haunting experience for Sybille with her childhood memories of the Tiergarten, the Siegesallee, the Herz house on Voss Strasse, now all images from a vanished past. On this occasion they were simply tourists, visiting the Kaiser Friedrich Museum, the zoo, the opera. "One evening we went to have a look at a large and glittering nightclub whose speciality was table telephones: middle-aged couples and a sprinkling of commercial blondes ringing each other up across the floor. The whole thing was of deadly vulgarity, a repulsive combination of facetiousness and lust . . . Aldous duly remarked how extraordinary it was and how depressing."

Even more depressing was the sight throughout the city of groups of Hitler Youth marching down the streets. "It was a mixed up and foreboding time, with daily clashes between communists and Brownshirts . . . There was an ominous feeling about the country." The atmosphere was heavy with violence and tension, and in this sinister and unsettling environment it came as little surprise that Sybille was refused permission to transfer her money, a refusal she accepted with courageous insouciance. "I found bureaucracy off-handedly blocking the way . . . [so] I let the future take care of itself and left Germany with Maria smuggling a couple of my thousand-mark notes hidden in her shoes."

Although there had been much to enjoy, Sybille had been profoundly shaken by what she saw taking place. Since childhood she had been brought up to love France and distrust Germany, the country of her birth, and now more than ever she felt the need to distance herself from her roots, as far as possible, to erase her nationality. "My German beginnings I discounted, sought to obliterate . . . I never felt I had the German identity, the Germanic mind . . . but the fact that I had any connections with this terrible country became a cause of guilt, and for some time I tried desperately to anglicise myself." It would be more than thirty years before Sybille set foot in Germany again, and now after returning to France she made determined efforts to camouflage her nationality, efforts which did not pass entirely unnoticed. The writer and philosopher Ludwig Marcuse, who was to spend several years as an exile in Sanary, remarked that Fraülein Schoenebeck was *"eine deutsche Halbjüdin, die englisch sprach, als wäre sie auf dem Campus von Oxford geboren . . . hatte nicht den geringsten Respekt vor Deutsche, innerhalb Germanias oder ausserhalb, von deutscher Literatur hielt sie noch weniger, worin sie vielleicht ihr Idol Aldous Huxley kopierte, der von den deutschen Schriftstellern Sanarys kaum Gebrauch machte—und tief verbarg, dass er deutsch verstand"* ("a German half-Jew who spoke English as if she had been born in an Oxford college . . . She hadn't the slightest respect for Germans, within the fatherland or abroad, and even less again for German literature; in so doing she perhaps copied her idol Aldous Huxley, who had no use for Sanary's German writers—and hid deep the fact that he understood German").

On her return to Sanary Sybille moved in to the Villa Huley as Lisa was away, undergoing further treatment at the clinic in Nice. With Raymond Mortimer and Eddy Sackville-West her fellow guests, she spent an enjoyable few weeks, swimming, reading, talking, dining with the Huxleys, with the Dincklages and Mimerels—Jacqueline by this time little more than a sentimental attachment: "much as I was inclined to admire, I no longer admired all the way." As a gesture of gratitude for the Huxleys' hospitality, Sybille for a couple of hours every day sat typing out Aldous's manuscripts, which she was more than glad to do, even if it left little time to concentrate on any writing of her own. "So much siesta and dining out and never any work," she noted in her diary. More and more it seemed she was following her mother's path, intending to write, full of ideas for writing, but somehow never getting down to it. Lisa always claimed that it was her frequent love affairs that had prevented her from writing, a problem which her daughter in time came to understand very well.

Within a few weeks Sybille was again on the move, leaving Sanary to join Eva Herrmann in Turkey. Eva had spent the past few weeks in Moscow, a city she loved. Shortly before leaving for Russia she had been profoundly shaken to learn of the suicide of an ex-lover of hers, and perhaps in need of distraction had had a brief affair with a young Polish architect, apparently without considering the possible consequences.

In the middle of July Eva and Sybille met in Constantinople, Sybille arriving on the Orient-Express: "*la journée passé vite . . . je lis, écrit, dors, et ai très chaud*" ("the journey passed quickly . . . I read, write, sleep, and am very hot"). From Constantinople they went to Athens, neither of them enjoying it much, Sybille pining for the south of France, Eva complaining about the food and the smell of food, the cause of her revulsion soon to become apparent. From Greece they returned to France to meet Sylvester Gates, an English friend of Eva's, and stayed in what Sybille described as "a horrid house" on an island off the coast of Brittany. It was here that Eva discovered she was pregnant, and so it was decided that the three of them should go to Switzerland, where Eva could have an abortion. After arriving in Zurich, Eva moved into a clinic where Sybille also stayed, while Sylvester rented a room nearby. Eva's condition proved complicated and it was nearly two months before she could undergo the operation, weeks that Sybille was delighted to spend in the company of Sylvester.

Sylvester Gates became not only a lover but a close friend of Sybille. Tall, slender, with a fine-featured, handsome face, Sylvester was a brilliant young barrister then in his early thirties. An outstanding scholar at Winchester and Oxford, musical and a talented linguist, he also had a highly refined appreciation of good food and wine, which naturally appealed to Sybille. His marriage, to a daughter of the Scottish industrialist Sir Charles Tennant, had recently ended because of Sylvester's terrifying explosions of temper, not infrequently culminating in physical violence. (As his Oxford colleague, Maurice Bowra, wrote of him, "Anger that ill becomes our kind, / Unbalancing the sober mind, was poor Sylvester's bane . . .") Yet despite his rudeness and irascibility, Sybille became and remained very fond of him, in awe of his intellectual ability, relishing his wit and cleverness as well as his sophisticated epicureanism.

During the few weeks they stayed in Zurich Sylvester found an understanding listener in Sybille, who was sympathetic to his unhappiness over his failed marriage. The two of them explored the city, went to the theatre, sat for hours over inexpensive meals—Sylvester was short of funds after his divorce—and when Sybille returned to her room in the clinic Sylvester accompanied her, the two of them spending much of the night talking, drinking and making love. When at the end of her life Sybille was asked in an interview whether she had ever fallen in love with a man, she replied, "Yes. I had one very serious attachment to a man." This man was Sylvester, and although their physical relationship may have been intermittent and had certainly ended long before 1936, when Sylvester married again, their friendship, founded on an intellectual compatibility and a strong emotional bonding, remained unbroken for forty years.

In October, when Sylvester returned to England, Sybille and Eva made their way back to Sanary. Here Eva, still fragile after her operation, remained until the following month when she left for New York, while Sybille went back to living with her mother. On New Year's Eve she and Lisa were invited to a dinner party at Villa Huley, a poignant occasion as the Huxleys were on the point of leaving to spend several months in Mexico and Central America. The New Year also marked the end of a period of relative political stability: on 30 January 1933, Adolf Hitler was sworn in as Reich Chancellor in Berlin, and on 27 February the Reichstag building went up in flames, an act of arson later recognised as pivotal in establishing the Nazi regime.

It was during the weeks after the Reichstag fire, with Jewish communities increasingly under threat, that the great exodus from Germany began. In France the government immediately declared the country's readiness to accept large numbers of German refugees, a statement that was to have a significant impact not only on Paris but particularly on the south. Within a very short time exiles began arriving in Sanary and Bandol, some to stay only a few weeks, others remaining for a number of years. Distinguished writers came to form one of the largest groups, among them the brothers Thomas and Heinrich Mann, Lion Feuchtwanger, René Schickele, Bruno Frank, Stefan Zweig, Bertolt Brecht, Ludwig Marcuse, Franz Werfel and Alma Mahler. Soon Sanary was being referred to as the secret capital of German literature, "a gregarious and gossipy world," as Klaus Mann recalled it, with the marble-topped tables of La Marine and La Veuve Schwob now occupied throughout the day by a galaxy of German literati. "A galaxy indeed. And didn't they know it," Sybille wrote later. "Their entourage, a gathering of secretaries, housekeepers, agents, referred to them—straight-faced—as *Dichterfürsten*, princes of poetry."

Most famous of the princes was Thomas Mann. Mann was not Jewish but his wife, Katia, was, and so therefore were his six children. It was his two eldest, Erika and Klaus, who had persuaded him to leave Germany, Mann agreeing with reluctance, loath to abandon his affluent life in Munich for the comparatively rustic conditions of the south of France. Arriving in May at the Grand Hôtel in Bandol, he wrote disdainfully in his diary, "*ich finde in diesem Kulturgebiet alles schäbig, wackelig, unkomfortabel und unter meinem Lebensniveau*" ("I find everything in this cultural milieu shabby, rickety, uncomfortable, and beneath my accustomed standard"). Fortunately he was obliged to spend no more than a couple of nights there before moving into a comfortable villa in Sanary, La Tranquille, the house which a few years earlier had been renovated by Nori. Indeed it was Lisa who had arranged for the Manns to take it. As a young woman Lisa claimed to have known Thomas Mann, had even, or so she said, turned down a proposal of marriage from him, ever afterwards referring to him pityingly as "poor Tommy."* Almost everyone else, however, regarded the great novelist with awe, treating him with the flattering deference to which he had long grown accustomed.

Not one of those who shared this view, Sybille found Mann pompous and conceited, and Katia's frequent references to her husband's "*Welt Ruhm*" ("world fame") ridiculous. To his two eldest children, on the other hand, Klaus and Erika, she quickly became devoted. Erika,

---

* Interestingly, Mann in his diaries gives no indication of ever having met "Frau Marchesani" before arriving in Sanary.

in her late twenties, the elder by only a year, was often taken as the twin of Klaus, partly because the two of them looked so alike—slender, pale, with dark eyes and short dark hair—and partly because they were so closely involved with each other, both emotionally and intellectually. Erika, a wild, exuberant personality, determined and tough, was an actress, winning much acclaim with her performances in Die Pfeffermühle ("The Peppermill"), the political cabaret she had recently founded. Both were heavy drinkers and smokers, with Klaus, but not Erika, dangerously addicted to drugs; Erika had affairs with both men and women, while Klaus was wholly homosexual. They were both passionate opponents of the Nazi regime, and Klaus spent much of his time travelling round the European capitals, attempting to organise anti-fascist protests among the various émigré groups. On 8 May, two days before the notorious burning of the books in Berlin—a campaign organised by the Nazis to destroy all works considered subversive—the names of both Klaus and his uncle Heinrich appeared on the blacklist of 136 writers whose works were to be banned in Germany.

It was Klaus, frail, complex and highly strung, to whom Sybille grew closest; with Erika she enjoyed "a sporadic camaraderie," while "for Klaus I came to feel much affection. I loved him as a brother in many situations and years to come." A dedicated writer, Klaus was the author of several plays, had published a couple of novels while still in his twenties, and in 1932 a first volume of autobiography which had made a considerable impact. His writing was crucially important to him, and as Sybille, too, was determined to write, she regarded Klaus's ferocious dedication with awe, while at the same time having reservations about his style. "I never knew anybody who was more *naturaliter* a writer, by temperament, steady work, everything; but the talent was not commensurate." She wholeheartedly sympathised with his courageous opposition to the Nazi regime, with consequences that were shortly to prove extremely damaging.

Not long after the Manns' arrival in Sanary, Willie Seabrook threw a garden party to welcome a number of the recent arrivals. It was a hot afternoon, and Seabrook, glass in hand, greeted his guests wearing nothing but a pair of khaki shorts, his hairy chest on full display. Sybille, who had arrived with the Huxleys, was amused to see the contrast between their host's rumpled dishabille and the formally dressed Mann brothers: Thomas, with his ramrod back, slick grey hair and trimmed moustache, famously compared to a walking stick, while Heinrich, in a high collar and black coat, extended, "like M. de Charlus, two fingers to anyone offering to shake hands." Most of the German *haute culture* kept themselves to themselves, only Lion Feuchtwanger, the celebrated novelist and playwright, talked to the other guests, "making the round of the younger and more attractive women telling about his latest sales figures." The reaction of some local residents, Sybille and the Huxleys among them, was slightly derogatory. "What struck the Huxleys was the regard some of them had for themselves. They threw their weight about; they were pompous."

Once settled in Sanary Thomas Mann and a number of his writer colleagues decided to form a weekly reading circle, their meetings to be held at La Tranquille. Here, *"der Zauberer"* ("the magician"), as his family reverently referred to him, sat at the centre of a table on the terrace, flanked by a group of compatriots, with their wives positioned on chairs behind them. When the performance was due to begin Erika solemnly placed her father's manuscript before him. In the garden below, perched on steps, cushions, a wooden bench sat the groundlings, among them Sybille, Lisa and Nori, Eddy Sackville-West, the Huxleys, all straining to hear as Mann mumbled his way through a section of *Joseph und seine Brüder*, his work in progress. *"Je n'ai jamais lu un de ses livres"* ("I've never read one of his books"), Aldous later confided to Klaus. Afterwards the high table was served with Riesling and chicken salad, while fruit cup and biscuits were distributed among the rest.

The following month, in August, Lisa gave a soirée to which she invited all the Manns, the Meier-Graefes, the Stefan Zweigs, the Huxleys, and also Willie Seabrook and Marjorie Worthington, who were shortly to leave Sanary for good. That evening Lisa was at her best, witty and charming, apparently in excellent spirits, although as it turned out this was one of the last occasions on which she was to appear in full possession of her faculties. Within a very short time it became clear she was suffering from serious depression, and for the first time in her life she began to drink heavily. She slept "long, sometimes into the afternoon. One day I came across the gin bottle in her bed. It fell out, it was empty." Sybille and Nori tried to take control by offering to make cocktails which the three of them could enjoy together, but now all Lisa wanted was to lie in bed on her own with whatever alcohol she had been able to lay her hands on. Worse was to follow: somehow, probably through the compliant Dr. Joyeu, she had again begun taking morphine. The smell of ether permeating the house was an unmistakable indication of her decline, as was Lisa's ravaged, emaciated appearance, "not a Giorgione any longer," in her daughter's words, but "a Rembrandt woman, an ageing Jewess howling by a wall."

At this stage there were still a few hours in the day when Lisa felt able to dress, go into town, see friends, but now she was careful always to lock her bedroom door before leaving the house. On one occasion she and Sybille returned only to find she had lost the key. Lisa "with quick resource fetched a flat-iron and smashed one of the lower panels of the door . . . leaving an opening roughly the size and shape of that of an average dog kennel. My mother got down on the floor and wriggled through this aperture with astonishing agility and invited me to follow her. I declined . . . Her head appeared near floor level. 'Then we must talk from where we are. Bring a cushion, I've got one.' I fetched a cushion and we soon began talking quite normally, each crouching by one side of the hole." This grotesque situation continued for several days, with Lisa on all fours crawling in and out of her bedroom, until Nori, who had been away, returned home. "When [Nori] came in and saw us, he swore—most rare—and slammed the passage door on what to him must have appeared the ultimate in disorder."

One of the friends who called at the house during this period was Maria Huxley, who was astonished by what she found. Returning to the Villa Huley she described to Aldous the extraordinary scene she had witnessed, a scene which, to Sybille's horror, appeared in excoriating detail three years later in his novel, *Eyeless in Gaza*. Not only is there a vivid account of Lisa wriggling her way into her bedroom but also a ruthlessly accurate picture of her alcoholic degeneration. "Hennaed to an impossible orange, a lock of tousled hair fell drunkenly across her forehead . . . A smear of red paint, clumsily laid on, enlarged her lower lip into an asymmetrical shapelessness, a cigarette end had burned a round hole in the eiderdown . . . The pillows were smudged with rouge and yolk of egg. There was a brown stain of coffee on the turned-back sheet. Between her body and the wall, the tray on which her dinner had been brought up stood precariously tilted. Still stained with gravy, a knife had slipped on to the counterpane." After Lisa's mother, Anna Bernhardt, read *Eyeless in Gaza*, she wrote resignedly to Sybille, "I hadn't known that AH had been one of her endless Leporello list."

When on the book's publication Sybille came across this passage she was appalled by what she regarded as Aldous's perfidy, shocked by the merciless detail in which Lisa's condition was described. "When I remonstrated, Maria told me that he would put anything he got hold of into the book; sooner or later and in his own way. So if I had a story I didn't want to see in print, 'Don't tell Aldous.' " And it was no doubt true that Maria's account as retailed to Aldous had been embellished by Sybille, who would certainly have discussed her mother's condition with the Huxleys. As Anna Bernhardt wrote to her granddaughter, "It is not you who wrote the book, but it is you who expressed your feelings to Mr. Huxley." Aldous had not intended to be cruel, but as his old friend Ottoline Morrell once wrote of him, he was "a scientific student of human behaviour . . . singularly lacking in the emotion of the heart . . . he listens and looks as if he were looking and listening at the behaviour and jabber of apes."

Fortunately, during this early period of Lisa's decline Nori was spending more time in Sanary than away, his girlfriend, Doris, having returned to Berlin. Despite his wife's unrelenting hostility towards him, Nori did his best to look after her, to do what he could to keep the house in order, leaving Sybille free to enjoy some life of her own. As soon as Lisa had retired to bed, Sybille would often walk into town, these nocturnal expeditions a vital escape from the stresses of life at home. Accustomed since early adolescence to eating alone in hotels and restaurants, she enjoyed sitting by herself in one of the cafés overlooking the harbour, drinking brandy and soda and watching the evening promenade. On summer nights there would often be dancing in the square to a couple of accordions, festivities in which Sybille, dressed in "the kind of sailors' clothes I liked," enjoyed taking part. Her partners were usually girls of her own age, with some of whom she found herself wandering off afterwards for a stroll, "*à deux* under the night sky . . .

with perhaps worse to follow." In her diaries the letters "*NR*" ("*Nuit Romantique*") are frequently noted in pencil.

At the end of the year, in November 1933, Sybille spent a couple of weeks with the Huxleys in Spain. She and Eva Herrmann, who had returned from New York, travelled together to Madrid, where they joined Aldous and Maria, the four of them embarking on "an exhilarating and happy time." From Madrid they drove to Toledo, Segovia, Ávila, where long days were spent sightseeing followed by "evenings of ease, theatre, late dinners, talk, affection, laughter." The only difficult moment came when they arrived at the airport for the flight home, to find in place of the regular Air France plane a Lufthansa aircraft with a large swastika displayed on its tail. As both Sybille and Eva refused to travel under the Nazi emblem, the Huxleys agreed to wait until the next day when they were able to take a Spanish flight onward.

Returned home, Sybille was depressed to find that her mother's behaviour was growing ever more violent and vindictive. Lisa's fury with her husband was unrelenting, her rages, fuelled by drugs and drink, now almost beyond control. She even tried to persuade her daughter to join her in taking morphine. "Lisa is the hole into which everyone sinks," as Nori glumly remarked. Then one night Sybille was woken by the sound of her mother screaming at Nori; frightened and appalled, she pulled the covers over her head and tried to go back to sleep. Early the next morning she was woken by her stepfather coming into her room, fully dressed, briefcase in hand. He could no longer cope, he told her; he was leaving, his suitcases already in the car. "Look after her," he said. "I shall send some money when I can." He embraced Sybille lovingly, and then he was gone, leaving her with nothing of his except his Remington typewriter.

From the moment of Nori's departure, the problems arising from Lisa's condition were to escalate rapidly, at times almost overwhelming her close friends and family. As before, Maria Huxley was to provide the most practical advice and support, with Katzi, too, giving what help she could, as did Lisa's mother in Berlin. More immediately, however, Sybille was confronted with a situation that potentially was far more threatening.

Since the arrival in Sanary of the Mann family, Sybille had spent

much time in the company of Klaus, whose courage in voicing opposition to the Nazi regime she passionately admired. Now Klaus was in
the process of publishing a literary review, to be entitled *Die Sammlung*
("The Collection"), essentially to provide an uncensored voice mainly
for German émigré writers and intellectuals. Within a very short time
the project had attracted considerable backing: Heinrich Mann, André
Gide and Aldous Huxley had agreed to stand as sponsors, while a distinguished list of contributors was soon assembled, among them Albert
Einstein, Bertolt Brecht, Jean Cocteau, Boris Pasternak and Ernest
Hemingway. Eager to be included, Sybille was thrilled when Klaus
agreed to accept an article of hers.

The first issue of the journal was to appear in September 1933. In
April Aldous Huxley's book on Mexico and Central America had been
published, and it was this, *Beyond the Mexique Bay*, that Sybille chose
for the subject of her dissertation. She wrote the essay first in English
before translating it into German, showing both versions to the novelist Lion Feuchtwanger for his comments. His reaction was far from
favourable: Sybille was told that it was "juvenile in concept, clumsy
in execution . . . My grammar and style pained him." Although Sybille was grateful for the care and patience with which he analysed her
text, she decided to change nothing, leave everything as it was. Most
of the article took the form of a lengthy encomium on Aldous's book,
but at the very end Sybille had decided to include a couple of damning sentences voicing criticism of Hitler's Germany: "*Huxley's vor ein
paar Monaten ausgesprochene Hoffnung, dass Furcht und Abneigung gegen
Hitler-Deutschland zu Verständigung und rationeller Zusammenarbeit der
anderen Nationen führen könne, scheint heute kaum mehr begründet . . .
[der] Abgrund, [in den] Leidenschaften ohne die Hemmungen der Intelli-
genz und mit Ermutigung der bodenlosen Dummheit führen können, ist das
Deutschland der Nationalmenschlichen.*" ("The hope Huxley expressed a
few months ago that fear and dislike of Hitler's Germany might lead to
compromise and rational collaboration between other nations scarcely
seems justified now . . . [the] abyss [into which] passion untrammelled
by intelligence and urged on by bottomless stupidity might well take us,
is Nazi Germany.")

Looking back on the episode many years later, Sybille wrote of her article, "I merely wanted—very strongly—to stand up and be counted." And counted she was. In Germany the reaction to the publication of *Die Sammlung* was punitive and immediate: Klaus Mann, whose works were already on the Nazi blacklist, was declared guilty of high treason and stripped of his citizenship. For Sybille, the consequences, if less vicious, were ominous nonetheless. One morning a document arrived in the post informing her that the money held in her name in Berlin had been confiscated. "That money . . . the capital from my father's estate . . . was gone. Irrevocably, it became clear. They— the regime—had taken *connaissance* of my partly Jewish descent." To protect her status the obvious first step was to apply for French citizenship, which surely would not be rejected; over the past years her *carte d'identité* had been regularly renewed without question. Now, however, her application was refused. The welcome offered by France to the first wave of émigrés had been short-lived; restrictive measures had recently been introduced, with many refugees denied entry, others escorted to the border to be returned to Germany. Those Germans already settled in France were no longer able to regard their residency as secure.

As before Sybille turned to the Huxleys for help, and they, understanding only too well the dangers of her situation, promised somehow to find a way of ensuring her safety for the future.

FIVE

SAILING INTO THE UNKNOWN

The furore caused by the publication of *Die Sammlung* was alarming, and Sybille was profoundly shaken by the experience, although she never for a moment regretted her involvement. Her loathing for Germany, which began in childhood and intensified over the coming decade, was never to leave her, and it was only many years later that she was able to bring herself briefly to return to the country of her birth.

More immediately, however, she was faced with the daunting problem of how to cope with Lisa, who had sunk into a drug-induced stupor after the departure of Nori. The only member of the family now prepared to take responsibility was Lisa's mother, Anna Bernhardt. Anna's relationship with her daughter had always been difficult, as Lisa, headstrong and impatient, resolutely resisted any attempt at guidance or control. After Sybille was born, Anna had transferred her maternal feelings to her granddaughter, to whom she had remained devoted, despite their long periods of separation. She wrote regularly to Sybille, long letters usually in English, giving detailed accounts of her daily life, her friends and relations, recollections of the travels she had so much enjoyed in the past; she wrote about her love of reading, in English, French and German; and also about her passion for good food: Anna was an accomplished cook and regularly included favourite recipes with detailed instructions on how to carry them out.

A member of a wealthy family, married in Hamburg to a rich man, Anna had been accustomed to a comfortable existence in a large house waited on by a staff of well-trained servants. Since the post-war inflation, however, her income had drastically diminished, and now in her early seventies she was reduced to living in near poverty in Berlin. "I prefer Berlin," she told Sybille. "It is so vast that I can conceal my shabbiness." Anna was currently lodging in one small room in a *pension* on Budapester Strasse—her window looking out not onto the Zoologischer Garten at the front but over a dank interior courtyard at the back. In such straits she was able to offer Lisa little financial help, although in practical terms it was Anna from this time onward who was to organise almost everything. Her feelings of hostility and resentment towards her self-centred daughter had grown over the years: Lisa was a vampire, Anna said, selfish, vain, hot-tempered, never considered anyone's interests but her own. "*Lisa n'a jamais supporté d'être éclipsée et persiste à être plus centre* in the scene" ("Lisa can't bear to be eclipsed and must always be the centre of attention"). Yet Anna never questioned the fact that the problem of Lisa was hers to solve, and despite the endless complaining, about Lisa herself, about the lack of money, about the complex legal issues, she remained unflinching in her determination to deal with the situation as best she could.

Lisa's condition, her alcoholism and reliance on morphine, was now so serious that Anna decided she must be brought back to Germany as quickly as possible. There was a private sanatorium at Lichterfelde, on the outskirts of Berlin, where the distinguished Austrian physiologist Manfred Sakel had developed a form of shock therapy for drug addiction, which at the time was considered highly successful. This, Anna decided, was the place for Lisa, and here she hoped her daughter could be safely interned. Sybille was dismayed when she learned what was planned for her mother. "I am worried and out of sorts," she told Toni Muir, "and have to write presently a long birthday letter to my grandmother to whom I must be nice because she is lonely and disappointed and also out of fear because she is behaving incredibly nasty [*sic*] towards Lisa, who is rather in her power. They want to intern her in a German asylum. Terrible. And what can one say against it."

Fortunately Lisa still had a modest income from her German investments, as well as a few pictures, some silver and china which could be sold to help cover her expenses. The most immediate problem concerned her citizenship. Since her marriage to Nori, Lisa had held an Italian passport, which would prevent her from claiming German nationality, even the right to residence in Germany. As it turned out, however, her Italian nationality was questionable: as both she and Nori were Roman Catholic, and as Lisa when she married him was a divorced woman whose first husband at the time was still alive, then technically her second marriage could be annulled. "If this statement is agreed by Court and Embassy," Anna triumphantly declared, "Lisa is free, Frau Schoenebeck and German!"

Nori, meanwhile, had lost no time in unshackling himself from his marriage, initiating divorce proceedings within days of his leaving Sanary. He had previously been in touch with Anna over various problems to do with Lisa's condition, and it was now that he arrived in Berlin to meet her. Their relations were extremely amicable, and together they dealt with the complex procedures required to obtain permission for Lisa's repatriation, with Nori agreeing to make over to her as much as he could afford from his own very modest finances.

After this first stage was completed, Nori departed for his family home at Bolzano. That early morning when he had suddenly walked out of the house in Sanary was almost the last occasion on which Sybille was to see her stepfather. Despite the unpleasantness of the divorce proceedings, however, the two of them stayed in touch, maintaining an affectionate if sporadic correspondence, Nori keeping Sybille informed of his eventual second marriage to an Italian wife and an agreeable existence running a golf club in San Remo. Here many years later Sybille went to visit him for what turned out to be a fond reunion, although for Sybille it was a somewhat strange experience: "I thought of Lisa, and asked her not to mind."

Meanwhile, on that morning of Nori's departure, Sybille, unable to cope with her mother, had moved to the Villa Huley, reliant as ever on the kindness of Maria. The following month, in February 1934, the Huxleys took her with them to Italy for several weeks, returning to Sanary at the end of April. During this time Lisa again stayed at the clinic in Nice while the complex bureaucracy involved in the move to

Berlin was set in motion. In the event it was not until June that she finally left France, accompanied on the train by a nurse, the expenses of the journey shared between Nori and Anna. Sybille and the Huxleys were present at her departure. "The last I saw of my mother was at Toulon station being lifted through the window of a wagon-lit carriage on a northbound express. Aldous & Maria stood with me on the platform." Sybille never set eyes on Lisa again.

During the stressful period of Lisa's addiction, Sybille had received help not only from the Huxleys but also from her sister. After Nori left, Sybille had written to Katzi in Paris, imploring her to return to Sanary. Katzi willingly agreed: she was fond of her stepmother, with whom she had enjoyed an affectionate and much easier relationship than that existing between mother and daughter. From the early stages of Lisa's dependence on morphine, Katzi had been aware of the problem, and now, seeing for herself the seriousness of the situation, she had determined to try to moderate Lisa's behaviour. Just as she had all those years ago with Sybille at Feldkirch—"Don't tell lies," "Have you washed your hands?," "*No, you can't have it*"—Katzi began laying down the law. "My sister, ferociously disgusted by drugs, had an aptitude for kindly and effective authority . . . Now my mother gave in to her up to a point. For a while."

Although they were so different in temperament, Sybille had been devoted to Katzi, who since her early childhood had been unfailingly supportive. And yet in later years when recalling this troublesome period Sybille was curiously ambivalent. "[I] could not love her as we had loved each other in my childhood and after . . . There was an estrangement, one-sided perhaps, not open." In fact there were serious reasons for what Sybille described as her "inner withdrawal," although she gave little indication of what these might be, referring only in passing to her disapproval of Katzi's passive acceptance of the deplorable state of affairs in Germany. "If she was against what was currently going on in Germany, she did not <u>detest</u> it enough. This grieved me." In reality the truth was far more complex.

From the time of the Dincklages' first arrival in Sanary in 1930, the couple had proved themselves popular. They were both sophisticated, charming and very good-looking, Katzi "*élégante et mondaine*," Spatz clever, amusing and delightfully flirtatious. They were excellent tennis players, loved parties—they themselves entertaining frequently at their own residence, La Petite Casa—and both willingly turned a blind eye to each other's sexual liaisons. In Paris they lived in a spacious apartment on the rue Pergolèse, Spatz comfortably supported by a large income provided, as was later revealed, by German military intelligence. An excellent linguist, Spatz held the post of cultural attaché at the German Embassy, although, significantly, he was not a member of the Nazi Party—a fact which his French friends, mistakenly as it turned out, found reassuring.

Sybille had always been wary of Spatz, "a ruthless social butterfly with a heart of steel," although she was glad of his presence in Sanary, which allowed her to spend time with her sister. Sometimes she and Katzi met alone, more often she and the Dincklages lunched and dined with friends: the Huxleys, the Meier-Graefes, and Pierre and Jacqueline Mimerel, Pierre in particular forming a warm friendship with Spatz. Unsuspected by any of them at this period was Spatz's undercover work for military intelligence, his mission to supervise an espionage operation focused on the French naval bases at Toulon and at Bizerte in Tunisia. In this he proved remarkably successful. Accompanied by Katzi, he himself had visited Bizerte in 1931, and while in Sanary had established a network of French as well as German agents, who in return for generous pay reported back to him in Paris. The Sûreté, highly suspicious, had kept Dincklage under observation for a number of years, although it was not until 1935 that a Paris newspaper publicly exposed him as a Gestapo agent.

Shortly before this revelation, Spatz had discreetly divorced Katzi, acting in compliance with the newly introduced Nuremberg Laws forbidding marriage between Jew and Aryan. The divorce was kept secret for some time to come, the couple continuing to appear as man and wife, until inevitably the rumours began—Sybille first learned about her sister's divorce when she overheard a German couple discussing it. Katzi meanwhile behaved as though nothing had changed, although she now spent more time on her own in Sanary while Spatz was constantly on the move, undertaking missions in Paris, London and North Africa. As before, the two of them continued to engage in a number of affairs, for Spatz the most significant a lengthy relationship with the *couturière*, Coco Chanel, while among Katzi's lovers were two Frenchmen, both at the time secretly working for Dincklage's intelligence network.

Profoundly as Sybille would have abhorred these liaisons had she been aware of them, there was one affair of Katzi's of which she entirely approved. Not long after Lisa left France, the Huxleys went to London and Sybille moved in with the Mimerels. Here Katzi often came to see her, and before long began an affair with Pierre. In the Mimerels' marriage up to now it was always Jacqueline who strayed, rarely without a good-looking young man following adoringly in her wake, with Pierre, the *mari complaisant*, tolerating his wife's infidelities while showing little interest in indulging in anything similar himself. Now for the first time he fell in love, he and Katzi embarking on a brief but happy romance. Sybille was delighted for both their sakes—"Pierre never looked back . . . My frivolous, life-enhancing sister had been the right thing at the right time"—and it was only many years later that she learned of the pain their liaison had caused Jacqueline. "*Il m'a forcé à prendre ta soeur chez nous*" ("He forced me to take your sister into our house"), Jacqueline told her, explaining how devastated she had been to find that Katzi "was the turning point in P[ierre]'s life, and that after her he never ceased *de courir après les filles* [to run after girls]."

While living with the Mimerels, Sybille enjoyed a freedom she had almost never known. The crushing burden of her mother's problems had disappeared, and for almost the first time she felt unfettered, able to do as she pleased, to embark seriously on the career to which she had always aspired, as a writer. For this, her present environment was ideal, her few weeks at La Pacifique encouragingly productive, as she began on a short story she had had in mind for some time. With a room to herself and no domestic responsibilities, she lived a well-ordered existence in a spacious, impeccably kept house, whitewashed inside and out, set among olive trees, well off the road, beyond earshot of any noise from neighbours. Every morning a maid came in to open the blinds and bring her breakfast in bed, making sure that a pile of ruled paper was correctly positioned on the table. After the chaos of the previous few years the serenity and order were inspirational, and Sybille found she was able to work with great concentration. "To my astonishment I found myself writing; not merely keeping regular hours . . . but actually <u>writing</u> . . . It was painful, hard work and a great joy."

In this undertaking, slightly to her surprise, she was encouraged by Jacqueline. Now, instead of the mocking, patronising treatment Sybille had received during the period of her infatuation, she found Jacqueline adopting an almost maternal manner, softer and more serious. "I became for her '*mon jeune écrivain* [my young writer],' whose career she nursed." After the day's work the three of them often spent the evening together, Jacqueline sewing while Sybille and Pierre read or played patience. Only once was the tranquil atmosphere broken, when during dinner one evening Jacqueline suddenly snapped at Sybille, who was casually helping herself to yet another large glass of wine, telling her she was drinking too much, that she should be careful as after all "*ta mère est une morphiniste*" ("your mother is a morphine addict").

After a few industrious weeks with the Mimerels, Sybille left La Pacifique to stay with Eva Herrmann, who had recently returned from New York, where she worked as an illustrator and caricaturist for several magazines. Eva, who had plenty of money, had rented a handsome villa with a large garden at Sainte-Trinide, an area in the back country about four kilometres inland from Sanary. La Bastide Juliette, set in a gentle landscape of vineyards and olive trees, was isolated and fairly primitive: there was no electricity, no telephone, and water was supplied from a cistern which had to be hand-pumped for ten minutes a day by a maid who came in every morning. The house itself was beautiful in an austere, rather monastic style. On the ground floor, giving out onto a pine-shaded terrace and a wide expanse of lawn, was a spacious whitewashed library with an enormous sofa piled with cushions. While Eva slept in a large room upstairs, Sybille's bedroom was below, almost bare of furniture, with a crucifix on the wall and a copy of Pascal's *Pensées* on her bedside table.

Both Sybille and Eva intended to devote themselves to their work, but inevitably there were distractions. Eva, after her return from New York, had enjoyed a couple of liaisons, including the obligatory brief affair with Aldous, but now she had embarked on a serious relationship with Lion Feuchtwanger, which his wife appeared to accept with much the same level of tolerance as that shown by Maria Huxley towards her husband's adulteries. Sybille for her part was still intermittently involved with her lawyer friend, Sylvester Gates, who came to stay at La Juliette for a couple of weeks in August. Despite his impatience and explosive temper, Sybille was delighted by his company. "He is so intelligent and agreeable to talk to which is rarely found, especially combined with a liking for food and wine . . . and till the next row we are all remarkably pleased with each other."

Another impediment to work was the summer social life, in which Sybille was always a keen participant, almost daily ferrying herself and Eva to and from town in her battered old Ford. Maria Huxley's sister, Suzanne Nicolas, described Sybille at this period as *"un personnage fascinant. Le centre d'un groupe d'intellectuels anglais et allemands et, lorsqu'on se rencontrait au petit café sur la rade à Sanary ou à Bandol, elle était l'animatrice des conversations"* ("a fascinating person. The centre of a group of English and German intellectuals and, when one met her in the little café at the harbour in Sanary or Bandol, she was the driving force in conversation"). At the many social gatherings, the longer-established residents, such as Sybille and the Huxleys, continued to show a slight air of condescension towards the ever-increasing numbers of German émigrés, a feeling of *de haut en bas* towards the newcomers which did not pass altogether unnoticed. The writer Ludwig Marcuse, recently settled in Sanary, described Sybille as *"eine grosser Snob"* ("a big snob"), adding perceptively that she had a kind heart while also showing signs of considerable insecurity—despite a voracious appetite for entertaining, *"immer in Bewegung, jemand zu bewegen, dass er etwas in Bewegung setze (im Zweifelsfalle allemal: parties)"* ("always in motion, to set someone else in motion, to put something in motion [parties, more often than not]").

At La Juliette, Eva and Sybille were now able to give parties of their own, supper followed by dancing on the terrace or leisurely luncheons in the garden. "We had a picnic party the other day," Sybille reported, "all the *Dichters* [poets] bringing their own fruit salad or mayonnaise or drink, it was rather fun . . . We go out a good deal now, about three of four nights a week, what with picnics and going 'a-bathing' in moonlight, and the Huxley Sundays and birthdays and an awful English girl we all dislike and find rather pathetic but gives very good dinner parties at a new restaurant."

By this time the friendship between Sybille and Eva was easy and affectionate, as it was to remain for the rest of their lives. In appearance and manner they could hardly have been more different. Sybille, with her pink cheeks and short blonde bob, was boyish and plump; straight-backed, brisk in movement, dressed always in a shirt with trousers or shorts, she gave the impression, said one of her friends, of a well-brought-up guards officer. Eva by contrast had a slender figure and thick dark hair; a fragile, romantic-looking beauty, she was always elegantly dressed, her manner reticent and shy, although underneath she was tough and determined in achieving her ambitions. Marjorie Worthington in one of her novels portrayed the pair of them as "Doris Grey, a pretty American girl who lived with Ilsa in a small house on the outskirts of Sanary, a slender brunette, who was as feminine as Ilsa was not." When entertaining at La Juliette, it was Sybille who did most of the organising, planning the menus, setting out plates and glasses, arranging the furniture, with Eva during the evening obediently carrying out instructions conveyed by Sybille's meaningful glances. The partnership worked well; their friends enjoyed coming to La Juliette, enjoyed hearing the laughter of the two girls, as one put it, sweeping over the company like the beam of a lighthouse.

With the onset of autumn, however, the two women settled down to a more disciplined routine, Eva painting, Sybille concentrating on the story she had begun while staying at La Pacifique. "I am really working at present," she reported, "so I only go to Sanary once a week, and that only in order to buy food for us."

"Mon Pigeon," written in English and the first surviving piece of fiction by Sybille, is a whimsical short story about an English couple, a painter and his wife, living in the south of France. One day in a field near their house the couple notice a pigeon perched unmoving on the branch of a large tree, apparently mourning the death of its mate. The bird is seen by the husband, the narrator of the tale, as a symbol of his own disintegrating marriage, the unravelling of which provides the momentum of the plot. "Mon Pigeon" is well written, the rural setting sensitively observed, yet the whole effect is slightly ponderous, mainly because of somewhat stilted dialogue and a cumbersome vocabulary—"puristically," "fusslessly," "arboreous," "pre-tempestial"; and the piece is heavily overloaded with literary references and quotations, from Emily Brontë and Jean de Joinville to Strindberg, Fielding, Rimbaud and Poe. When the story was finished Sybille took it to Maria, who persuaded Aldous to show it to his American publisher, Cass Canfield, currently on a visit to Europe. Canfield was polite, softening his rejection by saying if Sybille were to write a full-length novel one day he would be pleased to read it.

By the end of the year Sybille was making plans to join the Huxleys, who were spending the winter in England. Her resources were dwindling fast, and she was eager to find a job. *"Ernstlich . . .* don't you know about any literary work I could do?" she asked Toni Muir, with whom she had continued to keep regularly in touch. And indeed she had reason to be worried: the money smuggled out of Germany two years earlier was almost gone, leaving her largely dependent on friends to support her: the Huxleys, the Mimerels, Eva, with whom she lived at La Juliette rent-free, and also Anna Bernhardt in Berlin, who sent what money she could, coded in her letters as "eggs." But as Anna repeatedly reminded her, Sybille must stop depending on others and start earning her living—until, that is, she succeeded in making "a nice marriage," which would comfortably ensure her financial future.

In mid-November 1934, Sybille in her small car drove with Eva to London, where she was to stay with Aldous and Maria. The Huxleys had recently taken the lease of a flat in Albany, a handsome Georgian mansion overlooking Piccadilly where Lord Byron and William Gladstone had once lived. At the start of the nineteenth century the building had been converted into apartments for bachelors, with a courtyard at the front, and at the rear two parallel long buildings divided by a covered passage opening into Vigo Street, each entrance supervised by a uniformed porter in a top hat. ("Albany was both rather wonderful and a bit preposterous," in Sybille's view.) It was behind the main building, along the "Rope Walk," that the Huxleys' rooms, their "set," was situated, comprising a spacious drawing room, a couple of bedrooms, a kitchen in the basement, and a tiny gaslit maid's room, temporarily Sybille's quarters, on the top floor.

Here Sybille planned to begin the book which had been in her mind for some time. Aldous was diligently at work on his new novel, which might have set her an example; but Sybille, while she admired his self-discipline, found herself unable to imitate it. From childhood her sole ambition had been to write; yet she was always to struggle over writing, dreading it, avoiding it for long periods altogether, then battling furiously, sometimes for years at a time, with the current work in progress. "I sit before my hostile typewriter and sicken before the abnormal effort," as she later described the process. "What is this blight I have suffered from all my life that makes trying to write . . . such tearing, crushing, defeating agony."

A serious impediment at this period were the distractions currently on offer. In the weeks leading up to Christmas there were luncheons and dinners almost every day, not only with the Huxleys and their friends, but also with the Dincklages and Mimerels, who had come over to London for the holiday. On New Year's Eve, Aldous and Maria threw a party, attended among others by Sybille and Eva, Eddy Sackville-West, Raymond Mortimer and Lady Ottoline Morrell. In the early hours of the morning, after a great deal of champagne, Aldous with Sybille walked out into the courtyard to wave goodbye to the departing guests. "*Auguri*, we shouted, <u>Auguri</u>! Rather a nice beginning to the New Year, I thought."

It was not until the spring of 1935 that Sybille returned to France, as before living at La Juliette with Eva. Here in their tranquil haven they were joined for a while by Klaus Mann, in need of a retreat from his anti-fascist campaigning in order to work on a new novel, *Mephisto*. In June, after a peaceful few weeks, he took the two women with him to Paris to attend the first Congress of Writers on the Defence of Culture. They found the city in a state of extreme political tension, with street battles breaking out between the right-wing, anti-Semitic nationalists of Action Française and the socialist-communist Front Populaire. For five days in sweltering heat they were part of an audience of nearly 4,000, listening to speeches from distinguished literary figures from all over Europe, among them, E. M. Forster, Boris Pasternak, André Malraux, Bertolt Brecht, as well as Huxley, Feuchtwanger, Klaus and Heinrich Mann, all focused on the importance of defending intellectual freedom from the threat of fascism and war.

That same month news came from Anna in Berlin that Lisa had been released from her clinic; she had made a good recovery, Anna reported, was going out, seeing friends, even organising a little art exhibition in her small apartment. Anna, who had recently moved to be close to her daughter, remained as ferociously critical as ever. "Lisa looks frightfully old and *fanée* [withered] . . . and not a bit pretty (for <u>any</u> taste) and her nails are as dirty as ever . . . she is awfully fat now and looking <u>so</u> old, and always these showy outfits . . . I can't get along with her! Her way of always reproving me and snubbing me—my nerves are overstrained." The divorce case was at last reaching a conclusion, with the judgement at this point in financial terms going against Nori, who, it appeared, would be ordered to pay Lisa a substantial sum, a decision that in Anna's view was unjust. "The Court has decided against him in every concern . . . I am very sorry for him," she told Sybille, adding sarcastically that Lisa of course "is a white lamb who has never done the slightest harm and has only been ah! so ill!!! and abused by everybody."

Anna's letters rarely refer to the state of affairs in Germany, despite her own Jewishness and the rapid growth of a nationwide anti-Semitism. That year, in September 1935, the Nuremberg Laws were passed, withdrawing citizenship from German Jews as well as prohibiting their marriage to Aryans. Inevitably this resulted in greater numbers crossing the border into France, and as a consequence levels of anxiety were intensified among the French. In Paris the Parlement had approved an Act restricting the movement of refugees, requiring those who wished to change residence to apply for a special permit. Even those Germans who, like Sybille, had long been settled in France could no longer consider themselves safe. With the large number of émigrés in and around Sanary, the atmosphere was becoming increasingly charged, and "the locals were prolific in poison-pen complaints."

Alarmed by the precariousness of Sybille's situation, the dangers inherent in her German nationality, the Huxleys decided to act. The most effective method of securing her status, they concluded, was to obtain a British passport, the easiest route to which was marriage to an Englishman. A friend of Sybille who had done just that was Erika Mann, who had recently travelled to England to marry a man she had never met, the poet W. H. Auden. Inspired by this example, the Huxleys determined to make a similar arrangement—"We must get one of our bugger friends to marry Sybille," Maria announced. None of the bugger friends, however, seemed willing to oblige, and the project turned out to be more difficult than anticipated. Aldous sent numerous letters asking for help in locating a potential husband for their "German friend . . . The solution, it seems to me, consists in finding someone combining impecuniosity, honesty and homosexuality . . . She will give fifty pounds—which might, at a pinch, be raised to a hundred; but she can't afford more." Unfortunately, not a single volunteer came forward.

It was at this point that Sybille decided to consult Sylvester Gates. Sylvester responded immediately, and within a very short time had located a suitable prospect: an acquaintance of his had a butler whose ex-boyfriend had agreed to marry in exchange for a payment of £100. Walter Bedford (originally Walter Croan) was living in Soho and working as an attendant at a gentleman's club in St. James's.

Once the agreement had been confirmed, Sybille at the beginning of November travelled to England, accompanied by Pierre Mimerel, who at the time had business in London. On Sylvester's advice she stayed not with the Huxleys but in a hotel in Kensington, she and Pierre, again on Sylvester's recommendation, careful to take rooms that were not adjoining. The next morning, shaking with nerves, she went to Albany, where she found Maria in the drawing room with a stranger, "on the handsome side, in his thirties probably, rather more masculine than Maria's b. friends." This was Walter Bedford, in fact forty years old. The two of them shook hands, and shortly afterwards set off to the local registrar's office to apply for a licence.

Early on the day of her wedding, Sybille was dressing when the receptionist telephoned to warn her that an official from the Home Office was on his way upstairs. "He was in the room within seconds, a tall man holding a briefcase and a bowler hat." Immediately he began questioning her: "So you have been living mostly in France over the last few years. And you intend to marry a British subject this morning?" Unimpressed by her replies, the gentleman asked to see her passport, which he carefully examined before putting it in his briefcase; her marriage was not feasible, he told her before taking his leave. Shocked, Sybille telephoned Sylvester, who instructed her to go at once to the Huxleys in Albany. Here she remained, at night sleeping on the drawing-room sofa.

Several days passed, with Sybille in a state of acute anxiety, and then one morning a messenger arrived at the porter's lodge bringing her passport with him. "It was stamped with a Deportation Order. If I had not left the United Kingdom within forty-eight hours, I would be deported to the country of origin. (Germany.)" Sybille had already consulted a solicitor, a contact of Sylvester's, who had advised her to claim that she was of independent means, and thus no burden to the country of adoption, but this had had no effect. In desperation Maria decided to make one final attempt, going herself to the Home Office to lodge a personal and impassioned plea on Sybille's behalf. Miraculously, she succeeded. "Some hours later came a message by hand—the Deportation Order was rescinded."

Shortly afterwards, on 15 November 1935, Sybille was married to Walter Bedford in a civil ceremony at Caxton Hall, with Aldous and Pierre Mimerel as witnesses. That evening the Huxleys gave a cocktail party at Albany, with among the guests several of Walter Bedford's friends ("half a dozen showgirls . . . and some tough male bruisers"), as well as a Bloomsbury contingent, including the poet and playwright Robert Nichols, the Scottish novelist and poet Naomi Mitchison, Leonard and Virginia Woolf. Sybille was thrilled to meet Virginia, who "came up to me, took mine into her exquisite hand (I had not met her before, nor after). 'This,' she said, 'is a very queer party. I can't understand anything about it: one day you must come and tell me.' " Later in the evening, Mr. and Mrs. Bedford, as a present from Aldous, went to dine at the Trocadero off Piccadilly before attending a variety show. The two never saw each other again. Not long after her wedding Sybille finally found herself in possession of a British passport, the German document of "musty brown paper with a kind of eagle on the cover" replaced by the treasured dark blue and gold of the United Kingdom. When on her return to France she sent in her current *carte d'identité* for renewal, "they returned it with a '*devenue Anglaise*' [become English] scrawled by hand across a front page."

For the rest of her life Sybille carried with her a feeling of guilt and loathing, what she described as the "national shame . . . of a German origin." For some years after the Second World War she refused to visit the country or speak the language, and felt immediately uncomfortable if she found herself in the company of Germans. "I never felt I had the

German identity, the Germanic mind," she said once in an interview. "The fact that I had any connections with this terrible country became a cause of guilt, and for some time I tried desperately to anglicise myself entirely." English had become her first language, the language in which she wrote, and although by no means uncritical of her newly adopted country, her British citizenship was always of vital importance to her; from now on England was to be her "home base."

For the present, however, most of Sybille's time was spent in France. In December she was back in Sanary, staying with the Mimerels, as Eva with her lover, Lion Feuchtwanger, had left for Moscow; hoping to join them, Sybille had begun learning Russian but her application for a visa was refused. On Eva's return Sybille joined her in Paris, where the two women remained until the beginning of June 1936, when they settled at La Juliette for the summer. In October both women again left the south, Eva to return to Russia, while Sybille spent a few weeks in Eva's apartment in Paris, writing and also trying, without much success, to find a job.

Paris, together with London and Rome, was over the years to become one of the centres of Sybille's existence. Her first introduction to Paris had been at the age of fifteen while en route from London to Sanary; between arriving early in the morning at the Gare du Nord and departing in the evening for the south, Sybille had had almost a day at her disposal. Following Lisa's detailed instructions, she had obediently visited the Louvre, the Tuileries, the Musée de Cluny, Montmartre and the Sacré Coeur, yet none of it particularly impressed her. "I felt nothing very much . . . Nor did I know what to make of the unfamiliar facades of the *grands boulevards*, the slate-grey straightness, the compound gusts of smells: open *pissoirs* with tin screens like fire-guards . . . I wandered about, unnoticed, unmolested . . ."

Now ten years later, Sybille had come to feel a strong connection with the city, enjoying her long solitary walks after a morning's writing. "The thing about Paris for me are these afternoon hours of walking the streets . . . looking, seeing, thinking . . . It is a kind of *apprentissage* . . . Here one is alone, strange and at home, in the quiet streets and boulevards." A voracious reader, Sybille also spent many hours browsing in the two famous bookshops on the Left Bank, La Maison des Amis des Livres, owned by Adrienne Monnier, and Shakespeare & Company, owned by Monnier's friend and lover, Sylvia Beach. Monnier "was invariably polite . . . no more . . . At Shakespeare & Company I subscribed to the lending library . . . There one had to pay a deposit of 50 francs, about two dollars, against loss of books, for me quite a wrench . . . [on leaving Paris] I asked (sheer necessity) for the deposit back . . . I wish I had not, for Sylvia Beach, handing 50 francs to me, gave me a shocked, astonished look."

Despite the many distractions, Sybille had been determined to develop a disciplined routine, especially as she was now starting on what was to be her first full-length work of fiction. *Devil on the Brain* (originally entitled "The Expense of Spirit") recounts the amorous experiences of an eighteen-year-old Englishman spending the summer with his uncle and aunt in the south of France. The story begins with Charles in the process of disguising himself as a pirate in preparation for the fancy-dress party his uncle is throwing that evening. Among the guests, English, French and German, are a couple of scheming femmes fatales with whom Charles quickly engages, fancying himself in love with the beautiful Huguette while simultaneously indulging in an erotic *pas de deux* with a Madame Durand; it is Madame Durand who in the final section turns out to be spying for Germany. Both characters and location are clearly based on Sanary, its cafés and restaurants, its busy summer social life—with the fancy-dress party at the beginning a recognisable, if somewhat pallid, version of the pirate party thrown by Nori and Sybille seven years earlier. Although at the start the story shows promise, such signs quickly evaporate, the whole weighed down by two-dimensional characters, ponderous literary references, and a plodding, self-conscious narrative that quickly destroys all claim to conviction.

Returned to Sanary, Sybille continued working on the book, Maria typing it out chapter by chapter. Once it was finished Maria showed it to Aldous, who was damning in his criticism. "It was a bad, empty novel, and he told me as much . . . 'lack of vital relationship between the characters . . . issues of little significance . . . the book needs to be simultaneously shortened and filled up.' " Although painful at the time, many years later Sybille found herself in agreement with Aldous's verdict. "I had read too much and knew too little . . . My wretched words were derivative . . . I followed the master, but I followed him very poorly: watered-down Aldous Huxley was Huxley with flat water indeed." The manuscript was sent to several publishers, all of whom turned it down: "rightly so but to my desolation at the time." In fact it was to be another almost twenty years before Sybille was to find her own remarkable voice.

The failure of her novel marked the beginning of a period for Sybille of traumatic upheaval and emotional crisis. In the autumn of 1936 while staying in Paris, Sybille had met a young woman with whom she had become instantly infatuated. Joan Black, exquisitely beautiful, the daughter of a well-to-do Irish couple, was staying in Paris having recently returned from a motor tour in the south with her sister. Joan was currently living with an American divorcée, Eda Lord, whom Sybille had briefly encountered in Berlin in 1932; Eda at the time had been much taken with Sybille, who had barely noticed her. Now it was Sybille who was rejected: Joan, after a few weeks of tantalising flirtation followed by a short affair, returned to Eda, leaving Sybille so miserable that she left Paris to take refuge with the Huxleys in London. This minor episode may have seemed of small significance, and yet all three, Sybille, Joan and Eda, were over time to become part of a complex web of love and friendship—and occasional hostility—that was to last for the rest of their lives.

As always Sybille's spirits revived in the company of Aldous and Maria. On this occasion, however, the Huxleys were able to offer little comfort, Maria greeting her with the news that they were shortly to leave Europe and settle, at least for a while, in America. Although Maria was loath to abandon her beloved Sanary, she thought it "quite pointless to stay and risk so much when we are among the few people who have the freedom to be able to escape." Now, hoping to find a tenant for their set, they had moved out of Albany and with their son Matthew had taken three service flats in the Mount Royal Hotel near Marble Arch. Fortunately, however, Sybille was able to remain as before in their tiny maid's room, from where late every evening she would walk up Bond Street, across Grosvenor Square to Oxford Street to spend the night in bed with Maria, returning to Albany at dawn.

Meanwhile some troubling news was received from Anna in Berlin. By now the situation for Jews in Germany had become extremely perilous, particularly in the capital, where the authorities pursued a vigorous role in depriving the Jewish population of their rights. Increasingly, Jews were targeted, frequently spat at in the street and physically assaulted, with anti-Jewish propaganda placarded in shops and restaurants all over the city. Anna had always distanced herself from her Semitic origins, proud that her colouring—her blonde hair and blue eyes—gave her an Aryan appearance. In her view, most Jews, however wealthy and successful, were inherently inferior; both her children, Lisa and her brother, had been baptised at birth, with Lisa's conversion to Catholicism at the time of her first marriage a source of considerable satisfaction to her mother.

Now, however, to her extreme distaste, Anna found herself living in cramped conditions at close quarters with some offensively vulgar Jewish neighbours. Recently she had been obliged to move yet again, this time into a stuffy little room in a house crammed with lodgers, where she was reduced to doing her own cooking, washing and ironing. Her landlady, a Frau Jacobson, was "an insufferable Jew," who refused even to supply her with lavatory paper. The house, she complained, "is a kind of synagogue without any discipline. I never talk to anybody . . . [and] I've always my door locked . . . I had a row with my disgusting Jewish Jacobson. She wanted M[arks]. 5 more because I burnt too much light . . . She _is_ a beast . . . Today my room is so cold that I write in my seal coat and can't hold the penholder."

Anna's hostility towards her daughter was as vituperative as ever, and she appeared to take little pleasure in Lisa's recovery. The previous Christmas she had written to Sybille, "Tomorrow week is Xmas Eve . . . shut up in my room without children or grandchild . . . without a Xmas tree . . . But no need to worry about me. I'll go on living as long as possible—so that your mother shall wait for my death as long as I can help! May God grant it." Now, however, her attitude began to soften as Lisa became overwhelmed by depression, triggered by an unexpected reversal in her divorce case: it was now Nori who had been awarded almost everything, leaving Lisa with barely enough to live on. Her doctor said "it will take a _long_ time to get her sane again," Anna reported. "The worst is that she has no courage any more." Lisa's condition then deteriorated further when she developed appendicitis and had to undergo an operation. Afterwards, her depression intensified to such a degree that she tried to commit suicide by swallowing pieces of broken glass from the tumbler by her bed, and by the end of the year it was obvious she would not recover. "Your mother is now immensely *pitoyable*," wrote Anna. "She had tried to reconstruct her life with an admirable energy and brilliant success—and everything went to pieces by this devastating operation." Finally on 2 February 1937, Lisa, aged fifty-three, died in hospital in Berlin; her body was cremated two days later.

Sybille, staying in Albany at the time, first heard the news by telephone from Maria Huxley, followed a few days later by a letter from her grandmother. Now Anna wrote that she was "immensely sorry about our poor Lisa . . . they said it was *Entartung des Herzmuskels* [degeneration of the heart muscles] which didn't work any more and gave such horrid pains." Sybille's feelings about her mother's death remained ambivalent. For the rest of her life she felt remorse, blaming herself for her failure to love her mother; and yet with Lisa wholly lacking in maternal instinct, there had been small chance of any real emotional connection. During the last few years in Sanary Sybille had done everything she could to help and please her mother, whose problems had become an almost overwhelming burden for her daughter. And yet despite Lisa's often appalling behaviour, Sybille had always admired her, admired her moral courage, her vivacity and wit, and above all her powerful intelligence. "She taught me everything about literature and art and world affairs," Sybille said in an interview many years later. "She was a great influence on my intellectual life." And crucially Lisa was to remain one of the dominant figures in her daughter's imagination, this clever, wayward beauty to play a pivotal role in all four volumes of Sybille's published fiction.

Since her childhood, when she had spent months at a time staying with her grandmother in Hamburg, Sybille had encountered Anna only occasionally. Now the two of them agreed to meet. As it was out of the question for Sybille to go to Germany, they arranged to spend a couple of days together in Amsterdam, where they could talk about family history and the recent harrowing past. One morning they visited the Rijksmuseum and sat together on a wooden bench, silently studying *The Night Watch*. It was to be the last time Sybille was to see her grandmother. Some months later, Anna, fearing arrest and transportation, committed suicide.

Returning to London, Sybille was faced with the Huxleys' imminent departure for America. They had left Sanary in February, convinced—mistakenly, as it turned out—that they would eventually return, encouraging various friends and relations to stay at the Villa Huley and keep an eye on the house and garden. During the weeks before their departure, Sybille was with them constantly, helping them pack, running errands, joining their family and friends for dinner in the evening, all the time trying not to dwell on how desperately she would miss them. Finally on 7 April 1937, they sailed from Southampton on the SS *Normandie*, Sybille, wretchedly unhappy, accompanying them on the train from Waterloo. "When the bell rang for visitors to leave the ship, I said farewell to Aldous. Maria came up to the open deck—it was nightfall now—from where one took the launch. I was a symbol, the last of Europe, the last link . . . I was already down the gangplank when Maria took off her officer's cloak, keep this, she called, and let it fall."

Sybille remained in London for several weeks, living in Albany while working on a new novel, her stay coinciding with the enthronement of George VI, whose coronation procession she watched slowly winding its regal way along Piccadilly. Here as before, Sybille supported herself by giving lessons in English, her pupils mostly well-to-do businessmen, German Jews on their way to the United States. "The idea was that I might be able to give them a crash course in easy, competent everyday speech. It worked . . . I discovered that I much enjoyed, and had an aptitude for, teaching. I craftily avoided having to write anything down by my own hand, and skated over spelling . . . The fee for a private lesson then would be five shillings an hour or could be as low as 3/6 or even 2/6. I was paid 7/6 which felt and was quite [a] lot."

Rarely happy when living alone, Sybille during this period took comfort in the company of an acquaintance whom she had first met a few years before in Sanary. Charlotte Wolff, then in her early thirties, was a Jewish psychotherapist who, banned from practising in Berlin, had moved to the south of France. Here she had been taken under the wing of Maria, who had been fascinated by Charlotte's practice of chiromancy, or palm reading, which quickly became popular among the Huxleys' friends, Sybille among them. "Maria Huxley once asked me whether I could see literary talent in Sybille's hands," Charlotte recalled. "I answered: 'Yes, particularly as an interpretative writer.' I frequently had to tell Sybille what her hands disclosed . . . Like most artists, she had faith in the irrational and was very superstitious." Tall and lanky, Charlotte was strikingly masculine in appearance, always dressed in trousers, shirt and tie, her thick dark hair slicked back like a man's; an active lesbian since her student days, she was to become highly regarded for her writings on female homosexuality.

While living in Albany, Maria had found a small apartment off Piccadilly for Charlotte, who was now permanently settled in London. Depressed by the Huxleys' departure, Sybille was delighted to spend time with Charlotte: "two people affected in different ways by the Nazi upheaval became a comfort to each other." The pair took to dining together once a week in a small restaurant in Soho. "We generally occupied a corner table at the furthest end, where we sat eating, drinking and talking," Charlotte wrote later. "When I looked sideways at Sybille, I saw her eyes and mouth smiling. Nobody else I have known has managed to have such a worried and amused look at the same time. Her rapid speech was something one had to get used to. I often became nervous when, on some occasions, she could not keep still and walked about the room, talking; but chez Joseph she spoke in a quieter voice, relaxed by the good food and wine."

During the early summer Sybille returned to Sanary, again staying with Eva at La Juliette. It was the start of what was to be a particularly rackety season, Sybille just one of a group of friends who, lively and intelligent, were also capable of extravagantly outrageous behaviour. Among them were the two "Eddies," Sackville-West and Gathorne-Hardy; the former was at work on a novel, and spent several weeks at La Juliette, prancing about in brick-coloured shorts with a tiny knitted skullcap on the back of his head. Almost every day Sybille would drive Eddy and Eva into town to meet the rest of the gang, among them Gathorne-Hardy and another Eton and Oxford contemporary,

Brian Howard. Brian, a strikingly elegant figure with his black hair and large, heavy-lidded dark eyes, was charming, flamboyant, witty and malicious—later portrayed by Evelyn Waugh in *Brideshead Revisited* as that dissolute exquisite, Anthony Blanche. In his mid-twenties Brian had been sent to Berlin to be treated for depression, and while there had fallen in love with an old school-friend, James ("Jimmy") Stern. Brian's passion was unreciprocated, but the two men had remained close, and after leaving Germany made regular visits to the south of France. It was here that the fond friendship between Brian and Sybille began.

From their first encounter, Sybille had been fascinated by this exotic individual, despite his frequently deplorable conduct. At this period Brian's boyfriend was a young German, Toni Altmann, blond, stupid and exceptionally handsome, always referred to by Sybille as "the oaf." Night after night the two men would drink themselves into near insanity, with Brian beginning the evening witty and engaging before descending into violent argument and frequently angry brawls. After one particularly raucous evening at La Juliette with Eddy Gathorne-Hardy, Brian sent Sybille and Eva an apology:

> With humble gratitude and lowered eyes,
> Aware of folly, swearing to be wise,
> No longer tipsy, ribald or inept—
> The beastliest men in England, we accept.
> Eddie his lusts, Brian his tongue shall calm,
> No oaths shall mar, no grossness shall alarm
> Our twin Egerias' board! Yes, we will show
> > How high they sometimes fly, who
> > Sometimes fall so low.

Far worse, however, was the fracas that was to follow a few weeks later.

On most evenings Sybille, Brian, Toni Altmann and a group of friends met for dinner in a restaurant in Sanary, Sybille ferrying them there in her newly acquired convertible, an ancient eight-seater De Dion-Bouton recently found for her by Pierre Mimerel. After dinner the group often went on to a favourite bar in Bandol, "where one could dance, ambisexually, on a small floor-lit square," before ending the night in some seedy *boîte*; from there in the small hours, not entirely sober herself, Sybille would drive them all home. On one occasion, after a lengthy drinking session at a local bistro, where Klaus Mann and Eddy Gathorne-Hardy were also present, a row erupted near midnight with a small contingent at a nearby table. One of the group addressed a remark to Toni Altmann which Brian considered offensive. "Within seconds a general fight had broken out. The table overturned, carafes of red wine flowing forth, plates of spaghetti *pomodori* sliding on to our clothes and the floor . . . all the men seemed to be fighting each other, with fists and kicks." The result a few days later was a formal summons from the Mairie: "We, Brian, Eddy, myself, were arraigned for the fracas at the bistro . . . and of course were sent to pay, not very much—for the broken cutlery and glass."

A more decorous event, organised by Brian, was a theatrical performance one evening in the garden at La Juliette. The stage was the long terrace outside the house, and below it on the lawn sat an audience of nearly a hundred, the Kislings, the Mimerels, the "German *haute culture*." First was a one-act piece, *Le Cheval Arabe* by Julien Luchaire, followed by *The Secret of Mayerling*, Brian's mischievous retelling of the double suicide of Crown Prince Rudolf of Austria and his mistress, Marie Vetsera. In this version the object of Prince Rudolf's passion was not Vetsera but a handsome young huntsman, played, appropriately enough, by Toni Altmann. Brian in black satin breeches was the crown prince, Eddy Gathorne-Hardy, magnificent in court dress, wig and cardboard crown, impersonated Empress Elisabeth, while Sybille herself was "the Secret," a rent boy "in a tight drainpipe trouser suit, shaking with stage fright." The play, performed in English, was received with such rapture that the cast, intoxicated by their success, gave it twice more, ad-libbing first in German, then in French.

In between the summers in Sanary, Sybille spent most of her time in Paris with Eva. The two women shared a studio flat with a tiny garden off the avenue Victor Hugo, and it was here that Sybille hoped to finish her second novel. She was also acting as cover for Eva, deeply immersed in her affair with Lion Feuchtwanger. "The little Lion," as Sybille called him, came up from the south at regular intervals and often took the two women to lunch or dinner, sometimes dining alone with Sybille when Eva was engaged elsewhere. In June Eva underwent another abortion, and again it was Sybille who supported her, keeping in touch by telephone with an anxious Lion in Sanary. With the novel finally completed, Sybille was full of hope that now she would find acceptance, but this second work (which has yet to come to light) was rejected as firmly as the first. Eva, while sympathetic, was not uncritical, saying that in her view the book was overloaded with information, that Sybille was too "anxious to show how much you know."

One spring evening in Paris, on 10 March 1938, Sybille was sitting in the Café de Flore with a group of friends, among them Brian, Klaus Mann, Brian's old friend Jimmy Stern, and the exotic, left-wing activist Nancy Cunard. The intense discussion focused on the threatening situation in Germany, where Hitler's troops were gathered on the Austrian border ready to invade. Klaus, taut and febrile, was arguing for the probability of some form of compromise, while Brian and Jimmy Stern were predicting war. The atmosphere was charged; indeed Brian, who since the early 1930s had courageously spoken out about the dangers of Nazism, was in such an agitated state that he suddenly turned on his neighbour, Nancy Cunard, and snapped, "It makes me rather nervous, my dear, to watch you eat this horrible welsh rarebit, while our friends in Vienna . . . This means war, my dear!" Two days later came the *Anschluss*. As Klaus remarked, "Brian was wrong. It was not yet the hour . . . The fall of Austria meant bloodshed, but it did not mean war . . ."

Soon after this Sybille returned to Sanary, living at the Villa Huley. "[*Je veux*] *que la maison serve d'abri au plus de gens possible*" ("[I want] the house to act as a refuge for as many people as possible"), Maria Huxley had written to her sister Jeanne, and over the next few months, as well as Jeanne and her French playwright husband, Georges Neveux, a number of friends moved in, with Sybille appointed as housekeeper. "You probably know that La Gorguette is going to be a sort of camp all summer," Maria told Eddy Sackville-West, "with Sybille at the head of it and feeling important. I have good letters from Sybille. She seems to be getting along somehow and a little more tidily than in the past." During this period Eddy himself came to stay, as did Eva for a while, and also Katzi, who arrived from Paris after a brief period of internment as a suspected spy. Fortunately, she seemed unmarked by the experience, as cheerful and sociable as ever, currently conducting an affair with Pierre Gaillard, one of her ex-husband's French agents.

In September events took a more sinister turn, as Nazi troops massed on the Czech border, but the tension was briefly alleviated at the end of the month by the signing of the Munich Agreement, the British prime minister, Neville Chamberlain, famously returning to London from a meeting with Hitler triumphantly declaring "peace in our time." At this same period Sybille was in Paris, working on a new novel, giving lessons in English, and undertaking "volunteer work for a group of hard-up, left-wing refugees." Despite Munich, the international situation was growing increasingly threatening, and Sybille was alarmed by the hostility shown to foreigners, especially Jews, living in France: recently Brian and Eva had been spat at and threatened while walking along the quayside in Sanary. Now Sybille anxiously began to focus on the possibility of escape, writing to Maria to ask if she could arrange passage for her to the States; Maria, however, had been dubious. "*Je vais parler à des amis avant de lui répondre,*" Maria told her sister. "*Tout devient de plus en plus difficile ici pour les Allemands*" ("I'm going to talk to friends before replying to her. Everything here is becoming more difficult for the Germans").

Fortunately, however, the situation was not yet entirely grim, and it was now that Sybille was to embark on one of the most enduring and important relationships of her life. Allanah Harper, a handsome, forceful young Englishwoman in her early thirties, had been living in Paris for the past decade. The only child of a wealthy and well-travelled family—her father, a successful engineer, had built the first railway through the Andes—she had been educated in England, presented at court, and during the 1920s had become one of the leading members of the "Bright Young Things," with such friends as Cecil Beaton, Stephen Tennant, the Jungman sisters, and Brian Howard. At the age of twenty-five, Allanah, "well read and amusing without being brilliant," according to Beaton, had moved to Paris, and in 1930 launched a literary journal, *Echanges*, which published both French and English writers, among them W. H. Auden, Edith Sitwell, T. S. Eliot, Virginia Woolf, Paul Éluard, Henri Michaux and André Gide. For this she had

had the backing of three wealthy sponsors, Princess Pauline Terry, the half-English daughter of Maharajah Duleep Singh; Princesse Edmonde de Polignac, the Singer sewing-machine heiress; and the Aga Khan, to whom for a brief period Allanah had been engaged. (There is a photograph of Allanah with the Aga Khan at a fancy-dress ball, Allanah in costume as a white rabbit with a pair of towering white ears.)

Echanges did not last long, but Allanah continued to live mainly in Paris, "hurrying about in a large, handsome English way" between the worlds of bookshops, literary salons and a wealthy international society that migrated between the capital and the Côte d'Azur. It was in Paris on 2 January 1939 that Sybille and Allanah first met, over cocktails in the company of Princess Pauline, Joan Black, with whom Sybille had for a while been deeply infatuated, and Joan's partner, Eda Lord. Allanah, tall, handsome, with dark brown shingled hair, was about to leave for the theatre with Pauline, and during this brief encounter she and Sybille took little interest in each other. The following week they met again, at a dinner party of Pauline's, and everything changed.

Over the next half-century Allanah was to remain one of the most crucial figures in Sybille's life, first as her lover, then as friend and generous provider—as well as a sometimes scathingly stern critic. Tough, determined and extremely energetic, Allanah always knew what she wanted, and unlike Sybille rarely suffered from doubt or depression. Now during the months after their first meeting the two were constantly together, in Paris, at Gadencourt in Normandy, a tiny village in the Eure where Allanah owned a share in a small house, and in Sanary, staying with Princess Pauline, who had rented a villa for the summer. Allanah gave Sybille a gold ring as a token of their commitment to each other.

During this period Allanah left the south for a few weeks to visit her mother in England, and during her absence Sybille became very taken with a young woman currently staying in Sanary. Poppy Kirk, of American-Italian descent, married to a minor British diplomat much older than herself, was strikingly beautiful if not particularly intelligent; for several years she and Allanah had been lovers, and when their affair came to an end Poppy had started a relationship with Princess Pauline; it was in the company of Pauline that she first encountered Sybille. For obvious reasons it was essential this new relationship be kept undercover, Sybille renting a box at the Sanary post office so she could discreetly slip in "at some quiescent hour" to collect Poppy's letters. Inevitably on Allanah's return the affair was discovered; Allanah in a fury pulled her ring from Sybille's finger and swore she would throw it into the sea. Mortified, Sybille begged for forgiveness, and after a brief glacial period the two became reconciled; Allanah returned the ring, swore that she loved Sybille and would look after her for ever.

After this painful debacle, the two women stayed in Sanary. When in the New Year Princess Pauline left for Switzerland, the couple, together with Allanah's large brown poodle, moved into the Villa Huley. As before Sybille was responsible for running the household, if not always entirely to Maria's satisfaction. Sybille, *"très grasse mais contente"* ("very fat but happy"), had by now developed a somewhat entitled attitude, not bothering to thank Maria for the previous year's Christmas cheque, it appeared, nor had she yet paid her share of the electricity bill. *"Je suis vraiment plutôt découragée par l'attitude de Sybille,"* Maria wrote crossly to her sister. *"Je me demande pourquoi on les aide car il y en a beaucoup d'autres qui ont besoin d'aide et qui l'apprécierait"* ("I'm really rather discouraged by Sybille's attitude . . . I ask myself why one helps them when there are many others needing help and who would appreciate it").

During the summer of 1939, as the crisis in Europe intensified, the freedom of foreigners in France became increasingly restricted, with curfews imposed, permits required for travel over even the shortest distance. With the signing of the Nazi–Soviet Non-Aggression Pact on 23 August, the atmosphere darkened: all at once soldiers were everywhere, crowds of civilians on the move, holidaymakers rushing to return home, roads jammed with traffic as heavily laden cars and trucks full of troops heading north met hordes of refugees fleeing south. On 1 September the Germans invaded Poland, and two days later war was declared by Britain and France. In Sanary an order was immediately issued for all German males between the ages of seventeen and sixty-six to be interned, including, among many others, Eva's lover, Lion Feuchtwanger, and Brian Howard's boyfriend, Toni Altmann. Toni was driven by Sybille and Eva to the designated camp, Les Milles, a former tile factory near Aix-en-Provence. For the first few days the two women were allowed to visit the camp, bringing with them fruit, cheese, wine and cigarettes as well as rugs and pillows; but then on 15 September such rights were withdrawn.

The following month Eva left for New York, and a few weeks later Sybille and Allanah with her dog, Poodly, drove to Normandy, where they spent several weeks at Gadencourt. Here over Christmas they were joined by Joan Black and Eda Lord, all four of them struggling with food shortages and the intense cold. "We had deep snow then 14 below zero," Eda wrote to a friend. "Scarcely any cars dared try the roads which were ice by that time. We didn't move . . . for ten days."

By now Sybille's anxiety had become almost overwhelming. Despite her British passport, she was well aware that her German origins placed her in danger with the French as did her Jewishness with the Germans—later she discovered her name had been on the Gestapo's list of suspects to be arrested. Desperately she wrote again to Maria imploring her somehow to arrange passage for her, but with the enormous numbers queueing to cross the Atlantic this seemed improbable: as Maria told her sister, Sybille *"aimerait venir ici mais étant Allemande cela est presque impossible. Le quota est rempli"* ("would like to come here but being German it is nearly impossible. The quota is full").

On 2 January 1940, Sybille and Allanah left Gadencourt to return to the south. With strict petrol rationing in force, Sybille knew they would be unable to drive there and so, reluctantly, gave her beloved De Dion-Bouton to Mme. Guérinier, the *femme de ménage*. The two women made their way first to Paris, then Cannes, where Allanah's mother had been on holiday, Allanah succeeding with some difficulty in securing her mother's return to England.

In Sanary, they found the whole coast in a state of upheaval, the chaos intensified after the start of the German invasion of France on 10 May. Fortunately by now Sybille had heard from Maria that she had at last managed to obtain two tickets for the following month on an American ship leaving Genoa for New York. In the middle of May, Sybille and Allanah, with Allanah's poodle and nineteen suitcases, made their way across the border to Genoa, reporting immediately to the United States consulate, as the British consul had already departed. Here they were warned that Italy was about to enter the war, at which point they would be instantly arrested and interned as enemy aliens; the town was full of spies, the consul told them, and it was vital they not give themselves away by speaking English. The next few days were spent in a state of extreme apprehension, until finally on 20 May they were informed that their ship, SS *Exeter*, had docked and they must board as quickly as possible. Yet when they arrived on the quayside, their luggage piled up on a pushcart, they were appalled to see what appeared to be a vast crowd making their way up the gangplank, American diplomats and their families and staff, a group of Polish refugees, all given precedence over the two young women.

Eventually, however, they were allowed on board, shortly before the ship set sail. It was only afterwards they learned that *Exeter*, carrying in her hold half of Italy's gold reserves, was the last passenger ship to leave the port of Genoa for the duration of the war. They were gone just in time: the next week Mussolini declared war on France and Britain, followed four days later by the German occupation of Paris. Genoa, as Sybille wrote later, was "where Allanah and I sailed from in June 1940 out of the maw of war seven years into the unknown."

SIX

"A NEW EXOTIC OPULENT WORLD"

After seventeen days at sea, *Exeter* docked in New York on 6 June 1940. For Sybille and Allanah it was a moment of intense relief finally to arrive after nearly two and a half weeks of overcrowding and discomfort on board and constant anxiety about the future. When at last they emerged from the grey gloom of the customs sheds they found themselves in a seemingly enchanted environment: midtown Manhattan on a perfect summer's day, "the streets sunlit, glittering with bright awnings where tall doormen lifted hats to smiling men and well-dressed women. A new exotic opulent world." To Sybille's surprise and joy, Maria Huxley was there to meet them, by chance in New York on a brief visit from California, where the Huxleys were now living. With the luggage crammed into a couple of taxis, the three women were driven to the Bedford Hotel on 40th Street between Lexington and Park, where Maria had arranged for them to stay. Owned by a German couple, the Bedford, comfortable and expensive, had long been established as a centre for Jewish émigrés from Europe. As Sybille waited at the reception desk, she felt someone touch her elbow, turned round, and to her delight found Klaus Mann standing behind her.

Klaus, who for the past four years had spent much of his time in the States, tirelessly touring the country lecturing on the dangers of the Nazi regime, was now settled in New York, a permanent resident at the Bedford. Soon afterwards Erika, too, appeared, greeting Sybille with dramatic expressions of enthusiasm; she was shortly to leave for London, she told her, where she was to work as a correspondent for the German Service of the BBC. Although Erika appeared unchanged, Klaus, nervously chain-smoking, had visibly aged, paler, with the beginnings of a paunch and a small bald patch on the crown of his head. At once he began excitedly to describe his current project, the launching of a literary magazine, *Decision*, "on a much larger scale and infinitely more exciting than *Die Sammlung*." He already had promise of financial backing and a distinguished list of contributors, among them his father and his uncle Heinrich, as well as Brecht, Auden, Cocteau and the American novelist Sherwood Anderson. He hoped that Sybille, too, would write for the magazine.

Meanwhile Sybille and Allanah needed to decide on their immediate future. Soon after meeting them, Maria had left to return to California, where the two women intended to join her as soon as possible. Yet both were short of money: strict regulations had limited them to taking not more than £50 out of Europe; the Bedford was well above their means, as was the long train journey to Los Angeles. Fortunately a solution was quickly presented: two days after their arrival Erika took them to see her father, who was on a brief visit to New York. As formal and elegant as ever, Thomas Mann greeted them graciously before telling them of his plans. For the past couple of years he had been living and lecturing in Princeton, but the summer months he and Katia preferred to spend in California, where they were soon intending to settle. They would be leaving for Los Angeles in a few days' time, he explained, travelling by train, while their two servants, John and Lucie Long, would follow by car. If Sybille and Allanah cared to accompany the Longs they would be most welcome.

Delighted, the two women accepted gratefully, and a few days later left New York early in the morning for Princeton, where they found Mann, immaculately groomed, poised outside his handsome house waiting to receive them. "The Master was standing on the doorstep, hands raised high in greeting with impersonal Olympian benevolence: '*Wilkommen.*' " After breakfast the Manns left for the station, while Sybille and Allanah set off with the Longs, a mountain of luggage and two large poodles, Allanah's Poodly and Mann's adored Nico, John driving the Manns' large, luxurious Lincoln while Lucie followed in her own car.

It was a long and arduous journey, the heat growing more intense with every passing hour. John, it soon became clear, was an incompetent driver, and Sybille took over the wheel for most of the journey, steering day after day along "the endless flat roads, on and on through the corn plains of the Middle West . . . [stopping for] the ice-cold Coca-Cola at the gas stations, laced from the quart of rum I carried." While Allanah did what she could to keep Poodly cool, Sybille looked after "the sweating hot-furred" Nico: "I comforted him in the air-thin altitudes of New Mexico; when we crossed the desert, I laid ice packs on his curly head." But their main difficulty arose at night. The Longs were both black, and as most motels refused to take either blacks or dogs it was extremely hard to find a place to stay. "You can't appreciate the South," Sybille said later, "until you've tried travelling through it with a Negro. Everything was segregated in those days. The only place we all stayed together was in an undertakers' establishment in Texas where they woke us up in the middle of the night and asked, 'Where is your loved one?' "

The exhausted little convoy finally arrived at the Manns' house in the Brentwood district of Los Angeles on 1 July. As Sybille walked into the drawing room with Nico, the dog "went straight to his master, sat down by his side, head in air. When presently I came up to say goodbye to him, he ignored me. Slightly turned his head away."

On leaving the Manns, Sybille and Allanah went on to the Huxleys in Pacific Palisades. The moment of reunion with Aldous and Maria, after more than three years since they had set sail from Southampton, was intensely emotional. And yet although overjoyed to be in their company once more, it was not long before Sybille began to realise how much they had changed, and how little she was to find sympathetic in her new environment.

Pacific Palisades, or "Weimar by the Sea," as it was known in reference to the number of German writers and artists who had settled there, was an idyllic residential neighbourhood overlooking the ocean. Many of the exiles had been attracted to the area not only for its warm climate but also for its almost Mediterranean scenery, its wide beaches, palm-lined streets and lush gardens of lavender and bougainvillea, magnolia, sycamore and eucalyptus. Among the more recent arrivals were several expatriates known to Sybille from Sanary, including her beloved friend, Eva Herrmann, who had arrived in the States the year before and was now living in a large, luxurious house in Brentwood. Eva had been suffering agonies of anxiety over the fate of her lover, Lion Feuchtwanger, who at the time of Sybille's arrival was still in France. Fortunately, however, the Feuchtwangers were soon to reach California; as part of a small group including Heinrich Mann and Klaus's brother, Golo, they escaped by making a perilous night-time journey on foot across the Pyrenees into Spain, and thence by sea from Lisbon.

Within a short time of arriving Sybille and Allanah had found a property to rent on Iliff Street off Sunset Boulevard, a modest little dwelling, like "a dentist's suburban villa," as Allanah dismissively described it. The two women were delighted, nonetheless, to have a place of their own, where they could be alone together. Their deep love for each other, their strong emotional bond, was to remain intact for the rest of their lives, and if their friendship was sometimes stormy, their mutual devotion remained unchanged. While the sexual side of their relationship faded over time, each continued to depend on the other for encouragement and support, with Sybille especially looking to Allanah for practical advice, not only in her daily life but with her writing career. Inevitably, too, she relied on her for financial help. When after the war Allanah came into money left to her by her father, providing her with a more than adequate income, she immediately made over a portion of this to Sybille, hoping it would help enable her to launch a career of her own.

Iliff Street was within easy walking distance of Aldous and Maria, and Sybille looked forward to spending much of her time with them. The Huxleys had been settled in California for nearly three years, and were living in a small house on South Amalfi Drive, hideously furnished and dimly lit, Aldous working as industriously as ever, both as a screenwriter for MGM and on projects of his own. Disdaining the brash society of most of the Hollywood film world, they led a relatively quiet life, seeing only a small group of friends, among them Charlie Chaplin, Anita Loos and the astronomer Edwin Hubble. Although happy to be reunited, Sybille was disturbed to realise how much her old friends had changed: Maria, thinner than ever, was no longer the gaily exuberant figure she had been in Sanary but appeared tense, anxious and permanently exhausted, while Aldous looked grey and drawn, "like a man with a great burden of unhappiness severely locked away."

To Sybille's dismay both Huxleys were now strict vegetarians, Maria insisting on dining every evening at the distressingly early hour of 7 p.m. The tension during mealtimes was often palpable, with Maria desperately worried about the hardships and dangers to which her family in Belgium were constantly exposed. Aldous talked entertainingly about his work at the film studios, and yet if the conversation turned towards the war his mood darkened instantly: war was a forbidden topic. This veto shocked Sybille profoundly, as did the reason for Aldous's adamant refusal even to have the subject mentioned in front of him: he was too sensitive, it appeared, it distressed him too much. To Sybille such an attitude was incomprehensible: the terrifying reality of the war in Europe overshadowed everything, and now to look away and attempt to ignore it seemed to her a devastating moral failure. "It was of course a deeply unhappy time for most of us, but it seemed to me that the Huxleys were almost deliberately, if not consciously, putting themselves under the greatest possible strain, submitting themselves to some rigorous process of repression." One evening Sybille managed to manoeuvre Allanah into introducing the forbidden subject. "Aldous, don't you want England to win?" Allanah asked him. " 'Wouldn't it be *better* if England won?' Aldous remained mute for a second, then he said in a colourless voice, 'There won't be any England as we knew it.' "

Within a short time both Sybille and Allanah had settled into their new routine. To earn some money, Sybille occasionally cooked at local dinner parties, but mostly she concentrated on her writing and on spending time with old friends, among them Eva Herrmann, the Feuchtwangers, and on his occasional visits from New York, Klaus Mann. Klaus, who in his diary referred to Sybille and Allanah as "*deux curieuses bonnes femmes*" ("two curious good women"), was currently engaged in producing his new journal, *Decision*, to which Sybille had promised to contribute. At the moment, however, she was concentrating on revising a novel completed shortly before she left Europe.

"What Can We Ever Do?" focuses on a group of young English people in Paris. The time is 1938, shortly after the *Anschluss*, and all are deeply apprehensive about the threat of war, anxiously discussed during long sessions at the Café de Flore. Most passionately involved are Eleanor and her friend Desmond, the latter, clever and outrageously camp, an instantly recognisable portrait of Brian Howard, while Eleanor, plump, blonde, blue-eyed, with a passion for good food and wine, bears a striking similarity to her creator. Eleanor's brother, Basil, is infatuated with Rolande, a world-weary beauty married to John Fontenham, a successful English businessman. Unfortunately for Eleanor it is John with whom she falls unrequitedly in love, her misery eventually driving her to retreat to London, where she takes refuge with another brother, the rascally Jockie, in his set in Albany. Returning to Paris after some months, she rejoins her friends, who are now focused more intently than ever on the political situation—Hitler, Roosevelt, Chamberlain, the Munich Agreement; she meets John again, but by this time is able to part from him amicably. " 'Dear John,' said Eleanor. 'Silly little thing,' said John, smiling. Eleanor felt more light-hearted than she had for months." The novel ends with Eleanor and Desmond walking through the forest at Fontainebleau, the last line of the book Eleanor's statement, "I shall never get John Fontenham and there 'll probably be a war."

The Parisian setting, complete with nightclubs, parties and fashionable *maisons de couture*, is well drawn and a number of scenes are perceptively realised; as in Sybille's previous fiction, however, the main characters are mostly two-dimensional and the narrative heavily weighed down with lengthy quotations from favourite authors, among them Huxley, Isherwood and E. M. Forster. The major flaw, however, lies in the ponderous and interminable speeches, from Eleanor, from Desmond, from Basil—several over ten pages long—on the subject of European history, current politics and the threat of war, all delivered in the style of a school essay.

With the novel finished, Sybille left its promotion to Allanah, who sent copies of the text to two literary agents, both of whom turned it down. One, the Roginia Agency in New York, enclosed a detailed report. The work was not wholly unenjoyable, in the reader's judgement, but "it is so overloaded with literary references . . . nothing much happens . . . history obtrudes itself too much . . . it is the work of somebody who, whatever else she may be, is certainly not a professional writer and certainly not a novelist; though the book has wit it is not particularly interesting as writing." So crushed was Sybille by this dismissive judgement that it was nearly a decade before she regained the confidence to begin another book. "I had reached the age of twenty-nine when typescript number three was turned down," she recalled, "and this, except for a little journalism, brought me to a stop for—I must face it—many years."

By the time the novel was completed both Sybille and Allanah had had enough of California, Allanah missing the kind of bookish society she had known in London and Paris, while Sybille found much of the West Coast distastefully vulgar, appalled by the garish architecture, the screaming billboards and neon signs. As in Sanary, she was made uncomfortable by the numbers of German refugees who for the past couple of years had been pouring into Los Angeles, many behaving as if they owned the place, leading the locals to refer to them as the "bei-unskis," as their every conversation seemed to begin with a self-centred *"bei-uns"* ("with us," i.e. "in our view").

"Sybille is a silly little snob about it," Maria complained. "[She and Allanah] are not happy here . . . They are very very English with super English accents and as they have little money and an expensive dog they won't part with, life in America is not to their liking; they like the East better." Sybille's closeness to Maria remained unchanged—Sybille was *"probablement ma meilleure amie"* ("probably my best friend"), Maria told her sister, Jeanne—but Sybille's feelings for Aldous had altered. Aldous's determination to seal himself off from the appalling events taking place in Europe had upset her profoundly; and she was disturbed, too, by his recent change from rational intellectual to religious mystic, by a fascination with psychic powers and Hindu philosophy, his "yogi-bogey," as his friend Christopher Isherwood described it. Looking back, she defined her friendship with the Huxleys at this period as "a difficult time: of branching interests, emancipation; there was much friction then."

Eventually in January 1941 Sybille and Allanah, with Poodly, left Los Angeles for New York, again by car, driven across the country in a luxurious limousine owned by a wealthy neighbour. When they arrived in New York Sybille stayed at the Great Northern Hotel on West 65th, and Allanah nearby in a room rented by Prince Sergei Youriévitch, the father of an old friend of hers. A French sculptor of Russian birth, Youriévitch had arrived in the States the year before with almost no money at all, camping out in a shabby studio which he shared with his beautiful daughter, Princess Hélène, whom Allanah had known since before the war. The studio was filled with the prince's work, a bust of Mrs. Roosevelt, a statue of Pavlova, some dead frogs hung on a washing line, and, in one corner, a couple of mattresses for Allanah and Hélène. Sybille was responsible for finding more permanent accommodation; she started her search early in the morning, stopping for a quick lunch of coffee and a couple of hot dogs at Nedick's, in the evening joining the others to cook dinner over the prince's single gas ring. "In those New York years the Youriévitches were so hard up that we used to collect the chicken bones off our plates and cooked them up for next day's soup for Papa and Hélène."

It was after dinner that the partying began. The ringleader of their little group was Jean Connolly (née Bakewell), wife of Cyril Connolly, whom Sybille had last encountered some years earlier with the Huxleys in Sanary. Jean, now separated from Cyril, was voluptuously beautiful, hard-drinking, wealthy and sybaritic. Together with her younger sister, Annie, Jean was part of a highly cultured group mainly composed of writers and painters dedicated to leading an existence as hedonistic as possible. "In those American years," Sybille recalled, "Jean led, and induced some of her friends including me to lead, an apparently frivolous life. Parties given and gone to, orange blossoms (the cocktail) in the morning, improvisation of haute cuisine . . . dancing to old records into the small hours . . . Jean was re-enacting the early happy irresponsible years with Cyril, I was trying to live the youth I did not have under the benevolent, restrictive shade of the Huxleys; if Aldous had added ten years to Cyril's life, the Connolly spirit took ten years off mine."

Two of the most notable figures in this exotic milieu were the art critic Clement Greenberg, and the millionaire collector and socialite Peggy Guggenheim. Sybille first met Peggy, or "Guggers," as she referred to her, while staying at the Great Northern Hotel, where Peggy for a time had been installed with her soon-to-be second husband, the German painter Max Ernst. On leaving the hotel the couple had moved into an elegant town house, where Peggy immediately resumed her role as hostess, throwing lavish and flamboyant parties in which Sybille was often included. Many of the guests were painters and writers, and it was here that Sybille found herself in the company of Edmund Wilson, Mary McCarthy, Diana Trilling, the English photographer Olivia Wyndham, as well as friends such as the Bakewell sisters and Clem Greenberg.

It was Greenberg of whom Sybille became particularly fond. A regular contributor to the radically left-wing *Partisan Review*, Clem was also the highly respected art critic of the *Nation*. A friend of the Youriévitches, Clem was often present at the simple suppers cooked by Sybille, accompanying them afterwards to that evening's party. Then in his thirties, Clem, a dedicated womaniser, was tall and bald-headed, his hooked nose and blubbery lips giving him the appearance, according to one observer, of "a Yiddish bulldog." Yet although Sybille and Allanah regarded him as "ghastly physically," they both admired his intellect and found him most sympathetic as a friend. At the time Clem was attempting to extricate himself from a somewhat stormy affair with Jean Bakewell's sister, Annie, who was in the process of divorcing her husband. Annie's erratic behaviour, her constantly blowing hot and cold, Clem found both mystifying and enraging—until suddenly he realised what the problem was: "lesbianism."

Before long Sybille was able to leave the Great Northern, having found a suitable apartment at 56 West 58th, only a block away from Central Park. Here she and Allanah moved in, together with Jean, Annie, and Allanah's dog, Poodly, adored by his mistress, regarded by almost everyone else as excessively tiresome and "monstrously untrained." As Sybille was unable to contribute much towards the rent almost—her only source of income a monthly cheque of $25 from Eva Herrmann—it was she who took on most of the cooking and shopping, a job she enjoyed, especially the morning outings to the Italian fruit and vegetable markets on 2nd Avenue. Now and then she gave English lessons to German and French refugees, and occasionally undertook translation and secretarial work for Clem. For Sybille it was a period of great contentment, remarkably free of stress, surrounded by a group of interesting intellectuals, her relationship with Allanah, if physically less intense, as close and loving as ever.

Later, looking back on her life in New York, Sybille admitted she had felt uneasy, even guilty, that during the war years she had been able to live in safety and comfort while so many were experiencing conditions of extreme privation and danger in Europe—a fact with which she would be confronted with some resentment on her eventual return. After America entered the war in December 1941, Sybille enrolled in a first-aid course under the aegis of the American National Red Cross, and on a more personal level she was able, at one remove, to provide practical support for members of Maria Huxley's relatives in France.

Since leaving Los Angeles, Sybille had kept in close touch with Maria, who was in a state of intense anxiety about her family, particularly her mother and her sister Rose, who had recently escaped into France from Belgium. Desperate to arrange safe passage for them to America, Maria was also attempting to find a secure method of sending food parcels, which from California was an extremely uncertain operation. Sybille promised to organise both of these projects, and it was agreed that Maria would send Sybille money to buy the necessary provisions, and also instruct her how to have the relevant papers processed. "I have got all the information from the [Belgian] consul," Maria told her. "Not difficult to get them out. Can be done fairly quickly. But we need affidavits . . . It must be you to help me . . . I enclose a cheque for fifty dollars . . . I cannot guess how much the food costs and mailing and so on. We ought to send once a week don't you think. Chocolate is what my mother asks for . . . I kiss you very dearly and I cannot tell you what a comfort it is to know I can rely on you exactly as on myself."

Aware of Sybille's impoverished state, Maria had been sending small sums of money to help with her living expenses, but now, she told her, with her own family to support, these payments would have to stop. "*Malheureusement je dois dire que vous ne devez plus compter sur nous que dans la toute extrémité. J'ajoute cela parce que, vu la guerre, notre aide n'aurait plus de fin et que vous devez vous adapter à vivre à la guerre comme à la guerre. C'est toujours mieux que d'être en France ou en Hollande, n'est ce pas?*" ("Unfortunately I have to tell you that you can no longer count on us except in an emergency. I add this because, given the war, we can see no end to the help we must give my family and you must adapt to living in the war as if you yourself were at war. It's much better than being in France or Holland, is it not?").

Despite the slightly admonitory tone of this letter, the two women remained devoted as ever, Maria telling her sister Jeanne that although she and Sybille were so different she always looked on her as her closest friend, "my always dear Sybille." To her "very dear Sybille" herself she wrote, "it is good to say one loves. And dearly. You have always known it and so have I," while Sybille for her part regarded Maria throughout her life as "the most remarkable and adorable woman I ever knew."*

Shortly after Sybille left California, Aldous had published a book on which he had been working for some time, *Grey Eminence*, a biographical study of François Leclerc du Tremblay, otherwise known as Père Joseph, the famous *éminence grise* of Cardinal Richelieu. Sybille suggested to Klaus Mann that she write a review for his newly launched (and disappointingly short-lived) literary journal, *Decision*,† a suggestion received with enthusiasm by Klaus.

Sybille's article is of particular interest not only for its critique of the work but also because here for the first time she communicates in her own voice. There is none of the ponderousness, of the self-conscious bookishness that so weighed down her previous endeavours. Instead, she says exactly what she thinks, deftly summarising the subject as well as offering a perceptive analysis of the author himself, in particular his remote form of intellectualism and his failure to connect with ordinary humanity. Defining cowardice as the refusal to face "the difficult facts of life," she takes the opportunity to examine Aldous's failure to confront the horrors of war, his escape from it into religious mysticism. "Many have ceased to cope," Sybille writes, "and, instead, have sought a consoling substitute . . . [for the] irreparably sad and heartbreaking facts of reality. Once again, life has become too bad to be true. Therefore it is not true. Reality . . . is an illusion. Ultimate reality, so Mr. Huxley reiterates throughout *Grey Eminence*, is only in God . . . The man who

---

* Little survives of Sybille's correspondence with the Huxleys as all their papers were destroyed in a house fire in California in 1961.
† The article appeared in the magazine's final issue, January–February 1942.

wrote that 'to talk about religion except in terms of human psychology is an irrelevance' . . . now writes, unflinchingly, about the That and the Thou. To the world, jealous, and a little sad to have lost him, the change is somewhat disconcerting."

Although Sybille remained fond of Aldous, indeed continued in many respects to admire him unreservedly, she had been painfully disillusioned by his evasiveness. It appalled her to witness the dissolution of the irony, the steel rationality she had so admired in Sanary, now replaced by this flaccid and sentimental form of religious belief. Nonetheless she was relieved to receive Aldous's generous, if slightly "spiritual" letter written in response to her review. "I have just read your article on *Grey Eminence* in *Decision*," he told her, "& am writing to tell you how good I think it is. Painfully good, at times, so far as I am concerned; for you have said many true and searching things in it. I was born wandering between two worlds, one dead, the other powerless to be born, & have made, in a curious way, the worst of both . . ."

Meanwhile at the beginning of summer, in order to escape the stifling heat of the city, Sybille and Allanah moved to the country, initially staying with Jean and Annie in Edgartown on Martha's Vineyard, the following year in a house at Snedens Landing, a pretty hamlet in a wooded area west of the Hudson, about twenty miles from New York. Yet as well as providing a tranquil retreat, these locations were also the scenes of wild partying, particularly at weekends, with dancing and heavy drinking often continuing into the small hours. Here Clem Greenberg was a regular presence, usually accompanied by Mary McCarthy and a group of colleagues from *Partisan Review*.

Others included Jimmy and Tania Stern, a couple whom Sybille had known since before the war. Jimmy, dark-haired and strikingly handsome, was an old friend of Brian Howard, who for a couple of years had been unrequitedly in love with him. During the 1930s the two young men had become familiar figures in Sanary, Jimmy, like Brian, notorious for his promiscuous behaviour among the good-looking boys on the beaches at Bandol and La Napoule. In 1935, however, Jimmy had decided to change tack and to marry Tania, the daughter of Alfred Kurella, a prominent German-Polish psychiatrist from Berlin. Orphaned in childhood, Tania had been brought up by Ernst Freud, a son of Sigmund Freud, and while still in her teens had decided on a career as a therapist, working first in Paris, then New York as a teacher of "bodily consciousness." Before meeting Jimmy, Tania in the early 1930s had had a long affair with Eda Lord, who eventually left her for Joan Black, the Irish beauty with whom Sybille for a time had been infatuated.

The Sterns had left France in 1936 for Portugal, where they lived for a while with Christopher Isherwood and his boyfriend, before moving to the States in 1939. Jimmy had always wanted to write: during the 1930s he had published a couple of short-story collections, and during the war had a job at *Time* magazine. Sybille admired Jimmy's style, slightly in awe of his sharp, critical intelligence. At his suggestion she had sent him a typescript of her third novel, of which he had made a lengthy appraisal, concluding, dispiritingly, that "I was, on the whole, disappointed. Perhaps I expected too much." Her friendship with Jimmy was to endure nonetheless, with Tania, too, the three of them keeping closely in touch throughout the years to come. Sybille continued to rely on Jimmy as literary mentor and critic; and she was grateful as well for his generosity: the Sterns were comfortably off, and throughout most of Sybille's life continued to provide her with considerable financial support.

Returning to the city in September 1942, Sybille and Allanah moved into a spacious new apartment on East 75th, between Madison and Park. "It's frightfully underfurnished," Sybille told Tania Stern. "In fact, my room which is as large as the second best drawing room at Versailles, has nothing but crystal chandeliers, yellow draperies, looking glasses, a vast fireplace . . . However, I decided that space, high ceilings, French windows, streaming sunlight and a balcony on which we sit and dine of a summer evening, more than offset the incongruous furnishings." Here the two women continued their energetic social life, with Sybille again taking on the shopping and cooking, happy to have "a full-sized kitchen, which I garlanded with garlic and peppers and earthenware casseroles and which is my Mediterranean wish-fulfilment." She was also delighted to make several new friends who shared her serious interest in wine, chief among them the American painter and photographer Curtis Moffat. In London, where he lived after the First World War,

Moffat had been an early member of the Wine and Food Society and the Saintsbury Club, and after returning to America soon became known for the contents of his remarkable cellar. After one particularly vinous evening at his house, Sybille sent him a poem in thanks:

> . . . Of Hock and Fine your table be as sure
> As set with Lafite, Brion and Latour.
> Your cellar dry; bins full that may abound
> With rows of Corton in good bottles round,
> Richebourg galore and Pommard by the case,
> Montrachet, not Bâtard. And then to face
> The morning after: Fernet's bitter brine,
> Black preface to another day of wine.

Although at first the daily life of Sybille and Allanah continued much as before, in fact some profound changes were about to take place. Allanah, to her friends' astonishment, suddenly announced she was engaged to be married, her fiancé Robert Statlender, a young Frenchman whom she had met one evening with the Youriévitches. Robert had been wounded while fighting with the Free French in 1940, and had afterwards been transported by sea to America. Small in stature, charming, wealthy and very clever, Robert had impressed Allanah by his love of music and wide knowledge of literature, both English and French. When he proposed, she accepted immediately, a response which puzzled her friends, struck by the emotional awkwardness all too apparent between them. "Poor A. trying to prove to herself she is not Lesbian," Maria Huxley remarked to Sybille, while Tania Stern wrote, "I found myself a bit depressed . . . by the sight of two so hopelessly inefficient people as Allanah & Robert . . . [they] so obviously have no relationship with each other and don't even know it—because they don't know what it is to <u>have</u> any relationship!"

Like everyone else, Sybille was taken aback by the engagement, although she had always recognised that Allanah had a conventional streak, that, at least in theory, she valued the idea of marriage and a family. Sybille found Robert both clever and engaging, and she soon became accustomed to his almost constant presence in the apartment.

When plans for the future were discussed, Sybille willingly agreed to Allanah's proposal that after her marriage the three of them should stay together. Robert "is devoted to you and wants you to live with us always," Allanah told her, and "we could all three live much more comfortably with his money as well as ours."

Meanwhile the two women continued to move in the circle of writers and artists revolving around Peggy Guggenheim and Clem Greenberg. Clem, having amicably ended his affair with Annie, was now passionately in love with her sister, Jean. On one occasion when Clem was out of town, Annie sent him an account of a party given by Sybille and Allanah. As well as Jean and Annie, the guests included Jimmy and Tania Stern; the novelist James Agee; Curtis Moffat's son, Ivan, the British film producer and screenwriter; and Bush Meier-Graefe, whom Sybille had known in Sanary, now married to the Austrian novelist Hermann Broch. The dinner had been cooked by Sybille. "An extremely good dinner (as you can imagine)," Annie reported, "roast pork and mashed potatoes, Brussels sprouts, apple sauce, bread and wine, avocado salad, and ice cream, which we put coffee on . . . Everybody was gay and happy, I would say, and Sybille at her peak of gaiety so it was very nice."

Particularly nice for Annie, who had suddenly fallen in love with Sybille. Surprised by such an unexpected development, Sybille was nonetheless enchanted by this pretty young woman, small and slender, with thick dark hair and enormous brown eyes. Within a very short time the two became lovers, with Annie writing to Sybille almost daily to tell her how much she adored her, playfully addressing her as her "delicious white pig" or "my sweet *sale cochon* [dirty pig]."* "Darling, wasn't it fun last night or rather this morning, because going to bed with you last night wasn't fun so much as pure delight . . . Tonight I shall have to go to bed by myself. No delicious white pig to come into the place I've warmed for her . . . I am so sad I don't know what to do . . . How shall I get along without my sweet *sale cochon, je me demande* . . ." Yet while Annie was blissfully immersed in this new turn

---

* This was a habit adopted by nearly all Sybille's lovers in their correspondence. In their letters to each other Sybille and Allanah were "Rabbit" (or "Bun") and "Bull," while among later members of the epistolary menagerie were Horse, Rat, Turtle, Tortoise, Beast, Goat, Bear.

of events, Sybille remained slightly cautious. There was "a new *affaire de coeur*, I have to admit rather sheepishly," she confessed to her old friend, Toni Muir. "Someone rather young, and sweet and silly. Not at all what you'd expect. It may be most unsuitable, and I am quite frightened sometimes, as I don't know where it will lead . . . I ought to be sensible enough by now to look before I leap, but then I didn't do much of the leaping."

One of Annie's chief concerns was to keep the affair hidden from her mother. Mrs. Bakewell was a forceful personality, on whom her daughters depended for their generous incomes—"her nasty old allowance-power," as Annie resentfully described it. The sisters were living together, Jean anxious to conceal her current affair with Laurence Vail, an ex-husband of Peggy Guggenheim, while Annie knew her mother would be outraged to discover the nature of her new relationship. For this reason she decided to persuade Peggy's latest crush, Kenneth Macpherson, to act as her cover, a curious choice in a way as Kenneth was openly homosexual, his face always heavily made up, his hair dyed a startling blond.

For Peggy such details hardly seemed to matter. Her marriage to Max Ernst had soon disintegrated and she had become deeply infatuated with Macpherson, a tall, handsome Scotsman who had been married to the lesbian writer Annie Winifred Ellerman, always known as Bryher. Bryher, a generous philanthropist from a wealthy shipowning family, had left Macpherson very well off when they parted. He and Peggy were now living together in a large duplex, Kenneth maintaining the upper floor for his private apartment, a sumptuously furnished space, including a dressing room stocked with expensive cosmetics where he entertained his fellow "Athenians," a term he preferred to "fairy," "sissie" or "queer." It was during this period that Sybille first met him, running into him one day with Allanah, who had known him in Paris during the 1930s. He and Sybille took to each other at once, although it was not until after the war that their friendship was to become more firmly established.

As time passed Annie fell ever more deeply in love with Sybille. "I could never have enough of you, in bed and out of bed," she declared in the spring. "I want to be with you all the time. Will we ever be living together, I wonder?" In another letter of this period she included a drawing of herself and Sybille naked in bed, under which she wrote longingly, "If only you could be here tonight, then morning would show two contented sleepy pigs, only hungry for breakfast, nothing more. For I'm sure we would have made such a lot of love." Yet there was little possibility of moving in together; and just as Annie knew to be wary of her mother, so did she have to tread carefully with Allanah, whom, unsurprisingly, she disliked. "I feel so worried and constrained when Allanah is around," she admitted. "I never look at her any more than necessary." The feeling was mutual. Annie was "too boring for words," Allanah told Sybille. "Kenneth in the middle of lunch said that it was unbelievable that such a remarkably intelligent girl like you could like what he considered the stupidest girl he had ever met . . . I must say it does bring you down in my estimation, you liking a silly creature like Annie."

Eventually during the summer of 1943 the two women were at last able to spend some time alone. Annie and her sister Jean had rented a house for a couple of months in Gaylordsville, Connecticut, while Allanah, accompanied by Robert, had decided to return to Martha's Vineyard. At Gaylordsville Jean with Laurence Vail appeared only occasionally, so for most of the time Sybille and Annie had the place to themselves. This, as Sybille admitted, was "delightful . . . We were very cut off, with of course no car . . . A country store, poor at the best of peace times, making deliveries twice a week. We swam: and later when it got too cold for the lake, played croquet . . . And walks, also a new discovery. I can walk twenty miles in a day now . . . we used to go off for the day, with lunch in a bundle, through the woods, make a fire and cook sausages on a stick."

Allanah on the Vineyard, separated from Sybille, had plenty of time to ponder her friend's situation, which increasingly became a cause for concern. Allanah firmly believed in Sybille's talent as a writer, and she found it frustrating that she was idling away the summer in the country with Annie, and when in town doing little but attending parties and giving extravagant dinners for friends. Why could she not try to focus and begin work on a new novel? "Darling," Allanah wrote to her, "you are so unusually talented that it makes [me] ill to think that you do not write another book . . . Remember you are a writer not other people's cook." Fundamentally Sybille knew she was right, but when forced to confront the problem her guilt made her irritable with Allanah. "If only you were not so horrible to me all day I would love to be with you always," Allanah told her, "but you treat me rather like a poor relation . . . whose presence gets on one's nerves and who every time they open their mouths to speak one shuts up with a sharp answer because one does not really want to hear anything they have to say."

Despite these complaints, however, Allanah continued to do her best for her friend. When Sybille finally completed a short story it was Allanah who sent it to *Chimera*, a small literary magazine, whose editor, Barbara Howes, agreed to publish it in the issue of September 1944. "Compassionata at Hyde Park Corner" follows two friends, a middle-aged woman and her younger male companion, as they drive in heavy traffic along Piccadilly, all the while learnedly discussing the aesthetics of certain styles of architecture. At Hyde Park Corner Osbert, the driver, forced to come to a halt, is intrigued by the sight of an old woman in a bath chair on the road beside them and starts to imagine her history. Then as the car in front moves forward, he makes a sharp turn and accidentally runs her over. When referring to the story some years later, Sybille accurately described it as "quite bad."

Allanah meanwhile had problems of her own. Robert was putting pressure on her to marry him, a prospect which was suddenly causing her to panic. "I do not know what to do," she told Sybille. "I cannot bear the thought of you and I not living together, I love you more than anyone in the world, and admire your mind more than anyone I know . . . Please help me I am in such a dilemma." Her main fear was that if she turned down Robert to live with Sybille, then eventually Sybille would leave her for another woman, "and I shall be left too old to marry . . . [and] would go dotty with depression . . . I want you to answer this quite selfishly . . . [do not] ever let money considerations come into the question, because they do not exist, you are an economy for me, I could not live at all without your marvellous management." Until she had come to a decision, Allanah begged Sybille not to discuss the situation with Annie or Jean. "Annie repeats everything and Jean writes everything to Cyril [Connolly] . . . and he will read the letters out to a bunch of sissies [homosexuals] at the Café Royal, who will all titter about it."

A few months later, Allanah made up her mind and she and Robert were married in New York early in 1944. Robert moved into the apartment, the three of them amiably co-existing, apart from some grumbling from Robert over what he regarded as Sybille's insensitive invasion of his private space.

By this time encouraging news had started to arrive from across the Atlantic. In September 1943, Italy had finally surrendered to the Allies and shortly afterwards declared war on Germany, a reversal of immense significance, awakening in Sybille a passionate desire to return to Europe. "The news has been so exciting these weeks that one dares hardly breathe," she wrote to Toni Muir. "I long to get back, but what one will find, and how one will fit, is difficult to imagine. I have been here for three and a half years. Although it has been undeservedly easy, and comfortable, it has also been barren. Just waiting. I like being in America, but do not feel in the least at home or belonging, or ever could." She yearned to live again in France, "in a warm place, a Mediterranean place," although not in Sanary, which was too fraught with memories of the past. After the turn of the year, as the strength of the Allied position increased, culminating in the Normandy landings on 6 June, Sybille's longing grew ever more intense. All around her, friends were making plans and booking their passage home, but in fact it would be more than three years before she would be able to return.

One evening in June 1944, Allanah met a friend of hers, Esther Murphy, for cocktails in the bar of the Gladstone Hotel. During their conversation Esther remarked that she had enjoyed Sybille's article on Aldous Huxley in *Decision*, a compliment that Allanah lost no time in reporting back. Not long afterwards Sybille was introduced to Esther at a dinner party of Curtis Moffat's. She found herself spellbound by the older woman, thrilled to be in the company of someone so scholarly and well read. A few evenings later Esther came for a drink at the apartment before taking Sybille and Allanah out for dinner. When Allanah left to go home, the other two went on to the fashionable Stork Club, where Esther, although dressed in slacks and a shabby overcoat, was immediately shown to the best table by an obsequious maître d'. "I <u>must</u> warn you that Mrs. Bedford does <u>not</u> like ice in her highballs," she magisterially instructed him. Here the two women sat and talked until the club closed for the night, by which time both knew they had fallen in love.

Esther was from a wealthy family, her father, Patrick Murphy, the owner of the Mark Cross luxury leather goods company. Her brother Gerald was a close friend of F. Scott Fitzgerald, who in *Tender Is the Night* had modelled the characters Dick and Nicole Diver on Gerald and his wife. From childhood Esther had spent lengthy periods not only in New York but in Paris and London, where her father spent months at a time supervising his shops and factories. Born in October 1897, Esther had early on shown signs of a formidable intelligence; possessed of a restless intellectual energy, she was widely read in both English and French, with a passion not only for literature but also for politics and history, in particular the political history of the United States and of France in the seventeenth century. "The past is so satisfactory to me," she wrote once to Gerald. "Ah! Why could I not have lived at Versailles under Louis XIV!"

Esther had always wanted to write, over the years securing contracts for several biographies, none of which were ever completed. In her twenties and thirties, travelling ceaselessly between Paris and New York, Esther had become part of a mainly literary society, in New York a close friend not only of the Scott Fitzgeralds, but also of Edmund Wilson, Mary McCarthy, Muriel Draper and Dorothy Parker; and in Paris she was a frequent visitor at Gertrude Stein's, and part of the lesbian circle surrounding the American *salonnière* Natalie Barney, with whom for a while Esther had had an affair. Since her early twenties Esther had known her sexual preference was for women, although this had not prevented her from marrying twice, first, in 1929, to the British socialist politician John Strachey, secondly, in 1935, to Chester Arthur, grandson of the twenty-first president of the United States.* Although she remained on good terms with both her husbands, it had always been clear that Esther was not designed for marriage, a fact amicably acknowledged by Strachey, who had married her for her money, and by

---

* According to the writer and critic Edmund Wilson, "For Esther, to have married the grandson of Arthur means almost what it would have meant for Proust to have made an alliance with the Guermantes." *The Fifties*, Edmund Wilson (Farrar, Straus & Giroux, 1986), p. 252.

Chester, who was himself homosexual. During her brief first marriage Esther had lived in London, then moved to California after marrying Chester; but although it was nearly thirty years before she obtained her second divorce, she and Chester soon separated, he remaining on the West Coast, Esther returning with relief to New York.

Six feet tall, ungainly and very masculine in appearance, Esther had a large plain face, one slightly squinting eye, thick short brown hair and a somewhat mannish figure. Indifferent to her appearance—usually dressed either in trousers or an old tweed suit, with shirt, cravat and sensible shoes—Esther since the days of Prohibition had become a dedicated drinker, now spending much of her time at the Gladstone bar, glass in one hand, cigarette in the other, talking, talking, talking—about Louis XIV and Madame de Maintenon, about the Hanseatic League, the Catholic Church, about the war and President Roosevelt, for whose election she had energetically campaigned. As her first husband said of her, Esther was "proud, loyal, warm-hearted, generous and extravagant . . . [but] she never drew breath." Much more damagingly, however, she almost never stopped drinking.

Sybille, nearly fifteen years her junior, was immediately impressed by Esther's remarkable intellect, fascinated to hear that she was planning to write, indeed was currently under contract for a book about Madame de Pompadour. She felt an intense emotional connection with this remarkable woman, excited and moved, too, by the depth of Esther's feelings for her. "You crossed my path like a wandering apparition," Esther told Sybille not long after they met. "I have never in my life felt about anyone the way I feel about you. I ask you to believe this." When Sybille left town for a few days, Esther wrote passionately, "I love you and miss you much, much more than I can express or that I could have imagined missing anyone ever again. So I shall see you Monday night. Otherwise I shall send bailiffs after you so be careful."

Before long Sybille had moved into the Gladstone with Esther, an arrangement somewhat grudgingly approved by Allanah, who resented the fact that when the three of them were together it was always Esther who took centre stage. "Everything I say seems to irritate you," Allanah complained to Sybille. "I don't think I ever opened my mouth at dinner without your waving your hand at me, and saying schussh schussh.

Why should Esther be the only person allowed to speak. It is a form of selfishness and egomania to speak as much as she does. Of course it is because she drinks too much . . . People who drink as much as she does have little sense of the reality of what [is] happening at the moment." In time Sybille, too, would come to dread Esther's drinking, but at the start of what would develop into one of the most important relationships of her life she was too happy to care.

While Allanah had misgivings about her friend's new affair, it caused intense pain to another of Sybille's ex-lovers, Annie Bakewell. "I only love you more and more instead of less and less," Annie wrote after discovering what had happened. "I think of my Pig and long for my Pig all the time. And I have lost her, my darling. How suddenly and sharply it all happened. I now feel I will never get over you and when I see you I shall feel like dying . . . I will unwillingly address this letter to you at the hated Gladstone, care of the person who took you away from me." Indeed it was many months before Annie began to emerge from depression, wretchedly unhappy at Sybille's defection; in time, however, she began to recover her balance, first reigniting her affair with Clem Greenberg, before eventually marrying again, this time to yet another ex-lover of Peggy Guggenheim's, the very wealthy and famously foul-mouthed William ("Bill") Davis.

Meanwhile in New York euphoria over the end of the war was everywhere, with peace declared in Europe on 8 May and on 14 August in America. Sybille and Esther spent the summer on Martha's Vineyard, a time of real happiness for Sybille, who was deeply moved and impressed by what she described as her lover's "goodness of heart, her lovingness." The plan had been for the two of them to spend their time working, Sybille on a projected cookery book, Esther on her life of Madame de Pompadour, but in fact they did very little except enjoy themselves, Sybille swimming and cooking, while Esther, wholly undomesticated, spent her time smoking, drinking and endlessly talking about her yet-to-be-written biography.

The following winter the two women returned to the Gladstone, by which time it had begun to be clear how much Esther relied on Sybille. "Supernaturally erudite," Esther commanded respect, despite her shabby, tousled appearance, and yet there were areas of considerable insecurity. "She talks constantly," one acquaintance observed, "not as an exhibitionist but as a tireless defender of her own privacy . . . barriers of statistics must be piled up like sandbags to protect the small shy bird within." When Esther was asked to take part in a radio series, hosted by the journalist Dorothy Thompson, she readily agreed, but then suffered appallingly from nerves before each broadcast, turning to Sybille for support. For Sybille, the situation began to appear familiar: Esther's scholarly conversation, her alcoholism, her failure to write, inevitably brought back memories of Lisa, with her brilliant talk, her endless plans for books never written, and her destructive addiction to morphine.

As the weeks passed Sybille's longing to return to Europe grew ever more intense. Esther had agreed to accompany her, but, with vast numbers waiting to cross the Atlantic, tickets were almost impossible to obtain. Allanah and Robert had been among the more fortunate, in May 1946 sailing for England on the *Queen Mary*, still painted a wartime grey and, as it turned out, very overcrowded and uncomfortable. Allanah was miserable at leaving Sybille, begging her to follow as soon as possible. "The only thing that matters now is that our separation be a short one . . . I love you my darling White Angora, and shall miss you every day until we meet again." Arriving at Southampton, Allanah immediately reported back to describe her joy at returning home, of hearing gentle English voices—"everyone shrieks in America"—of seeing once more the luscious green countryside, the fields covered in wildflowers. Within a month she had left for France, reviving in Sybille a feeling of acute homesickness—"Oh Bull how you made me long to rush to Paris . . . your letter excited and unsettled me . . . I couldn't hear enough of the streets, and your feelings."

As well as from Allanah, there were letters from friends in France with whom during the war communication had been blocked. After the Liberation, Joan Black, once so adored by Sybille, wrote to her from the village in Normandy where she and Eda Lord were living. "It is over five years since we had the smallest word from you," Joan complained. "We survived, which sometimes seems a miracle . . . we are absolutely starved for outside news and people. So I hope you will answer this by a very long and complete letter." Inevitably there was a certain resentment felt towards those who had lived out the war in safety and comfort abroad. In a lengthy postscript to one of Joan's letters, Eda described the hardships they had been forced to undergo, particularly the persistent hunger resulting from the scarcity of food. "Poor Joan started reading detective novels, English ones, for the bacon and eggs, whiskey and sodas. Literary bacon and eggs are not very sustaining . . . Normal life is coming back to us—but so very slowly." Allanah, too, was faced with a barrage of reproaches, including from her one-time lover, Poppy Kirk, who said she never wanted to see her again, and from Joan, who felt deeply hurt that neither Allanah nor Sybille had once made contact with her. Looking back Sybille wrote of this period, "What one also did not know was that one would not be able to receive letters from or write to Occupied France, and that when this became possible again, one often *did not write.* The gap, in every sense, had been too great."

It was shortly after arriving in Paris that Allanah discovered what had happened to Sybille's sister, Katzi. The two met in a bar in the rue de la Paix, where over several glasses of champagne Katzi told her story. "She looked very well and smartly dressed as usual, but her hair is grey," Allanah reported. "She has had an appalling time, she was put in prison in 1944 and only got out this May, so it was two years in prison, in the most filthy conditions and for months only bread and water. She said, typically, that it was amusing in the beginning because the prison was full of marquises and countesses who had collaborated, but after a few months they were all let out through influence, but she remained on with only '*les femmes de ménage et des grues*' [charwomen and tarts]. She thinks she was put in because of her husband, but I think it was for going about with officers." Soon afterwards Sybille received a fuller version in a letter from Katzi herself. Interned by the French at the beginning of the war, she had been released after a short period only to be arrested again, this time by the Germans, who on account of her Jewishness made her wear a yellow star and threatened her with transportation to Poland. It was at this point that Katzi was rescued by her ex-husband, Dincklage, then part of the *Kommandantur*, after which she remained in Paris unharmed throughout the Occupation, supporting herself by selling lingerie on the black market.

Katzi's final period in prison, for collaboration, a charge of which she was eventually cleared, had left her in a fragile condition. "Her health has suffered a great deal, especially her teeth, complete under-nourishment," Sybille told Allanah. "I am trying to send her food and cigarettes . . . she seems very lonely too. I am very affected." Despite Katzi's marriage and her dubious wartime record, from now on she came to harbour a loathing for Germany, an "*aversion insurmontable*," as she described it, which made it easier for Sybille to deal with her sister's somewhat unsavoury past, even if she could never quite bring herself to forgive her for it. Katzi "was no collaborator . . . she loved France as much as I did, was alienated by most things German, but had little conscience about what she called 'just politics.' Some of her con-nections, men and milieux she was capable of associating herself with, were to me a source of deep distress, and this unspoken discord under-laid our relationship."

With Allanah gone and the papers full of news from Europe, Sybille felt an almost frantic desire to escape. She missed Allanah painfully. "I suppose I feel closer to you than to anyone else alive," she told her. "I wish we would have some kind of future to look forward to—being neighbours in a house in France or Italy." She longed to return to Paris, but the waiting lists for transatlantic passage were impossibly long and the tickets were expensive. Sybille was wholly reliant on the generos-ity of friends, while Esther's finances were currently in chaos thanks to the irresponsible behaviour of her husband. More and more Sybille was driven to reflect on how little she had achieved during her years of exile. "I am very desperate in many ways," she told Allanah. "I feel that I have wasted the remainder of my youth in America . . . I am not writing, and I do not like my present life . . . I am rather frightened that unless I make some drastic change in my own life it may be too late."

It was at this point that Sybille decided she must leave the States, she must travel, and as Europe for the time being was out of reach then she would go south. "I had a great longing to move, to hear another lan-guage, to eat new food; to be in a country with a long nasty history in the past, and as little present history as possible." She and Esther spent many hours poring over maps and examining the possibilities of Peru, Uruguay, Montevideo, all of which turned out to be far too costly. So they settled on Mexico. "It only costs just over a hundred dollars to get to Mexico," Sybille told Allanah, who had agreed to pay for the journey. "I am longing to see it and in a way quite wild with joy, though nervous and apprehensive . . . Esther is reluctant to leave and depressed . . . it does not make it easier. Still we should be pleased enough, going off with plenty of books, not too much luggage and a picnic basket."

After much planning and anxiety, Sybille and Esther finally left New York on 30 June 1946. Booked onto the St. Louis Express, they boarded the train at Grand Central Station, seen off by Esther's husband, Chester, and by Annie, who provided a modest picnic of wine, cold chicken, pumpernickel and cheese. For the first part of the journey they had an air-conditioned compartment to themselves. Time passed slowly, Esther spending much of the day drinking in the club car, Sybille lying on her bunk reading and playing patience. At St. Louis they changed trains, spending the night with other passengers in the curtained sleeping car as they slowly made their way south towards the Texas border. Here at Laredo all passengers were submitted to the "malevolent rigmarole" of a lengthy customs inspection, before finally boarding another train which arrived a day and a half later in Mexico City. "I am delighted to be here," Sybille wrote at once to Allanah, "delighted NOT TO BE in the USA."

From the very first day of what was to become a nearly eight-month sojourn, Sybille was determined to experience as much as she could of this unknown country. Once settled into their hotel, an old colonial palace with a peeling pink facade, Sybille, impatient to begin exploring, at once set off into the noisy, crowded streets, fascinated and bewildered by the sheer foreignness of what surrounded her. "As one picks one's way over mangoes and avocado pears one is tumbled into the gutter by a water-carrier, avoids a Buick saloon and a basin of live charcoal, skips up again scaring a tethered chicken, shies from an exposed deformity and bumps into a Red Indian gentleman in a tight black suit." Over the next few days, as they gradually became acclimatised, she and Esther visited many of the sights of the capital, churches and palaces, galleries and museums, as well as the murals of Diego Rivera in the Palacio Nacional.

If a matter of indifference to Esther, for Sybille an important priority, after years of the bland, boring fare of America, was to sample

Mexican cuisine. Recalling one of their first meals, luncheon in a small restaurant near their hotel, she described in fascinated detail the long succession of courses placed before them: two kinds of soup, then an omelette, followed by "two spiny fishes covered in tomato sauce . . . Two thin beefsteaks like the soles of children's shoes . . . two platefuls of bird bones, lean drumstick and pointed wing smeared with some brown substance. Two platefuls of mashed black beans . . . Everything tastes good, nearly everything is good." The local wine, by contrast, was deplorable. "I sniff before tasting, so the shock when it comes is not as devastating as it might have been. I yell into the darkness to have the bottle removed . . . Cheap ink dosed with prune juice and industrial alcohol, as harsh on the tongue as a carrot-grater . . . It begins to dawn on me, Mexico is not a wine country."

After a few days the two women left the city, as Sybille was eager to explore the dramatic beauty of the countryside, the prairies and forests, lakes and volcanoes. Their first destination was by Lake Chapala in the state of Jalisco, about 250 miles north-west of the capital. The Villa Montecarlo, part of a small family estate on the edge of the lake, had recently been converted into a hotel, the new arrivals lodged in a comfortable hacienda a little way from the main house. Sybille was overwhelmed by the beauty surrounding her: "a sun-splashed loggia above a garden white and red with the blooms of camellia, jasmine and oleander and the fruits of pomegranate, against a shaped luxuriance of dense, dark, waxed, leaves; and below the garden lay the lake." Entranced by her surroundings, she was equally enchanted by the hotel's owner, Don Guillermo González Hermosillo Brizuela, a gentleman of exquisite courtesy, elegant if somewhat effeminate in manner and appearance. "The place belonged to the governor of Jalisco," Sybille explained to Allanah, "and now after the revolution, his son, that rare thing a Spanish sissy, has turned it into a hotel."

So charmed were they by the villa and its owner that the two women decided to stay on for some time. The climate was temperate, the hacienda, with its view of the lake, clean and very comfortable, the food was delicious, and there were large numbers of servants to do absolutely everything. Sybille and Esther, familiar figures by now, the small boyish blonde with her tall, gaunt companion, lunched and dined almost every day with Don Guillermo and his many friends, Mexican, English, German, American. After dinner, while Esther smoked, drank and lectured the company on seventeenth-century France or the Truman presidency, Sybille and her host sat quietly together playing piquet. Don Guillermo's conversation, his friends and acquaintances, the feasts provided, the expeditions arranged were like nothing else, baroque and bizarre, and, as it turned out, an almost miraculous inspiration for Sybille.

Contented although she was at the Villa Montecarlo, eventually Sybille grew restive, anxious to investigate as much as possible of the rest of the country. There was no question of her going alone, but Esther, the "born anti-traveller," proved difficult to dislodge. Esther "hated to travel—God, she hated to travel," Sybille recalled. "I laugh when I think of her in Mexico . . . this tall Don Quixote figure, with a head like Jefferson, bowing to everybody and saying, 'Viva Mexico,' with an American accent. It's the only Spanish she learned." Eternally good-natured, Esther soon submitted, and the two women set off on their hazardous road trip from one coast to the other, moving erratically across country, to Cuernavaca, Morelia, to Mazatlán, Acapulco and Veracruz, none of it of much interest to Esther. Together they covered hundreds of miles, cooped up on rackety trains that were always late, in taxis driven at hair-raising speed, on crowded buses stuffed to the gills with turkeys and pigs, Esther with her height jammed under a low roof in a seat that was much too small. Yet despite the discomfort Esther remained calm, uninterested in the passing landscape, rarely looking up from her volume of Trollope or Jane Austen. "I am more and more enchanted with Mexico," Sybille told Allanah, "but Esther does not like to move, and stalks past colonial palaces and Aztec pyramids much as Doctor Johnson must have stalked through the Hebrides."

Inevitably over the course of their journey there were many delays and frustrations, even the threat of danger. During a stop for dinner one evening their bus was plundered by bandits. While the passengers watched helplessly from the roadside, "three or four men in fine hats and bandanas tied over their faces" helped themselves to the luggage piled on the bus's roof, including a suitcase containing all Esther's clothes and notes for her biography as well as the recipes for a planned cookery book of Sybille's. An unpleasant experience of a different kind was that of a bullfight in Guadalajara. While living in France Sybille had attended occasional bullfights in Arles and Nîmes, but now for the first time she was appalled by the cruelty. "The actual fight sickened and depressed me beyond belief," she told Allanah. "What horrified me perhaps most was that I had once enjoyed or professed to enjoy the spectacle of an animal being slowly slaughtered . . . I really owe it to you that I have now again a feeling for animals, that was blotted out for years through selfishness, opposition to my animal-mad family and intellectual silliness. I should say that I owe it to you and to Poodly."

Fascinated as she was by the country, Sybille remained largely unimpressed by most of the people she encountered. With the exception of Don Guillermo and his extended family, she despised the Mexicans. The indigenous population she found "dirty and illiterate . . . A people so naturally unintellectual is unfathomable to a person like myself. As to the middle class . . . they seem dishonest, mindless, dumbly and lecherously Latin . . . The men with their small moustaches and enormous conceits are soft and sneery . . . The womenfolk are just womenfolk. Such members of the upper class as I have met seem desiccated." There was little to be said, either, for the expatriate society. "Old Virginian ladies who call the natives niggers . . . the dreadful middlebrow arty Anglo-American colony of Ajijic and San Antonio . . . Then there are some fantastic *wandervogel* Germans who smell of Nazi three miles off, who walk about with guitars and talk about good German blood."

Long an admirer of D. H. Lawrence—it was while reading his *Mornings in Mexico* that she first became interested in the country—Sybille was intrigued to meet Lawrence's old friend, Witter Bynner, but he, too, turned out to be a disappointment, drunk and talking unstoppably to a small group of admirers with the "spinsterish primadonnaism of a trout among the minnow intellectuals." Even less to her taste was the American writer Neill James, author of a series of travel books in which Neill herself starred as "the Petticoat Vagabond" ("if that doesn't make your flesh creep," as Sybille caustically remarked). She and Esther were taken to meet Neill at her house near Lake Chapala, where a furious row broke out on the subject of Huxley's mysticism, the visit ending abruptly when Neill in a rage told her visitors they were "rude as Yankee peddlers," hurling a large lacquered plate after them as they hastily made for the door.

Eventually, towards the end of the year, Sybille began to long for departure. She had been away for nearly six months, and while recognising how much she had benefited from her Mexican experience she was now looking forward to a more settled way of life. "Mexico has made all the difference to me," she told Allanah. "I feel much younger and infinitely more contented having no longer the sense of having wasted all these years in America. The reanimation, of travelling, of seeing one's surroundings in a fresh way, have sloughed off years of stagnation." It had been good for Esther, too. "You would not recognise her, sitting almost silent before her heaped plate and eating it, vegetables and all, like an ordinary human being. I should never have thought that Esther could live without alcohol, but she does here . . . Of course it won't last." Sybille's plan was to leave for Europe as soon as possible; she wanted to write about her Mexican experience, a short book to be completed in a few months, for which she was sure Allanah would find a publisher. Allanah's response, however, was dispiriting: in Europe at the moment there was no point in thinking of books and publishing: "everyone is too concerned over daily living, getting enough coffee or wine, fearing communism or war, to think about anything else."

Meanwhile all plans for departure were delayed, first by Sybille falling ill with a painful sinus infection, confined to bed at the Villa Montecarlo for several weeks, then by a crisis over money. Esther, who for years had lived off her share in the family business, now discovered that the Mark Cross Company was in trouble and her income consequently diminished. To make matters worse, her husband, Chester, who had run through his own considerable fortune, was demanding money from his wife. Alarmed by his threats and reluctant to start proceedings for an inevitably contentious divorce, Esther feared she would have to remain in the States, a prospect which appalled Sybille, divided between her love for Esther, which would require her to stay, and what she described as an "almost frantic need to return to Europe." For a while the two women were stranded, but then Esther, realising she must act, wrote "a few firm letters" and the immediate problems were solved.

With Sybille fully recovered, the two women returned to Mexico City to prepare for the journey home. Allanah, critical of what she regarded as her friend's dowdy attire, had sent her money to be spent on new clothes. "I got a good black suit," Sybille gratefully reported, "a grey and blue large check worsted suit, and a gay green herringbone jacket with an olive grey flannel skirt and trousers . . . I also had some warm trousers made, dark blue corduroys . . . and a canary yellow pair with a waistcoat; and a scarlet corduroy coat; and some cheap but rather gay Mexican cotton shirts . . . I feel so ashamed fitting myself out on Bull's money."

On 13 March 1947, Sybille and Esther left Mexico City by air for New York. Sybille felt overcome by gloom when she found herself again in what she now saw as "the bogus city . . . the galvanised grave." However, she was pleased to see her old friends, including Annie, who on Sybille's birthday, 16 March, gave a small party for her. Yet while grateful for Annie's kindness, Sybille was too anxious to enjoy the occasion. With the war over, it seemed everyone was on the move, and passage by sea still almost impossible to obtain. Eventually, however, a couple of places were secured on a recently converted troop ship, six to twelve people sharing a cabin, "the last word in discomfort." At Allanah's request, Sybille amassed quantities of supplies. "I can bring a thousand cigarettes . . . a great deal of tea, 50 or 60 pounds of the best green coffee . . . Also rice, black pepper, curry powder, candles, pease pudding and 20 pounds of sugar . . . a few jars of marmalade and jam . . ."

Finally on 9 June, Sybille and Esther sailed from New York, reaching Cherbourg ten days later, where they found Allanah on the quayside to meet them. Happy and intensely relieved to be once more in France, Sybille looked forward to a period of settled contentment. In this she could hardly have been more wrong. "After a universal cataclysm, return into a previous world is apt to be convulsive," she wrote later. "And in my case it was . . . One might describe what followed . . . as a kind of disordered game of chess . . . I did not come out of it well."

SEVEN

THE LOVELINESS OF ROME

After an absence of seven years, Sybille was overjoyed to find herself once again in Europe. Now thirty-six, she was anxious to settle, to live in France, where she could concentrate on writing the book whose inspiration had come to her during her first weeks in Mexico. She had before her, or so she believed, a rewarding period of peace and stability, in the company of her two most loved companions, Esther and Allanah. It was not long, however, before Sybille's excitement, her happiness at her future prospects, were to be tempered by a series of complex situations unfolding around her.

During her long absence, all Sybille's hopes had been focused on a return to the south, to the Mediterranean, on living again in Provence. Allanah, however, had no desire to move: she loved Normandy, loved her little house at Gadencourt, the green fields and wooded hills of the Eure valley. "I cannot tell you what joy it is being in France again in my own village," she had written. "How agreeable it is to live amongst the French . . . despite their amorality, one is charmed by their spontaneous gaiety, their livingness [sic] and their right feeling for wine and food." Another significant advantage was that Gadencourt was within easy reach of Paris, where Allanah's husband, Robert, lived during the week, visiting his wife at weekends, when he enjoyed working in the garden, mowing the lawn, sawing wood for the fires.

While Sybille looked forward to reunion with friends she had not seen since the beginning of the war, their reception was in some instances distinctly chilly. For those who had remained to survive the Occupation it was difficult not to resent the escapees. As Allanah's one-time lover, Poppy Kirk, had expressed it, "If one has been through the bombing, one has little in common with people who went off to America; we have changed, life can never be the same again." Joan Black and Eda Lord, too, were clearly resentful of the new arrivals. Their experience had been particularly harrowing: at the time of the German invasion they had fled to Aix-en-Provence, a terrifying journey on roads jammed with thousands of fellow refugees, in cars, on bicycles, on foot, frequently strafed by German aircraft. Shortly after arriving in Aix they were arrested and transported to Paris to be interned as enemy aliens, later taken back to the south and confined to house arrest under Gestapo surveillance. When after the Liberation they eventually returned to Normandy, it was clear both had been marked by the trials they had undergone.

On Allanah's arrival from the States, she had been treated with reserve by Joan and Eda, but the three of them had eventually resumed an amicable relationship. Allanah had sent detailed reports to Sybille in Mexico of her visits to Vernon that were sharply critical of Joan, with whom, inexplicably in Allanah's view, Sybille had once been so infatuated. "Nice as she is, it amazes me how you could have thought her so wonderful," she wrote. "She is completely inartistic, and has no fantasy or imagination, and were she not an L[esbian], you would think her a nice middle-class woman with the most conventional ideas." Describing the balance of power between the couple, she saw Joan as stupid and overbearing, while Eda, who did all the shopping and cooking, was treated as her slave. Joan took centre stage, venting her loathing for the Germans, Russians, Americans, French, while Eda remained quietly in the background. "Eda as usual does not express an opinion, only says yes, or no in a gentle voice." Allanah's hostility towards Joan was further intensified when she found herself falling "madly in love" with Eda.

By the time she reached France, Sybille had been well informed by Allanah of her new-found passion. Joan predictably had been furious when she discovered what was going on, while Robert on the contrary had quickly come to accept his wife's extramarital affair: he "has been wonderful about it. He says he would never tolerate a man, but he likes

Eda, only fears she is a morbid type. But of course he does not think I will ever leave him, that he says he could not bear."

It had been arranged that Sybille should remain with Allanah at Gadencourt, while Esther would stay with her American sister-in-law, Noël Murphy, who lived a short distance away at Orgeval. ("I could have Esther here of course," Allanah had said, "but would she not object to the outside lavatory?") Noël Murphy, a tall, blonde beauty, was the widow of Esther's elder brother, Fred, with whom Noël had lived in France until his early death in 1924. Subsequently she had bought a small farm at Orgeval, soon becoming part of the cultured expatriate society that was to flourish in the region both before and after the war. For Sybille such company was highly rewarding, and she came to relish lunching and dining with visitors such as the novelist Malcolm Lowry, Natalie Barney, as well as with Nancy Cunard, who owned a house in the neighbourhood, and with the distinguished *New Yorker* columnist Janet Flanner. Janet, who was to become a good friend of Sybille's, was based in Paris but came to Orgeval most weekends to stay with Noël, the two of them having been lovers in the early 1930s.

From time to time Sybille left Gadencourt to spend a few days in Paris, staying at the Saints-Pères, a small hotel on the Left Bank. It was here one day that she came upon her old friend from Sanary, Pierre Mimerel, "sitting in one of the stiff armchairs in the narrow ante-room . . . wearing riding breeches and a hacking jacket." Delighted to see her, Pierre immediately asked her to stay at his new property in Touraine, an invitation that was eagerly accepted.

Pierre's situation had radically changed since the pre-war days. He had parted from his wife, Sybille's once-adored Jacqueline, and was now married to Simone, a woman he described as the love of his life. Leaving Sanary soon after the Occupation, he had spent the war years farming in the Savoie, before eventually purchasing Les Couldraies, the hunting lodge of the magnificent Château de Chenonceaux in the Loire valley. The property included a farm and a vineyard, and Sybille during the long, hot summer spent happy hours riding with Pierre over the estate, as well as picking grapes and bottling wine. After her father, Pierre of all her friends was the most knowledgeable about wine, and he and she spent many hours tasting and judging the contents of his cellar, talking with intense absorption about labels and vintages, fermentation, tannins, bouquet and various *crus*. Sybille had taken immediately to Simone, so much calmer and less egotistic than her predecessor, and she relished the country-life routine of "vast meals on time, wood fires, cards and Monsieur le Curé in the evening."

To please Sybille, Pierre invited a number of her friends to join them, among them Janet Flanner and Noël Murphy, and also Esther. Uninterested in the farm and vineyard, although ready to consume quantities of wine, Esther came into her own over dinner in the evenings. "She spellbound her hosts," Sybille recalled, "with her broad evocations of French and American history delivered in an oratorical voice . . . while she vaguely stirred about the *noisette de porc aux pruneaux* congealing on her plate." While Sybille described Esther's French as grammatically "near-flawless," another of Esther's acquaintance, the writer and critic Edmund Wilson, was rather less complimentary. "How is it that she has lived in France so long and still speaks French so badly?" he wondered. "It seems to me that she actually gets worse: she aspirates the *h*'s in *hélas* . . . and talks about *Madame Bovairy*. She is fluent in her rugged and rocky way . . . [but] pays little attention to genders." To Sybille's relief Pierre obviously knew nothing about the nature of her relationship with Esther. "The Mimerels were entirely out of it . . . there was a chaste austerity about Pierre . . . [who] had already begun his habit of addressing me as '*ma fille*.' "

Returning to Normandy, Sybille was prepared for the tensions surrounding Allanah's affair with Eda; what she had not expected was Esther's sudden infatuation with Joan. Almost from the start Allanah had been critical of Sybille's devotion to Esther—"I wish you would fall in love with someone else, who does not drink, and rave about politics from nine in the morning till 12 at night"—but had never questioned the solidity of their relationship. Now, faced with Esther's infidelity, Sybille felt shocked, angry and hurt. With Esther, her "dear monster," she had felt settled and secure, committed to an enduring alliance that perfectly balanced the physical side of love with the emotional; it had never occurred to her that their powerful bond would not, as she expressed it, "weather the years." Esther's "moral stature has been diminished," she wrote to Toni Muir. "That for me is the beginning of the end of any love. The Trusted and Trusting alliance . . . the feeling of security . . . has of course gone down the drain."

Deeply unhappy, Sybille felt she must escape, and within a very short time had made up her mind to leave France for Rome, remembered fondly from her visits there years before with her mother and Nori. From Rome, she wrote to Allanah, "I am rather sad and quite lonely. And it is rather humiliating to say the least to think of ALL the misery and destruction brought about [by] that ass [at] Vernon. A wilful, minor maniac of a rather uninteresting kind." Within a few weeks, however, a very contrite Esther arrived to join her, full of abject apologies for her behaviour. "I know I have forfeited all claim to your love," she told Sybille. "I have played fast and loose with our relationship and I would not blame you at all if you felt that my conduct has killed something in it that cannot be revived"; Sybille must understand, however, "how unspeakably I love you . . . and how completely I realise that you are utterly indispensable to my life."

Although undoubtedly true that Esther's love for Sybille was genuine and unchanging, her relationship with Joan was to continue for some time, with Esther regularly commuting between Italy and France. At first Sybille continued to feel betrayed, as well as miserable at being left for long periods on her own, but after a while she came to tolerate and eventually to forgive. Nonetheless from this time onward her feelings for Esther began to change, gradually evolving from love affair into a devoted, if not uncritical, friendship. And in due course Esther's infidelity was to give Sybille the freedom to indulge in affairs of her own.

Meanwhile there was Rome, the city which Sybille now claimed she loved more than anywhere else in the world. "Some people can write love letters and some can't," she once said. "I can't, but if I could I'd write them about Rome." Life in Rome in the early post-war years was glorious; with little traffic and the crowds of tourists yet to return, the city was a walker's paradise, with "the sun, the sweet air, the new near quiet." While Esther was with her the two women stayed at the d'Inghilterra, a hotel in the Via Bocca di Leone, a narrow street near the Piazza di Spagna. The d'Inghilterra was far from luxurious—there was no food and only a skeleton staff—but immediately inside the entrance there was a small bar with a cosy, club-like atmosphere; much patronised by English and Americans, it had become a well-known meeting place, a fact which had immediately appealed to Esther.

When after a few weeks Esther returned to France, Sybille, needing to economise, rented a room in a private house in the Via Angelo Brofferio, a cheap if not particularly comfortable location. The family were pleasant, but it was a bleak winter, "the cold is breaking me . . . and THERE IS NO SIGN OF A BATH EVER." Here she had intended to start on her Mexican book, but apart from taking classes in Italian she did no work at all, spending her time exploring the city and lunching and dining with friends. "I am not writing," she told Toni Muir, "but momentarily the sense of guilt and failure is held at bay by some of these inexplicable periods of light-heartedness that descend upon one as fortuitously, though more rarely, as the periods of staleness and depression."

A few months after her arrival, in the spring of 1949, Sybille left Rome to visit her sister, Katzi, now living in Austria. Following the end of the war Katzi had remained for a while in Paris, but her situation there had been precarious, associated as she was with her ex-husband, Dincklage, and tainted by rumours of collaboration. Finally she had been persuaded to leave France for Austria, where she was taken in by a cousin, Carl-August von Schoenebeck, a nephew of Maximilian, who had a small estate at Hinterstoder, in the Austrian Alps east of Salzburg. Carl-August had had a distinguished war as a Luftwaffe general, but was later arrested by the Americans and confined for two years as a prisoner of war; he understood very well the importance for Katzi of leaving France but also of changing her name and nationality. Much as the Huxleys had done in finding Walter Bedford for Sybille, so Carl-August paid a young Dane—Axel Nielsen, an impoverished homosexual—to marry Katzi.

Katzi, who had startled the locals by wandering around the village in a pair of bright red trousers, cigarette in hand, her now grey hair tinted blue, had looked forward to her wedding. Expecting at least a new dress and a bouquet of flowers, she had been disappointed that she was simply taken one morning to the registry office in Hinterstoder, where she met her future husband for the first and only time. Once the process was completed, Nielsen instantly disappeared, refusing even to come back to the house for a glass of champagne.

Subsequently Katzi was to remain in Austria for several years, supported by Carl-August. Sybille's visit was of importance to both, but while Katzi was cheerful, open and affectionate, Sybille, although as fond of her sister as ever, was deeply uneasy. Austria was not Germany, but she nonetheless felt a profound hostility to the people surrounding her and to their political views, which often "made my hair stand on end with antagonism." But for Katzi there were no such problems: she "remained the loving, generous sister often seeking my advice, more often mocking my preoccupations, '*Oh, la grande intellectuelle!*' On my side there was a good deal of cowardice, sad to admit. Her uncertain standing with the French authorities never ceased to resurrect my own fears."

For Sybille it was a relief to return to Rome. "I can't tell you HOW lovely Rome is now," she told Allanah. "The streets are full of tables with people drinking wine, and stalls bursting with fruit: cherries, strawberries, plums, tomatoes, early peaches . . . One cannot live in Italy long without feeling proud to be alive, and connected with a kind of human eternity." Thanks to Esther's generosity, Sybille had been able to move back into the d'Inghilterra, occupying a spacious room on the top floor: "French windows giving on to ochre-and-apricot facades of the side street, a huge almost square bed, my own bath, a well-swept fireplace and a marble-topped sideboard on which I kept the paraphernalia for my breakfast—an economy the *albergo* [hotel] never commented on."

By now Sybille had made a number of friends in the city, among them two Americans, Peter Tompkins and Donald Downes, both of whom had worked at high levels in U.S. intelligence in Italy during the war; the writer Constantine FitzGibbon and his wife; Patricia Laffan, a young actress friend of Allanah's; and there was also Janet Flanner, a kind and constant ally of Sybille's, who came regularly to Rome not only to research subjects for her *New Yorker* column but also to see another of her close attachments, Natalia Murray.

Now in her fifties, Janet was grey-haired, strong-featured, rather masculine in appearance ("a gentleman of the press in skirts," as she was once described). Janet had been writing for the *New Yorker* under the byline "Genêt" for twenty-five years, reporting mainly from Paris, but also from other European cities, and, during the war, from the

States. Married in her twenties, she had shortly afterwards fallen in love with Solita Solano, a young journalist, with whom she moved from New York to Paris, where she was to remain for most of her life. It was while in France some years later that Janet began her affair with Esther's sister-in-law, Noël Murphy. On returning to New York in 1940 she had met her third love, Natalia Danesi Murray, Italian, dark-haired and very pretty, who was working as a newscaster for NBC. Somehow Janet managed to maintain close relations with all three, with Solita in Paris, Noël in Orgeval, and from the late 1940s with Natalia, who by then had moved back to Rome.

As always, Sybille sent regular reports of her daily life to Allanah, who never hesitated to speak her mind. While congratulating Sybille on "the enormous moral progress you have made during the last seven years," Allanah was disparaging of her social deportment. After Sybille's arrival in Rome, Allanah had provided her with several introductions, among them to the British ambassador, Sir Victor Mallett, and also to Roger Hinks, head of the British Institute. But with both men, Allanah had learned, Sybille's manner had been ridiculously timid. "I cannot understand," she scolded her, "why you behave like a maid being interviewed when you first meet people like that? . . . Behaving with ease and a certain boldness on meeting new people, whoever they are . . . [is] a class thing, and for a person of your breeding and obvious upper class and even aristocratic family . . . [your manner] is impossible . . . It gives people the wrong impression about you; it is only after they have met you several times that they discover your brilliant mind." Sybille knew Allanah was right and thanked her for her "rather nasty letter about my behaving like a housemaid," admitting that her shyness was "not an amiable quality."

It was shortly after her return from Austria that Sybille heard the shocking news of Klaus Mann's suicide at the age of forty-two. Having returned to Europe from America, Klaus had lost his sense of direction, failing to make progress with his new novel, reduced to translating his English works into German simply because he needed the money. "Klaus could no longer find himself in the post-war era," said his brother Golo. "The times were against him." Always vulnerable to depression, Klaus had attempted suicide at least once before, and now while staying in a hotel in Cannes he had finally succeeded. Sybille was profoundly saddened by the news. The image of Klaus killing himself, she told Allanah, "goes on like a great heavy wheel slowly turning inside one's mind and heart." Despite disapproving of his "romantic, German fixation on death," she had always admired Klaus, regarded him as one of her closest friends, with whom she had shared not only nationality, culture and generation, but actual experience, in particular "that fear of arrival, angst and loneliness in strange places . . . I loved him very much."

While Esther continued to visit Sybille in Rome, insisting that her feelings were unchanged, and that she felt mortified by her infidelity, Sybille for her part began to enjoy a new sense of freedom. Planning to start work on her book, she was also determined to enjoy herself to the fullest. "I am free of Esther," she wrote to Toni Muir, "and it has probably saved me as an independent person and a writer . . . My one idea now is to make something of my life or such abilities as I may have . . . I have the feeling that for the moment I am out of the wood of human relationships. I've never felt so free."

In the immediate future such freedom did little for Sybille's literary career; it did, however, enable her to enjoy a particularly carefree summer. While Janet Flanner had been in Rome, Sybille had come to know her lover, Natalia Murray, attractive, intelligent, "a woman of radiant vitality." Born and brought up in Rome, Natalia had married an American, and spent much of her earlier life in New York, which is where, after divorcing her husband, she had first met Janet. As Janet was often away, Natalia now spent much time on her own, very ready to enjoy an affair with Sybille. Natalia was charming, Sybille told Allanah. "Not educated in our sense but with a natural emotional sense of style and beauty. She is also very smart indeed which I think is so much nicer than dowdiness in a travel companion."

The two of them went to Florence for the music festival in May. "I had what is called a good time in Florence," Sybille reported, "a sort of fullness of doing the things I like so much: ballet, opera, pictures and pictures and pictures." While in the city, the most memorable encounter was with a fellow guest at their hotel, Una, Lady Troubridge. Una Troubridge was the "widow" of the lesbian novelist Radclyffe Hall, author of that notorious work *The Well of Loneliness*. One evening Sybille and Natalia joined her for cocktails, or "cocktailinos" as Natalia always referred to them, both intrigued by this stern-faced, masculine figure sitting very upright in her tailored suit and tie. "I never met a more self-righteous woman," Sybille recalled. "There was something very hard about her and it wasn't just the stiff collars and the monocle . . . [she] went to early Mass every morning (in the bitter dawn), was rather good company, intelligent about music and Italian art, preposterous about politics, ungiving about friends, and a source of much amusement."

Returning to Rome Sybille and Natalia continued to see each other although they were careful to keep their relationship secret. "How guilty one feels," Sybille confessed to Toni. "The jerk at the collar. I've been letting go too much lately, you know; it frightens one."

The following month Sybille let herself go again, involved in an even briefer liaison, this time with an actress friend of Allanah's. Patricia Laffan was taking part in a film, *Quo Vadis*, an epic of ancient Rome, with Peter Ustinov as the emperor Nero and Patricia as his wife, Poppaea. "Your friend Patricia Laffan seems charming: warm and open and such zest. I liked her," Sybille reported to Allanah. Shortly after this first encounter Sybille found herself dining with a group that included Patricia, who "took me aside and made a declaration that could not have been more straight from the shoulder and direct. God, the young are crude . . . She's twenty-seven, very pretty, without the slightest mystery." Later the two of them retired to bed, afterwards making a date for the following night, a commitment that Sybille almost immediately regretted. "I tried to dodge my actress, but apparently one had been far more of a success than one thought, and it became absolutely impossible to get out, without great show of ill grace, of that 2 a.m. rendezvous. The awful thing is I rather like her. I went, and fell asleep in five minutes. With the young one can't even laugh about it."

Despite her good intentions and much nagging from Allanah, Sybille was yet to make any progress on her book. The previous year Allanah had completed a work of her own, *All Trivial Fond Records*, a childhood memoir dedicated both to her husband, Robert, and to Sybille; well reviewed in the States, it was shortly to be published in Britain. Pleased by her success, Allanah had renewed her efforts to promote

Sybille's writing career, generously continuing to provide her with an income so that she could devote herself to her work. Recently while in London Allanah had lunched with Diana Gollancz, daughter of the publisher Victor Gollancz, who had expressed enthusiasm for Sybille's Mexican project. "She was very excited about it," Allanah told Sybille, "said, 'That is just what Father wants now. I am nearly certain he will take it.' So for heaven's sake get on with it."

Galvanised by Allanah's prodding and ashamed of her constant procrastination, Sybille once more resolved to start writing. "Very well," she replied. "I will do the book to the best of my ability, and I will do it immediately. But please do not underrate the expense of guts and discipline it will need . . . I have not done any serious work for a long time. I lead the kind of life I am least suited to (loneliness, irregularity, lack of domesticity) . . . I know it is going to be damned difficult . . . [but] the book is a promise . . . If one is going to be a failure as a writer, it will have to be for lack of talent or originality, but it mustn't be because one didn't have the guts to try. So there."

Fortunately Sybille had recently made a new friend, who over a period of years was to provide her with much of the help and encouragement she so badly needed. Martha Gellhorn had made her professional reputation as a war correspondent, reporting on the Civil War in Spain, on the rise of Hitler, on the war both in Europe and the Far East; she had been the only woman accompanying the Normandy landings on D-Day, and had reported on the liberation of the Dachau concentration camp. Martha, very much a man's woman, had had a number of lovers, and in 1940 had married Ernest Hemingway, but the couple had divorced five years later. Now living on her own in Mexico, Martha was on a visit to Italy, where she hoped to adopt a child.

Sybille first met Martha over dinner with friends, immediately struck by this handsome, slender, tough-talking American. "Meeting Martha," Sybille wrote later, "was like being exposed to a fifteen-hundred-watt chandelier: she radiated vitality, certainty, total courage. Add to this the voltage of her talk—galloping, relentlessly slangy, wry, dry, self-deprecatory, often funny. Add to this her <u>looks</u>. The honey-coloured hair, shoulder-length, the intense large blue eyes, the fine-cut features, the bronzed skin, the graceful, stalwart stance." In a letter to Allanah,

Sybille defined Martha's character as "proud, solitary, faintly snobbish . . . She may appear very hard-boiled; I don't think she is. She is
very intelligent; very disciplined; very sad and devastatingly disillusioned. I like her immensely."

At this juncture Martha was on the point of departing for Capri, to
conduct a series of interviews for an American magazine, and needed
someone to drive her car from Rome down to Naples. For this Sybille
eagerly volunteered, excited at the prospect of the drive almost as much
as the prospect of spending time with Martha on the island.

The night before she left, Sybille had stayed up late at a party, leaving Rome at dawn after no sleep at all, reciting poetry to keep herself
awake as hour after hour she drove south. "By full morning I had to fight
drowsiness . . . [but] in the end I got there." In Naples she left the car
in a garage before lunching with friends, among them Constantine and
Theodora FitzGibbon, who were then based on Capri. Afterwards, in
the company of the FitzGibbons, Sybille boarded the island ferry. Once
disembarked, she was thrilled to see among the crowd Martha waiting to
welcome her; the two of them walked up the steep hill to the main piazza,
then on to the *pensione* where Martha had taken a couple of rooms.

Sybille had first visited Capri the year before, when she had spent
several weeks there with Esther. Although enchanted by the island's
beauty she had been repelled by some of its expatriate community.
"The island is full of the old and titled from out of every rat hole in
Europe . . . Italian princesses . . . Russian princesses . . . German princesses who saved nothing but their family trees . . . German barons
who try to be house agents; gaggles of countesses perched in rocky her-
mitages knitting socks . . . Most are pathetic, some are rogues, and all
are bores." Fortunately there had been other, more sympathetic figures
in whose company she had delighted, among them the FitzGibbons,
and also a friend from her time in New York, Kenneth Macpherson.

After the war Kenneth had left the States to return to Europe, eventually settling on Capri, where he lived with a handsome English boyfriend. Kenneth's property, the Villa Tuoro, was an airy, white-painted
house with a beautiful garden, its flower-laden terraces looking out over
the famous rocks, the Faraglioni, rising high up out of the sea. Kenneth
had built the villa not only for himself but to provide a home for his

old friend, the distinguished writer Norman Douglas. For many years Douglas, now in his eighties, had relied on the financial support of others, among them Kenneth and his ex-wife, Bryher. Admired as a writer, particularly for his novel *South Wind*, Douglas had also been notorious as an unregenerate paedophile—"I left England under a cloud no bigger than a boy's hand," he used to quip. In his old age, however, he had come to be regarded with awe, enjoying the homage paid to him as a literary celebrity. It was to write a biography of Douglas that Constantine FitzGibbon had come to Capri, and it was with the FitzGibbons as well as with Kenneth that Sybille and Esther on a number of occasions had found themselves in Douglas's somewhat daunting company.

Now on Sybille's first evening on the island, she and Martha decided to dine at the Savoia, a small trattoria near the main piazza. The moment they entered they saw Douglas, white-haired and rosy-faced, sitting at a table by himself, his customary paraphernalia of pipe, snuff-box and tobacco tin set out before him; he waved to Sybille, beckoning her over to join him. Sybille immediately felt apprehensive: Martha had read none of Douglas's works, and, puritan by nature, disapproved of homosexuals, "sissies" and "lizzies" in her vocabulary, while it was soon clear that Douglas for his part had failed to recognise in Martha the famous and formidable war correspondent. Fortunately, however, the misunderstandings on both sides resulted in a cosy and enjoyable evening—"The talk, as I remember, was chiefly about fish"—with Douglas, "bubbling and bawdy, and kind," playfully addressing Martha as "my poppet," while she saw in the pederastic Norman simply a charming and courteous old gentleman.

After dinner the two women returned to their *pensione*. It was a warm evening and the shuttered windows were high up near the ceiling. To reach them they stood on a pair of stools, and there for some while they remained, elbows on the windowsill, breathing in the scented evening air, Sybille listening fascinated as Martha talked far into the night, about her war experiences, her love for her mother, her miserable marriage to Hemingway. "I felt privileged. *I was captivated*," Sybille recalled. At its start this new friendship seemed made of solid gold, with Martha "the brightest, most honourable and virtuous being one had ever met." In time their relationship would lose its shine, painfully descending, from Sybille's perspective, from one of awed respect to bitter disillusion. In the immediate future, however, and indeed for some time to come, Martha was to prove a loyal friend to Sybille and in professional terms both an exemplar and supportive ally. "I owe her a good deal in one way and another," Sybille wrote later, "and it may well have been that it was her dazzlingly robust verbal style which provided the final kick that set my writing free."

At the end of June Sybille left Capri, returning for a couple of weeks to Rome before departing again, this time for Ischia, accompanied by Esther. For Sybille the purpose of the expedition was to provide the time and seclusion necessary for her to write. Constantly nagged by Allanah and now bracingly encouraged by Martha, she knew she must make a beginning or the whole of her Mexican experience might fade, the compulsion to write about it evaporate, and the work never materialise. While on a previous expedition to Ischia she had been offered the chance of somewhere to stay, with no domestic duties, where she could devote herself to her writing.

This fortuitous opportunity had materialised when she and Martha were on Capri and had decided to visit Ischia for the day. While strolling up from the port, Martha *soignée* and elegant, Sybille in shirt and shorts, with a faded blue baseball cap shading her eyes, they suddenly came to a stop. "By golly!" Martha exclaimed. "Don't look round—there's the *baronessa* . . . the Kraut who was in with Ciano and Franco and all . . . I can't believe it, how dare she show her face? She must be one of the wickedest women in Europe." Describing the incident afterwards, Sybille wrote, "My God, I thought, it can't be! But it was . . . She walked up to us, made straight for me and said, 'Billi.' "

The bad *baronessa* was Maria Ursula ("Mursel") von Stohrer (née Gunther), whom Sybille remembered as a close friend of her mother, a frequent visitor to the schloss at Feldkirch. Although Mursel was nearly twenty years younger than Lisa, the two women had much in common, both sophisticated, highly intelligent and well read. Sybille as a young child had loved and admired Mursel, and thus it had come as a shock when she learned later of Mursel's marriage to Baron Eberhard von Stohrer, a high-ranking diplomat, who during the war had served for a time as German ambassador in Madrid. Appalled by this association with the Nazi regime, Sybille had resolved, should the occasion arise, to avoid any further contact with Mursel.

Now for the first time in nearly twenty years Sybille had come face-to-face with the villainess herself. But in place of loathing and hostility, she found herself fascinated, seduced by the older woman's charm, impressed by her blonde beauty, her elegance, if not wholly at ease with her slightly sardonic manner. Mursel "gave me an affectionate if a tinge ironic smile. 'Billi,' she said, 'what are you doing here?' She took me in with one amused glance. 'You look a bit shabby,' she said. Another mocking smile. 'I suppose that comes from having been on the winning side.' " The Stohrers owned a luxurious hotel and spa on the north coast of the island, and it was here that Mursel suggested Sybille should stay for a while; she would be offered a special rate, and with everything provided would be able to concentrate on her writing.

A few weeks later when Sybille returned to the island with Esther, she found herself in a grand if somewhat eccentric environment. At the Villa Castiglione the two women were shown to a separate guest house, an arrangement which turned out to be less than ideal. Their accommodation, Sybille told Martha, "though charming and comfortable for ONE, consists of two rooms, one above and one below connected by an outer staircase . . . The upper room is the bedroom, and I am sharing it with E . . . In the sitting room, I work and try not to share it with E. Actually, she could not be nicer about it. But you can imagine what it's like: driving somebody out to sit in a bedroom immediately after breakfast, hearing them pace overhead." Sybille did everything she could to persuade Esther to go out on her own, for instance to call on her old acquaintance, W. H. Auden, who was staying with his boyfriend, Chester Kallman, in the town of Forio, but Esther's inertia was too deeply embedded. "Nothing will induce her to take the bus to the Forio sissies by herself. She agreed to walk into Porto d'Ischia the other day because I promised I'd bicycle down after seven and take her back. I found her, hours later, on a milestone halfway, 'My sandal's broken, I can't move.' (It was not broken, only undone.)"

Every evening the two women joined the hotel's other guests for dinner on the terrace. Here they were placed at a separate table, "set out with gleaming linen, silver, china . . . polished candelabras . . .

coroneted napkins, silver dishes, trembling peasant boys decked out in the grey and scarlet livery of the German Embassy at Madrid." Sybille, nervously self-conscious, would begin making conversation, watching with dread as Esther grew increasingly intoxicated, talking about "the most unsuitable topics in a loud, public voice."

Despite her uneasiness over the Stohrers' past, Sybille could not help but enjoy their company. "One cannot think much, oddly enough, of the political angle once one is under their roof." As before in childhood she was bewitched by Mursel herself and fascinated by her stories. "The *baronessa* tells them extremely well," she reported to Martha, "devastating anecdotes about Franco, Goebbels, Eva Braun . . . She seems to have made a lot of valuable connections in Spain, and is hand in glove with the Vatican." As for her husband, "I find him a fountain of joy . . . without a ray of imagination or humour; longing to talk. It all comes out, one is convinced, exactly as it happened. The Führer at Hendaye, Ribbentrop . . . When she isn't about, he forgets to say Adolf and says der Führer . . . I am not so sure whether their teeth are really drawn . . . [but] they are not Nazis, and honestly don't consider themselves Nazis."

Meanwhile, Sybille was determined to make a start on the Mexican story, the idea of which had first come to her over three years ago, "one warm night, on the terrace of a hacienda, lying on a deckchair under the subtropical sky." When Esther had arrived from France before their departure for Ischia she had brought with her the letters Sybille had written to Allanah describing her Mexican experience. Since Sybille had kept no diary nor taken any notes, these letters were invaluable, long extracts eventually appearing almost unaltered throughout the book. She intended to present it as a kind of travel diary, she told Allanah, "an extremely subjective book that relies entirely for its coming off on being well written and on the quality of the author's mind and sensibility . . . But amusing in parts, even burlesque, with perhaps bits of narratives about the stranger and more eccentric characters there; but with always the sense of what a remote, strange (the incredible Otherness of Mexico) place it is."

Sybille found the beginning unexpectedly difficult. "I haven't written for much too long. It's as though a muscle were gone . . . I feel exhausted, discouraged and depressed . . . Buckling down is much harder than I thought." In a notebook kept at this period the entries read: "July 20th No work—no excuse. 21st Thinking Fiddling—Dawdling . . . 25th Thinking—Dawdling—Dreaming—Fiddling . . . 22nd Aug Hungover." Eventually, however, she began to gather momentum, and "now it's a bit better, as one has forced oneself into a routine . . . There have even been a few of those moments of sheer joy when one thinks one has caught it." The highs and lows continued, but Sybille was determined to persevere, often taking stimulants, up to three Dexedrine a day, to keep herself going. "I've been wrestling all afternoon with getting myself off the High Plateau of Northern Mexico where I am stuck," she reported to Allanah at the end of the first month. "It took me three weeks to cross the U.S., and I'm only just across the border . . . Constant descriptions of the countryside are wearing me out."

Inevitably there were distractions, chief among them her feeling of guilt about Esther, the constant awareness of Esther's solitary presence in the room overhead. Nonetheless, Sybille soon found herself working for up to six hours at a time, and before long she came to realise that her discipline and determination were proving productive. "What mattered was that the book was moving and with it the discovery that I was writing in a voice unlike the one I had assumed before. My inner ear no longer echoed the cadences of Aldous Huxley."

In September, Sybille with Esther returned to France for the first time in over a year. Here she found that much had changed, the sexual carousel once more in full swing. Esther, who had planned to visit Ireland with her lover Joan Black, now discovered to her astonishment that Joan was about to marry. Her English fiancé, Peter, Viscount Churchill, was regarded with suspicion by Joan's friends, his reputation that of "a worn-out international fairy . . . who could not be trusted around the corner." Luckily, however, the shock of Joan's defection instantly cured Esther of her infatuation. "My whole feeling about her has vanished so completely," she told Sybille, "that I am honestly amazed by my own indifference to the whole thing." Then Eda Lord, who two years earlier had left Joan for Allanah, had suddenly gone to live in Wales with Hilary Williams, a woman with whom she had had a brief affair at the beginning of the war. The two were "madly in love," according to Allanah, who had been devastated by Eda's departure. Allanah's husband continued to be supportive, "and could not be sweeter or nicer to me," she told Sybille. "But I miss Eda so terribly and am so utterly heartbroken and miserable without her . . . I feel I cannot get through the days and nights."

Fortunately, Allanah was engaged in a new project which was to help take her mind off her unhappiness. Recently she had bought a house in the south of France, at La Roquette-sur-Siagne, a tiny village in the back country, just over six miles north of Cannes. Here Sybille soon after her return came to join her, immediately entranced not only by the house but by its location deep in the heart of her beloved Provence, "to me one of the most heavenly countrysides in the world." At Les Bastides she found herself in an "abode of permanent peace . . . We look out into a Virgillian valley, silver with olives, flanked by exquisite hills . . . It is still fine; but there is an autumn coolness in the evening air, and the warm summer scent of thyme and pines is already mixed with woodsmoke where they burn the leaves. The grapes are still on the vines . . . [the house is] simple, whitewashed, large square rooms, built-in lights and built-in bookcases, and books and books. It sort of exhales peace and order." During the next few weeks Allanah, her husband Robert and Sybille spent their days swimming and taking long walks in the country, in the evenings after dinner playing cards, reading and listening to music on the gramophone.

For Sybille it was a time of peace and enchantment, Les Bastides providing a precious haven from the stresses of the world—and so it would remain for the next nearly forty years of her life.

Arriving back in Paris, Sybille's intention was to return to Rome as soon as possible and continue work on her book. It was now, however, that she was faced with a serious obstacle, a deterioration in her eyesight affecting her ability to read and write. Familiar with Aldous's lifelong problems with his eyes, she had read with interest his recent account of the dramatic improvement to his vision resulting from following the Bates Method, a process of "visual re-education." Today almost wholly discredited, the Bates Method at the time was heralded by many as a revolutionary development, its popularity significantly boosted by Aldous's book on the subject, *The Art of Seeing*. Sybille was determined to try it for herself, first consulting Maria Huxley's sister, Jeanne Neveux, who was a Bates practitioner in Paris. After her appointment, however, Sybille came away unimpressed by what she described as "the Bates Sorcery Chamber—blackboards, cut-outs, beads, balls, cardboard fans," disappointed to find the exercises made no difference at all.*

Fortunately Allanah decided to take the matter in hand. In London she booked appointments for Sybille with three different specialists: the first two were unhelpful, but from the third some simple instructions were to prove invaluable: "Write on green paper, not white: less glare. Never read or copy looking down on a flat surface: hold the page or book at an angle. Never stare." After the two women returned to Paris, Allanah for good measure insisted on one final consultation, which at last seemed to offer a correct analysis. "The occulist," Sybille reported, was "quite first rate . . . [and] I'm convinced his diagnosis is right (increasing sensitiveness to light due to congenital lack of pigmentation; you see I was very fair as a child; brought out by advancing age and aggravated by astigmatism) . . . One can alleviate it (drops, ointments for lids, dark glasses, wearing a shield) . . . Writing is the last kind of profession for me, he said. But my eyes are good, and sight too. It is a relief that nothing is basically wrong."

For the first three months of 1950, Sybille remained in France, commuting between Gadencourt and Paris, where she stayed with Esther at the Hôtel Saints-Pères. It was often with Esther that Sybille went out in the evenings, on several occasions dining with old friends such as Janet Flanner and Noël Murphy, and also Poppy Kirk. Poppy, in Sybille's view "still one of the liveliest and aesthetically most pleasing people alive," was now ensconced with a new lover, the flamboyant Mercedes de Acosta, adored by Poppy, despised by many others, Sybille, Esther and Allanah among them. While living in California, Mercedes, a glamorous Spanish-American, nicknamed "Countess Dracula" for her vampire-like costume—black cloaks and trousers, white face powder,

---

* When *The Art of Seeing* was published in 1943, the distinguished ophthalmologist Stewart Duke-Elder wrote in the *British Medical Journal*, "For the simple neurotic who has abundance of time to play with, Huxley's antics of palming, shifting, flashing, and the rest are probably as good treatment as any other system of Yogi or Coué-ism. To these the book may be of value. It is hardly possible that it will impress anyone endowed with common sense and a critical faculty."

blood-red lipstick—had been famous for her affairs with, among others, Greta Garbo and Marlene Dietrich. Sybille had met her first with the Huxleys in Los Angeles, when she had found her "unbelievably tiresome." Now in Paris her opinion of this "Lord Byron of the Ladies" was unchanged. "Smart, celebrity hunting, deadly dull, and not nice. She's been called Countess Dracula, but I believe the only thing she minds is being called Old Merc."

One of Esther's regular haunts was the literary salon of Natalie Barney, whom Esther had known since the early 1930s. Among the many distinguished guests now frequenting the rue Jacob were Alice B. Toklas, Jean Cocteau, Colette, Virgil Thomson, Janet Flanner and Nancy Cunard. Despite Natalie Barney's formidable reputation both as literary hostess and promiscuous lesbian, Sybille remained unimpressed. "Quick change and off to Miss Barney rue Jacob with E very dull indeed—Alice B. Toklas creeping about," she reported. Sybille disliked the stuffy, darkly lit drawing room and was repelled by what she considered as Miss Barney's solipsistic showing off.

Feeling under obligation to return Natalie's hospitality, however, Sybille gave a small tea party for her at the Hôtel Saints-Pères. The atmosphere was uncomfortably formal, Natalie not bothering to conceal her boredom, until suddenly there was a knock on the door and a little girl appeared holding a telegram for one of the guests. "Suddenly," Sybille recalled, "Natalie snapped awake, her eyes sparkled and she began to praise the child—'quelle jolie fille'—salivating over her and stroking her arm the way an old man would drool over and pinch the bottom of a chorus girl . . . She is a monster," Sybille concluded, "entirely selfish . . . with no moral compass . . . The entertaining, brittle world of Paris, it makes me sick."

Rather more congenial were the evenings Sybille spent with Allanah in the company of a group of hard-drinking Americans, all writers, gathered at a small hotel in the rue de l'Université, among them Truman Capote, Carson McCullers, Eudora Welty, and the very eccentric Jane Bowles. "Allanah and I shared many of their views if not their habits," Sybille recalled, "were captivated by their writings, deplored their drinking . . . Allanah on principle, I for the delay of dinner." Some of the group they had met while in the States during the war, most often the talented, unpredictable Jane Bowles, described by Sybille as "an angelic, witty, suicidal imp." Jane had recently written her first play, which was about to go into production, and thus she was planning to return shortly to New York. It was unfortunate, therefore, that now, during her brief stay in Paris, she and Allanah should have fallen passionately in love.

Sybille was sympathetic to her friend's new affair, on several occasions dining with Allanah and Jane, yet all the while she remained restless with longing to return to Italy. Then at the end of March Pierre and Simone Mimerel arrived in town and to Sybille's joy offered to drive her to Rome.

Within a few days of arrival Sybille had found somewhere to live, at 54 Piazza di Spagna, only a short walk away from the d'Inghilterra. The apartment was minute, a tiny bungalow built onto the roof of a five-storey building, but the location was ideal and the views spectacular, of the Spanish Steps, the Trinità dei Monti, and the magnificent gardens of the Villa Borghese. Before leaving for Capri, the FitzGibbons had lived there, and had loved the little dwelling, the single room lined with bookshelves, the terrace covered with flowering plants. To begin with, however, Sybille was less than enchanted, describing it as "a horrid Dog Kennel: dilapidated, with every stick of scarce furniture fit to be burned." The accommodation was limited, one bed-sitting room, a small kitchen and a tiny bathroom with a large marble bath, but after spending a week washing and scrubbing, she began to see the appeal of the place, and was particularly pleased with the spacious terrace. "I have my tea there in the morning . . . Lunch out of doors, and dinner. It is like living in the country."

As spring evolved into summer, Sybille began to realise how happy she was in her rooftop eyrie. In many ways it was an ideal existence: there was a maid who came every afternoon to clean; and Sybille's friend, Peter Tompkins, constructed a miniature summer house, open on one side and made of bamboo, where during the day she could sit in the shade. Although she continued to suffer problems with her eyes, obliged to wear very dark glasses when out-of-doors, she was now able to read for several hours at a time, emerging in the evenings to water the plants and gaze at the view. "I have acquired a new joy, gardening," she told Allanah. "Thirty-five potted creepers (raised from seed); hon-eysuckle, jasmine, geraniums, moon flowers and morning glory, ole-ander and a pergola of vine; and the bamboo house full of greenery." Here on the roof she regularly entertained friends for cocktails, after which they would go on to dine at Toto's, a little trattoria round the corner. Among the regular visitors were her beloved Natalia Danesi, accompanied by Janet Flanner when she was in town; Peter Tompkins and his wife; Donald Downes; and "awful" Patricia Laffan, still filming at the Cinecittà studios.

One morning while looking through letters at the concierge's lodge, Sybille found an envelope addressed to her, inside it a note from an acquaintance in New York introducing a young American couple recently arrived in the city. Sybille immediately responded, inviting them to meet her the next evening in the bar at the d'Inghilterra.

Milton and Evelyn Gendel, both in their early thirties, small in stature, slender and dark-haired, had come to Rome after Milton had been awarded a Fulbright scholarship. Sybille enjoyed their company, and after an hour or so the three of them went on to dinner at Toto's. "Conversation flowed. Milton amusing, brief, detached; Evelyn chat-tered. Happily, disarmingly." After that first evening, Sybille began to see the Gendels several times a week; they went to concerts and the opera together, dined at various local trattorias, and took to going for long walks through the city after dark, sometimes into the early hours of the morning. Before long the Gendels became regular visitors at the Piazza di Spagna; Milton reorganised the electrical system and installed lights on the roof, while Evelyn hemmed curtains, taught Sybille how to touch-type, and during the afternoons read aloud to her so that she could rest her eyes.

As soon became clear, the Gendels had differing attitudes towards the Eternal City, Milton finding it disappointing—"I felt I'd moved to Yonkers or Westchester or somewhere . . . There was a very provincial feel to it"—while Evelyn was utterly enchanted. It was her first experi-ence of abroad and she was eager to explore the ancient ruins, the gal-leries and palaces, everything the city had to offer. Unlike Milton, she was also passionately interested in food, which naturally endeared her to Sybille.

During this time Sybille learned much of the couple's history. Both had been born and brought up in New York, Evelyn's father a schoolteacher, Milton's in the rag trade. They had known each other since their schooldays, after which Evelyn went on to NYU, Milton to Columbia, where he left with a BSc as well as an MA in the history of art. They married in 1944, immediately before Milton, now in the army, was sent out to China, having become fluent in Mandarin after a four-month course at Yale. When the war ended, Evelyn found a job in publishing, while Milton stayed on in Shanghai for a couple of years before returning to the States. After several months with the War Department in Washington he finally rejoined Evelyn in New York. Awarded a Fulbright scholarship, Milton immediately made plans to return to China, plans that at the last moment were cancelled by the newly appointed Chairman Mao. It was at this point, somewhat reluctantly, that he accepted the State Department's alternative offer of a year in Italy.

Sybille was impressed by Milton's clever, laconic and self-assured manner, although she found him not altogether sympathetic: he could be boring and seemed a little too pleased with himself, "one of those rather sarcastic, stuck-up young New York intellectuals." Evelyn, on the other hand, was enchanting: "young in some ways; but steady, disciplined, mature in others . . . Intelligent, with a will of her own . . . She looks a little like a ballerina, with a curious Byzantine face, with those slanting inhuman eyes of the mosaics." Curiously, both Milton and Sybille regarded the gap in age between them as a barrier to closer friendship. "I didn't especially take to Sybille," Milton recalled, "but then there was twenty years' difference in our ages," while Sybille stated, "Yes, I did like the Gendels well enough. But. They were *young*. The gap between their mid-twenties and my late thirties was too great." In fact, both Gendels were in their mid-thirties and Sybille was thirty-nine, so the gap was far smaller than they believed.

As her vision improved, Sybille was able to spend several hours a day reading and writing, her eyes protected by a white tennis visor lined with green. Gradually she felt able to return to her book. "I bit a nail, sat down before my pages and the typewriter every morning. I worked, and it worked." In the early afternoon, she left her desk and went into the kitchen to assemble her lunch, which was then carefully placed on a small card table in a shady corner of the terrace—"tomatoes, an egg or two, salami, fruit, a large glass of water." As the day cooled she emerged onto the roof to spend time pruning and watering the plants, then in the early evening settled back with a glass of wine to watch the swifts swooping overhead, later either going out with friends or eating on her own while listening to music on the radio. As always, Sybille took care in preparing her dinner, concentrating intently not only on the cooking, but also on a meticulous *mise en scène*. "The Gendels, who occasionally came to pick me up for our late-evening walks—seemed overtaken with mirth finding me *à table* formally set with hot plate, first course, main course and the right-sized spoon for every grain of Parmesan."

One afternoon Evelyn arrived unexpectedly, on her own and clearly nervous. Sybille asked her to help take down some laundry hanging out to dry on the terrace. "Evelyn and I were facing each other across the washing line folding pillowcases, kitchen towels, when I heard her clearly enunciate what I call the three fatal words." Although Sybille had recently become aware of an emotional tension in the atmosphere the declaration took her by surprise. "I knew all the time, and yet did not know a thing, and the feather could have knocked me over. We talked and talked, it turned out that she had been married for twelve years,* but that the marriage had been rather dead for the last three or four." Sybille for her part felt disconcerted, but also flattered and suddenly intensely excited, as Evelyn described how deeply she had fallen in love with her, how she longed to leave Milton and to live for the rest of her life with Sybille.

Suddenly there was a knock on the door and Janet Flanner and Natalia appeared; Janet had come to say goodbye as she was leaving Rome the following morning. Soon after they left, Milton arrived, and he, Sybille and Evelyn went out for dinner, the two women revealing nothing, all three as usual spending an equable evening together. But "after that day," Sybille wrote of Evelyn, "I ceased to lump her together with her husband in my mind and judgement."

Over the next few weeks, Sybille, by now feeling "rather madly in love," did her best to arrange as much time alone with Evelyn as

---

* In fact the Gendels had been married for only six years.

possible. "We had to be extremely careful, as her husband was not to know, and therefore of course, for decency even more than prudence, nobody else." Every day Evelyn arrived in the early afternoon, when the two of them would have lunch and then talk while Evelyn sewed, both impatiently waiting for "the maddening, slow maid" to leave. By the time she had gone they usually had only a couple of hours to themselves before Milton presented himself, ready to go out to dinner. In her pocket diary Sybille briefly noted the emotions she experienced during this period: "overexalted & feeling oats . . . overwhelming longing . . . tired & v. nervous . . . frantic, active, happy." As she admitted to Toni Muir, "It was a strain. Those curiously intense days of talking, and too little privacy. Weekends were worse, as Evelyn had to spend at least all Sunday with her husband . . . Once or twice, we worked an elaborate edifice of opera tickets given to me for two only . . . *Rigoletto*, the stars be thanked, lasts until 2 a.m. in Italy."

Finally both decided they wanted to live together—"that notion of For Ever which is so attractive, and so frightening at the same time"— and that Evelyn must tell her husband that their marriage was over. "I was beside myself with heat, nerves and worry," Sybille recalled, but Evelyn remained relatively calm, explaining to Milton, who had known nothing at all about the affair, that she was determined to leave him. Initially Milton was both shocked and angry, feeling humiliated and betrayed. "After Evelyn left me I hated her for a while, though the relationship had been going wrong for some time . . . [but then] my anger evaporated. I realised the relationship had been over anyway and that that had nothing to do with Evelyn leaving me for Sybille."

In the middle of July 1950 Sybille left Rome and travelled with Evelyn to France. While in Paris, Sybille broke the news to Esther, who reacted with her customary kindness and understanding. Shortly afterwards Allanah arrived from London, "and thank God she and Evelyn get on well. We motored down to the South together in Allanah's car." By this time Sybille had recovered from the emotional turmoil of the last weeks in Rome and felt ready to enjoy herself. "I found the first weeks slightly worrying (I had rather wanted to live alone for some years) . . . Then I got over that, and I am peaceful and happy now." In fact her relationship with Evelyn was to be one of the most rewarding of her life. "Many attachments have improbable beginnings," she wrote later, and "this one for me was the most abrupt; it also turned out one of the happiest, due mainly to Evelyn's innate goodness and serenity of nature."

To Sybille's relief, Allanah accepted the new relationship, although, true to form, she was not entirely uncritical. Evelyn, she admitted, "was very nice and very intelligent, but she never opens her mouth without making some kind of gaffe . . . [and] her manner is too familiar." However, at this juncture Allanah was more concerned with her own problems; now amicably separated from her husband, Robert, she was currently torn between her passion for Jane Bowles and a new affair, with an Englishwoman, Frances ("Fay") Blacket Gill, a successful lawyer with a practice in London. "I love Jane as much as ever, but I am more in love with F[ay]," she confided to Sybille. "I want to live always with F yet the very thought of having thereby to give up Jane, appals me." After much agonising, Allanah finally decided that a life with Fay would be the sensible choice: Fay was well off, her house "a haven of luxury and comfort . . . With Fay I feel that I would be marrying the kind of Englishman and successful lawyer that I should have married had she been a man."

Sybille and Evelyn returned to Rome in October, Sybille determined now to finish her book. And yet although happy with Evelyn, she remained restless, over the next couple of years moving every few months between Italy and France, while Evelyn remained in Rome. Here she and Evelyn had squeezed themselves into another cramped little rooftop premises, this time in the Via della Fontanella; but while in Paris, by contrast, Sybille enjoyed the greatest luxury and comfort, staying in Esther's recently acquired apartment in the beautiful rue de Lille.

Sybille's relations with Esther were better than they had been for some time, peaceful and loving, with all the past tensions and jealousies behind them. Now at last with a place of her own, Esther was clearly enjoying herself: "thank God [she] has a little more money and it has made all the difference to her," Sybille reported to Allanah. "She is so changed, gay, buying herself clothes, and I'm afraid much too generous and spending most of it on other people." Sybille was delighted by the elegance of her new surroundings, the carved marble chimney pieces and Directoire furniture, the handsome rooms hung with pictures and gilded looking glasses. The inner courtyard was planted with a magnificent chestnut tree, "the L-shaped inner facade, plain, grey, patinaed of a late eighteenth-century *hôtel*. Just the view one would want in Paris . . . Nothing could be nicer and I am very very pleased."

Also pleasing was the fact that her sister Katzi, recently returned from Austria, was also in residence, employed as a housekeeper by Esther. Here Katzi was in her element, busily organising Esther's social life, planning the menus, even doing much of the shopping and cooking herself—Esther, according to Sybille, did not even know where the kitchen was. Thanks to Katzi, the cuisine was excellent. "We are going to have [a] marvel for dinner it appears," Sybille reported to Evelyn. "Champagne, Oysters, Roast Poulet de Bresse, with, if fancy does not deceive, a bottle of Château Lafite Rothschild, and a hot cheese savoury." In the evenings, Katzi sometimes visited friends or accompanied Sybille and Esther to the theatre, but her favourite occupation was staging elaborate dinner parties at the apartment, the marble table strewn with roses, crystal glasses gleaming in the candlelight. As in their childhood, Katzi kept a sharp eye on Sybille, and when dining in the company of her sister Sybille was careful to appear neatly dressed, in black jacket, shirt and trousers, her short blonde hair carefully slicked down; yet even so she came in for criticism. "*Je mange du cochon, mais je ne mange pas* comme *un cochon*" ("I eat pig, but I don't eat like a pig"), Katzi remarked meaningfully at lunch one day as Sybille gorged on a plateful of new potatoes. "*Tu peux être insupportable*," she told her on another occasion, "*et c'est pire maintenant que tu vis avec une personne* [Esther] *qui pense que tu es un ange*" ("You can be unbearable, and it's worse now that you're living with someone who thinks you're an angel").

To Evelyn in Rome lengthy descriptions were despatched not only of Sybille's social life but also of her working routine. Each morning she spent several hours at her desk, before taking long walks through the city in the afternoon. At the rue de Lille the atmosphere was cheerful— "Katzi well and easy . . . Esther merry as a grig"—and with everything so well organised Sybille was able fully to concentrate on her book.

These letters to Evelyn also included detailed accounts of Sybille's preparations for lunch, much appreciated by Evelyn, whose interest in food was as passionate as her own. "Yesterday," Sybille reported, "buckled down to a little work, interrupted by lunch . . . Ryvita, butter, duck drippings, smoked fish roe, boiled eggs, and a large plate of cold cuts on table. Beer, Nescafé . . . I ate half a slice of ham . . . and two Ryvita with fish roe (it looks and has the consistency of *Mettwurst* but tastes like soft not very salty *botarga* and partakes of the nature of *oursin* and red caviar. I have a savage passion for it, always drawn between eating or saving it). I took my second cup of Nescafé to my desk and worked undisturbed (Wanda Landowska tinkering Bach in the background)."

For her part, Evelyn in Rome responded with meticulous records of her own daily activities. In their correspondence the two women had amorously adopted the habit of referring to themselves in the masculine third person, as "he," often characterising themselves as animals, "Tortoise," "Turtle," "Goat," "Hare," "Great Beast." "This afternoon, he changed the ribbon and cleaned his typewriter," Evelyn reported. "THEN he will begin to think about his DIN . . . Porker, and beans and salad, and then he will eat it, very gentlemanly, with red wine, and he will listen to Beethoven 4th piano concerto and 3rd symphony . . . and all the time, thinking lovingly of his dearest creature . . . his Great BEAST. SO sweet. So kind. It makes HIM CRY. Bless you my darling." A few evenings later, "He was ravenous, so he put on his roast at seven, and peas pud at the same time . . . Roast, he will tell him honestly, was quite good—tasty, and edible—but nothing like his darling's . . . THEN he mended, stitch stitch stitch . . . then he made the rounds, spoke to all the dear plants." Sybille's letters meant everything to her, Evelyn wrote. "They are yourself, in conversation, with your face with the eager and talkative look it gets, when he begins to rock back and forth, caught in the flow of his own story."

Sybille treasured these missives, acutely missing Evelyn's company. "I think of my Dear constantly and with great tenderness," she told her. Yet after the intense excitement of the affair's beginning she had soon become aware that although she loved Evelyn dearly she was not in love with her. "I cannot really love my lovers," she confessed to Allanah.

"There IS something false about a relationship between two women. At least for me. But I do not suffer from it. Only one does not give enough: and then of course some day the tables are turned on one."

Nonetheless over the next couple of years as she continued her peripatetic existence, moving between Rome, Paris and the south of France, Sybille felt increasingly protective towards Evelyn, guilty about leaving her so much on her own, worried that she was imposing too heavy a burden. It was Evelyn, after all, who now undertook all domestic duties, and Evelyn's small savings that largely covered their rent and household expenses. "I do feel," Sybille wrote to Allanah, "that Evelyn should share some of the good things of my life, and not only slave for me . . . [Evelyn] has changed her life, milieu, everything, entirely for me; she has given up everything in fact including earning a decent amount of money in America . . . my life as it is now is entirely thanks to her: how could I work all day . . . be read to in the evenings, have all dates and historical business looked up for me, doing all the errands . . . I should be very unhappy if I were completely alone. This almost ideal setting for a writer is perhaps paid for by the future of another human being . . . Evelyn is not a second-class appendage and I will not treat her so."

Mainly due to Evelyn's care and kindness, Sybille had been able to write uninterruptedly for hours a day in order to meet her deadline. "Yes he realised that he will have to work and work, and it makes him happy to think so," Evelyn replied. "He will type and type for him, with pride and pleasure. And make him thermos tea, and his lunch-munch, and love him, and answer the telephone for him . . . It is very coocoo and happy for him to think of his Beast in his room snorkling and mumbling and tapping." For Sybille it was a period of intense concentration, at her desk all day, wearing her tennis visor to protect her eyes, only emerging in the evenings to water the plants and eat dinner prepared by Evelyn. Finally by the autumn of 1951 the first section of the book was done, the typed pages parcelled up and posted to London. "It is gone," Sybille told Allanah, "and this morning I tidied my desk and tore up the notes . . . It is no pleasure at all. How long will it take one to make such an effort again?"

It was now that Allanah, as before, took control, sending the manuscript to the publisher Victor Gollancz. The following January Sybille learned to her joy that Gollancz was prepared to offer her a contract on condition that the second part was of as high a standard as the first. They wanted to talk to her as soon as possible, she was told, and a meeting was arranged for early February. Delighted by such a positive response, early in the New Year Sybille arrived in London.

Evelyn, who had worked in publishing while in New York, was anxious that Sybille should present herself in the best possible light. It was important that she should not appear too masculine, she told her, but instead give the impression of a conventional lady writer. "Please," Evelyn begged her, "will he NOT wear stocks . . . [but] a pretty chiffon instead?? . . . He wants them to see a fair and feminine creature." Evelyn also tried to calm Sybille's nerves. "Don't make a nonsense by clinging to your idea that it will be an ordeal. It will only be a conversation, between you and people who like your work, and who want to know . . . what you have in mind. And so, tell them, without any of this false modesty . . . HE IS RIGHT. DO AS HE SAYS. And don't mumble."

In London Sybille stayed in Chelsea at the house of Allanah's new attachment, Fay Blacket Gill. On the day of her appointment with Gollancz she awoke acutely anxious, well aware of the firm's distinguished standing, of its list of famous authors, among them Elizabeth Bowen, Ivy Compton-Burnett, Orwell, Kafka and Colette. When she arrived at the address in Henrietta Street, Covent Garden, she was surprised to find how shabby the premises appeared. The interior of the house was ramshackle, "even for an English publisher," she reported to Evelyn. "Up a narrow uncarpeted staircase, a tiny office, complete with coal fire, teapot, gas ring, hideous cheap pine furniture . . . rattly sash window." However, she found Sheila Hodges, who was to be her editor, a "very nice girl, young and simple." Sheila offered Sybille an advance of £100, rather less than Sybille had hoped, on the understanding that the second half of the book was delivered within six months.

Slightly to Sybille's relief she had not had to encounter the head of the firm himself, "a tricky old bird," as he was known in the trade. She did, however, catch a glimpse of him on her way out. "I had been warned that old Victor Gollancz might come in to have a look at me. He did not. I left the office, and hopped down the stairs much relieved . . . I muttered, though inaudibly, to myself, that's over; how mean they are. Then I looked up: and in the door, on the lower landing, poking his head round the jamb, stood watching me VG himself: great wreath of white curls, like Einstein on the stage. Our eyes met, he wriggled back and closed the door."

The second section was finished at the end of May 1952, and posted to London. Meanwhile Sybille had been trying without success to think of a title, "something that gives a hint at the Marx Brothers quality of Mexico." Her first choice had been "The Mango on the Mango-Tree," a quotation from T. S. Eliot's poem "The Hippopotamus,"* but that, it turned out, had recently been used by another Gollancz author. Finally it was Martha Gellhorn, recently returned to Rome, who provided the solution. Martha had been enthusiastic about the book—Sybille "has written a travel book about Mexico which is as funny and perceptive as anything I have ever seen," she told her friend, the composer William Walton—and had written to Sybille with two suggestions, "The Train of the Day Before Yesterday" and "The Sudden View." Sybille found it difficult to make up her mind, but eventually chose the latter.

Finally on 23 February 1953, *The Sudden View* was published, dedicated to both Esther and Allanah. Sybille was in Rome on the day of publication, sitting reading in the flat by herself, "when the door flung open and in came Martha and Evelyn bearing a champagne bucket and a cake, like a birthday cake, but saying BOOK on it . . . a very happy moment . . . We drank two bottles of champagne (but did not get raving), then I struggled out of my old corduroys, and Martha took us out to dinner."

The Sudden View, Sybille's account of her eight-month journey through Mexico, part memoir, part invention, makes for one of the most engaging travel books ever written. Accompanied by "E," her unnamed companion, Sybille keeps herself at the centre of the frame, an endearingly fallible figure, constantly frustrated, often delighted, occasionally enraged, from the very beginning avid to explore all levels of experience, from squalid to sublime. As the two women begin their

---

* "The 'potamus can never reach / The mango on the mango-tree; / But fruits of pomegranate and peach / Refresh the Church from over sea."

travels, everything is observed with close attention, Sybille graphically describing her surroundings and vigorously engaging with the people she encounters en route—nuns, hoteliers, shopkeepers, as well as resident expatriates from Europe and America, many of the latter regarded with a frigid disdain. Food, of course, is the focus of intense examination, but so is the way of life at every level of society, from aristocrat to peasant. Sometimes the travellers find themselves most eccentrically lodged, as in Guadalajara, where at their hotel, a magnificent sixteenth-century palace, they discover the staircase to their first-floor room has yet to be installed and there is no running water. ("There doesn't seem to be any water in our bathroom." "Of course not, Señora. It has not been laid on. One thing after another. Perhaps next year?") Elsewhere, by contrast, they find themselves living in exquisitely serene surroundings, most notably on the property by Lake Chapala belonging to "Don Otavio." And as in life, so in the book, it is Don Otavio and his luxurious estate that provides the central focus of the adventure.

A particularly beguiling element of the story is the contrast of Sybille's enthusiasm to the languor of her companion. "E" is a fond and accurate portrayal of Esther, who throughout her time in Mexico showed a complete lack of curiosity in her surroundings. " 'I have not the slightest desire to see the wonders of nature' . . . '*I will not go to this volcano,*' said E in the manner of Edmund Burke addressing the House of Commons." Yet despite her reluctance to explore the sights, it was Esther who had guided Sybille in much of her study of the country's history, from Aztecs and conquistadors to the modern era, all of which Sybille found invaluable for her research. When she had first begun reading about the country she had been unimpressed by most contemporary accounts, naming only Graham Greene's *The Power and the Glory* and Malcolm Lowry's *Under the Volcano* as outstanding, with D. H. Lawrence's *The Plumed Serpent* dismissed as "weak and hysterical," and both Huxley and Waugh as "uninteresting." Ultimately it was Esther's suggestion of two nineteenth-century works—William H. Prescott's *History of the Conquest of Mexico* and Frances Calderón de la Barca's *Life in Mexico*—that contributed most to her understanding of the country's past.

The vivid, highly personal account of Sybille's adventures recounted in *The Sudden View* was to make a significant impact, establishing her as a talented member of the profession to which she had always yearned to belong. It was with *The Sudden View* that Sybille finally emerged from the heavy Huxleyan influence in which up till now she had been immersed, here that she found her own voice, that clear, distinctive voice which in the years to come would win her recognition as one of the outstanding writers of her time. The work "was an immediate critical success," Sybille recalled in an interview many years later. It "made a great difference to me. It meant that I had reached the identity I wanted—that of a writer."

Shortly after the day of publication Sybille received a letter from Allanah. "Great Rabbit, A thousand thanks for the dedication, for which I feel deeply honoured . . . I read about thirty pages without a stop, one cannot put it down, and then tears streamed down my face and I cried out every few minutes, HE CAN WRITE, HE CAN WRITE, IT'S A GREAT BOOK . . . Oh, Rabbit, what an achievement. The book is so funny every page has some anecdote or some description that makes one laugh." Sybille was profoundly grateful to Allanah, who had not only encouraged her to write the book—"Without you," Sybille told her, "I should [still] be sitting in a café, talking about writing"—but with her wide range of literary contacts had been instrumental in promoting it. Although Allanah had failed to persuade Aldous Huxley to contribute an introduction ("his eyes were too bad to permit him to read anything that was not connected with his work," Allanah explained), she had shown the book to several influential figures, among them Cyril Connolly, who described it as "first class," and to Raymond Mortimer, who reported that he thought it "brilliant, quite an extraordinary performance for somebody who, so far as I know, has had little experience of writing."

Mortimer was also among several critics who reviewed it in the press. "This book can be recommended as vastly enjoyable . . . radiant with comedy and colour," he wrote in the *Sunday Times*. "The frequent snatches of dialogue that enliven the descriptions might be the work of a skilled novelist, so sharp the eye for character, so alive the ear to the run of speech." John Davenport in the *New Statesman* was equally enthusiastic, while Peter Quennell in the *Daily Mail* described the book as "Absorbing . . . Its account of the lake and the garden, and the flowers and birds of the subtropical landscape around Chapala, has made me long to go to Mexico." It was also recommended by the Book Society and extracts were read aloud on the BBC.

Early the following year *The Sudden View* was published in the States. At first, to Sybille's disappointment, it had received a number of rejections, but then Cass Canfield, head of Harper's in New York, agreed to take it on. Nearly twenty years earlier, Canfield, while visiting Aldous Huxley in Sanary, had read one of Sybille's short stories, writing to her afterwards that although he did not think it worthy of publication he would be pleased to see any of her future work. Now he reacted with enthusiasm. *The Sudden View*, he told her, "is one of those rare books which a publisher is fortunate to encounter once every few years." Although extremely pleased by Canfield's response, Sybille had been unimpressed by Gollancz's handling of the American offer. "They did very badly indeed. Rotten contract, v. low advance. I am afraid it is rather a mess, and I am sick of them." Nonetheless she was gratified by the book's reception. "A delightful, unclassifiable, and shimmering book," wrote Alfred Kazin in the *New Yorker*; "one of the travel books of the year" said the *New York Times*, while the *Washington Star* described it as "something new in travel literature . . . [with its] vivacious and malicious narrative."

Translated into Italian, French and German, *The Sudden View* in years to come was to be rarely out of print. With its title subsequently changed to *A Visit to Don Otavio*, the book was later reissued by the New York Review of Books Classics, and in Britain was published in turn by William Collins, by Picador (with an introduction by Bruce Chatwin), and by Eland Books, whose edition remains in print today.

Exhilarated by her success, Sybille felt she must not lose her impetus, must start work again as soon as possible. Both Martha and Allanah were begging her not to waste time, to begin exploring some of the many themes for the novel she had talked about over the past couple of years. Sybille knew they were right but somehow inspiration failed to arrive. "*Maintenant il ne reste que commencer un autre livre*" ("Now it remains for me to start another book"), she told Allanah. "But what has one got to say?"

EIGHT

"THAT OGRE, THE SNAIL NOVEL"

The lack of inspiration was short-lived. Since childhood Sybille had known that writing was her métier, and now at last, after years of failure and procrastination, her ambition had been realised. "The impulses behind writing are obscure in everyone," she told Evelyn. "<u>Why</u> one wants to tell a good story, for instance, is mysterious to me . . . [but] I do want to." Impatient to start work, and with several ideas for a novel in mind, she was finding it difficult to decide which direction to take. Initially she had been drawn to the subject of an eccentric *ménage à trois* she had known in New York,[*] but then abandoned that in favour of focusing on Mursel von Stohrer, "the bad *baronessa*," who had been much in her thoughts since their meeting on Ischia. However, it was not long before she decided on a story that had been with her since childhood, that of her father, Maximilian, of his family and early life, and of his two marriages.

Sybille when writing required hours of solitude a day, but she also strongly felt the need of a writing colleague, someone with whom she could discuss in minute detail the problems involved, talk about her progress or lack of it, with the firm understanding that each would be honest and outspoken when criticising the other's work. While engaged on *The Sudden View*, she had relied on Esther for advice on the histori-

---

[*] The trio in question was made up of the English photographer Olivia Wyndham, Olivia's lover, the African American actress Edna Lewis Thomas, and Edna's husband, Lloyd Thomas.

cal background and had read occasional passages aloud to Evelyn, but
Esther, although impressively well informed, was reluctant to criticise,
while Evelyn simply seemed bemused: "her boredom with the text was
evident . . . she said she just did not know what to make of it." Fortunately, by the time Sybille began work on her new project, she had
found the perfect partner in Martha Gellhorn.

Martha was now living in a rented farmhouse a few miles outside
Rome, together with Alessandro ("Sandy"), the little boy she had
recently adopted from an orphanage near Florence. Martha, too, was
about to start work on a novel, and the two women immediately became
engaged in a close critical alliance, meeting several times a week to discuss their work (always referred to by Martha as "bilgers"), and cor-
responding almost daily, their letters often running to seven or eight
closely typed pages. As Sybille explained to Allanah, Martha's "arrival
showed how much I needed someone to talk to in exactly that way,
someone intelligent, sensitive, entirely different from myself, who is,
apart from very amusing, and so witty, entirely serious, entirely in the
grip of the same questions that beset me: conduct, human destiny, writing, the use of minor talent, the ordering of one's life and efforts." And
Martha for her part was equally reliant on her dear "Sib" or "Sibbie," as
she usually addressed her. Sybille "has become my bosom companion,"
she told William Walton. "She is the best person to talk writing with
that I have ever found; she loves going over, by the hour, words, effects,
motives; she is such a help it isn't even true; has a fine literary education
so one can listen to her; and I like her own work."

Several times a week Martha drove into the city in her little Fiat
Topolino to see Sybille, and the two women spent hours intensively
picking over not only the act and art of writing but the minutiae of
each character, the nuance of every scene. Although their literary styles
were very different, the two shared a number of personal character-
istics: restless, perfectionist, and given to frequent periods of anxiety
and depression. For both, writing was a vital part of their existence,
although Sybille was less methodical, less accustomed to routine than
Martha; while Sybille had periodic bursts of working hard, Martha,
an experienced journalist, was ruthlessly disciplined, long used to the
intractable demands of the deadline. Sybille explained to Martha how
important to her their partnership was. "This letting me in on your

work is a true pleasure for me, a stimulus for my own work, and I think it's a privilege, something <u>you</u> give." And Martha for her part was equally enthusiastic. "Sybille dear . . . I take everything, I take greedily, with both hands, without consideration, sparing you nothing . . . There is absolutely no sense in my being in Italy except this astounding, unexpected sense of having you to do my work with." Sybille was very moved when Martha made her one of two dedicatees of *The Honeyed Peace*, a collection of short stories published during this period.

Although devoted friends and colleagues, in some areas the two women were somewhat less compatible. Martha found lesbianism distasteful ("There is nothing I do not know about Lesbians," she told Walton, "except how they make love; I couldn't bear to ask that for fear of hearing"); while Sybille for her part was critical of what she saw as Martha's streak of American vulgarity. When for the first time Sybille visited Martha at her farmhouse she was appalled by the interior, which to Sybille was distastefully reminiscent of California. "All windows closed . . . everything spotless," she reported to Allanah. In the bedroom "the servants (3) had switched on the electric blanket, laid out a white nylon *plissée* nightgown, a bed jacket, white mules, the dinner table laid with doilies, little salt arrangements . . . My dear, I had a cold shiver . . . M's workroom is padded, noiseless, cut off. It gave me the creeps." Worse was when they sat down to dinner and Sybille to her horror was served with tinned tomato soup. But then she already knew that Martha was shockingly indifferent to what she ate, while Martha for her part was irritated by what she regarded as Sybille's gastronomic obsessiveness. "Do you realise that not a chapter of your present book is without detailed eating?" she complained of the novel in progress. "People do meet at meals; good. It cannot be avoided. But the menus can be skimped. I <u>know</u> I am right. There is too much of it . . . PLEASE Sybille."

Meanwhile Sybille continued to commute between Paris and Rome. While in Paris Sybille was constantly in touch with Evelyn by letter, always guilty at leaving her so much on her own, yet reassured by Evelyn's stability and goodness of heart. "She has the most astounding qualities," she told Martha. "Not only unselfish, but <u>incapable</u> of self-pity or dramatisation. I really believe she is happy."

And it was true that Evelyn by temperament was both sensible and calm, neither given to panic nor easily annoyed. Sybille was the centre of her life, and her admiration and respect never wavered. "Her heart and mind are so good and absolutely uniquely giving," she noted in her diary. "And the work, the writing, the scrupulous love of writing, that's altogether wonderful." At the same time Evelyn recognised her lover's failings, and understood very well that although Sybille was undoubtedly devoted, she had many different worlds and levels of emotional attachment that had little to do with her. During Sybille's absences Evelyn profoundly missed her, and yet she peacefully continued with her routines, writing almost daily to her "DEAR Beast" to report on what she had done, whom she had seen, and, most important, the meals she had prepared and eaten, described in minute and sensuous detail. "Oh his pot-roast: he took off the lid of fat, and put it back into the oven (mod-slow) until his fagiolini and potatoes were ready . . . Ate quantities of meatie and sauce (pure meat-glaze, my how strong and good) and strips of pancetta and grasso di vitello, and small boiled potatoes and fagiolini with oil and lemon too, and then had potatoes and salad with sauce and oil and lemon, MY it was good."

When in Paris Sybille as usual stayed with Esther and Katzi, Esther having recently moved into a comfortable apartment in the rue Madame. Sybille's relations with Esther continued affectionate and relaxed, helped by the fact that, at least for the moment, Esther's drinking was under control. Katzi, however, she soon came to find intolerable. With her now blonde-streaked hair, her painted nails and showy costume jewellery, Katzi exasperated Sybille, banging and clattering about in her full skirts and high heels, cigarette in hand, arguing with almost everything Sybille said. "My sister is an amoral nitwit. Her every touch rubs me the wrong way, and she knows it, resents it." There were constant spats between the two, their shouting matches entertaining Esther and making her laugh. Nonetheless the three of them continued to live together, spending most evenings in each other's company, and often entertaining friends to dinner at home.

One evening a new guest appeared at the rue Madame, Eda Lord, with whom Allanah had previously been deeply infatuated. Eda, who was briefly in Paris with her lover, Hilary Williams, had encountered Sybille one afternoon as she was walking past Les Deux Magots in

Saint-Germain. "A soft voice called Sybille—I turned and there was Eda. Will you speak to me, she said. My dear, I said, of course. And we sat down, and drank Coca-Cola (only thing one could think of to ask the insistent waiter) and talked, and I was really very pleased. Eda has great charm . . . I asked her, and her friend Mrs. Williams, in for drinks here, later in the evening." When at the appointed hour Eda and Hilary arrived, Sybille was in the kitchen stirring saucepans and opening bottles of wine. Esther, hospitable as ever, immediately insisted they stay for dinner, which they did, and Sybille found the evening exceptionally enjoyable. "Eda was very affectionate, and I found myself being so too." The pleasure and excitement Sybille felt was to remain with her for some time.

Towards the end of 1953, when Sybille was again in Paris, Evelyn for the first time was invited to stay. The prospect made her uneasy: well aware that neither Esther nor Katzi had the slightest interest in her, she nonetheless believed she must accept for Sybille's sake. And indeed from the moment of her arrival, Evelyn felt an outsider. "They don't care for me," she noted in her diary, "but I must not let them see I know that." Katzi, true to form, was particularly brusque and impatient. "Says: 'why don't you go out?' Says: '*comment, vous avez bouffez tout le pain?* [what, you've gobbled all the bread?]' . . . Says: '*alors, vous êtes fini?* [so, have you finished?]' Because I sit on chewing slowly after she's left the luncheon table . . . E is bored, squirms visibly. Katzi is angry and bored . . . S says nonsense, nonsense, enjoy yourself, but that's impossible, one cannot be happy feeling unwanted."

In the morning Evelyn remained in her bedroom, reading, sewing, writing her diary and making plans for a children's book she had in mind. In the afternoon she explored the city and once or twice met friends she had known years before in New York. After a few days, much to her relief, the atmosphere lightened and she began to feel more welcome, Esther smiling and benign, Katzi much friendlier. Evelyn was perceptive about the relationship between the two sisters, the tensions and unspoken resentments that simmered below the surface. "I am so surprised to hear that S 'never laughs,' that she is so 'serious' poor K has to retire in the evenings for boredom. The point is of course, that S laughs all the time, only her jokes and interests are incomprehensible to

K, and K's easy nightclub gaiety is not merely incomprehensible to S, but she disapproves, sees it as symbol of all the easy vulgarity, the lack of taste etc, which it is. I feel a fool, laughing with K when she dances about, singing her nightclub songs (as she did last night, before bed, weaving about, reminiscently, in her peignoir); she looked so happy then. 'Oh, that's the life,' she seems to say."

For Evelyn, her stay in Paris, if not wholly enjoyable, had provided her with a much deeper understanding of the complexities of Sybille's situation; it had also served to clarify the relationship between them. By the time she returned to Rome, Evelyn had regained her emotional stability while also attaining a new sense of liberty. "Felt free, and also, more independent . . . for the first time truly . . . independent of S. NOT less loving—but independent . . . My life depends on ME, so finally, possibly along with this small drama, it has become a practical working REALITY. Darling S, the most valuable of human beings I know, is my beloved valued creature, not my prop or my crutch."

While in Paris, Sybille had been working not on her novel but on a long article describing a journey she had made earlier in the year to Switzerland. In Rome during the spring she had felt particularly restless, "trapped in my recluse life here . . . trapped also by the complete lack of money which makes even an evening at a Roman trattoria something as financially impossible as say an evening at Glyndebourne." Fortunately she was rescued first by Martha, who gave her a generous $200, enough to live on for several months, with the promise of more whenever she needed it; then by the final payment from Harper's in New York for *The Sudden View*; added to this was the magnificent sum of $1,200 from the American magazine *House Beautiful* for four cookery articles she and Evelyn had written together. Temporarily relieved of financial worry, Sybille immediately began planning her escape. Esther wanted to spend the summer in the mountains, and as Austria was out of the question for Sybille—"I still cannot bear a Germanic country"—they eventually agreed on Switzerland. "I am rather looking forward to it," Sybille told Martha. "I long for surrounding order and responsibility."

In August 1953, Sybille from Rome and Esther from Paris met at the station in Geneva, from where they travelled by train to Berne, then on to Gersau on Lake Lucerne. Although Sybille was enchanted by the scenery glimpsed from their carriage window—"past the vineyards, past grey-stone chateaux . . . past orchards, fir trees, cuckoo-clock houses, village spires"—Gersau itself was a disappointment, "clean, honest, stolid, but no charm, no mystery, no magic." Far worse, however, was the discovery that her fellow guests at the hotel were German Swiss. This appalled her, particularly as she was obliged to speak to them in German: "one is automatically taken for a *Reichs Deutsche.* God forbid." When Sybille went down to the lake to bathe she found the dreaded *Schweizerdeutschen* already in the water. "The Germans talk about my slow descent into that liquid Frigidaire (*'sie hat ja Gänsehaut* [you have gooseflesh]' . . . HOW I HATE THEM) When I was in they all said, snuffling in the water, *'herrlich, herrlich* [glorious, glorious]' to each other. Well it wasn't magnificent it was just extremely steely bone-touchingly cold."

From that moment on, however, Sybille began to enjoy herself. Every morning, dressed in shorts, striped jersey and espadrilles, a cardigan tied round her waist, knapsack on her shoulders, she left Esther at the hotel while she strode off into the mountains for day-long walks by herself, "smelling the moss, hay, with the sound of the brooks, passing the goitered localry saying *Grüsse* [greetings] . . . E is most considerate," Sybille reported to Evelyn, "but has expressed a wish to walk herself, which means 30 minutes (perhaps) to a café with a view." As the days passed, Sybille came to love the country more and more. "A resurgence of health, physical activity and traveller's curiosity. The excitement of discovering a new country. I <u>have</u> fallen for it . . . its happiness, innocence and kindliness."

But after a week this peaceful existence was suddenly disrupted by a telegram, followed by a telephone call, from Martha announcing her imminent arrival. Martha had been in Yugoslavia, it appeared, and now, restless as ever, had decided to drive nearly 1,000 miles to join Sybille in Gersau. Privately Sybille was dismayed, knowing how disruptive Martha's presence could be. "M said isn't it 'rather fun.' To me it's rather grave," she told Evelyn. "Also will she stay one night, two, three, hate it . . . Will she turn me against it all? One of the points here for me was inner freedom. So you see. Yet I feel ungrateful . . . I suppose I don't want to be another paving stone on M's road of disillusionment." The next day Martha's little Topolino drew up outside the hotel. "It made me feel odd, unsettled, unreal. There was M sitting & powdering her face, then I opened the door and said Hello, and she said Hello, isn't this fun. And I felt heavy and shy, but swiftly we got up to her room and into sneakers and off we were for a walk . . . and then we were sitting on a bench above Gersau under an apple tree, looking at a view I had often looked at . . . and there she was *en Chair et Os* [in flesh and bone], and it felt flat and strange."

The immediate problem was with Esther, whom Martha had met briefly in Rome and instantly disliked. Sybille's "beloved," she had reported to William Walton, "is six foot two, wall-eyed and talks like an early American primer." Now, as Sybille feared, this second encounter was equally awkward. Esther, who joined the two women for tea, was silent at first, then suddenly launched into an unstoppable spate of name-dropping anecdotes about people of no interest to Martha. Martha for her part made little attempt to hide her boredom, within a very short while leaving to spend the rest of the evening in her room. Upset, Sybille went to find Esther "and explain and be nice—and that meant beer in a v. noisy *Gasthaus* . . . I feel I am taking this trip from E somehow. I don't know. It should be more joyful."

The next day she and Martha set off for a whirlwind five-day tour of the country, hurtling along in the Topolino, up tortuous mountain passes, by the side of lakes, through valleys and orchards, past castles and picture-book villages. Whenever they stopped to look at a view, within minutes Martha would say, "Let's shove"—and on they shoved, pausing only to eat and sleep. Luckily Martha was in a good mood, and Sybille quickly found herself enjoying the expedition, particularly happy that for once Martha was tolerant of her love of food. "Oddly enough M and I ate superbly and often, though at odd hours. Toblerone is what M likes best," while one of Sybille's greatest treats was Turkish cigarettes, "the most expensive, and I think the best in the world . . . They are the only cigarette that comes near a cigar in enjoyment . . . I smoked mine to the last fraction of an inch."

Shortly after Martha left, Sybille and Esther also departed, Sybille sad at leaving a country she had by now come to love. After a brief stay in Rome, she returned to Paris to work on an article about her Swiss experience. Entitled "The Anchor and the Balloon," the piece gives a lively, impressionistic account of the people and places she encountered, and in particular her travels with Martha, endearingly portrayed with all her impatience and curiosity. Sybille's sentences, sometimes a paragraph in length, whirl the reader up mountains and into pastures, through long walks in the country, swimming in icy rivers and lakes, exploring Berne, Geneva, Zurich, Lucerne, shopping and lunching, idling over coffee while reading the paper. In Lucerne she listens to Mozart played in the open air. "It was pitch-dark and music and musicians came curiously distorted over the intervening water. The strings, now muted, now carried, floated thin; conductor and violins were reflected, enormously agitated, tail-coated cardboard frogs . . . The whole quite unreal; lovely, though perhaps too charged with romanticism. Mozart does not need this setting." With her keen novelist's eye, she also portrays with notable elan the characters she meets en route, most memorably the hotel manager in Gersau, "in black coat, silk tie and polished boots," unfailingly courteous as he beadily assesses his customers. The tone is powerfully subjective so that the reader is always aware that they are seeing the country through the author's eyes.

"The Anchor and the Balloon" was submitted first to *Cornhill*, which turned it down, then sent by Allanah to Stephen Spender, editor of *Encounter*. Spender replied he would be delighted to run it if Sybille would cut it by half; this she did, and the article appeared in the issue of August 1954.[*]

Although keen to return to work on her novel, Sybille felt restless and dissatisfied, longing for change, tired now of both Paris and Rome. "I don't like living in Rome any more," she wrote of the city which she had once loved so passionately. "I am not at all happy here . . . everything grates, from the slovenly mindless careless humourless people to the noise, to the dirt, the general unreliability." This was a pattern that was to be endlessly repeated, ecstatic love for a city alternating with deep distaste. Over time London, Paris and Rome, the three capitals in which Sybille spent most of her life, would in turn be both vilified and

---

* "The Anchor and the Balloon" was later included in a collection of Sybille's articles, *As It Was: Pleasures, Landscapes and Justice* (Sinclair-Stevenson, 1990), then in *Pleasures and Landscapes* (Daunt Books, 2014).

adored. London, where she was to live the longest, was the ideal city with its magnificent trees and peaceful parks, and alternately "horrible, plebeian, ugly, confused . . . and so dirty." Similarly, Paris was found to be ravishingly beautiful and at other times repulsively ugly, "a monstrous agglomeration of filth and greed, disguised as civilisation." Now it was the turn of her beloved Rome, considered deeply depressing, the weather intolerable and the Italians "mindless, mechanical, dirty, dishonest."

Fortunately for Sybille's state of mind, at the beginning of 1954 she was able to leave Rome for a couple of weeks in England. Her visit had been arranged by Martha, whose situation had substantially changed. Recently Martha had agreed to marry Tom Matthews, a wealthy American widower, previously editor-in-chief of *Time* magazine in New York. Martha was not in love, but she liked and respected Matthews, was tired of Italy, and was particularly anxious to secure a stable home for her young son, Sandy.

On arrival in London Sybille stayed in Chelsea with Allanah and her lover Fay Blacket Gill, but the atmosphere quickly curdled as a mutual dislike developed between Sybille and Fay, whom Sybille described as "philistine and difficult." Fortunately Sybille was soon able to escape by joining Martha for a few days in a house she had taken in the country, although this turned out to be little better as Martha was in "a murderous mood" and Sandy a source of constant irritation. "Sandy burst in at 8.45 . . . chatted through my pot of tea, dropped my pen, put on my rings . . . he may be insecure, but he is spoilt too . . . [and] I am not in such a state of awe at the sacred demands of childhood this morning as I ought to be." Soon afterwards all three returned to London, Martha's wedding to Tom taking place at Caxton Hall on 4 February 1954, with Sybille and Moura Budberg, an old friend of Martha's, as witnesses.

A few days later Sybille returned to Paris to join Evelyn, who was again staying with Esther and Katzi. As before Evelyn had kept devotedly in touch, almost daily sending long letters interspersed with little notes written in their private baby-talk. ("He LOVE him-y . . . Now is lunch, he go, den he post this, to his DEAR . . . spruce himself a little, fluff his hair, scent himself . . . and out he go.") To Sybille's relief, relations between the three women were far easier than before, Evelyn, now amused by Katzi's snapping, had grown genuinely fond of Esther, the two of them "instinctive conspirators against K . . . I don't find E boring at all, anymore," she told Sybille, "except when drunk, but that's something else."

During this period Sybille worked hard on her novel, regularly reporting her progress, or lack of it, to Martha. "[I] must say how I thank you. I had been trying to work on that beastly novel before your letter came . . . and at last today the ice broke . . . I seem to need words, your kind, so much. It's like cranking up those old motor cars, so that their own engine can start running." By the end of March, Sybille and Evelyn were back in Rome, where Sybille looked forward to an uninterrupted period of writing interspersed with some vigorous rooftop gardening. But then in early summer, to her surprise, the Huxleys arrived; on their first visit to Italy since before the war they were planning to spend a couple of weeks in the city, then go on to France to stay with one of Maria's sisters.

At first Sybille was apprehensive: it was now nearly fourteen years since she had last seen them and she was unsure what to expect. When on their first evening she walked up to their hotel at the top of the Spanish Steps she found to her relief that the couple were almost as she had first known them, Aldous relaxed and more handsome than ever, Maria pale and thin but cheerful and lively. "All is joy and ease," Sybille reported to Martha. "Very happy. And such jokes . . . Aldous angelic . . . giving out a plenitude of serenity, calm, benignity . . . It is all as though one had never parted, not going back to youth, but a circle. Happy family feeling . . . almost a sense of roots." Later Sybille described Aldous at this period as very different from the strained, tormented figure she had known during the war. "There was a sleekness, a smoothed-outness . . . and this had an extraordinary peace-inducing effect as though one were sitting . . . at the feet of a large and benign cat." Initially Maria, too, seemed much the same, "*en beauté*, animated, gay," although it was not long before Sybille noticed a sudden sinking into tiredness, which seemed to be more than ordinary exhaustion.

During the next couple of weeks Sybille saw the Huxleys almost daily, usually in the evenings after they had returned from a day's sightseeing. Over the past few years Aldous had become immersed in the study of various forms of parapsychology, then much in vogue in California, and to Sybille's slight unease the subject of Aldous's own "magic" was now at the centre of attention. When at one point she mentioned she was suffering from a period of insomnia, he immediately offered to cure it with what he called his "animal magnetism." Submitting somewhat reluctantly, Sybille sat with her back to Aldous, who rolled up his shirtsleeves, then started pummelling with his right hand up and down her spine, while the fingers of his left rested lightly on the base of her neck, "like a violinist's hand on his keys. 'Aldous, what is that for?' 'Ah,' he said, 'I haven't the faintest idea, that's where the abracadabra comes in.' " The first phase completed, Aldous continued by making wave-like motions with his arms, while intoning in a solemn, slow voice, "You are going to have a deep, deep sleep, a restful sleep, a deep refreshing sleep . . ." Later Sybille refrained from telling him she had stayed awake throughout the whole of the following three nights.

In the course of one of their evenings together, Maria began talking of a friend of theirs whom she said she would like Sybille to meet. Laura Archera, born in Italy, now living in California, was a lay psychotherapist, currently on a visit to Rome. Shortly afterwards the Huxleys brought Laura with them for drinks on the roof with Sybille and Evelyn. Laura, in her early forties, slender and dark-haired with large brown eyes, was high-spirited and attractive, not at all "the forbidding esoteric therapist I had half expected." Sybille took to her at once, finding her charming and sympathetic. At one point while Aldous was in full flood expounding another of his theories, Maria and Laura quietly disappeared indoors, where they remained talking together for some while. "There was a scent of honeysuckle, jasmine, tobacco flower," Sybille wrote of the evening. "Above us, garlands of vines and in their interstices the sky. There was Aldous's voice . . . and I knew as if I had been there that Maria was speaking at last about her illness."

As was soon to become clear, Maria was terminally ill with cancer, a diagnosis she had accepted with characteristic equanimity. "To me," she had told Laura, "dying is no more than going from one room to another." Maria was anxious, however, both to protect Aldous from the reality of her condition and at the same time to make provision for his future well-being. Aldous for his part understood at one level how serious the situation was but on the surface at least preferred to remain in denial. "Of course he knew," said one of his sisters-in-law. "But he pushed it away. Didn't want to talk about it. He was protecting himself from a truth that was unbearable." Maria's most urgent project had been to find a replacement for herself, a second wife, and it was about this that she had talked to Laura. Bringing Aldous together with Laura, Sybille wrote later, "was a kind of consecration." On the Huxleys' last evening in Rome, Sybille and Evelyn joined them for dinner at a trattoria near the Piazza Colonna. "Afterwards I went with them as far as their hotel. At the door, Maria turned from me. 'We don't have to say goodbye,' she said, 'we've had our goodbye.' "

Sybille was never to see Maria again. After Rome the Huxleys went on to France before returning to California, where on 12 February 1955 Maria died. A little over a year later Aldous and Laura Archera were married.

Meanwhile, soon after the Huxleys' departure, Sybille arranged another meeting with Laura. Maria had talked of Laura with enthusiasm, praising the effectiveness of her unconventional form of therapy, which she was sure would cure Sybille's increasing vulnerability to anxiety and depression. Over the next fortnight Sybille saw Laura for several long sessions, during which the two women formed an affectionate friendship, Sybille convinced, at least for a time, that Laura had finally enabled her to achieve a new stability, both mental and emotional. "No orthodox analyst or doctor could do what I think Laura Archera can . . . It has made a total difference to my life. To everything," she told Martha. "The effect was extraordinary . . . It has filled me with lightness, strength and hope . . . liberation from fear, a new ease and openness . . . And I believe now, entirely, that everything is curable."

In August Sybille left Rome for a prolonged stay in the south of France with Allanah at Les Bastides. Here she planned to immerse herself in her novel, energised by the "tremendous experience" of Laura's "voodoo," as she later referred to it. Unfortunately this buoyant mood was not to last, and before long Sybille found herself irritated and depressed, constantly distracted by the extensive building work under way on the house and by the people around her, in particular by

Terence, a little English boy whom Allanah, together with Fay Blacket Gill, had recently adopted. "Bastides quite the wrong place," she complained to Martha. "[I am] stuck, in writing, in everything, hedged in, repressed, angry, trying, trying, trying, getting nowhere. Not been able to write a word since end of August, though at desk, and quite frightened about it." Martha, accustomed to Sybille's complaints about staying with Allanah, was brisk in her reply. Les Bastides "has always been a disaster," she told her. "You are like a repetitive lemming, going annually to your doom."

The following month, however, Sybille was able to escape for a fortnight, travelling to Switzerland, where she experienced much the same lightness of spirit as before. The purpose of the expedition was to buy a car, a little grey Citroën 2CV, a present from Esther, which had been found for her by her old motoring colleague, Pierre Mimerel. A couple of days after the sale went through, Sybille set out on the long journey from Berne back to Rome, relishing every moment of the "monotonous, strenuous, solitary driving days." As it was too expensive to run the car on a daily basis, it was to be used for long journeys only, kept meanwhile near the tomb of Augustus by the Tiber, "with an anti-aircraft balloon to cover it, and an old scoundrel to keep an eye on it occasionally for a thousand lire a month. I sometimes go and polish it. I love that car," she told Martha. "It will carry one, if God wills it, to London . . . So look at it not as wickedness but a bid for freedom."

Cheered by her acquisition, Sybille settled down to a final bout of intense concentration on what she described as "that ogre, the snail novel." Finally in January 1955 it was done, and as before Sybille turned to Martha, not only for her critical opinion but also for help in finding a new publisher as she was determined not to return to Gollancz. Although Martha had her reservations about the book—"the novel seems to me almost too carefully embroidered, as if you never let yourself go"—she promised to do everything she could to help. First, however, Sybille had to decide on a title, her initial suggestions—"The Choice & the Moments," "A Wheel," "All that Was Possible," "Failure and Interference," "An Inheritance"—all disliked by Martha, particularly the last, which "sounds like Anthony Powell to me, and I cannot say worse." Finally, after a few further weeks of struggle Sybille came up with *A Legacy*, which both agreed was by far the best choice.

Sybille had been disappointed by the slow sales in England of *The Sudden View*, and was excited when Martha arranged for her to meet her publisher friend, George Weidenfeld. Weidenfeld, from an Austrian Jewish family, had arrived in London as a young man not long before the war, setting up his firm, Weidenfeld & Nicolson, in 1948. Short and plump, with dark eyes and a pasty white face, George was clever, sociable and intensely ambitious; immediately sensing an interesting opportunity, he invited the two women to luncheon at the Ritz. The occasion went well, Martha later reporting that Sybille was now "certainly established in George's mind as the next best thing to Henry James." As George himself had little interest in fiction, the manuscript would be read by his chief editor, Sonia Orwell, George Orwell's widow, who had previously been employed by Cyril Connolly on his magazine, *Horizon*.

Before any contract could be signed, however, Sybille needed to extract herself from Gollancz, who was reluctant to release her. Again it was Martha who took control, introducing Sybille to her own literary agent, Elaine Greene. A New Yorker, married to the brother of Graham Greene, Elaine was director of the literary branch of MCA (Music Corporation of America) in London. When Sybille first met her at her office in Piccadilly, she found Elaine both practical and friendly. Elaine was impressed by *A Legacy* ("It will not, of course, be everybody's meal, but no one ever expected—or wanted—you to dish up anything but the finest quality caviar") and agreed to arrange matters with Gollancz. Privately, however, she was dismayed that Sybille had chosen to be published by Weidenfeld: "no fait accompli has ever distressed me more," she was later to tell her. Weidenfeld meanwhile was reported to be delighted at the prospect of Sybille joining his list, offering her £200, exactly twice the amount paid by Gollancz for *The Sudden View*.

It was at this point that Sybille was introduced to Sonia Orwell, "a pretty, blowsy, reddish blonde, full of *joie de vivre* and generous to a fault." Although Sybille later claimed that Sonia had had reservations about *A Legacy*, she was nonetheless an excellent editor, whose comments and criticism her author willingly accepted. The two women took to each other, enjoying long, gossipy conversations about their mutual acquaintance. On a couple of occasions Sybille was invited to dine alone with Sonia at her little flat in Percy Street, where the two of them downed quantities of red wine while Sonia provided divertingly salacious accounts of Weidenfeld's current affair with Barbara Skelton, Cyril Connolly's second wife.

Sybille signed her contract almost a year before the date of publication, a period full of restlessness and unease. Her financial situation was particularly precarious, with Esther currently paying the rent on the flat in Rome, which Sybille, now hoping to settle in England, was longing to leave. After finishing her book in January 1955, she spent the next twelve months almost constantly on the move, in February travelling from Rome to Sanary to stay with the Mimerels, then to Paris, where Esther had recently moved back to the rue de Lille, into another spacious apartment; after this there was a holiday in Switzerland with Martha and Tom, then back to Rome before moving on to London in August; then to Paris again, followed by several weeks at Les Bastides with Allanah. In September Sybille left for a month's motoring tour of Spain and Portugal with Esther and a couple of American friends, her first experience of Spain since her visit there with the Huxleys before the war. Then it was a return to Provence, followed by a few days in Geneva, then Paris, and finally in November to London, where, remarkably, Sybille was to remain for over six months.

During this peripatetic period, Sybille inevitably saw little of Evelyn, who spent much of her time on her own, working on a children's book, *Tortoise and Turtle*, "which I find delightful: very simply written; full of jokes," Sybille reported to Martha. As the flat in Rome was to be let, arrangements were made for Evelyn to move to London, where eventually she and Sybille hoped to settle. Meanwhile, Evelyn needed to find work; her first job was in Surrey, as paid companion to a Mrs. Torrens, a widow, a position Sybille had found for her through that famously genteel employment agency, Universal Aunts. It was Evelyn's first experience of England, but although she saw Sybille only occasionally, she settled contentedly into her new existence, looking forward to the day their life together could be resumed. To supplement her small income, Evelyn had taken to making lampshades—"he rather loves working the raffia," she reported—which she was soon selling to a number of shops and decorators and eventually to Selfridges.

By the beginning of 1956, Sybille in London was living in a tiny apartment in Osten Mews, South Kensington, while Evelyn, whose job with Mrs. Torrens had come to an end, rented a room in Ashburn Place, only a few minutes' walk away. Finally in March *A Legacy* was published, dedicated to Evelyn. "Yes—Evelyn Gengel,"* Sybille told her. "The Book, such as it is, is dedicated to you. And quite Right TOO! (<u>Such</u> a pleasure to me.) Love, my Love. S."

A Legacy, regarded by many as Sybille's finest work, is closely based on recollections of her own childhood and of what she had absorbed of her parents' history before she was born. The story follows the interlinking through marriage of three families in a newly unified Germany. Like the Herzes, her father's first parents-in-law, the Jewish Merzes are wealthy industrialists, inward-looking and resolutely uncultured, living in suffocating luxury in Berlin, while the Feldens and Bernins, both Roman Catholic, have long been established in the country, in the bucolic south, near the border with France.

The novel opens with a magnificent description of the Merzes in their over-stuffed mansion on Voss Strasse, indolent and self-indulgent, with no interest in politics or the arts or indeed in anything except their own comfort. The Merzes "never went anywhere, except to take a cure, and then they went in a private railway carriage, taking their own sheets." The head of the family, Grandpapa Merz, still regards himself at nearly ninety as a dashing Lothario, while Grandmama, short, placid and very stout, rarely moves from her armchair, her sole domestic duty to interview the cook for half an hour every morning. One son is an idle bureaucrat, while another, Edu, a compulsive gambler, is married to Sarah, a wealthy wife with whom he moves, according to season, from Berlin to London, Paris and the Riviera.

Of the two rural families, the Feldens, like the Schoenebecks, are "old, landed, agreeably off without being in the least rich and of no particular distinction . . . the centre of their world was France. They ignored, despised, and later dreaded, Prussia." The eldest son marries into the Bernin family, while the second, Julius ("Jules"), leads a solitary and sybaritic life, wandering between France and Spain, devoted to a large menagerie of animals and to the courtship of beautiful women.

---

* A joke spelling of Evelyn's surname which Sybille occasionally used.

The third son, Johannes, a docile simpleton, brings disaster on the family after running away from his regiment only days after his enrolment. At first vigorously pursued by the army, he is eventually left in peace for over thirty years. Then suddenly his case is revived by the War Office, Johannes is arrested and accidentally shot dead. The event is seized upon by the press, with "the Felden scandal" purveyed to the nation in slavering detail to the horror and humiliation of Johannes's family.

On receiving the news of his brother's arrest Jules, by now in his fifties, reluctantly returns to Germany from Spain. After the early death of his first wife, Jules had married again, to a beautiful and affluent young Englishwoman. Caroline, strong-willed and intelligent, had quickly become bored with her life in Spain, but before she can leave her husband the news reaches them of Johannes's death, and it is while on the long train journey back to Berlin that Caroline realises she is pregnant. With the press feeding ravenously off the Felden scandal, and with her own condition to consider, Caroline feels trapped, accepting her obligation to stay with Jules, at least for a while. She buys a small estate in the south of the country; a daughter is born; when the little girl, Francesca, is a few years old her mother finally returns to England, leaving the child in the care of her father. It is only after Jules's death a few years later that mother and daughter are eventually reunited.

A Legacy is an extraordinary feat of recollection and reconstruction on Sybille's part, powerfully evocative and indicating an exceptional clarity in vision and understanding. The story draws copiously on Sybille's own childhood memories, which, as she later remarked, "must have stayed in me suspended in amber." Vivid, sensual, impressionistic, the complex plot is shot through with wit and irony, as well as with a disturbing portentousness, a hint of darkness to come. The story moves between first and third person, with the little girl, Francesca, appearing intermittently as narrator, a version of the Cheshire cat, as Sybille herself phrased it. From her earliest childhood Sybille had been alert to her surroundings and fascinated by family history, both when living with her parents at Feldkirch and while staying with the Herzes in Berlin. "The sources of *A Legacy*," as she later explained, "were the indiscretions of tutors and servants, the censures of nannies, the dinner-table talk of elderly members of a stepfamily-in-law, my own father's talks, polished and visual; my mother's talent for presenting private events in the light of literary and historical interpretation." The characters of Jules and Caroline are immediately recognisable portrayals of her parents, Maximilian the isolated aesthete, Lisa with her flamboyant sexuality and love of sophisticated society. The depiction of Jules is particularly intriguing, with the balance between his exquisite courtesy and a ruthless self-absorption never quite explained—even perhaps not wholly comprehended by the author.

At a slightly further remove from actuality is the harrowing story of Johannes, concocted from the experience of two families, the Schoenebecks and the Gunthers. Like Johannes in the novel, Maximilian's elder brother, Gustav, had been cruelly mistreated at his military academy; while Sybille remembered Lisa's great friend, Mursel von Gunther, describing the sadism of a family tutor, which had resulted in the death of one brother and the lifetime's confinement of another to a mental institution. The repercussions caused by the fictional Felden scandal closely echo the Allenstein affair, when Gustav, then a major in the Prussian army, was shot dead by his wife's lover, the story seized upon by the campaigning journalist Maximilian Harden and spread widely throughout the country and abroad. In *A Legacy*, Sybille gives voice to her rage at the pain this caused her family, with Harden appearing barely disguised as Quintus Narden, "one of the most ruthless and accomplished publicists of the day."

As it evolves, the military theme in the novel begins to take on a more sinister significance, a foreshadowing of Germany's future, as do the final stages of the Merzes' history. After Grandpapa's death their fortune is found to be almost depleted, their wealth no longer sealing them off from the threat of an emerging anti-Semitism and the rapid rise of Prussian military ambition. "Much of what was allowed to happen in these decades was ill-conceived, cruel, bad," Sybille wrote later. "Is some of this a foundation of the vast and monstrous thing that followed? Did the private events I lightly draw upon leave some legacy? Writing about them made me think so."

With *A Legacy* based so closely on fact, Sybille was particularly anxious about the reaction of her sister, Katzi, who appears in the novel under her baptismal name, "Henriette." Katzi had not only lived for years at Voss Strasse but, unlike Sybille herself, was a blood relation of the Herzes. To Sybille's relief, however, Katzi told her that she liked the book, thought it "*admirablement écrit*" ("admirably written"), although she admitted she had been shocked by the lack of discretion about their father, and by the fact that Sybille had not troubled to disguise the Herz family name other than by changing the initial letter.

It was this last point that proved unexpectedly contentious. Not long after the book's publication, Sybille was summoned to meet several members of the Herz family, who had recently arrived on a visit to London. After a frigid half-hour she was left alone with the eldest of the group, Marta Strich, née Herz, daughter of the heiress portrayed in the book as Sarah Merz and of the rakish Edu. The conversation that followed was extremely uncomfortable as Marta, white-haired, discreetly elegant in a plain tweed suit, coldly described to Sybille the pain inflicted on the family by her "ghastly book." Why had Sybille made so little attempt to disguise the family name? Why had she not changed the name of the street where they lived? "You did not think? That is your answer? You just did not think? . . . My mother was not like that. Not like that at all." Sybille, mortified, offered profound apologies and gradually the atmosphere relaxed. " 'We were very angry with you, we wanted to make a libel suit.' 'And now you are no longer angry?' 'No, it is over now. You didn't think. It wasn't malice.' We shook hands and she said breaking into German '*Nichts fuer ungut* [no offence].' "

A Legacy was published on 17 March 1956. A few days earlier George Weidenfeld had invited Sybille to lunch, again at the Ritz. A little nervous but looking forward to the occasion, she was dismayed to find her publisher sullen and depressed. Weidenfeld "was in an awful mood, tired, sloppy, low," she told Martha. "He seems most tepid, tired, unenthusiastic about this book. Publishing going to the devil anyway, no one wants quality, we won't advertise before we get reviews . . . I hope we get some . . . [and] no, he doesn't know anyone special to send it to." To begin with it seemed such pessimism was justified, the first few notices unencouraging in tone, several reviewers bemused by the disconcerting non sequiturs and long passages of unattributed dialogue. "Some of Miss Bedford's creations might creep as 'extras' into the kind of world Proust created," wrote *The Times* condescendingly.

On the radio the reaction was even less favourable: the "critics on the Third Programme . . . tore it to pieces," Sybille reported gloomily to Allanah. "They called it pretentious feminine drivel."

It was now, with Sybille's spirits descending lower by the day, that Esther came to the rescue. A passionate admirer of the novel, Esther had been enraged by what she saw as Martha's disastrous interference, resulting in Sybille's move to "Weidengeld," as she disparagingly referred to him. Dismayed by the publisher's lethargy and lack of interest, Esther decided to take matters into her own hands, giving a copy to a friend of hers in Paris, Nancy Mitford, and asking Nancy to send it to her old ally, Evelyn Waugh. After reading the novel, Nancy wrote to Sybille. "My dear Mrs. Bedford," her letter began, "It would be absolutely impossible for me to tell you (I mean really to convey) how much I admire your book. It is certainly one of the very best novels I have ever read." There was only one small error that Nancy, supernaturally alert to such matters, felt she should point out. "The *Almanach de Gotha* (surely, I'm sure I'm right) only deals with princely & ducal families—?"

Three days later Nancy received a response from Waugh. "I am hugely grateful to you for sending me *A Legacy*. I read it straight through with intense pleasure." Inevitably he had a number of criticisms, in particular the author's distressing lack of knowledge about Catholicism, but overall he had been fascinated by the book and, he added teasingly, was very curious as to who "this brilliant 'Mrs. Bedford' could be. A cosmopolitan military man, plainly, with a knowledge of parliamentary government and popular journalism, a dislike for Prussians, a liking for Jews, a belief that everyone speaks French in the home." To this Nancy, who had recently met Sybille for the first time, replied, "The real Mrs. Bedford is a small, fair, intensely shy woman, about forty I suppose, half German. There is something very sweet about her, but never would you suspect talent & when a mutual friend sent me the book I dreaded having to read enough to be able to comment . . . Of course I was immobilised for days."

On 13 April, a short review by Waugh was published in the *Spectator*. "A novel has just appeared by a new writer of remarkable accomplishment," his article began, "a book of entirely delicious quality . . .

cool, witty, elegant." This was not to say the work did not have its weaknesses—a disruptive time sequence, for instance, in which "the daughter relates things she cannot possibly ever have known as though she were an eye witness." There were also indications of theological ignorance, a certain clumsiness in narrative technique, especially in the second half, "as though the author had taken a deep, unaccustomed draught of Henry James." But overall it was an exceptional work and "we gratefully salute a new artist."

For Sybille, Waugh's review changed everything. "Nothing that has been said about my work has given me so much pleasure," she later remarked. "It's the one thing I hang on to sometimes when I start to wonder what I have done with my life." Other laudatory reviews soon followed, among them one by Francis Wyndham in the *London Magazine*, who described the book as "original, witty, entertaining, informative, elegant, intelligent." Another, in *Encounter*, by Waugh's old friend Christopher Sykes, acclaimed Sybille as "a writer of extraordinary power. Her book is unconventional, bold, experimental . . . It has considerable faults and is probably not a masterpiece for that reason, but it is written with genius." It was Sykes, then working at the BBC, who also produced a dramatised version of *A Legacy*, to be broadcast on radio the following year.

Nine months after its British publication, the novel appeared in the States. Initially there had been little enthusiasm in New York, where it had been turned down by five firms, among them Knopf, Random House, and also by Cass Canfield at Harper's; Canfield, who had published *The Sudden View*, was reported as saying it was one of the dullest books he had ever read. But then Sybille, through her agent, Elaine Greene, received an offer from Simon & Schuster, which was gratefully accepted. Here her energetic young editor, Robert Gottlieb, "fell madly in love" with *A Legacy*. Convinced he had a masterpiece on his hands, he at once began promoting the book, writing dozens of letters to critics and well-known writers, publicising it as widely as possible. "We did everything," he later recalled. "And it worked."

A Legacy came out on 30 January 1957, and for several weeks appeared on the bestseller list of both the *New York Times* and the *Herald Tribune*. The book was bought for $1,500 by the Readers Subscription Club, whose editors were W. H. Auden, Lionel Trilling and Jacques Barzun, and to Sybille's particular delight received a laudatory review from Janet Flanner in the *New Yorker*. "Cosmopolitan, ironic, penetrating," Janet described it, "the most interesting, entertaining, and illuminating novel about high-class, old-fashioned Germans since Thomas Mann's *Buddenbrooks*, which it in no way resembles." Before long Simon & Schuster had sold 20,000 copies, which, as Bob Gottlieb later remarked, for such a European and elitist novel was "a highly unlikely success back in the fifties." To Sybille he wrote appreciatively, "We are simply delighted with the way the book has been received. It is for us a wonderful proof that we can publish books we really love and still MAKE MONEY."

While *A Legacy* was significantly to raise Sybille's professional reputation, it was now that her private life, too, was to change dramatically. At the beginning of the previous year, 1956, Sybille had been somewhat nervously awaiting the day of publication. She and Evelyn were still living apart in London while hoping soon to find a place they could share. They saw each other almost daily, Evelyn working industriously on her lampshades, helped by Sybille, who in her little Citroën took on the job of collecting the supplies of raffia and wire frames that Evelyn required. Sometimes the two of them had supper together in Sybille's tiny flat in Osten Mews, South Kensington, but more often Sybille, usually accompanied by Evelyn, spent the evening with old friends, among them Allanah and Fay Blacket Gill, Joan and Peter Churchill, Toni Muir, and Sybille's old friend from her Sanary days, Sylvester Gates, now a successful banker and contentedly settled with his second wife.

And there was also Martha, at this period still one of Sybille's closest and most trusted confidantes, now living with her husband in a large house in Chester Square, Belgravia. It was Martha who suggested one January day that the two of them should drive out to the country to see the famous gardens at Luton Hoo in Bedfordshire designed by Capability Brown. Afterwards they went to a local pub where they lunched off beer and beef sandwiches, an ending to an expedition that Sybille recalled as both pleasant and unremarkable. Returning to London in the late afternoon, Martha dropped Sybille off at Osten Mews. That same evening Sybille noted in her diary, "Everything changes."

It had been almost three years since Sybille had last seen Eda Lord, when they had encountered each other while in Paris in 1953. Now Eda and her lover Hilary Williams, with whom she had been living in Wales, had recently arrived in London, and were staying with Joan and Peter Churchill in their apartment near the Strand. It was almost certainly with the Churchills that Sybille and Eda met again, and on this occasion the effect on both was tumultuous. Over the next couple of weeks Sybille's brief diary entries chart her emotional state as she and Eda, now passionately in love, planned to meet whenever possible, Sybille in the grip of an overwhelming emotion, sometimes ecstatic, often in an agony of tension and anxiety. "A held-in day of pacing and inner monologues and waiting . . . Wait for telephone all day . . . Walk the block again and again at night. Not good . . . Desolate." Then one day, after lunching with Martha, "Come home and find message . . . Babbling with relief. Very warm . . . Radiant day . . . Everything more and more wonderful . . ."

As the weeks passed, the two saw each other whenever they could, intently discussing their plans for a future together. At this point they had known each other for more than twenty years and had many friends in common, even, in one instance, a lover: in France after the war Eda had had an affair with Allanah, who had been devastated when Eda subsequently left her for Hilary Williams. At forty-eight, Eda was four years older than Sybille, slender, fragile and pale-faced, with large dark eyes and beautiful thick hair streaked with grey. Shy and retiring, Eda gave the impression of "a wounded bird," in the words of one acquaintance, always arriving at social occasions clutching a thermos of coffee as in the past she had been a serious alcoholic. Now both she and Sybille were faced with uprooting their lives, breaking out of long-established relationships in order to begin again with each other, neither for a moment in doubt that this was what they must do. Being with Sybille, Eda said, "makes me feel as though I were a tail attached to a very bright comet."

Keeping the affair secret would not be possible for long, and both were deeply apprehensive about the impact of revealing the situation, Eda to Hilary, Sybille to her beloved Evelyn. For Sybille this was a traumatic period: she was restless and impatient when away from Eda, especially when in the company of Evelyn, who was now constantly on her nerves. After one evening at Evelyn's flat in Ashburn Place Sybille recorded, "I'm irritated bored and caged. Missing, missing, missing," and after another, this time at Osten Mews, "Ev[elyn] for din. Irritable. Do not behave well. But Ev does not seem to have noticed thank God . . . very restless; these evenings are painful . . ." Fortunately Hilary was often away, allowing Eda and Sybille to spend whole days and sometimes nights together. "First day to ourselves and the sweetness of it all," Sybille wrote on 22 March. "I go out quickly to do some shopping lunch here—work . . . D wonderful we make our dinner and eat it, then d leaves I do letters and tidy . . . to my joy she is back by 11 and still here till tomorrow . . . Happy, happy happy, bless -d-."* Eventually, as spring moved into summer, Sybille began to feel emotionally more stable, even on one occasion summoning up the courage to issue an invitation to a woman with an intimidating reputation, a writer whose work she had long admired. This was Ivy Compton-Burnett, whose novels Sybille had first begun reading when in her early twenties. In 1952 while living in Rome Sybille had spent six weeks composing a long letter to the revered author, earnestly analysing her works and expressing in great detail the reasons for her veneration. The letter, over 10,000 words, twenty-two pages long, was finally posted on 10 August. Some weeks later Sybille received a reply. "Dear Mrs. Bedford, Thank you so much for your letter. I shall always treasure it as a possession. Yours sincerely, Ivy Compton-Burnett." Four years later in London Sybille finally met the distinguished author, now in her seventies, at a luncheon party of Allanah's: "sticky" was the adjective used to describe the occasion in Sybille's diary. Undeterred, Sybille a little later wrote inviting Miss Compton-Burnett to tea.

Both nervous and excited, Sybille went to great trouble to prepare for the occasion, enlisting the support of Eda and also of a new friend, Jane Stockwood, features editor of *Harper's Bazaar*, who had already met the notoriously difficult author. As a gesture of respect, Sybille "struggled into a skirt" before carefully laying the table, covered in

* In writing her diary Sybille struggled with finding a coded abbreviation for Eda's name. "E" was not possible as that had always belonged to Esther. Instead she used the middle letter: thus Eda is usually referred to as "D," "-d-" or simply "d."

a borrowed white linen cloth: three kinds of biscuit, a Fuller's walnut cake, toast, butter, jam and Gentleman's Relish. At 4:15 the doorbell rang. "I opened manfully. Miss CB tottered in . . . black kid-gloves kept on, mackintosh and moth-holed felt tricorne hat." As Sybille later described the experience to Martha, her guest "gave a sharp look round. 'You know Miss Stockwood?' 'No.' Miss S never recovered from this. It was like having a corpse on hand. I was kept nose to teapot and toast rack; the burden resting on Eda's magpie chatter. There was a very slow sentence every other five minutes. Miss CB ate steadily and we sat at the tea table for five quarters of an hour. She would break up a slice of toast into a mound of mice dice and butter every single dice, and then dab it with Gentleman's Relish. Same with jam . . . Conversation languished. I cut the Fuller's cake (6/6, six and sixpence, oh). Miss CB declined. I almost cried . . . She stayed till nearly 7 . . . We were all dead flies afterwards . . . What a hold this strange (put-on?) dragon has over people. Why?"

Subsequently, hospitality was returned and Sybille was invited to tea by Ivy at her "stark lugubrious flat in Braemar Mansions . . . [I] went through trepidation as the time drew near . . . and awaited future approaches of her tea hour, a strict 4 p.m., as one awaits the tumbrel." Despite the daunting nature of these encounters, Sybille continued respectfully to keep in touch, and for the rest of her life continued to regard Ivy Compton-Burnett as one of the greatest novelists of the age.

During the weeks following the start of Sybille's affair with Eda, the knowledge that she must eventually tell everything to Evelyn filled her with dread. When the moment came, however, Evelyn was typically generous, entirely sympathetic, promising Sybille her wholehearted support. And in a way the situation provided Evelyn with a welcome chance of release. While in London Evelyn had increasingly felt she was wasting her time: she had few friends of her own, her work was little more than a hobby, and it began to appear obvious that she should return to the States, which she had left over six years before. Sybille agreed that this was the right decision, although well aware of how painful their parting would be. "I shall miss her very much indeed," she confessed to Allanah. "I am awed when I look upon these years of unflagging unselfishness and kindness." And to Martha she wrote of Evelyn, "Her conduct to me, all those years, and during the last months is of such quality that one can only think of it with bated breath. And where did it get her? She would not even ask herself that question." Finally on 22 July Evelyn sailed from Liverpool to New York, where she was to live with her parents. Soon after arriving she wrote to Sybille, perhaps in part to prevent her "dear Beast" from worrying, that "I cannot imagine London . . . cannot even force [*sic*] to recall one instant in England . . . This here and now is so immediate everything else has simply receded . . . Darling heart & beloved creature, all is well."

The following month Eda made the break with Hilary, and she and Sybille were at last able to live together openly. Although both knew that this was what they wanted, nonetheless the process had been painful. Finally, however, they were able to start making plans for the future, Sybille taking Eda with her to Provence to stay with Allanah at Les Bastides, her habitual haven, where they could recuperate in peace. Although she may not have foreseen it then, for Sybille her time with Eda, "in terms of fulfilment, life affection," was to be one of the most rewarding periods of her existence.

NINE

"HEAVEN BLESS YOU, MRS. BEDFORD"

To those who knew Eda in the post-war period, she appeared a timid, fragile creature, shy and retiring, clearly reluctant to attract attention or to express any opinion that might be considered remotely contentious. In her younger days, however, Eda had presented a very different image, a dark-haired beauty, sociable, intelligent and high-spirited, attractive to both men and women, eager for adventure and determined to make a successful career as a writer.

Born in Mexico on 30 July 1907, Eda was the only child of Harvey Hurd Lord, an American mining engineer, whose first wife, Eda's mother, died shortly after giving birth to her daughter. Lord soon remarried, and Eda's childhood was subsequently divided into six-month intervals, between living with her father, who was always on the move, and with her wealthy maternal grandmother in Evanston, Illinois. Eda enjoyed the summers spent with her father's family, living in a series of rented houses mostly in the Midwest, their easy-going domesticity in marked contrast to the strict regime imposed by her grandmother, a woman apparently incapable of showing affection.

When Eda was nine, her father died and her grandmother, taking Eda with her, moved to California. At school in La Jolla, Eda did well both academically and in sports. "She exuded vitality and was one of the most popular girls on campus," recalled Mary Frances Kennedy, a fellow pupil who had developed a passionate crush on Eda. Although

Mary Frances, later to become celebrated as the food writer M. F. K. Fisher, stayed at the school for only a year, the two formed a significant friendship which was to last for the rest of their lives. Recalling those early days, Mary Frances wrote of Eda, "I remembered her firm strong body, and the way she could always do anything, anything at school better than we could, and how she was more exciting and brilliant than any student had ever been."

At eighteen Eda began a course at Stanford University, and it was then, with the country in the grip of Prohibition, that she began to drink. Not long after leaving Stanford she found a job in advertising in New York where, still in her early twenties, she met and married Karl Robinson, an executive in the oil business. Robinson was based in China, and it was while on their way out east that Eda realised the mistake she had made to marry. After little more than a year she decided to leave her husband, travelling on her own across Russia to return to Europe. Here, while making her way through France she was delighted to encounter Mary Frances again, soon afterwards indulging in a brief affair with a friend of Mary Frances, the writer Lawrence Powell. Powell later portrayed Eda in his novel *The Blue Train* as the heavy-drinking Joyce, a green-eyed beauty "veiled in smoke from the strong cigarettes she favored."

Eventually Eda moved to Berlin, where she was to stay for some time. It was here she began writing, working as a journalist and also publishing a number of short stories. Eda had several affairs, one of which resulted in her undergoing an abortion, an experience that led to a period of almost suicidal depression. From this she was rescued when she fell in love with another woman, Tania Kurella, later the wife of Sybille's old acquaintance, Jimmy Stern. Their relationship ended in 1935 when Tania married Jimmy and Eda began an affair with Joan Black, a union that was to last for over ten years.

For the rest of the decade Joan and Eda lived in Paris, yet while Joan just about kept her drinking under control, Eda did not, describing herself at this period "as fat as a mountain and too hazy with drink to notice a kerb." Both women were unrestrainedly self-indulgent, rarely awake before noon, spending hours downing cocktails and gorging in restaurants. When on one occasion Mary Frances encountered the pair, she was appalled by the change in Eda's appearance, the slender beauty transformed into a drunken hulk: "fat . . . with compact hips and very heavy, almost bull-like shoulders. Her head stuck forward . . . and there was a roll at the back, like a caricature of a German burgher, so that the close-cropped hair made unattractive bristles . . . [her face] was dead white, with the close-pored vaguely dirty whiteness of an alcoholic's."

Sybille first met Eda not in Paris, but in Berlin, when in 1932 she had been visiting the city with the Huxleys. Eda had been struck by this blonde, blue-eyed young woman, who had barely noticed her. "You were so occupied and preoccupied," Eda recalled, "that you seemed truly impatient with any outsider tugging at your sleeve." Towards the end of the decade the two met again, by which time Eda was living with Joan Black in France. When after the war Sybille returned from America, she found Eda strikingly changed, pale and thin, very anxious and shy, clearly traumatised by her wartime experiences: the terrifying flight from Normandy to the south, where she and Joan had been imprisoned by the Gestapo, half starved and in fear of their lives. After the war ended the two women had continued to struggle with the severe food shortages, Eda drinking large quantities of the cheap red wine then available, with disastrous results. It was not until 1947, when she began her brief affair with Allanah, that Eda started to make a serious effort to bring her alcoholism under control, an attempt at which, "with unrelenting effort—and the crutches of cigarettes and caffeine," she was mainly successful.

In 1953, when Eda encountered Sybille again in Paris, she had been living for several years in Wales with her lover, Hilary Williams. With Hilary she made occasional visits abroad and also to London to see friends, and it was in London in 1956 that the crucial encounter between Eda and Sybille had taken place.

Sybille had been thankful and relieved by Evelyn's generous acceptance of her successor. "I am so happy, on air, about what you say about Eda . . . Pink with pleasure," Sybille told her. "You know, I do adore Eda. I think she is very, very vulnerable, and could shrink away at a cold or violent touch. All now is so easy and light. I never thought she would be so very good and sweet to me . . . It is all very warming: I am deeply grateful and still incredulous." Eda, too, seemed happy with her new relationship, deeply in love with Sybille, whose talent, perspicacity and intelligence she had always admired.

At the end of the summer, Sybille and Eda left London for France, staying for a couple of days with Esther in Paris before driving down to the south, where they were to spend nearly three months with Allanah. Sybille had been looking forward to a peaceful interlude with Eda at Les Bastides, but not everything proceeded as smoothly as expected. While driving down from Paris, the two women were crashed into by another car, leaving Eda covered in blood, while Sybille was taken by ambulance to hospital, badly bruised, with a broken rib and a lacerated tongue which had to be stitched up, "an extravagantly painful process." She and Eda were obliged to spend three days recuperating before continuing south by train, and Sybille was acutely anxious about the damage done to her car, which was not covered by insurance. "The car is reparable," she told Evelyn, "but will cost 250–275 frs . . . Pretty hopeless." A few days later, however, two cheques arrived, one from Martha, another from Esther, who wrote reassuringly, "I want you to worry about nothing—the car or anything else. Take care of yourself, my darling, and get over your injuries."

As always at Les Bastides there was much to enjoy—swimming, lunching out-of-doors, sitting and talking in front of the fire after dinner. Relations with Allanah, however, were far from easy, she and Sybille angrily snapping and constantly on each other's nerves, while Allanah was "so beastly to Eda, so <u>resisting</u> the fact of her presence that it had me isolated from her and sad, and cross too." Allanah's bad temper stemmed partly from the awkward fact that in the past she and Eda had themselves been lovers, and also from her current unhappiness over the end of her affair with Fay Blacket Gill; Fay had recently fallen for Patricia Laffan, the actress with whom Sybille had enjoyed a brief interlude while in Rome. Allanah was miserable over the rupture, and it was not until the beginning of the following year that she regained her good humour, happy with a new lover, Charlotte ("Charley") Delmas, member of a wealthy shipping family, who owned a large house only a short distance from Les Bastides. By this time, good relations with Allanah had been restored, and Sybille reported to Evelyn that "Things are loving now . . . being very much in love, she has softened."

By the start of the New Year, 1957, Sybille and Eda had returned to Paris to stay with Esther and Katzi in the rue de Lille, a lively few weeks, with theatres, dinners and cocktail parties almost every evening. Katzi was in high spirits, immersed in an affair with a handsome Italian nearly twenty years her junior, whom she had met while on holiday in Positano. Gino Atanasio, by profession a chartered accountant, had spent the past few years looking after his ailing parents, and now finding himself almost penniless was hoping to settle in France and marry Katzi. "*Gino malgré son caractère extrêmement difficile est un idéal délicieux*" ("Gino despite his difficult character is a delicious ideal"), Katzi told her sister. Sybille was happy for her, although she had little liking for Gino; as she admitted, however, "that is neither here nor there. Katzi loves him very much indeed—and I think that he will be loyal to her as long as there is a decent modus vivendi."

For Sybille the endless comings and goings in the apartment soon became a tiresome distraction. "Eda and I never seem to have a moment *dans cette maison*," she grumbled to Evelyn. "We read, we talk, we pour more water onto tepid leaves, and bang, the front door shivers: it is K back from *son marché*." And to Martha she complained, "Paris stupefies me; the hot radiators, the lack of air, the people, the noise. We do too much and see too much and go to bed too late . . . Moreover I find Paris repulsive (obsessively this time) . . . We long for home life, work." Professionally there was one piece of good news: the French rights to *A Legacy* had been bought by the distinguished firm of Hachette, which, under the title *Une Vue Impartiale*, was to publish the novel the following year. "Yesterday I went to see my translator Beatrice Beck," Sybille told Evelyn, "shy, farouche, left wing. No visible command of English. As she had only managed to do fourteen pages since October, I can hardly report on more."

Fortunately at this point Eda, who had a modest but regular income, found a flat to rent for a few months in London. The first-floor apartment was in a Georgian terrace in Elizabeth Street, Pimlico, and reported to be "new, clean, and warm." On arrival, however, both Eda and Sybille felt disappointed and depressed. The flat, situated above a car showroom, was "everything it was not expected to be," Sybille complained, "not clean, not pretty, convenient, heatable or even ready for human habitation . . . No char: none in sight." Eventually, however, they managed to make the place comfortable, Sybille pleased with the large desk at which she worked in the sitting room, while Eda enjoyed the quiet and privacy of a small study at the back, where she could concentrate on the novel she had had in mind for some time. And fortunately their fellow tenants turned out to be agreeable, the well-known racing driver Patricia ("Speedy") McOstrich, and the children's novelist Noël Streatfeild.

Sybille was impatient to return to her writing, but first she had to deal with a number of tiresome chores, "the kitchen of life," in Martha's disparaging phrase. Recently she had applied to become a British resident, a process requiring her to fill in dozens of forms, appear at numerous interviews with accountants and tax inspectors, re-register her now repaired car, and as well open a British bank account, with Coutts & Company, "the oldest private bank in England. God it's grand! . . . they all wear frock coats with velvet froggings." Yet as the days passed, despite the tedium her spirits rose, and she was soon reporting to Evelyn that she felt more relaxed, happy to have returned to England. "I think I have that sense of both bounce and ease I have in Swiss (different) and had once in Rome; and did not have at the Bastides, or Paris."

Before long an active social life was under way, with Sybille and Eda going out most evenings, Eda never without her thermos of coffee and packet of cigarettes. Among the friends old and new whom Sybille saw at this period were Martha and Tom Matthews, Sylvester Gates and his wife, Jane Stockwood, the novelist Rosamond Lehmann, "so charming, so good, so distinguished," and also Charlotte Wolff, "the German witch doctor" first encountered in Sanary before the war. Sybille's "return to London," Charlotte wrote later, "meant more to me than I had anticipated. It not only led to an intimate friendship, but infused into my life the warmth and inspiration I had been starved of . . . Our friendship automatically included Eda . . . [who] was not given to much speech and only got a word in edgeways. But when she did speak it was with a perceptiveness and wisdom that made one prick up one's ears. Sometimes our evenings extended into the early hours of the morning."

Two other friends from Sanary whom Sybille now encountered were Eva Herrmann and Brian Howard. Eva, whom Sybille had last seen in California during the war, had arrived in London for a brief visit from Los Angeles, and during her stay she and Sybille were constantly in each other's company. They lunched and dined together, made expeditions into the country, all the while absorbed in talking about their past, renewing a friendship that, after Eva's return to the States, was to remain close for the rest of their lives. Brian, however, was far from easy since his heavy drinking and explosive rages frequently disrupted the occasions on which they met, leaving Sybille feeling both pity and disgust at his behaviour.

Her first encounter with Brian since the 1930s had been in Rome, where he had turned up with Sam Langford, his sailor boyfriend. On this occasion Sybille had been appalled by what she described as his "continued, unabated racketeering: drunkenness, waste, waste, waste and calling it naughtiness." Not long afterwards Brian materialised again, this time at Les Bastides, since his mother had recently bought a house near Nice. One evening, just as Sybille and Allanah were sitting down to dinner, he had unexpectedly appeared, "drunk and ill, taut and angry from the first. He stayed till half past 11. It was very bad all the time." Yet despite his behaviour Sybille remained fond of Brian, continuing to see him from time to time, their final meeting taking place in London in December 1957, when Brian, accompanied by Sam, gave Sybille and Eda a lavish dinner at Claridge's. "He was very sweet that evening," Sybille recalled. "Eda and I started tucking in with a will. 'CROCODILES,' said Brian." Not long afterwards, in January 1958, Sam died, poisoned while in the bath by an accidental gas leak, and four days later Brian took an overdose and killed himself.

Another death, in 1957, was that of Eda's one-time lover, Joan Black, Peter Churchill's wife, who died in May, leaving her husband "a broken man," Sybille wrote to Evelyn, and "I am very worried about Eda, all this has been very bad for her." Despite Sybille's brief passion for Joan during the 1930s, the relations between the two had remained contentious, but since Joan's marriage their enmity had largely dissolved, the two maintaining an amicable if somewhat wary truce. "She never let me much into her life, but we shared some laughter and some of the good carefree things of living."

The shock of these premature deaths had compelled Sybille to focus on her own life and the direction in which it was leading. She had achieved so little, wasted so much time, she admitted to Evelyn. "I feel that I have made *fausse route* in my life and that it is irretrievable now . . . I suspect that the foolish truth is that I have never grown up, and did not do so because I always missed having a real mother and father: parents in fact, a family. I don't know whether even now I am ready for a life with one other adult. What I always wanted was somebody else's home to be welcomed in: foster parents, a home: Pierre & Jacqueline; Aldous & Maria . . . rue de Lille. Of course this is too simple and pat, put like this. But there is truth enough in it, and it isn't very nice because I am too old now, and no parents will want me, and anyhow I should have changed a long time ago. And I don't feel being a writer is a substitute at all. It's an odd moment for it all to come to the surface; but it has."

To make matters worse, Sybille was again in a serious predicament financially, despite yet another large "loan" from Martha, this time of £1,000, accompanied by an irritable letter instructing her old pal to pull herself together and start earning a regular living. Yet as over the years Sybille had grown accustomed to accepting money from friends, she now resented such criticism. "The most unlikely people turn out wonderful when it counts. Others not," Sybille remarked bitterly. Martha "has the human touch that withers." Fortunately, however, the situation soon began to improve: the money from Simon & Schuster for *A Legacy* finally arrived, and as well Sybille was paid a generous fee by *Vogue* for an article she had written the previous year describing a trial at the Old Bailey.

Since attending her first court case nearly thirty years before, with Kate Muir at the Royal Courts of Justice, Sybille had been fascinated by legal process. "Going to law courts is a good education for a novelist," she said later. "It provides you with the most extravagant material, and it teaches the near impossibility of reaching the truth." Over the past couple of years she had attended court on several occasions, initially with the help of Fay Blacket Gill, herself a practising lawyer. Subsequently Sybille had sold the idea to *Vogue* of a report of an unexceptional trial at the Old Bailey, involving a young man accused of stealing a van-load of apples and cheeses.

"10:30 at the Old Bailey," published in October 1956, is a remarkable piece of reporting, witty, dramatic, intensely visual, deftly recreating the procedure, the courtroom itself and its dramatis personae. As each actor comes on stage a graphic impression is given of appearance and manner, of the judge, with "the face of a very old woman," of the prosecuting counsel, "bursting with self-importance" as he flamboyantly performs before a jury of "thin-boned, grey, absent-faced, thin-suited people." By the end of the day the pale young man in the dock is found guilty and sentenced to thirty months in prison. "One does not like to look at the Prisoner and yet one does. During the last half-hour the Court has filled with broad-built men with close hair-cuts and despatch cases. They are Police Officers. The moment of truth has come. It is very sordid."

The following year Sybille found herself eagerly focused on covering a trial about to open, a murder case that was to make an enormous impact and remain notorious for generations to come. The case was that of the "Bluebeard of the time," John Bodkin Adams, a doctor from Eastbourne suspected of murdering over 160 of his patients. First, however, Sybille had to find a publisher whom she could interest in the project.

After the success of *A Legacy* in the States publishers in London had woken up to the fact that its author was now a writer of significant promise, this change in Sybille's status a cause of considerable anxiety to George Weidenfeld. Mortified by his failure to promote the novel, Weidenfeld, "whiny and kind," did his best to woo Sybille, begging her to stay with his firm and offering her a contract for a travel book; Sybille, however, was determined to leave, a decision that delighted her agent, Elaine Greene. "George just phoned me, full of anguish, and I have, I hope, persuaded him that he can do nothing but let you go quietly and without argument. I do think you are quite right to change; he was never the right publisher for you." Meanwhile among other firms now circling were Rupert Hart-Davis, Hamish Hamilton and also William Collins, one of whose directors, Mark Bonham Carter, seemed the most sympathetic to Sybille's plans.

Over lunch at the Ritz, Sybille explained to Bonham Carter that she had two projects in mind, first a book on the Adams trial, and then a novel. "He said yes how much," Sybille reported to Evelyn. "Was screwing courage to ask for 500 when MBC said, as Adams was an interim book, what about an advance for that and a novel, over a period from now to 2½ years . . . [and] would 2,500 pounds seem reasonable . . . Tortoise! That's a 1,000 pounds a year." Next Sybille went to meet the head of the firm, William Collins, at his office off St. James's Street. During their discussion it was agreed that Collins would pay her £1,200 a year for two to three years on the understanding that both books would be delivered within that period. "Also they wish to buy—if poss—both *A Legacy* and *The Sudden View* and republish the lot. Golly." For publicity purposes, Sybille was photographed by the young Antony Armstrong-Jones, who posed her leaning out of a window looking slightly startled, her heavy eye-shade almost but not quite concealing her eyes; before her on the wide sill is her typewriter, her fingers placed delicately on the keys.

The trial of Dr. Bodkin Adams at the Old Bailey began on 18 March 1957, and continued for seventeen days, up till then the longest murder trial in British history. Sybille, who had attended the committal hearing at Eastbourne in January, was present throughout, on the first day arriving in the early hours of the morning, well wrapped up in a camelhair coat, to be sure of a place near the front of the queue. "Two muffled individuals were standing in the Public Gallery entrance, another was crouching on an orange crate. It was night. 'Good morning,' said I. 'Good morning,' said the individual, 'you're the first female tonight; this gentleman and I have been here since midnight.' Glorious." By the second day such an early arrival was no longer necessary as Fay Blacket Gill had obtained a press pass for Sybille, allocating her a seat on a bench near the dock, "a position which, if far from ideal, is worlds apart from the isolated heights of the public gallery." Throughout the trial, from 10:30 in the morning to 4:30 in the afternoon, Sybille sat in the oak-panelled courtroom watching with absorption. "It is completely fascinating," she told Evelyn, "with very dull stretches indeed."

John Bodkin Adams, then in his late fifties, was a general practitioner, whose patients were mainly rich, elderly ladies, an unusual number of whom had died in questionable circumstances, nearly all bequeathing him substantial legacies. Although suspected of killing many of his patients, he was to be tried for the death of only one, a Mrs. Edith Morrell, the case provoking intense interest around the world, "the murder trial of the century," as it was described in *The Times*. From the day of Adams's arrest in December the previous year, Sybille had been absorbed in the case, determined to write about it, "to give an accurate and detailed coverage of what happened in court—minute by minute, hour by hour." Shortly before proceedings began, she told Evelyn, "I've not had such a feeling of having come across the right material for myself for a long time."

The Best We Can Do, Sybille's lucid and informed account of those seventeen days in court, is a remarkable achievement. Watching throughout with intense concentration, she provides a compelling re-enactment of the entire procedure, tracking every argument, every change in pace and mood, showing us the stage—the court itself—and describing the performance of each member of the large cast. "I had often wanted to put down a trial exactly step by step," she wrote later, "and in such a way that the reader would have all the evidence and nothing but the evidence, but also the manner in which it was given and extracted." Arriving on the first morning, she finds the Old Bailey under siege, "police vans and press vans, cameras and cameramen, detective sergeants and CIDs . . . a line of special constables at every door, and thirty quarts of milk left for the cafeteria." Inside, however, in Central Criminal Court Number One, "there is more than silence, there is quiet."

Throughout the process the judge, Sir Patrick Devlin, a handsome figure in his grey wig, listens attentively, taking detailed notes, occasionally concealing a delicate yawn "behind his fine hand." Below him the actors play out their parts, chief among them the large and aggressive prosecuting counsel, Sir Reginald Manningham-Buller, whose questions "rolled up sluggishly like so much thunder"; and for the defence Mr. Frederick Lawrence QC, deft and theatrical, who time and again presents with a flourish unsuspected evidence devastating to the prosecution. One by one the witnesses are summoned, the three nurses who looked after Mrs. Morrell, three doctors, intensively examined on the effects of the large doses of morphine and heroin prescribed; the police, led by Detective Superintendent Hannam of Scotland Yard; and the accused himself, Dr. Adams, who declines to bear witness, sitting silently day after day watching the case unfold, "spherical, adipose, upholstered in blue serge, red-faced, bald."

After nearly three weeks the trial reaches its final stages, when over a period of two days the judge provides, with expert clarity and grace, a detailed résumé of the proceedings for the benefit of the jury. "You sit to answer one limited question," he tells them, "has the prosecution satisfied you beyond reasonable doubt that the doctor murdered Mrs. Morrell?" The twelve men and women rise and leave the court, retiring for exactly forty-four minutes, after which they return, "settle themselves, consciously, in the box . . . 'And have you reached your verdict?' . . . 'Yes . . . Not guilty.' "

In *The Best We Can Do*, Sybille gives a meticulous and absorbing account of each day of the trial. Her narrative draws partly on her own memory and the notes taken at the time, but more substantially on the detailed reports that appeared in *The Times*, as well as on the printed version of Sir Patrick Devlin's summing-up. Sybille completed the book in under a year, delivering the manuscript to Collins in March 1958. Dedicated to Eda, *The Best We Can Do* was published in October, receiving a number of respectful notices in the press, including one in the *Daily Telegraph* by John Sparrow, describing the work as vivid and skilful, with the characters in court coming "convincingly alive." Particularly gratifying was an appreciative letter from Patrick Devlin. He had read the book with enjoyment, he told her. "You have made it sound so exciting & have produced something so readable (which I should have thought was almost impossible out of seventeen days of transcript) & so much of the writing is so good that it leaves me full of admiration."

Yet, as before with *A Legacy*, it was in New York that the book was received with real enthusiasm; and as before it was Bob Gottlieb at Simon & Schuster who was largely responsible for its success. Gottlieb was said to love the book, to be "jumping with joy" at the prospect of publishing it. His excited reaction was reported by Evelyn, who had recently been taken on as one of Bob's assistants, an ideal job for her as she had worked in publishing during the war and had always hoped one day to return. Now she was at Bob's right hand as he set out to publicise *The Trial of Dr. Adams*, as it was titled in the States, contacting numbers of important judges, lawyers and academics for their opinions. One eminent scholar targeted by Bob was Eugene Rostow, dean of Yale Law School, who found it "A brilliant account. I know of no piece of trial reportage, save possibly Rebecca West's, to compare with it in literary power." After the book's appearance in the spring of 1959 there were many adulatory reviews, including one in the *New York Times* by Martha's husband, Tom Matthews, and an article in *Esquire* by Dorothy Parker. *The Trial of Dr. Adams* "is the book of my heart," wrote Parker. "I think, and I do not say this lightly, hers is the best account of a murder trial I have ever read. Heaven bless you, Mrs. Bedford."

In May 1958, almost six months before the book's publication in London, Sybille and Eda had left for Portugal. Hoping to find a quiet refuge where they could work undisturbed throughout the summer, they had rented a small house in the north-west of the country, near the coast at Afife. The drive from England was long and arduous, both women in a state of nervous exhaustion. By the time they reached the border between Spain and Portugal it was pouring with rain, and "I had to go back some way, still in the rain, to find two soldiers, thin as crows under their black lacquered hats, to stamp our exit; three hundred yards further along, the Portuguese customs sat squat and mute in a trim, white house, sparkling rings on their fingers." When they finally arrived at the Quinta S. José they were relieved to find the house much as they had hoped, "quiet, clean as whistles, in its own untidy garden and vineyard. Orchard and sea view. V. v. pleased."

Looking forward to weeks of hot sun, to swimming, exploring the countryside and sampling the local cuisine, they were to be disappointed at almost every turn. Apart from a pleasant few days spent staying at a vineyard in the Douro valley, nothing was as they had hoped: the weather was appalling, with drenching rain and far too cold to bathe. "We've had two dips each in the sea during the whole summer," Sybille complained to Martha, confessing she had done no writing at all, overwhelmed by depression and homesick for England; she was "going through a very difficult time of self-hatred, ineffectualness, lovelessness, misery and guilt." And Eda's condition was even more wretched, she worryingly thin, unable to sleep or work and profoundly unhappy. It was now that Sybille began to understand how deeply Eda had been damaged, how her wartime experiences had changed her from a sociable, cheerful personality into a fragile depressive, irrationally frightened, prone to intense anxiety and wholly lacking in confidence. Although Sybille was as much in love as ever, she was unable to forget Martha's words. "Eda will never decide anything because she cannot, and her motives are not what you think (gratitude, duty, affection etc) but plain terror."

Longing to leave but with nowhere to go, the two women had to resign themselves to remaining in a country regarded as "deeply alien and disturbing." Fortunately, however, towards the end of their stay the atmosphere was lightened by the arrival of Pierre and Simone Mimerel, who had driven from France with their nineteen-year-old nephew. "I am so pleased they are here, and it is fun too," Sybille noted in her diary. After a few days all five set off for a tour of the south of the country, then on to Seville, Cadiz, Ronda, and finally to Barcelona, Sybille cheered by the liveliness of Spain after what she described as "the hog slumber of Portugal." When the Mimerels left, she and Eda decided to spend a few days on Ibiza, of which Eda had happy memories from before the war, but that, too, turned out to be disappointing. They soon became "fed up" with the island, "a German and lower-middle-class English holiday colony with dumb natives."

Despite her feelings of antipathy towards Portugal, Sybille was nonetheless determined to write about it, delivering an article for *Vogue* which appeared in January the following year. In "Notes on a Journey in Portugal," Sybille gives little overt expression of her antipathy, concentrating instead on the beauty of the countryside and especially of the architecture—"All Portuguese towns are pretty; some are very pretty; a few are exquisite." She discusses the wine, is politely dismissive of the food—"agreeable, fresh, plentiful and uninspiring"—describes the difficulty of learning the language, and portrays the people as "placid, kindly, patient, slow." Her lack of engagement is discreetly downplayed, although few readers can have been encouraged by her account to visit such an apparently dreary country.

Sybille and Eda finally returned to London at the end of the year, having first spent several weeks with Allanah at Les Bastides. Having recently been received into the Roman Catholic Church, Allanah was calm and cheerful, clearly happy with her new love, Charley Delmas, and Charley's world of "the Riviera rich." It was not, however, a world in which Sybille felt at home. Allanah "makes us feel very dingy and literary and unwanted," she complained to Martha. "She took us to one of her friend's houses the other night but explained before that it was only a dinner for writers, and would not be the same food as a dinner for fellow rich, which made me absolutely furious." To Evelyn, Sybille described at length her irritation with Allanah's silly "expatriate jabber," and the tediousness of her wealthy friends. But Evelyn, who had heard all this before, was reassuring. "You swing from her regularly, ever since I've known you. And then again, come the times of sympathy, and the affinity is there, mysteriously warm as ever."

Once back in London Sybille found she had a similar problem with Martha, who now appeared to regard her as on a lower social level than the Matthewses' other friends. Shortly before Christmas Martha had telephoned to suggest that "when all festivities are over we must meet and have a nice walk round empty Belgrave Square," a proposal that held little appeal for Sybille. "This does not take into account that I too like festivities, a friend's warm house," she complained. "I'm fed up with being M's poor relation . . . [with] M's way of fitting one in between her engagements . . . Seldom a drink, never 'a hot meal,' it is not my conception of enjoying the company of friends."

Fortunately for Sybille's peace of mind she soon found somewhere to live well outside Martha's orbit. Conveniently close to London, Little Wynters, a cottage in the hamlet of Hastingwood, near Harlow in Essex, was "very comfortable, above all entirely quiet. 1¼ mile off the main road, no neighbours, no traffic; garden ending in fields . . . a glasshouse for sitting in the sun." The cottage was part of a property belonging to Air Chief Marshal Sir Thomas Pike and his wife, who warmly welcomed Sybille and Eda on their arrival, inviting them on their first evening to their house for drinks. As Sybille entered the drawing room her heart sank. There were "twelve people, sherry glasses and the neighbourhood to meet us. All majors and vicars, and ladies in tweeds, all military . . . I got my 'I'm afraid I am an RC' in, after having been told to join the Women's Institute." Nonetheless, the Pikes were friendly and helpful, and once the two women had settled in, to Sybille's relief, left them largely undisturbed.

Both she and Eda were much in need of tranquillity, both hard at work, Eda on a novel, Sybille on a second book about the law. Although it had been agreed with Collins that *The Best We Can Do* should be followed by a novel, she was now so absorbed in her study of jurisdiction that Mark Bonham Carter had agreed to accept another book on the subject first. This second project was of considerably wider scope, examining legal systems in England, Germany, Austria, Switzerland and France. Now while in Essex Sybille began her research, driving across the county to attend local courts in Chipping Ongar, Dunmow, Chelmsford and Saffron Walden. Fascinated by the experience, she was also shocked by much of what she observed. "I came back quivering with indignation," she told Martha. "Avaricious farmers on the bench, wicked Tory old ladies, retired military chaps . . . Most of the judges fiends." When she tried to begin writing, Sybille found herself struggling, sitting for days at her desk, "doing typing exercises and playing patience. Sick with disgust, discouragement, heaviness." Suddenly, however, the paralysis lifted and she found herself working "like blazes" for up to six and seven hours a day.

As spring moved into summer, both she and Eda took pleasure in tending their garden, an acre of lawn with a few fine trees as well as a large bed for fruit and vegetables. In the early evenings after the day's work was done, the pair spent an energetic couple of hours digging and weeding, chopping logs, gathering strawberries, raspberries, tomatoes, lettuces, peas and beans. "Tomatoes growing nicely, little yellow flowers," Sybille reported to Evelyn in June. "The strawberries are ripening, fought over one by one between the birds and me. I cover them with *The Times*." By the following month the first crops had ripened. "A basket with 3 dozen young peas, a dozen mangetouts, 6 fava, 2 small lettuces . . . dinner of odds and ends: the vegetable done in 2 mins, 1 min, 30 seconds respectively—all freshest green on same dish; gnocchi di olio . . . Followed by the year's harvest of raspberries picked by Eda." Sybille was charmed one day to see a baby hedgehog slowly crossing the lawn. "I ran for a saucer of milk which they are said to like . . . Put it down; hedgehog came straight away, dipped in its nose and little hands and very slowly drank up the milk, it took ten minutes; then, so heavy that it could just waddle, it made off to its woods."

In July the two women left to spend a fortnight by Lake Constance, as Sybille had been commissioned to write an article about the region for *Holiday* magazine. Returning to Little Wynters at the end of the month, they departed again in October for Switzerland, Germany and Austria, where Sybille was to spend several weeks examining the legal systems of the three countries. "The material I am finding fascinates me," she told Evelyn. "My Austrian . . . [and] Swiss court experiences are hallucinating, all as different as can be. The Swiss helpful, but so slow. Their idea of fun (*lustig*) is for me to be at their office at 7.45 a.m." Her experience in Germany was rather more complicated, although on the whole she was pleasantly surprised "by the fairness of their law courts. It reflected the new spirit of the Germans." Nonetheless there were some extraordinary differences. "Bavaria is the part of Germany where . . . murderers are quickly hanged, instead of soft Germany without—now—capital punishment. The authorities have become squeamish about taking life, the populace apparently not." Towards the end of the year the two women arrived for three weeks in Paris, where Sybille completed her research, witnessing a number of cases at the magnificent Palais de Justice on the Île de la Cité.

Interestingly, Sybille gives far less space to the French courts in her book than to those in Germany and Switzerland, but then, as she complained to Evelyn, she continued to find Paris repugnant. "Paris grates more than ever: a vast garage; insolently expensive." She was not happy, either, with the situation at the rue de Lille, noting in her diary, "Bad atmosphere in house . . . E[sther] cross."

Esther's irascibility was a recent development, a consequence of her currently fragile state of health. Six months previously her condition had begun seriously to decline; she refused to go out or to see friends, retreating for days at a time into an alcoholic stupor, a cause of increasing anxiety to Katzi. It worried her that Esther, gaunt and grey-haired, often stayed in her room for most of the day, supposedly working on a new book, a life of Madame de Maintenon, but in fact doing little except lying on her bed in a heavy wool dressing gown, smoking and drinking; she was skeletally thin, ate almost nothing, and was clearly in a state of severe depression. "*Esther boit beaucoup*," Katzi had told Sybille. "*Ivre tous les soirs . . . devient très difficile et capricieuse . . . fument sans arrêt*" ("Esther drinks a lot . . . drunk every evening . . . becomes very diffi-

cult and capricious . . . smokes non-stop"). She was frequently inconti-
nent, too, not only in bed at night but often when sitting in an armchair
in the drawing room, not troubling to get up and leave the room. *"Personne peut vivre avec Esther,"* Katzi complained, *"elle est folle—et sale"*
("Nobody can live with Esther, she is crazy—and dirty").

Further adding to their difficulties was the fact that Esther was in
a precarious position financially as payments of her share of the divi-
dends from Mark Cross were increasingly delayed, obliging her to rely
on gifts from her brother Gerald and sister-in-law Noël Murphy, and at
times to beg for loans from her friends, Sybille among them. The strain
on Katzi was growing almost unbearable, as she wanted her sister to
understand. Sybille had had such luck in life, always able to do exactly
as she pleased, whereas Katzi was locked into this intolerable existence
from which there seemed no escape. *"Je suis très déprimée . . . Et pour
une fois je n'ai plus de courage du tout!"* ("I am very depressed . . . And
for once I have no courage at all!").

Before long Esther's condition grew sufficiently alarming for her to
be taken to hospital, where she was diagnosed with epilepsy, a disorder,
she was told, almost certainly activated by a lifetime's heavy drinking
and smoking. She was prescribed barbiturates and forbidden both alcohol and cigarettes, a veto that was to be largely ignored. The immediate improvement, however, was dramatic, as Janet Flanner reported.
"Esther's nearly fatal illness—& it was that—was like a gigantic purge
that wiped out all her habits of exaggeration, mental & physical. She
[talks] only nearly all the time, not entirely all, & with a moderation
that is touching, brilliant in a new way because devoid of glitter." With
Esther rapidly recovering, Katzi at last was able to take a much-needed
holiday, spending three weeks with her beloved Gino on Capri. *"Gino
et moi—nous nous aimons vraiment"* ("Gino and I—we truly love each
other"), she wrote cheerfully to Sybille.

At the beginning of 1960, back in England and with her research
completed, Sybille was able to concentrate on her writing. As before,
there was greater enthusiasm for the project in New York than in London. Mark Bonham Carter, disappointed at the postponement of the
promised novel, had shown little interest in the book, languidly enquir-
ing after its progress over lunch one day, but "he is cold (at least to me)

not interested in writing; and not I think terribly in publishing." Bob Gottlieb, on the other hand, could hardly restrain his excitement, promising that Simon & Schuster would do everything they could to assist their author. "I know Sybille's had extraordinary expenses in preparing for this book," he told Evelyn. "We'd like to help, and we propose to pay her an exceptionally large advance, and to pay it before the manuscript is ready, to help her bear these expenses. If you agree, we'll give her $2,000, payable April 15 1960."

His generous offer was passed on to Sybille by Evelyn. Now amicably divorced from Milton, Evelyn lived with her parents, commuting daily from their apartment in the East Village to Simon & Schuster's office on 5th Avenue. She and Bob worked well together. "I liked her very much, [and] she liked me," Bob recalled, describing Evelyn as small and lively, "extremely not pretty . . . [but] active and quick and funny. Evelyn was very capable . . . [although] she had a minor position . . . [and] didn't have that much to do . . . Evelyn was useful, she was a useful person." Evelyn for her part liked and admired Bob, enjoyed watching him move restlessly about the office, polishing his spectacles, pushing back the heavy lock of dark hair that flopped across his forehead. Despite "an American brashness, let alone the way he wears his hair . . . he's in many ways endearing . . . [and] with all his commercial grasp, he has, he really does, the taste for real writing."

Without a great deal of pressure at work, Evelyn had been able at last to finish the children's book she had begun writing while living in Rome. *Tortoise and Turtle*, with drawings by Hilary Knight, the illustrator of the famous *Eloise* books, is a charming tale of the close friendship between the dignified, knowledgeable Tortoise and the far more light-hearted Turtle. For those in the know, Tortoise was instantly recognisable as Sybille, Turtle as Evelyn, the names they most frequently used in their correspondence with each other. Tortoise is "very fond of pleasure and comfort, and also of learning," Turtle "quite young, with a happy nature and a great deal of curiosity." Tortoise eats with concentration and discernment, his meals always exquisitely ordered. "Turtle liked to munch back and forth, changing the tastes. Tortoise did not." The story follows the planning of a party, to which one by one they invite their various animal friends, Turtle at every stage looking to

Tortoise for instruction and definition. " '*Entertain*,' said Turtle, 'what is that?' 'Party,' said Tortoise. 'Party is to go *out*,' said Turtle. Tortoise said, 'Entertain is to come here.' "

Published by Simon & Schuster, the book was dedicated to Sybille, although initially Evelyn had had trouble deciding on the exact wording. "As you know very well," she told Sybille, "*T&T* is your book. & I am now asking a delicate question—just how shall one put it . . . 'For G[reat]B[east] and T[ortoise] and Little Billy and S[ybille]. With my love . . . To the Baroness Billy. To the Bossy Little Baroness.' "

In the end it was decided to list mostly by initial all the names by which Sybille in private was known to Evelyn: "For GB and T, Billy and S." "I never loved a dedication more: it is like a red carpet unfurling for one to step on," Sybille told her appreciatively.

Under Gottlieb's supervision, Evelyn had edited the American edition of *The Trial of Dr. Adams*, and was now to do the same for *The Faces of Justice: A Traveller's Report*. When in July the finished version finally arrived in the office, Bob was beside himself with enthusiasm. "I love it. I am crazy about it," he told Sybille. And indeed, *The Faces of Justice* is another remarkable achievement on Sybille's part.

As in *The Best We Can Do*, she writes with exceptional clarity and grace, here conveying the complex workings of the courts of law in England, Germany, Austria, Switzerland and France. Mainly in magistrates' courts, or their equivalent, the cases she witnesses are frequently trivial, minor thefts, drunkenness, traffic offences, a young man accused of siphoning petrol from a car, another of smuggling in thirty-five cigarettes over the legal limit of 200. Many of the convicted are given small fines or suspended sentences. However, there are several serious cases resulting in heavy sentencing, one of the most disturbing instances in England, where a married man with children, despite pleas for leniency from his family, is condemned to years in prison for a homosexual offence. In Germany, by contrast, a Dr. Brach, found guilty of shooting dead a man who had repeatedly exposed himself to the doctor's young daughter, is given a deferred sentence of only four months. While describing this latter case, Sybille remarks how impressed she was by the judge's manner: "it seemed informed by moderation, good sense and a respect for other people's feelings. I should perhaps say that it was a performance of high human quality and that a German court of law was the last place where I should have dreamt to encounter it."

Beginning her tour in England, Sybille travels to Karlsruhe and Munich in Germany, spends a brief period in Austria, then continues on to Switzerland and France. With an elegant lucidity she explains the legal system of each country, describing in compelling detail the setting, the persons involved, the scenes witnessed not only in court but also backstage, where, unusually, she is allowed to talk freely to judges, magistrates and clerks. On one memorable occasion during the trial of Dr. Brach, she joins a small group, including both judge and accused, who go to the local park where the murder took place. Here as elsewhere she shows a remarkable ability, not only to make clear what is unfolding in court, but also the reasoning behind the judgements and the characters themselves. It is a difficult challenge and Sybille meets it triumphantly.

The Faces of Justice was published in May 1961, dedicated to her old friend Janet Flanner, who had herself covered a number of famous cases, her law reporting much admired by Sybille. To Sybille's relief, the book was well received on both sides of the Atlantic. In Britain the most appreciative critique was from Rebecca West, who praised the author's "powerful and original intelligence . . . The interviews with officials in this book show that they were swept off their feet into candour, as conventional people sometimes are, by a person unconventional but rather grand and of integrity as indisputable as their own. This is a gay, humane, animated book . . . [which] also tackles its serious subject seriously." Most gratifying of all was a review in the *Pittsburgh Press* by Michael Musmanno, a distinguished judge who early in his career had been involved in the notorious Sacco–Vanzetti case and later had presided at the Nuremberg trials. "A new book by Sybille Bedford should be proclaimed by silver trumpets, for she is a mistress of English prose," Musmanno wrote. "Crisp, informative, reassuring . . . it is the most delightful court book I have read in many years."

As always when working on a book, Sybille had interspersed periods of intense concentration with time spent visiting her friends. Among them were Jimmy and Tania Stern, who had recently left New York to settle in England, buying a handsome manor house in Wiltshire, which over the years both Sybille and Eda came to know well. Another figure from the past was Constantine FitzGibbon, last encountered in Rome and now living for a brief period near Sybille and Eda in the country. He and his wife had recently divorced, and Constantine was about to marry again; his fiancée, Marion Gutmann, was delightful, Sybille reported to Evelyn. "German Jewish banker's daughter . . . family comes from Baden." A friendship dating further back still was with the Muir sisters, Toni and Kate, who had played such an important part in Sybille's early years in London. Kate had never properly recovered from her lover's, the judge's, suicide, and it was Toni who ran their lives and with whom Sybille had kept most closely in touch. Yet fond though she was, they also irritated her. "Both the M[uir]s are so uncompromisingly, innocently, non-U," she complained to Evelyn. "Toni is much the better of the two . . . Toni is difficult but still alive, Katie is solid stone dead."

It was during this time that Sybille was introduced to two friends of Eda's, a couple with whom she was to remain close for decades to come. William and Elaine Robson-Scott, both academics, highly qualified in German and French, had first met in Vienna before the war, where William had been teaching at the university. Previously William had spent several years in Berlin, becoming a good friend of Eda, who was living and working there at the time, and also of Klaus Mann and of Christopher Isherwood, with whom he shared a keen interest in good-looking boys. Tall and bespectacled, William was fearless, even-tempered and polite, yet when the occasion demanded, as Isherwood recalled, "he would become imperious in an old-fashioned British way, brushing difficulties aside like insects." After their marriage in 1948, Elaine, thirteen years younger, had given up her university career to devote herself to looking after her husband and their daughter, Markie.

When Sybille first met the Robson-Scotts, they were living in a large, somewhat dilapidated flat in Dorset Square. It was here that she and Eda were invited to tea one afternoon, Sybille immediately impressed by her hosts' intelligence and warmth, as well as by their familiarity with German and French literature. "We had huge Scotch tea," Sybille recalled, with "a well-behaved small child and an ill-behaved but charming wire-haired dachshund. My first meeting: impression people of one's own

kind, so rare; warm, intelligent, liberal . . . Charming Oxford voice."
Sybille, usually wary of children, was also captivated by nine-year-old
Markie, described as "v. v. bright and well brought-up." It was Markie
who tried, unsuccessfully, to improve Sybille's illegible hand. "Dear
Sybille," she wrote in a childish but beautiful italic, "Here is your first
exercise. Please begin on the letters, and go on then to the days of the
week, writing them underneath mine. I will mark them and send it back
to you, with your second exercise. I am sending you a postcard of some
little horses, to cheer you up while you work."

Towards the end of 1960, not long after Sybille had delivered *The
Faces of Justice*, news broke of a trial shortly to take place at the Old
Bailey and quickly to become infamous: a charge brought against Penguin Books for publishing *Lady Chatterley's Lover*. Determined to cover
it, Sybille immediately wrote to Evelyn, now acting as her agent for
journalistic assignments, asking her to try to secure a contract with *Life*
magazine in America. She herself contacted *Esquire* in New York and
the *Listener* in London, both of which immediately made her an offer.
Sybille was delighted. "Instant, unalloyed, deep joy," she wrote to Evelyn on receiving the news, wholly unprepared for the tone of Evelyn's
reply. "NOW LISTEN TO ME," Evelyn's letter began, "you are NOT
to get in touch with *Esquire* yourself directly AT ALL. NOT, NOT,
NOT, except through me." Clearly Sybille had not understood that it
was wholly unacceptable to go behind her agent's back, to negotiate the
same deal with different publications simultaneously. "You haven't a
clear conception what 'Agent' means," Evelyn continued. "Your agent
is not only acting for you, he IS you: YOU are bound, YOU must honour your agent's commitment . . . [and] I cannot be in the position of
perpetual hair-raisers, of terror at what you may do next!" Sybille was
immediately contrite. "You do not often scold me. When you do I feel
crushed . . . I did not mean to do wrong."

The trial, *Regina* v. *Penguin Books Ltd*, began on the morning of
20 October 1960, at Court Number One at the Old Bailey. Penguin had
previously published a number of novels by D. H. Lawrence, and had
now decided to risk issuing *Lady Chatterley's Lover,* which had never
before appeared in Britain. This was a deliberate challenge on the part
of the firm, putting to the test the recently passed Obscene Publications

Act, the main purpose of which was to distinguish between literature and pornography. Penguin had assembled a group of thirty-six witnesses, most of them distinguished writers or academics, who during the six-day trial were successfully to contend that there was no case to answer, that despite the realistic descriptions of sexual intercourse, the frequent use of words such as "fuck" and "cunt," this was undisputedly a work of literature, with no intention to deprave or corrupt.

In her article for *Esquire*, Sybille gives a clear account of the proceedings, infiltrated by a delicate irony remarkably effective in illustrating her disapproval of the case for the prosecution. Beginning by explaining both sides of the argument, she goes on to describe the main players, drily portraying the judge, Mr. Justice Byrne, as "seemingly a man with little taste for fiction"; the red-faced prosecuting counsel, Mervyn Griffith-Jones, is "embarrassing to watch," while Gerald Gardiner for the defence appears "unemotional, cool, undramatic." Among the many famous names appearing as witnesses are E. M. Forster and Rebecca West, although most space is given to the two most effective testimonies, both from university academics, Helen Gardner from Oxford and Richard Hoggart from Leicester, whose courteous and informed statements were disastrously to damage the clearly ill-prepared Griffith-Jones. As the case continues it becomes ever clearer that the bullying Griffith-Jones is losing his grip. "He had never in his life been conditioned to regard with respect any modern classic in the realm of purely imaginative writing," which explains why his "cross-examinations were so indignant, so ineffective and so very much beside the point."

While in court Sybille was seated between the writer Penelope Gilliatt, who had commissioned Sybille's first article on the Old Bailey, and the theatre critic Kenneth Tynan. Although Sybille later reported that she and Tynan had been threatened with expulsion for laughing at some of the more ludicrous interactions, in fact the case had deeply disturbed her. "I felt so desperately strongly about it," she wrote to Evelyn only days after the trial had finished. "I sat . . . shaking with anguish and fury." Writing about it, she said, had been important to her on a personal level. "I really felt I had to pay back, put down some of what one had lived. But it has made me hate England. Curious, when I was young I never thought of DHL the whole year around, until the month one spent in London: then he seemed like the prophet in the wilderness, and one hated what he had hated, and I could not bear to get back to France."

Soon after finishing her long article, Sybille was delighted to hear from Evelyn that Simon & Schuster were offering a generous advance for her next novel. Bob Gottlieb, aware of her dissatisfaction with Mark Bonham Carter and Collins, was keen to have Sybille regard his own firm as her primary publisher. He felt that "you are ours and we are yours," he told her, and "though you're English and England is your base, we think that we are your publishers."

Anxious to begin work on a story that had been in the back of her mind for some time, Sybille at the end of the year was pleased to leave "wet, grey, cold, dreary" England for a couple of months in France. After a few days in Paris, she and Eda continued on to the south, staying with Allanah until the end of January. Despite a moderately merry Christmas, however, it was not a productive period for Sybille, who had sunk into one of her paralysing depressions. "Dawdle time away whining to and leaning on Allanah: and nothing lifts," she noted in her diary. "I am a weak fool. Now it is after twelve noon. God help me. I looked at work for about ten minutes, then went down to make and eat lunch with Allanah in the chilly kitchen. Lamenting went on; near tears some of the time. Allanah very sweet. That is always consoling: the help of others. Deserved?"

At the end of January 1961, she and Eda returned to England, both restless, both anxious to leave again as soon as possible. April saw the publication in London and New York of Eda's first novel, *Childsplay*, on which she had been working for some time. Closely autobiographical and written with an elegant simplicity, the story follows her early years with her father in the Middle West, her grandmother in Chicago, continuing on to her schooldays in California, then at Stanford University, and ending with her brief career in advertising in New York. Sybille declared herself deeply moved by the book, and there were a number of appreciative reviews, among them one in the *Manchester Guardian* describing *Childsplay* as a "masterpiece, tour de force, work of art." To Eda's particular gratification, her old friend Jimmy Stern, himself a reputable writer, told her he was overwhelmed by the work. It "is an amazing achievement . . . there isn't a dull paragraph . . . one is left not kissing or hugging the child but kneeling at her feet."

By this time Sybille and Eda had again left England, in March travelling south to Aix-en-Provence, where they were joined for a few days by the Robson-Scotts; from there they went to spend a week with Allanah, before going on to Rome. This was Sybille's first return to the city for over six years, an experience she found strangely disturbing. "I feel so much older," she told Allanah. "This country needs a certain vitality and flexibility and toughness. Youth, in a word. I've loved it too much, and now one is back like a revenant." There was much that had changed for the worse—the swarms of tourists, the heavier traffic, the often intolerable noise—but nonetheless the beauty of the city was "intact, incredible." Staying once more at the d'Inghilterra, Sybille took pleasure in seeing a number of her old friends, among them Donald Downes, and also Kenneth Macpherson, who had moved from Capri to live in Rome after the death of his old associate, Norman Douglas.

During this period Martha, too, arrived in Rome, her presence not entirely welcome. As before in London, Sybille felt she was regarded by Martha as "a grade B acquaintance," an attitude she resented, particularly as, in Sybille's view, she herself was of a higher social standing, and "never for a moment am I not imbued with the cast iron belief that M belongs to a different class than oneself." She and Eda met Martha for dinner on a couple of occasions at Toto's, their favourite trattoria— which "I am sorry to say she calls a Trat"; Sybille was made impatient by Martha's indifference to the beauty of the city, her current absorption in shopping and dinner parties. "She worries me," Sybille confessed to Evelyn. "One of the troubles is that what was possible for the free-wheeling journalist, all her rashness and brassiness and saying people were bums or one doesn't need to eat, is not so for Mrs. T. D. Matthews, with the house in Chester Square and all the rest."

Despite the resentments and complaints, however, at this period there still remained a solid basis of friendship, Sybille grateful as ever for Martha's support, particularly with her writing. It was Martha on whom she relied for advice on her work, and Martha one of a number of friends who continued to lend her money whenever she needed it. "You're a good friend," Sybille had written to her not long before their meeting in Rome. "Your part in my life has been strange: almost miraculously fruitful to me in some ways. The whole material basis of my present existence is chiefly due to strategic interventions and exertions at some turning point on your part." The letter was signed "Love, dear girl, Your grateful & tearful old chum, S."

In June 1961, shortly after Sybille and Eda returned to England, Aldous Huxley arrived in London, on his own as Laura had been obliged to stay in California. Only weeks before, in May, the Huxleys had undergone a shocking experience: their house in Los Angeles had caught fire and been burnt to the ground, with almost everything, including Aldous's books, manuscripts and correspondence, destroyed. Sybille had been appalled by the news, and within the first few minutes of their meeting in London had asked him how on earth he had coped with such a catastrophe. "Well," Aldous replied, as calm and rational as ever, "I went out and bought a toothbrush." Worried to see how thin and gaunt he appeared, his thick hair now mostly white, Sybille was soon reassured by Aldous's energy and cheerfulness. On a warm evening the two dined together at Rules in Covent Garden, then set out on a long walk, through Holborn and Bloomsbury, eventually on up to Marylebone and Dorset Square, where Sybille was staying with the Robson-Scotts. "Only then, with no sense of urgency, did Aldous decide that he might as well go back to Kensington in a cab . . . It was a curious and rather moving evening for me," Sybille reported to Allanah. "The first time we met since Maria died."

Shortly afterwards Aldous left England to attend a conference in the south of France. From there he wrote to Sybille, telling her "how good it was to meet again after all this time," and suggesting the two of them might take a short motoring holiday together. "If you can provide the car & the driving, I will provide the petrol and the living expenses. It might, I think, be fun." In the event, however, Aldous was unable to spare the time, returning to the States in September. Two years later, on 22 November 1963, Aldous died of cancer, the news of his death overshadowed by the assassination the same day of President Kennedy. Sybille learned of the circumstances from Eva Herrmann. "Eva writes that he did not suffer," she reported to Evelyn, "and wrote until two days before he died. An essay on Shakespeare, and finished it. Something consoling in that."

Sybille was very shaken by Aldous's death, by the loss of the man who for so many years she had regarded as her father figure, "the greatest moral influence on my life." In her contribution to a memorial volume published two years later, she recalls the pleasure of her early years with the Huxleys in Sanary, fondly remembering "Aldous's <u>unfailing</u> goodwill, his patience, his readiness to help . . . his inability to lie or hate, to form a petty thought or a malevolent emotion; his fortitude. Only now, can I see him then as the man who practised what he later preached. *Era tanto buono* [He was so good]."

Meanwhile, Sybille had continued to work on her novel, with which she was now making good progress. Yet while she and Eda were glad of the privacy and quiet provided by Little Wynters, they now found the solitude depressing. There is "no counter lift in the evening in this wretched Essex wilderness," Sybille complained. "I like to fling myself out into the street of an evening, friends, talk, drink." Nonetheless, the lack of diversion had its rewards as Sybille finally completed the book at the end of March 1962. The news was excitedly relayed by letter to a number of friends, among them Evelyn, the Robson-Scotts and also Jimmy Stern, now regarded by Sybille as one of her most important literary mentors. "I have now finished my novel. It has nearly killed me," she told him. "The relief is so great that I'm not used to it yet. It also feels like a cold silence after an incessant rush of noise."

As before with *A Legacy*, *A Favourite of the Gods* draws significantly on Sybille's own family history and experience, although, curiously, in an introduction to a later edition she states that the novel was "my one attempt at fiction with almost no autobiographical sources or associations." Certainly the first section, about an aristocratic family in Rome at the end of the nineteenth century, draws closer parallels with the novels of Henry James than with Sybille's own story, yet from the very beginning the similarities are indisputable.

In *A Favourite*, dedicated to Eda, the plot revolves around three generations of women in the same family: Anna, a wealthy American married to an Italian nobleman, her daughter, Constanza, and Constanza's daughter, Flavia. In a short prologue, Constanza and the child

Flavia are travelling by train from Italy to France in the 1920s, the same journey that all those years ago Sybille had made with her mother and Nori before settling in Sanary. When the train stops at the border, Constanza is shocked to discover the large ruby ring she had been wearing has disappeared. Desperate to find it, she decides to break her journey while an investigation is undertaken, eventually spending the night in a small fishing port on the French coast. And it is here, as it turns out, that she and Flavia will remain for many years to come.

From there the reader is taken back in time, to Rome in the 1890s and a marriage between Rico, an impoverished Italian prince, and Anna, the independent-minded daughter of an upright New England family. While Anna plays hostess to a group of diplomats, intellectuals, clergy and visiting Americans, Rico, a charming if negligent husband, spends his time playing cards with his men friends and visiting his mistress. Inevitably the time comes when the naive Anna discovers her husband's long-standing infidelity: enraged and implacable, she leaves Rome for ever, taking her daughter with her to live in London.

Here Constanza immerses herself in a sophisticated social life, her friends and many lovers mostly clever and ambitious young men, one of whom, shortly after the outbreak of war, she agrees to marry. Not long afterwards her husband is wounded while fighting in France, and it is shortly after his return to England that Constanza gives birth to their daughter, Flavia. The marriage soon founders, and after the divorce Constanza, accompanied by Flavia, returns to her peripatetic life of independence and adventure, eventually deciding to settle in the south of France, where she meets the Frenchman who will be the love of her life.

The character of the beautiful Constanza, clever and self-assured, bears an undeniable resemblance to Sybille's mother, reflecting Lisa's beauty and intellect as well as her promiscuity; similarly, Constanza's father Rico shares many attributes with Maximilian, a handsome philanderer, benign, unintellectual and emotionally detached. Their daughter, Flavia, as literary and inquisitive as Sybille herself, comes to develop, as Sybille did for Lisa, a protective fondness for her somewhat wayward mother. The small French fishing port in which the two of them eventually settle is an accurate depiction in every detail of Sanary, and the life the two women lead there, a mirror image of Sybille's adolescence, the draughty little villa in which the family first settled, the afternoons she and Lisa spent playing cards in a café overlooking the harbour, the evenings when Flavia, like Sybille, would walk "down to the village with napkin and bowl . . . [to bring] back a takeaway dish from the caterer."

Similarly the early section of the story clearly derives from Sybille's experience of Italy and of Rome. She demonstrates a flawless sense of period, even if the picture of her chosen stratum of society, the combination of Italian aristocracy and wealthy Americans, unavoidably evokes the world of Henry James, Sybille even naming one of her characters "Mr. James." (This was a mistake, as she later admitted: although Mr. James "was a New Englander with a Harvard link, he was in no ways related, connected, or alike his illustrious namesake.") Memorable, too, is the account of the prince's estate in Umbria, much loved by Constanza when a girl. "Lyre-horned oxen moved the hand-ploughs along small patched fields; on the slopes goats pegged to stumpy trees tore at harsh shrubs, there were lizards on the walls and the days were strident with cicadas and the nights loud with frogs."

Rather less successful is the portrayal of the two heroines, Flavia and Constanza. While the chivalrous Rico and naive Anna are subtly drawn, both wholly convincing, Constanza and Flavia, with all their formidable intelligence and determination, appear somewhat two-dimensional. Constanza's intellectual conversations are ponderous, and although high-minded and, we are told, frequently in love, she never appears to feel sufficiently for any one person or cause to convince the reader of the reality of either. Flavia as a little girl appears most unchildlike, sharing her mother's egotism, wholly lacking in both humour and charm. As Sybille's friend and mentor, Jimmy Stern, told her after reading the book, the two were difficult to envisage, too vague and unreal. "I do think you are inclined to make your characters talk a little too much in the same idiom, the same tone of voice. Now & again I could not tell them apart."

Fortunately, responses from other friends were more enthusiastic. Allanah described *A Favourite* as a novel of "technical perfection," while Martha wrote to "Sibbie my hero . . . the writing is the best, clearest, strongest you have ever done." From New York Evelyn described it as a flawless masterpiece, a work which had "in itself the power to soar . . . as though angels might take wing . . . The writing, the sheer writing, is plain virtuosity. Breathtaking." Her opinion was shared by her boss. "The book is wonderful," Bob told her. "Glorious Constanza and beautiful Flavia and awful Anna, I love them all . . . all of them so beautifully controlled and displayed, all of it so economical yet <u>there</u>."

Despite these encouraging reactions, Sybille was nervous about the book's public reception, and with reason, as it turned out. When *A Favourite* appeared in Britain early in 1963, reviews were mixed. The *Daily Telegraph* described the book as elegant and civilised, the *Spectator* judged it "an exceedingly good novel," while *The Times* praised the author's mind and style which "while capable of subtleties are vigorous, gay and direct." But V. S. Pritchett in the *New Statesman* was one of several who wrote in a more disparaging tone, complaining that after an excellent start, "the design vanishes into a flashy stream of mere chronology. As a feminist argument, Constanza is attractive; as a character she is totally unrealised." In the States, too, despite a few mildly appreciative notices, the majority of critics were unimpressed. "Miss Bedford is often too consciously literary in her technique," complained the *New York Review of Books*. Although her style is "supple and functional," the plotting is over-elaborate, and the novel fails because "she appears to forget human models, or to bear them in mind only fitfully." Even more condemnatory was the *New York Times*, which described *A Favourite* as "a mediocre novel . . . [that] drags and sags and finally expires in a burst of ingenious plotting."

Two readers who had expressed enthusiasm for *A Legacy*, Nancy Mitford and Evelyn Waugh, had been eagerly awaiting publication of the new work. When the time came, however, both confessed themselves disappointed. "It has been tremendously advertised by the Lesbian World here as better than *A Legacy* which it is certainly <u>not</u>," Nancy told Evelyn. "There are of course excellent things . . . but to me there is a certain naivete, underlying a sophisticated story . . . & then the characters are of wood. Wooden figures after Henry James. The strange thing is that this tough little person & ferocious Lesbian, always dressed as a motor racer should choose to write about an age of elegance . . . A sort of Golden Bowl upside-down . . . The beginning—the first quarter—is excellent & one thinks it is the prelude to an unfolding which doesn't happen—in fact the flower dies in the bud." To this Waugh replied that he, too, had been dismayed by the book's inadequacies. "Lovely first chapter—then it went to pieces . . . what is more, full of solecisms & anachronisms. I pointed out a few hundred of the more glaring ones to Mark Bonham Carter & advised him to withdraw & correct it, but he hasn't answered. Umbrage perhaps."

Fortunately Sybille never learned of these opinions, depressed enough as she was by the reactions of the press. "I am very sick and sunk," she wrote to Evelyn in New York. "I feel poisoned by those reviews . . . It has been rammed home to me, that I am not in the latest phrase 'with it.' The time for my kind of writing is pretty nearly over." She had felt humiliated, too, by a television interview on the BBC with the formidable reporter Ludovic Kennedy, whom she described as "loud-mouthed and hostile . . . He told me . . . he had looked at my new novel, not read it through, and not liked it. And so we went off to the cameras. A degrading business. If I weren't heavily in debt to Collins I should not have done it."

Sybille had finished *A Favourite of the Gods* in March 1962, but so bruised was she by its critical battering that it would be several years before any inspiration returned.

TEN

"THE TREMENDOUS TRIALS OF OUR TIME"

D uring the interval between delivering the manuscript of *A Favourite* and its publication, Sybille was delighted to be given the chance of leaving the country for a while. She had been commissioned by *Esquire* to interview a writer whom she much admired, Karen Blixen, who, under the pen name Isak Dinesen, was the author, most famously, of *Seven Gothic Tales* and *Out of Africa*. In July 1962, Sybille and Eda left for Denmark, a country Sybille had visited only once, when she had been taken there as a small child by her mother. For this occasion Sybille had rented a chalet at a seaside resort not far from Baroness Blixen's family estate at Rungsted, a few miles north of Copenhagen. "I love the look of it, the fields, the trees, the duck ponds and white manor houses," Sybille reported, but "oh dear, it is cold . . . Worse, much worse than England . . . We buy our food at Elsinore . . . Had Shakespeare really seen it, it would not have inspired him to setting his tragedy there."

A few days after arriving, Sybille was driven to Rungsted to meet the distinguished author, now in her late seventies. The house, a seventeenth-century coaching inn overlooking the sea on one side, a wood and orchard on the other, was "lovely"; the rest of the experience, however, if fascinating, was something of a disappointment. The baroness herself was tiny, fragile, gaunt-faced and skeletally thin. "She weighs 35 kilo . . . and is so weak that she cannot make a step unaided. She is dressed: narrow trousers, rough, white and black make up like Arlequin. She has the most extraordinary large eyes . . . She ate, during the whole longish meal, exactly one quarter of one strawberry. But as soon as the rest of us finished our chicken she began to smoke . . . and when she was carried back onto the verandah she clutched her package of cigarettes and a huge metal lighter . . . Later she drank cup after cup of black coffee, smoking all the time." Sybille's three fellow guests were Blixen's secretary, a Danish literary critic, and an Italian academic, none of whom were given much chance to speak as their hostess, despite her physical frailty, dominated the conversation, "very conscious she was, one felt, of being a baroness . . . Her talk was pretentious and not very interesting . . . *haute literature* in a rather *vieux jeux* way: 'Who would you say were the three greatest Englishmen? Shakespeare, Queen Elizabeth, Newton?' "

In the event, Sybille's article was never written. After leaving Denmark, she and Eda had driven to the south of France to stay with Allanah, where, not long after they arrived, news reached them that Karen Blixen had died. Sybille fulfilled her commission by writing a travel piece describing Copenhagen and its surrounding territory, her lack of interest in the country on the whole tactfully concealed.

After a pleasant couple of months at Les Bastides, Sybille and Eda returned to England in October, where they were met by some unwelcome news. Their landlord, Sir Thomas Pike, was on the point of retiring and wished to end their tenancy of Little Wynters. Inevitably this threw Sybille into a panic, and the prospect of returning to "horrible, plebeian, ugly" London appalled her. And where were they to live? Fortunately Sybille's old friend, Charlotte Wolff, came to the rescue, finding a flat for rent in Tregunter Road, Chelsea. "I don't like it, Eda doesn't like it . . . [but] dirt cheap for London," Sybille told Evelyn. The contract was signed and the move from Essex planned for the New Year.

Over the past few months, Sybille had received a number of letters from both Esther and Katzi, which had caused her considerable anxiety, each angrily complaining about the other. Although they had lived together for years and were close in age, the two were widely different in temperament, with almost no interests in common. Now, with Katzi in love with Gino and longing to spend time with him, she increasingly resented her domestic duties and what she regarded as Esther's patronising manner. "*Esther . . . toujours très distante . . . jamais un mot personnelle*" ("Esther . . . is always very distant . . . never a personal word"), Katzi complained. "*Elle m'a accusé de chose que j'ai jamais dite . . . A t-elle recommencé a boire? . . . C'est parce que Gino est ici? . . . Enfin je commence presque à croire—qu'elle est furieuse de me voir heureuse*" ("She accused me of something I never said . . . Has she begun to drink again? . . . Is it because Gino is here? . . . Ultimately I begin to think—she's furious because she sees me happy"). How was she to cope, Katzi demanded, with "*ces angoisses perpétuelles*" ("these perpetual anxieties")?

Esther, although by nature tranquil and benign, was being driven to extremes of irritation and despair by Katzi's behaviour. "I am afraid the situation between me and Katzi cannot continue," she told Sybille. "I cannot afford to live in this apartment with her . . . with Katzi taunting me all the time and saying how '*moche* [ugly]' everything is and how she hates France. Forgive me for saying it, but in addition to her <u>many fine qualities</u>, there is a good deal of the German and the bully in your sister, and I have let her get out of hand . . . I do not think Katzi and I can continue to live together. I don't blame her—this man means everything to her and she would walk over unborn babes' skulls to keep him. It is '*la dernière passion* [the last passion]' of an ageing woman . . . I do not think she ought to live with any woman—she is purely and entirely a man's woman—least of all with a woman like me. I know how difficult I am and that I should probably live alone."

The battle between the two, begun during the summer and continuing well into the autumn, left Sybille feeling helpless, unable to see how they might ever become reconciled. Esther, despite her kindness, was "a kind of monster," with her endless talking and drinking, while Katzi "is one of the stupidest women I know . . . The small brain has never learnt to order the emotions."

Then on the morning of Friday 23 November, while Sybille and Eda were still ensconced at Little Wynters, Esther in the rue de Lille woke late as usual, dressed in a leisurely manner and prepared for her customary walk across the Seine to Galignani, the English bookshop on the Right Bank. Before she had the chance to leave the apartment, she suffered a violent stroke, dying instantly. She had turned sixty-five only a few weeks earlier.

Sybille was in Harlow when the news reached her. On the Sunday, in a state of shock, she went by train to London, staying the night with the Robson-Scotts and arriving in Paris the following evening. Here she found Katzi alone in the apartment, although Esther's sister-in-law, Noël Murphy, had been with her most of the time. It was Noël, only hours after Esther's death, who had arranged for a priest to give the benediction, the body afterwards packed in dry ice as the cremation was not to be held for several days. As Esther had had no religious faith, a simple ceremony had been organised for the following Tuesday, Sybille one of a small cortège leaving the rue de Lille shortly before 9 a.m. for the cemetery of Père-Lachaise. The brief rite was well attended, and among the mourners was Nancy Mitford. "Oh dear I shall miss her," Nancy wrote afterwards to Evelyn Waugh. "Esther was a large sandy person like a bedroom cupboard packed full of information, much of it useless, all of it accurate. I was truly fond of her." A few days later there was a funeral mass at Saint-Germain-des-Prés, after which Esther's ashes were shipped to America, where her brother Gerald had them buried in the family plot in East Hampton.

During the next few days, Sybille, assisted by Katzi, spent hours going through Esther's papers, the notes for her unwritten biographies as well as a vast body of correspondence; Sybille burned almost everything, including all her own letters to Esther, spanning a period of over twenty years. When the will was read, unchanged since 1948, it was discovered that Esther had left the apartment and her few possessions to be divided equally between Sybille and Noël. The two women immediately agreed to make both their legacies over to Katzi, who since Esther's death had been left with no source of income at all. For this Katzi was deeply grateful, later writing to her sister to thank her for "*ta grande générosité envers moi—c'est finalement toujours toi dans ma vie qui m'a aidé et pouvait de vivre . . . J'éspère que un jour—ça sera mon tour*" ("your great generosity towards me—in the end it's always you in my life who's helped me and enabled me to live . . . I hope that one day— it will be my turn").

On Sybille's return to England, Eda, who had met her at Epping Station, was shocked by her appearance—she "returned in a state of collapse: white, shaking, exhausted," Eda reported to the Sterns. "Going to Paris was a terrible ordeal, physically and mentally . . . S. has such a very unhardened side and Esther's death touched it more closely than it has ever been touched before." And indeed for the rest of her long life, Sybille continued to be haunted by memories of Esther. She had loved her dearly, missed her gentle nature, her intellect and unfailing generosity, yet at the same time suffered a feeling of frustration that Esther had never come near to achieving her remarkable promise: those planned biographies, those endless rivers of explication, all in the end resulting in nothing. "What's the use of being brilliant," Sybille later remarked, "if you sit at a café all day and are considered the greatest bore because you don't know when to stop talking and never write anything down?"

Not long after Sybille's return from Paris, she and Eda left Essex for London, both in a state of depression, Sybille grieving for Esther, Eda miserable at leaving Little Wynters, which she had come to love. Fortunately, however, they were not there for long, as Sybille had taken a house in Asolo, the famously beautiful medieval city in the Veneto region of Italy. Casa La Mura, where Robert Browning had stayed shortly before his death, was a handsome building, set into the wall surrounding the city and immediately inside the arched gateway; on one side was a view of the cathedral and the central piazza, on the other of an undulating plain covered in fields and vineyards; at the back of the property was a shady garden planted with roses and olive trees. "The view from every window is like an Italian painting," Eda told Tania Stern, while for Sybille La Mura on first sight appeared to be everything she wanted, "ravishing and no noise . . . [only] thirty-five miles from Venice, from Vicenza, Padua. Italian spring: mountains, sea." Here they intended to stay for the best part of a year, looking forward to a peaceful period in which to write and gradually recover from the upheavals of the recent past.

The two women left London by car at the beginning of May 1963, arriving in Asolo a few days later in torrential rain. Within the first twenty-four hours they realised the mistake they had made: although the interior of the house was spacious and comfortable, outside the noise was incessant and appalling. La Mura was like living in "the inside of a meat grinder," Sybille complained; "large motor coaches, not to speak of scooters and road-races pass through our very marrow . . . Below our bedroom windows is the narrow gate . . . revving, hooting, belching diesel fumes." The noise continued until late at night and began again shortly after dawn, making it impossible to sleep into the morning. To make matters worse, it almost never stopped raining, and the maid, whose wages had been included as part of the rent, had fallen ill, so "we find ourselves again making beds and washing up, and paying 30,000 francs a month and her food for doing it."

Apart from a couple of excursions to Venice, there were few breaks from this dismal existence, one exception being an invitation to tea twice a week from the famous explorer, Freya Stark, resident in Asolo since the 1920s. Sybille had first met Freya while on a previous visit to Italy, and she now came to enjoy these somewhat austere occasions. "She's a kitten compared to ICB [Ivy Compton-Burnett]. I find her likeable (what she allows to appear) and the first English resident in Italy I've talked to who shares my views about the hideous nature of the Fascist regime in the 20s and 30s." But then again, agreeable although these visits were, there was much else that was objectionable about the town's social life. "Too many English," in Sybille's view, while both she and Eda resented the fact that there was "no possibility of coming and going and dressing as one pleases. A bothersome idea to have to wear stockings in blazing sun. Skirts when slacks are better for country walks. Gloves when hands are cooler. Hats, when one isn't used to hats. One somehow felt the unsaid rules."

Eventually Eda and Sybille decided they could endure it no longer, and although their landlady refused to refund any money, they left Asolo at the beginning of July, driving to France to spend a recuperative few months with Allanah. Arriving at Les Bastides Sybille immediately felt happy. "Allanah is being so very very sweet, and really seems to like to stuff her house with a selfish old creature like myself. Then the climate, the air that is like an element, the few clothes one wears, the sense of outdoor life and freedom. Being in the open air is bliss to me." Allanah, too, seemed very contented: divorced from her husband, Robert, she had also surrendered her maternal role, giving up her rights to the little boy she and Fay Blacket Gill had originally adopted together. Despite their occasionally embattled friendship, Allanah and Sybille remained close; Allanah confessed to Evelyn that when Sybille was in England she missed her "terribly. I love her more than anyone and would do anything for her."

Over the next couple of years, Allanah was to make some significant alterations to her property, her aim to provide Sybille, in return for a modest rent, with the space, privacy and quiet she needed to write. Close to the main house were a couple of small farm buildings, one of which was now converted into a separate two-storey dwelling, with jasmine and honeysuckle climbing the walls, and a vine-covered terrace overlooking the garden and beyond it the sea. The interior was whitewashed, the rooms lined with bookshelves, the air kept cool by "shutters closed from dawn to sinking sun." There was even a small wine cellar in an area dug out between wall and rock, "a true cave," as Sybille described it, "pitch-dark, very low . . . I had to squeeze in on all fours . . . extracting bottles one by one, pocket torch held in the other hand, then back out again." Here in their adjoining studios Sybille and Eda were able to spend the mornings peacefully at work; in the afternoons they drove down to the beach to swim, before joining Allanah in the evening for dinner. "This place is bliss," Sybille reported, "bare, clean and spacious; sun-drenched, large French windows opening south onto olives and wild country . . . No noise except cicadas. We dine out of doors every night. And there is a soothing stillness from morning (when Allanah goes off in her boat) till five in the afternoon when the *femme de ménage* clatters in."

This idyllic period was to be interrupted only once, when in mid-July Sybille returned to London for a couple of weeks, commissioned by *Esquire* to report on the trial of Stephen Ward. Ward was an originally peripheral figure in what had recently become notorious as the Profumo scandal. In March 1963, John Profumo, a distinguished member of Harold Macmillan's government, had been forced to resign after denying the truth about his relationship with Christine Keeler, a beautiful young "model" suspected of connections to a Russian naval attaché. It was Stephen Ward, described in the press as a "society osteopath," who had introduced Keeler to Profumo, and when further investigation revealed his close connection to a number of other young women of dubious reputation Ward was charged under the Sexual Offences Act of living off immoral earnings.

The trial began on 22 July at the Old Bailey, and from the beginning Sybille found herself both fascinated and appalled as the increasingly disquieting story unfolded over the following few days. Among the many witnesses called to testify, by far the most striking were Christine Keeler herself and Mandy Rice-Davies, both close friends of Dr. Ward. Keeler, a dark-haired beauty, was described by Sybille as "devastatingly sexually attractive," but whose absence of emotion gave a curiously chilling impression. "Not only the mean little voice is a giveaway, the look on the face is avid, stubborn, closed . . . At times there might have been a puppet in that box." Rice-Davies, by contrast, "festively decked out," was blonde, pert, giggly. "After Christine Keeler's wan automatism," Sybille observed, "we were back to flesh and blood. Miss Rice-Davies was at ease in the box like a cheerful predatory cat who knows she's got a good many mice under her paw."

Not until the fourth day did Dr. Ward enter the witness box. "His presence came as a shock, the shock of fresh air . . . Within two minutes one knew that he had two qualities which had not been associated with him publicly before, intelligence and dignity." Ward was interrogated for nearly six hours, responding with unfailing courtesy and calm, repeatedly making clear that although he enjoyed the company of pretty girls, he had plenty of money of his own and had never procured women for financial gain. Towards the end of the trial, the judge, Sir Archie Marshall, began a summing-up widely regarded as highly prejudiced against Ward. When at 4:30 the court closed for the day, "a kind of flat gloom set in. It must have sprung from a growing conviction among many of us that if Dr. Ward were not acquitted, justice would not have been felt to have been done."

On leaving the Old Bailey, Sybille found herself sharing a taxi with Ward. He was clearly in a desperate state, and she held his hand while trying to comfort and encourage him—to no avail, as it turned out: that night, 30 July, Ward took an overdose of barbiturates, and when discovered lying unconscious was rushed to hospital. After the court reconvened the following morning, the jury in his absence found him guilty of living immorally off the earnings of both Keeler and Rice-Davies, the judge suspending sentence until the accused was well enough to return. But Ward never did return, dying three days later, so "what that sentence would have been we shall never know."

Sybille had been shocked by the whole experience, "a case of judicial murder," as she later described it. "A very, very ugly page of English history." Writing to Evelyn the day after the trial ended, she told her how the "strange, doomed business" had left her with "a heavy feeling of tragedy, muddle & waste . . . a blatant and distressing manipulation of justice, and very frightening for us all." Her long article on the trial, entitled "The Worst We Can Do," was completed within weeks, but shortly before publication it was withdrawn, judged to be in contempt of court.*

With the case completed, Sybille returned to France, where she was to stay till the beginning of the following year. By now her journalistic career was well established, and she was receiving frequent requests for articles; her willingness to accept these often trivial commissions resulted in an admonitory letter from her agent in New York. "Tortiss Tortiss Tortiss," Evelyn began, "Pull up short—WHOA. I feel as if my T[urtle] has turned into a runaway horsie with bit-in-teeth. Darling you must STOP this galloping off in all directions on every nonsense piece of journalism that offers . . . It's not good for you when you simply take job after job as it's offered, so you're a perpetual journalism factory with no time for serious work for months on end." Only days after this letter was written, however, an offer arrived on Evelyn's desk which she realised would be out of the question for Sybille to refuse: to report for *Life* magazine on the trial in Dallas of Jack Ruby, accused of the murder of Lee Harvey Oswald, the assassin of President Kennedy.

"Darling listen," Evelyn wrote excitedly, "you surely must know that this will be one of the tremendous trials of our time . . . Bob says it's the greatest thing for your career that ever was." The offer from *Life* included all expenses paid, "plus, of course, the highest money in the US for every single piece . . . If this trial lasts 3 weeks—you can

* As Christine Keeler had yet to be tried, it was considered that the publication of the article could damage her defence. I owe this explanation to Desmond Browne QC, who gave it as his opinion that "the account of Christine Keeler's lifestyle, coupled with Sybille Bedford's doubts about her truthfulness, were potentially prejudicial. There is always a danger in a court report in which the author interpolates their own assessment of the evidence."

make a minimum of 15,000 dollars, repeat minimum. Bob says, this is a different class of money—beyond anybody's sanity."

Sybille did not hesitate to accept, and at the end of January 1964, she and Eda sailed for New York; Eda then left for California to stay with her old schoolfriend, the now well-known writer M. F. K. Fisher. Sybille meanwhile spent a week at the luxurious Weston Hotel in Manhattan, where she found herself "rushed off feet. The LIFE business is so tough I don't see how I can survive it." At a luncheon given by "the Top Brass on LIFE/TIME," the company, to Sybille's disgust, spent an entire two hours drinking cocktails before the first morsel of food appeared. Among her fellow guests was Ruby's counsel, Melvin Belli, a large, handsome man with thick white hair, pompous and vain, "a monster who'd be debarred in England." After arriving in Dallas, "the most hideous town I have ever seen," she was given a suite at the Sheraton Hotel, "2 TV sets & 4 telephones. No natural air; all food iced . . . Last night at dinner I sat next to the Prosecuting Attorney who chewed a cold cigar while he spoke." Later, looking back, she wrote, "I had five mortal weeks at Dallas and hated nearly every minute of it."

The trial of Jack Ruby, who had shot Oswald only two days after Oswald had murdered the President, was the focus of attention all over the world. As the shooting had been caught on camera, there was no question that Ruby was the killer; the case to be proven was not whether he were guilty of the act, but whether he had been in his right mind while committing it. Well aware of the gravity of the forthcoming trial and of its overwhelming national importance, Sybille was shocked to find how casually the proceedings were conducted in court, how undisciplined the behaviour of the legal teams. In a tone of barely concealed contempt, she describes the district attorney, Henry Wade, "lying back in his chair, chomping on his unlit cigar," while the judge, Joe. B. Brown, "bumbles about the scene . . . calls for water, swallows a pill or stands still to be photographed, or does his go-out-and-get-a-cup-of-coffee stuff." Meanwhile the accused, Jack Ruby, watches the proceedings "with a kind of dead-chicken stare. He looked . . . like a wretched, scraggly, half-plucked broiler, blinking or staring under a strong hypnotic light."

When after nearly three weeks the trial reaches its final stage, the courthouse is "overflowing with humanity and litter, with counsel, staff and newsmen in an indescribable state of grubbiness, nervous exhaustion, fatigue." By the time Melvin Belli begins his "wildly theatrical" closing speech, it is after midnight and everyone is exhausted. Belli speaks in a style reminiscent of "the long-discarded forensic art of the Victorians, the courtroom style of blood and thunder and tears . . . Dickens would have been at home here." When at 1 a.m. the case is finally referred to the jury, the judge instructs them to leave for a night's sleep before reconvening the following day. Next morning a consensus is quickly reached: Ruby is declared guilty of murder and sentenced to death.

After the trial finished, Sybille immediately returned to New York, the pressure of meeting her deadline intense. "I did sixteen thousand words . . . between one Saturday afternoon and the next Wednesday morning," she told Allanah. "I got up at 3.30 every morning and worked till 9 or 10 in the evening." In her report, her distaste for what she regarded as the "clownishly conducted" procedure in court and her shock over Ruby's sentencing are modified only up to a point. Perhaps unsurprisingly, her article attracted some negative criticism. "The summary of the testimony Miss Bedford presents seems reasonably objective," stated an editorial in the *Salt Lake Telegram*. "But by using one of the oldest, most transparent and discredited reportorial tricks of the business—the use of highly subjective adjectives to describe participants—she sets about discrediting judge, prosecution attorneys, and state witnesses." Miss Bedford was entitled to her opinion, but it was shameful "for a supposedly responsible national publication to spread this sort of womanly emotionalism on its news pages."

Once the article was written, Sybille, "feted everywhere" and living in luxury at the magazine's expense, was able to enjoy herself. Eda had returned from California, "has put on some weight, thank God," and the two of them now embarked on a round of cocktail parties, luncheons and dinners. One of the most memorable evenings was spent with Bob Gottlieb, Bob excited finally to meet the author whose work he so much admired. As Bob was indifferent to food and cared nothing about wine—"I only know there's red wine and white wine and that disgusting thing called rosé"—he had left the preparations for dinner to his wife, Muriel. Fortunately, "with the help of Manhattan's finest butcher she came through and produced a *filet de boeuf* that passed muster." The evening was clearly a success; Bob was fascinated by Sybille, impressed by her intellect and knowledge, while at the same time aware of a slight air of condescension in her manner towards him. "We had a good time together," he recalled, "but she was formidable . . . [Sybille] was arrogant, not a cosy person . . . She thought publishers and editors were tradesmen, didn't see them as equals."

Inevitably, the most emotionally charged element of Sybille's time in New York was her reunion with Evelyn. For the past fifteen years, Evelyn had provided the cornerstone of Sybille's professional and emotional life, while for Evelyn Sybille remained her dearest love, her closest confidante and friend. After Sybille's departure at the end of April, Evelyn wrote to her, "I miss you so much you can't imagine . . . And also feel consoled because I miss you: it's such a proof of the realness of the loving tie . . . And no I didn't see you sail. Stood on shore . . . and munched a hot dog off a hot-dog stand. Just stood and stared and stared and ate the hot dog then went and took the cross-town to office. OH and missed you so much."

Sybille and Eda left New York on the *Queen Elizabeth*, disembarking at Cherbourg rather than Southampton, as they were to return immediately to the south of France. And here over the next few years the two of them were to make their base, although several expeditions were also undertaken to other countries, to Italy, Germany, Yugoslavia, and to England. As ever, England and France were the two countries Sybille loved the most, despite their numerous faults and failings. "I'm deeply, intrinsically attached to France and to the French way of living," she said once in an interview, while "my ties with England are language, profession, institutions—and friends."

Among those friends Martha Gellhorn was one on whom Sybille continued to rely, grateful for her continuing financial help and for her open invitation to stay in Chester Square. On a personal level, however, she was beginning to find Martha increasingly difficult, resenting her bossiness and bad moods. "I admired her so," she told Evelyn, "and it animated my life at times. Now I do not admire her . . . [she] bores me. That is the worst . . . [her] reactions to me are so *déjà vu* and brash and empty . . . She is unhappy now, footloose, in despair . . . but all so self-made." The cause of Martha's current unhappiness was the sudden collapse of her marriage to Tom Matthews, recently discovered to have been conducting a secret affair for some time. The role of wife had never been easy for Martha, who had always hated the "absolute, pure, nameless, indescribable loathsome hell" of domesticity; "the plain fact is I should never have married . . . marriage is murder for me," she had confessed to Sybille only months after her wedding. Now, enraged by Tom's betrayal, Martha had decided to leave him, impatient to escape a relationship in which almost from the beginning she had felt trapped. Despite Sybille's misgivings about Martha, she was sympathetic to her situation. "One was very sad for M," Sybille told Evelyn, "who felt the human disappointment in Tom most and her wasted years and found it hard to see another side."

Two old friends with whom Sybille remained in affectionate contact were Jimmy and Tania Stern, now settled in England at Hatch Manor, a handsome sixteenth-century house with a large garden in Wiltshire. Here Sybille and Eda were often invited to stay, both enjoying the intellectual talk, the good food, the spacious book-lined sitting room with its open fire and comfortable chairs and sofas. The Sterns had been married for nearly thirty years, Jimmy as tall and handsome as ever, with his fine features and thick grey hair, Tania pale and delicate; both were always elegantly dressed, Jimmy in finely tailored tweeds, Tania with a metropolitan chic reminiscent of pre-war Paris and Berlin. Jimmy was very much the dominant partner, clever and amusing, insatiably demanding, quickly irritable, his main target Tania, whom he condescendingly referred to as "the LW," the little wife—"*Bist du da?*" ("Are you there?"), he would call to her throughout the day. Both Sterns were avid talkers, and with friends at dinner Jimmy before long would grow resentful of the audience at Tania's end of the table; rising from his chair, often half drunk, he would summon a chosen guest to go with him to his study, leaving Tania to entertain the rest of the company, the second rank, in the sitting room.

From the first, Sybille treasured her visits to Hatch. She relished Tania's excellent cooking, was fascinated by Jimmy's conversation, impressed by his profound knowledge of European literature, and she loved the fact that as guests neither she nor Eda ever had to lift a finger. "The bliss of no housework . . . talk talk talk, sheer joy and never without a full glass of champagne to hand. How I love that." Sybille was grateful, too, for Jimmy's generosity, for the large cheques that arrived every year on her birthday and at Christmas, and she enjoyed the glamorous parties hosted by the Sterns on their visits to London. In November 1960 Sybille and Eda had been invited to a fiftieth-birthday dinner for Tania at the Etoile, along with the Robson-Scotts, John Lehmann, William Plomer and Nigel Dennis, Sybille, to everyone's surprise, arriving dressed in a chic black evening dress and pearls.

An added attraction of staying at Hatch was the company of near neighbours, Billy and Jenny Hughes. Sybille had first known Billy Hughes over a decade earlier in Rome, where Billy had been chief of staff to the general commanding the Allied forces. Now a distinguished judge, tall, stout and very handsome, Billy was a man of enormous warmth and charm, witty, exceptionally well read and a talented raconteur. For Sybille he possessed almost every quality she admired. "I love Billy Hughes," she told Evelyn. "He is gay and kind and full of life, bursting with intelligence." His much younger wife, Jenny, was amused to see how taken Sybille was with her husband. "Sybille was obsessed with legal process, and if she found a lawyer who was also obsessed with poetry it was irresistible." Jenny for her part was intrigued by Sybille, although she often found her behaviour arrogant, particularly her bossiness and egotism, her habit of briskly brushing aside any intervention she considered irrelevant. In some respects, said Jenny, "she was a very difficult person to be fond of . . . with friends, she was quite secretive and it all had to be on her own terms, all of it."

Another significant friendship formed during this period was with a young film producer, Anne Balfour-Fraser. Anne and Sybille had first met at Little Wynters, where Anne had arrived for dinner one evening with her lover, Elizabeth ("Betts") Montagu, daughter of the Earl of Sandwich. Betts, whom Sybille had originally encountered through a shared fascination with the trial of Bodkin Adams, was a novelist, clever, acutely observant and with an ironic sense of humour. She was also a heavy drinker, and during the drive from London had insisted on stopping at a number of country pubs, with the result that the two of them arrived not only long after they were expected but with Anne tipsy and Betts extremely drunk. "Sybille was furious," Anne recalled, "as the meal (roast lamb) was late and ruined."

Sybille next encountered Anne while staying with Allanah in France, as she and Betts owned a house only a short distance from Les Bastides. Like Betts, Anne was well-born: her grandfather was the Earl of Balfour, brother of the Conservative prime minister, Arthur Balfour, while her great-grandfather was the famous novelist Edward Bulwer-Lytton. Intensely musical and highly intelligent, Anne had won a first at Cambridge before studying singing in London and Milan, afterwards becoming a successful documentary film producer. She had been married to a distinguished general, Sir David Fraser, by whom she had a daughter, but the couple had divorced after only a few years. Sybille was immediately attracted by Anne, with her handsome face and thick wavy brown hair, but her proposal of lovemaking was politely declined.

Despite this potential embarrassment, the two became close friends, Anne never failing to provide generous support, both emotional and material. As Sybille wrote to Evelyn, "I am devoted to Anne who is plump and gay and loves rich food and has three helpings when asked out, and sets a fine table herself. Above all she has a first-rate mind." On a number of occasions when Sybille and Eda had nowhere to stay in London, Anne lent them her "peach of a house" in Pimlico. And when in the south of France, they were frequently invited to the villa Anne shared with Betts at Valbonne. After a party there one Boxing Day night, Sybille wrote, "it was so beautiful . . . so magical . . . Anne singing Purcell and Italian arias accompanying herself on the clavichord—she has a fabulous sensuous voice, Milan trained—and the candlelight and the handsome honest English faces, all the upper-class boys and girls of the Balfours and Montagu families on hols. It was like something out of Trollope, only finer."

As before, Sybille found Les Bastides an almost ideal place in which to write, a much loved and familiar haven. There were of course the usual irritations, Allanah's bossiness (her disapproval of Sybille wearing trousers to dinner parties, of Eda's mannish haircut), and now there was her adored new dog, Bumbo, a wholly undisciplined boxer puppy, fast developing into as tiresome a member of the household as the previous generations of poodles. Nonetheless Sybille remained grateful to Allanah, especially as she was currently hard at work on a number of magazine articles, her anxiety increasing as each deadline approached. She was also suffering from the old problem with her eyes, of an extreme sensitivity to sunlight, obliging her to remain indoors during the day, wearing her green-lined tennis visor and with all the windows shuttered. While under such pressure she inevitably relied on Eda to cope with all domestic duties.

The previous year, 1963, had seen the publication of Eda's second novel, *A Matter of Choosing*, as before based on her own experiences, this time as a young woman at Stanford and later in New York. Although it had attracted little attention, she had already begun on a third work of fiction, and like Sybille had looked forward to a peaceful period at Les Bastides; but this proved impossible. For some time Eda had been suffering from an almost paralysing depression, had grown very thin, living largely off cigarettes and coffee; more and more she was finding it difficult to cope with Sybille's anxieties as well as with her own. When Sybille was under pressure, Eda said, it was "like living with a caged tiger," and because of the demands of her deadlines, it was Eda who was responsible for all the daily chores. "I've been nurse, housekeeper, errand boy, and the huge garden S wanted for her healthful exercise was tied round my neck with heavy chains. It didn't rain once all summer . . . I had to water by hand with a watering can . . . every evening without fail . . . Sybille at work like a beaver, and I . . . I sit staring at old chapters I haven't touched for a long time." Sybille was aware of Eda's dark moods but felt unable to help. "One could not ask. If I asked there was no answer. That wretchedness was neither admitted, nor discussed; it was concealed."

In October 1964, the two of them left France, driving across the border to Italy, to Alba for the truffle season. On this expedition they were accompanied by Katzi, now living with Gino in Nice. After Esther's death, Katzi had sold the apartment in the rue de Lille for a sum sufficient to provide her with an adequate income for life; unfortunately, Katzi had quickly spent the lot and was now in urgent need of support. Gino, currently working as a night porter at a hotel, earned very little, and as Sybille explained to Noël Murphy, Esther's sister-in-law, it was essential that Katzi find employment. "Katzi can work . . . her age (don't ever tell her I told you: or let prospective employers know it) will be 68 this summer. Her health is reasonably good, thank God, but she is not as strong . . . as she used to be." Noël held out little hope of Katzi finding a job, but in memory of Esther provided her instead with a small annuity.

After Italy, Sybille and Eda went on to London as Sybille, contracted to write an article on the House of Lords, was keen to attend the opening of Parliament at the beginning of November. Here again, while Sybille immersed herself in her subject, spending long afternoons in Westminster, Eda was left to cope with the domestic duties, driving about town collecting possessions stored with various friends, "sorting, packing, rearranging . . . then nose-to-grindstone when Sybille needed secretarial work done." After returning to France in December, their nomadic existence continued. As well as frequent visits to England, there were several weeks spent in Tuscany staying with Kenneth Macpherson, who had moved from Rome to a large and beautiful house near Siena; and in the late spring of 1965 the two women motored to Yugoslavia, as Sybille was to write about the country for an American travel magazine. "Yugoslavia was very exhausting," she reported to Martha. "So splendid, unique, visually; such a wretched place otherwise. Glad to be out of it."

On a different level altogether was a commission Sybille undertook for the *Saturday Evening Post* to cover what would become known as "the Auschwitz trial." The trial of twenty-two former guards at the Auschwitz concentration camp was to take place in Frankfurt and expected to last for six months. In the event the process continued for over one and a half years, the court during this time convening for only three days a week, as "anything more would have been unendurable." Sybille was present for the first week of the proceedings, in December 1963, and again for the final five days in August 1965. Inevitably she found the experience traumatic. "It filled me with a sick loathing," she said afterwards. "I tried so hard not to put Germans in a different category . . . I wish I could convey the utter misery of the trial."

For her own version of the process, Sybille relied mainly on reports in the German press, most specifically on the detailed accounts in the

Frankfurter Allgemeine Zeitung. As in all Sybille's court reporting, her observation is acute, her tone calm and lucid, despite, in this case, the horrifying content of much of the testimony. The trial, she explains, is "the first large-scale case of its kind tried by Germans, before a German judge and jury; the charges were murder and collective murder." As one by one the defendants are called for questioning, the same charges are made again and again. "Some killed by injecting disinfectant into human hearts, others by making people stand in freezing water, others operated the poison gas." As each of the accused takes his turn, the answers come almost by rote, denying guilt, unaware of what was going on. "What did you think these camps were for?" the judge asks one of the guards. "Protective camps. Where enemies of the Reich were being re-educated . . . I wanted to liberate the Reich from the Jews." As day after day the trial continues, Sybille notes the courtesy with which these "nightmarish figures" are treated. "Each one was asked if he would like a chair; all were given the *Herr* before their name; all were treated with detached politeness."

The summing-up began on 7 May 1965, and continued until 19 August, "a hot, grey, leaden morning." By this stage the chief judge, Dr. Hans Hofmeyer, was obviously under considerable stress, and at the end of his summing-up, "he said in a voice no longer quite audible or controlled that for nearly two years the bench had been under an almost unbearable emotional strain . . . Then the judge pulled himself up and icily addressed the convicted men. It was his duty, he said to inform them of their right to appeal. All but one have done so."

Sybille worked for over six months on her article, "The Worst that Ever Happened." After reading the ninety typewritten pages her editor at the *Post*, David Lyle, told her that he found the piece both powerful and compelling. It was, however, far too long and there were some significant changes to be made. In her response Sybille remained polite yet resolute: yes, she would agree to a few cuts, but most certainly not to any rewriting. "In my entire writing life," she told Lyle, "I have never had anything approaching this degree of, let us call it, editorial collaborations . . . Even LIFE MAGAZINE . . . emerges as a relative respecter of writers' words . . . not once did they query or touch my beginnings, ends, opinions, withheld opinions, presentation of opinions." She would of course understand if he declined to publish, but there was no question of making the alterations he demanded. The correspondence between them continued for some time, but in the end Lyle backed down, even raising her fee from $3,500 to $5,000, "because the published length will be substantially greater than had been foreseen."

"Relieved," Sybille told Evelyn when the matter was finally settled. "I feel drained; it's gone on too long. I'm not a bulldozer. And yet, and yet: one does feel strongly about writing. And there is this new thing of interfering with writers which is taking on truly frightening dimensions . . . Have we forgotten that it is writers, original writers not hirelings, who change and make and breathe life into language, not the editors with their levelling tools who limp behind?" Her resolve was rewarded when the following year her article was chosen by the Overseas Press Club of America as the "Best Magazine Reporting from Abroad during 1966."

The Auschwitz trial had been a horrendous experience, and Sybille was relieved to have it behind her. Now she felt ready to take a new direction, to start on a work of fiction, a sequel to her previous novel, *A Favourite of the Gods*. It was to be "a story about people and events belonging to a daylit world . . . free (within the, always tricky, human condition) to shape their own achievements and misfortunes." Before she began work, however, terms had to be settled for a contract she had been offered to write the life of Aldous Huxley.

Since Aldous's death the Huxley family had been intensely focused on the search for a suitable biographer. Several writers had been proposed, among them V. S. Pritchett, Alan Pryce-Jones, Cyril Connolly and Lionel Trilling; Pritchett had been their first choice, but when approached he had turned the offer down. It was Aldous's ex-daughter-in-law, Ellen, who then put forward Sybille's name, suggesting her to Cass Canfield at Harper's, who would be commissioning the book. But Canfield had not been keen. "Bedford is of course a brilliant writer," he told her, "but, so far as I know, has not written a biography so I am not too much carried away by this suggestion." At almost the same time, while Sybille was in New York after the Ruby trial, in 1964, she and Aldous's brother, Julian, had dined together, after which Julian decided the book should be offered to Sybille. Canfield was easily persuaded to change his mind, and immediately telephoned Bob Gottlieb to arrange the transfer of his author from Simon & Schuster to Harper's.

It was at this point, according to Evelyn, that "Bob hit the ceiling," making it very clear to Canfield that such a proposal was entirely unacceptable. After a number of lengthy conversations, however, the two men finally agreed terms for a joint publication, after which Bob contacted Chatto & Windus, publishers of Aldous's work in Britain, which, in association with William Collins, was to bring out the book in London. It was only then that a formal offer was made to Sybille—who, to everyone's surprise, turned it down. The book would take at least two years to write, the research involve dozens of interviews and extensive travel; but more important, as she explained to Evelyn, she believed she was simply not capable of it, "don't think up to it, good enough. Apart from fact never having done a biography. I meant not good enough intellectually, humanly. Not advanced. Not ready . . . So I have decided No."

Shortly afterwards, she changed her mind. In a letter to Ian Parsons at Chatto, Sybille explained that "Aldous's influence on myself, on my whole life, has been immense; so perhaps after all it might be the right thing to do. I think now that, in my own way, I could make a good job of it, and I would like to do it." She had after all the advantage of having known Aldous well, and if not perhaps a commercial enterprise, his biography would be "something of the first importance within the literary world." The more she thought about it, the more enthused she became. "Do you realise," she asked Bob, "that it just could be—with God's grace—a very good book?"

Before signing the contract, however, Sybille was determined to make her conditions clear. First she wanted to write her novel, which might take up to two years. Then it must be understood that "the use and organisation and writing of the book is my own . . . No nagging . . . no showing of sample chapters, no hurrying. When the thing is finished, DV [*Deo volente*, i.e. God willing], I shall be open to suggestions, corrections, but it is up to me whether I will act on them or not . . . I am not going to be a tame biographer." As well, her publishers must agree to provide assistance in the search for material and pay for the transcription of all handwritten letters; travel expenses must be covered and some form of secretarial assistance provided. Finally, as she explained to Bob, she expected to be paid a substantial advance, "something commensurate with the kind of book you expect, your costs, my standing as a writer."

Somewhat taken aback, Bob discussed the matter with Canfield, and between them they agreed to offer the sum of $10,000, which, with $5,600 coming from Chatto and Collins, would make a total of over $15,000. From the publishers' perspective this was a generous offer, although Sybille confessed herself disappointed, as she told Bob, that she was not to be allowed what she considered "an appropriate living wage." What upset her more, however, was the refusal on the part of all four publishers to cover her costs. "This really does distress me," she complained, that "the writer, the author, is made to pay for the expenses of the book." Surely Bob must understand how unjust it was that writers "have to accept their financially inferior status, and to live, uncertainly, on something no editor or publisher would accept." Bob was sympathetic but there was nothing further he could do. "You say there must be something odd about the publishing business, and there certainly is: it's economics. Here we sit, flushed with influence and status, and bringing in less money and profit than the meanest button factory." At this point accepting defeat, Sybille signed the contract and put the problems behind her, setting down to work on her novel.

Begun in the spring of 1967, *A Compass Error* was finished in under a year, on 1 February 1968. A sequel to Sybille's previous novel, *A Favourite of the Gods*, the story is focused on seventeen-year-old Flavia, who at the end of *A Favourite* had settled with her mother, Constanza, in the south of France. Now Constanza is living in an unknown location in Spain with her French lover, whom she hopes to marry after he has obtained a divorce. Only Flavia knows where they are, a secret it is vital to keep if the divorce is not to be made public, which would ruin the reputation of both. Flavia, meanwhile, is living alone in the small French port, working hard for her Oxford entrance examination, ambitious for an academic career in the future; clever and independent, she enjoys her solitary life, dining every evening in one of the restaurants beside the port, choosing her dishes with care, concentrating intently on the wine list.

One evening she is invited to join a neighbouring table, and it is here that she meets Therese, wife of a well-known painter. A handsome woman, outspoken and fiercely energetic, Therese soon becomes a maternal figure to Flavia as well as an occasional lover: as Therese makes clear, "it doesn't really matter very much which of one's friends one goes to bed with." Shortly after her first night with Therese, Flavia encounters Andrée, a cold, cynical, manipulative beauty, with whom Flavia becomes helplessly infatuated. Before long Andrée completely dominates Flavia, alternately spoiling and tormenting her; it is not until some way into their relationship, however, that she reveals she is the wife of the man Constanza is hoping to marry. Determined to sabotage the divorce, Andrée by tricking Flavia succeeds in finding details of the couple's location; the theft devastates Flavia when she discovers it, knowing it will ruin her mother's chance of marriage.

As might be expected, the picture Sybille draws of the harbour town is similar in every detail to Sanary, just as most of the characters owe their origins to the people she knew while living there. Therese, "the great handsome monster . . . [with] a smile of serene, archaic sweetness," is an accurate portrayal of Renée Kisling, while the wicked, fascinating Andrée bears an incontestable similarity, as Sybille later admitted, to her first great love, Jacqueline Mimerel. Yet, just as in *A Favourite*, the character of Flavia remains somewhat wooden and two-dimensional, formidably well read, full of literary theory and philosophy, but somehow unconvincing as a seventeen-year-old girl.

But for many, the most serious flaw, as a number of critics pointed out, was the author's decision to relate substantial sections of the story already told in *A Favourite of the Gods*. For readers unfamiliar with the earlier novel, such large quantities of information were difficult to absorb, while many of those who knew the story were exasperated at having it rolled out again and at such interminable length. Mr. James, for instance, a minor character from *A Favourite*, writes a letter of many pages charting the end of the life of Constanza's father in Rome. But the longest passage by far is that spoken by Flavia herself, who, during her first night in bed with Therese, decides to narrate in relentless detail almost her entire family history, in a section that is over fifty-two pages long, nearly a quarter of the entire book. When Flavia finally turns to her companion after coming to the end, she finds Therese "peacefully lying asleep."

After the typescript was sent to New York, Evelyn told Sybille that both she and Bob had loved the book; they did have a few reservations, however, chief among them the disproportionate length of Flavia's monologue. Sybille was taken aback. "Let me say at once that I do not agree," she replied, but "don't let us argue about it. It is quite horrible to have to explain and defend one's own work." A number of her friends expressed similar views, among them Jimmy Stern ("I found that early monologue far too long") and also Allanah. The "one colossal error in the construction . . . was the fifty pages recalling the *Favourite of the Gods*, it should have been reduced to five . . . It made one want to put the book down and not go on."

In the event, no cuts or changes were made, and it was not until nearly thirty years later that Sybille came to change her view about the novel's construction. "I was making an experiment. Deliberately. I was not recapitulating, or repeating events in *A Favourite* for new readers—that was far from my intention. I wanted to try what painters sometimes do—the same subject in a different format, light etc . . . Anyway, today I think it was a mistake. I wouldn't try that way again."

As with *A Favourite*, reviews were mixed. Bernard Levin in the *Daily Mail* described the novel as "beautiful, civilised, clear-eyed, haunting, evocative," while the *Observer* judged it "a work of distinction." Others were less complimentary, however, the *Sunday Times* finding it "slightly maniacal about explanation and biographical detail," while the *Times Literary Supplement* described the novel as "curiously irrelevant, dated, and mannered . . . [not] one to reaffirm those high-flown hopes which *A Legacy* inspired."

With the novel finally behind her, Sybille could now turn her attention to her biography of Aldous Huxley. She would have two years in which to write it, and as she was careful to clarify, the result would be a short, compact book, "scholarly (in a modest way) . . . a straight narrative . . . and not too long." The work was to take her nearly six years to complete.

ELEVEN

"FOOD IS PART OF THE LOVE OF LIFE"

I love food, good food, simple, authentic," Sybille said once in an interview. "Taking food with friends has a sacramental dimension for me. It is part of the love of life." Since early childhood, when she was introduced by her father to the highest levels of fine cuisine, Sybille had been alive to the perfection of simplicity, to the finely tuned balance of taste and texture. Over time she had met a small number of amateur cooks whose talents she admired, one of the most gifted her early mentor, Renée Kisling. But it was not until the mid-1960s that Sybille came to know some of the most influential exponents of the period, among them the English writer Elizabeth David. Elizabeth, like Sybille, had lived in France and Italy, and since the early 1950s her books had had a significant impact on transforming the eating habits of the English middle classes. Her first, *A Book of Mediterranean Food*, had been published in 1950, four years before food rationing had ended, at a time when olive oil was still sold in miniature bottles as a medicament in Boots. *Mediterranean Food* had been followed by *French Country Cooking*, *Summer Cooking*, *Italian Food*, and in 1960 by *French Provincial Cooking*, all five works revered by Sybille, who was in awe of the author's knowledge and discernment, impressed by her outstandingly elegant style.

In 1963, after reading an article by Elizabeth on the markets and restaurants of Venice, Sybille had written to express her admiration. "Dear Mrs. David . . . I read 'Point de Venise' about six times . . . It is so beautifully written . . . so exciting, and so true . . . I do so like every word you write about food and cooking and eating." Within days she received a gratifying reply. "Dear Mrs. Bedford, It isn't every day that one gets a fan letter from one of one's own most admired writers . . . Your own writing about food is so beautiful, and the passage about Melanie and the *loup de mer* in *The Legacy* [*sic*] is to me one of the most luminous and moving of expressions of the impact of the Mediterranean that I know."

Not long after this exchange, Elizabeth invited Sybille to dinner at her house in Chelsea. Sybille was immediately excited by the prospect while at the same time feeling a certain level of apprehension, well aware not only of Elizabeth's distinguished status, but of her formidable reputation for speaking her mind.

Arrived in Halsey Street, Sybille was led by her hostess along a narrow hallway and into the drawing room, "books, and books and books, up to the ceiling, on the floor, rather beautiful furniture, Edwardian photographs, objects (many, too many, but somehow right), bowls and platters of pomegranates, melon, nectarines." Here Elizabeth introduced her sister, Felicité, who acted as her secretary, the three of them settling down to talk over a bottle of vintage Gewürztraminer, Sybille's favourite white wine. After an hour or so Felicité was despatched to her room upstairs while Elizabeth took Sybille down to the kitchen in the basement. Here they sat at a long wooden table, Elizabeth with her back to an old gas cooker, a packet of Gauloises close to hand. A great beauty in her youth, she was still at nearly fifty very handsome, with large dark eyes, her thick grey hair now worn in a chignon at the back of her neck. The dinner was simple and delicious, shish kebabs and a fresh green salad, followed by cheeses and apricots, to drink a white Beaujolais, a wine Sybille had never tasted before, and a premier cru Sauternes.

The two women talked intensively for hours, about food, but also about painting, Shakespeare, poetry, and one or two friends they had in common. Both, as it turned out, had known Norman Douglas, Elizabeth in the south of France at the beginning of the war, Sybille a few years later during her visits to Capri. It was during her first stay on the island that Sybille had assisted Norman with a cookery book he had been working on, *Venus in the Kitchen*, a collection of mischievously aphrodisiac recipes. In his preface Norman had expressed his gratitude to Sybille, "without whose friendly help and expert knowledge of matters culinary many mistakes might have crept into the text." With so much gossip, so many subjects to cover, Sybille and Elizabeth remained at the table for hours, talking absorbedly until nearly midnight, when Sybille, "v. v. tipsy," finally took her departure.

From that time on, their friendship continued to flourish, Sybille almost in thrall to Elizabeth, admiring her natural authority as well as her scholarly understanding of her subject. When during the following year the *Sunday Times* approached Elizabeth to commission an article about her, she agreed on two conditions: that Sybille should write it, and that there should be no personal detail, nothing about her marriage and divorce, nor indeed about any aspect of her private life. Once this was settled, she and Sybille met on several occasions, mainly over dinner at the flat off Sloane Square where Sybille and Eda were currently ensconced. As Sybille needed to concentrate on interviewing Elizabeth, it was Eda who undertook the cooking, "oddly enough," as Eda remarked, "because Sybille is almost a professional in that line and I am not. All went well, but it took up a good deal of time and thought."

Published on 1 January 1967, Sybille's article focuses on two aspects of her subject, Elizabeth David the writer and Elizabeth David the scholar cook. "If one had to sum up in a few words Elizabeth David's own contribution to the development of cookery," Sybille states, "one might say that it was her postulate of the authentic . . . her outspoken stand against the non-foods of every kind." To Sybille's relief, Elizabeth not only approved of the piece but told her how much she had relished her company. "I enjoy talking to you so much," she wrote. "You make me forget the nonsenses I've created, and take me to another world, out of my own little pool in which I lie too much. You have, and give out, very great strength." Over time the friendship remained firm, although it took Sybille some while to realise just how difficult Elizabeth could be, that their relationship would be conducted solely on Elizabeth's terms, not hers. "I was an innocent in those days," she later recalled. "I thought we were equals."

During the next few years Sybille was to become ever more deeply embedded in the world of gastronomy, forming significant friendships with some highly distinguished members of the fraternity. Meanwhile, however, there was the Huxley biography, on which it was essential that she begin work as soon as possible. The contract had been signed nearly three years ago, and her publishers were beginning to grow anxious, Ian Parsons in particular expressing his frustration that Mrs. Bedford had still not started work on a book "which—even if she began next week—couldn't possibly be published before the spring of 1970."

At this point Sybille's procrastination had been due mainly to her dissatisfaction with the terms of her contract, in particular her publishers' refusal to pay the costs of her research. As she told Bob Gottlieb, she thought it a disgrace that the author should be responsible for the expenses "for the biography of one of the world's most distinguished men of letters." This injustice, as she saw it, had continued to rankle, and eventually, without informing either Bob or Evelyn, Sybille placed herself in the hands of a literary agent in London, Jan van Loewen. Van Loewen was reassuring, promising that he would negotiate a more profitable deal, at which point Sybille wrote to Evelyn to tell her what she had done.

Both Evelyn and Bob reacted with fury. Sybille's behaviour was wholly unacceptable, Evelyn told her. "If you had serious objections, T, you should have voiced them then. It seems to me very wrong to expect Bob to reopen negotiations after two years' time." Bob, enraged when he heard the news, was equally outspoken. "PUBLISHERS ARE PEOPLE TOO!" he wrote to Sybille. "It was agony working out that contract . . . Now Mr. van Loewen reopens the very points we settled after endless discussion . . . I don't know how to answer him, Sybille, because—I have to tell you the truth—I feel we have been treated badly in this matter . . . Forgive me if I sound petulant about this. I'm really disturbed."

But Sybille stood firm: she had no intention of putting herself permanently in van Loewen's hands, she explained. "When I have, DV, ordinary books, not involving research expenses and a thousand of other considerations . . . I propose to continue as before . . . All that is being asked now is slightly increased expenses." Over the next few weeks letters were exchanged between all four publishers, anxiously discussing how to respond to Sybille's demands and to what they regarded as van Loewen's objectionable intrusion. Finally an agreement was reached: the advance would be slightly increased and, crucially, the delivery date extended by two years: according to van Loewen, Mrs. Bedford felt it would be unfair "if a delivery date were inserted in the contract which may harass her over much."

A further upheaval occurred when shortly after these altercations had ended Bob Gottlieb left Simon & Schuster for the firm of Alfred Knopf, taking Evelyn with him. Fortunately, as Sybille told Martha, "S&S rather generously let one choose where to go, and that Eda and I chose to go with Bob." From then on Sybille had no further dealings with Simon & Schuster.

During the previous year, with Sybille almost constantly at work, Eda had been attempting to write a third novel, but had made little progress; this was partly on account of the demands of her domestic duties ("Eda the general handyman," as one of her friends referred to her), but also because of long periods of severe depression. "Last year's depression was very, very bad indeed," Sybille reported to Jimmy Stern, Eda "ill, depressed, unwilling to go on . . . it was a tragic situation: an oozing away of any hold on or pleasure in life." Recently, however, Eda's condition had improved, largely due to her discovery of the antidepressant drug Drinamyl, which had been recommended to her by Martha. Thanks to these pills, Sybille told Martha, Eda is "as well and strong this summer as she was ill, depressed, unwilling to go on last year . . . now she is working away, without great faith but with tenacity and courage, on her novel, struggling to finish it before we set off on our travels."

The travels, in the United States, would turn out to be extensive, but first there were a number of conversations to be conducted nearer home, both with the Huxley family and with friends and colleagues of Aldous's. As Sybille recognised, verbal testimony was of particular significance as the bulk of Aldous's papers had been destroyed when his house in Los Angeles had burned down. One of her earliest interviews had been in Italy with Laura Huxley, the two meeting for the first time in nearly a decade. Laura was both friendly and helpful, eager to talk about Aldous and about the memoir* she had recently written about her marriage, an account Sybille found admirable in many ways, while

---

* *This Timeless Moment: A Personal View of Aldous Huxley*, Laura Archera Huxley (Chatto & Windus, 1969).

also shockingly "unprivate." Sybille also met and talked to Aldous's brother Julian and to Maria Huxley's sister, Jeanne Neveux, as well as to friends of Aldous such as Leonard Woolf, Bertrand Russell and Enid Bagnold. Returning to Les Bastides, she settled down to read Aldous's works and to organise her notes. For Sybille as biographer this was a new discipline to be learnt, sitting hour after hour, day after day, putting herself through "the sheer drudgery . . . of sifting, noting, filing facts, checking and sorting like a book-keeper, and at the same time trying to remember and to forget, to think and simmer. It is fascinating and rewarding work, and I believe in it."

After the summer in France, Sybille, accompanied by Eda, sailed in October 1968 for New York. Before her was the lengthy process of tracking down and interviewing Aldous's friends in America, an undertaking that was to extend over six months. After a few weeks in New York, Eda left for California while Sybille travelled to Washington to see the Huxleys' son, Matthew, and his wife in their large, comfortable house in Chevy Chase. "The Huxleys most kind and hospitable . . . [I] did enjoy Washington. How curiously old-fashioned it is . . . [but] the boredom of the social life! My goodness . . . The US seems the nadir in voluble vapidity."

From Washington, Sybille went on to California, joining Eda, who was staying with an elderly aunt in Del Mar. Aunt Margaret "is kindness herself," Sybille reported, "but the days are spent in maddening slow rounds of trivia: cookie making, cousins to call, sing-song parties . . . Dinner is at six . . . Eda tells me every morning: 'This is why I left.' " And indeed for Eda, "shrivelled with boredom," the situation was particularly depressing, struggling to write her novel but almost never allowed a minute alone, constantly at the beck and call of her inexhaustibly social aunt. Hardest of all was the strong disapproval repeatedly expressed of Eda's smoking. "Smoking is the very devil to Margaret's friends," she complained to Jimmy Stern, "which gives [me] the intense longing for it as Prohibition did for drink. A sensible time to give it up but human nature doesn't work that way; especially under a glaze of boredom." Fortunately she and Sybille were allowed at least some time to themselves, taking long walks on the beach, "miles and miles of broad sand. Seals & surf bathers in the sea. Hot hot sun."

Sybille's parents, Lisa and Max, on their wedding day in Berlin, 1910

Sybille as a small child playing with her dolls

Sybille with her half-sister, Katzi

Sybille and her mother, Lisa, surrounded by Lisa's beloved dogs on the beach at Sanary in the south of France

Nori Marchesani, Sybille's stepfather and loyal ally

Sybille walking on the beach with her good friend Pierre Mimerel, 1929

Renée Kisling, "a great handsome monster" and wife of the artist Moïse Kisling, who acted as both lover and guardian to Sybille

Sybille during her visit to Berlin with the Huxleys in 1932

Sybille gazing adoringly at her idol,
Jacqueline Mimerel

Preparing drinks under the eyes of a much-
impressed Sylvester Gates

Sybille and her friend Eva Herrmann,
the artist and caricaturist, in 1932 while
living together at Sainte-Trinide

Aldous Huxley and Sybille engrossed in conversation with the literary critic
Raymond Mortimer

Sybille and English writer and memoirist Allanah Harper in Normandy with Allanah's adored dog, Poodly

Sybille spending the summer with Allanah in Edgartown, Massachusetts, 1941

The highly literate and extremely voluble historian and academic Esther Murphy

Maria and Aldous Huxley in California, 1940s

Tuesday night
27 April
1943

Dearest

S. says she will rush out & catch the 11:30 mail so I must hurry with this and it won't be in French but if it were it wouldn't say what I want to say.

S. has just put on "A media Luz", awful for me but nice — she's been so sweet with Miss Curse bringing soup & biscuits before going to Tania's, cooking dinner, making quickies, clearing table, coffee, and now the night cap for all. Such nice things have been said about my darling Sybille, I wish she were here, my darling sweetie.

Marco had, yes, some tidbits, & about A. Is she serious or just making with Sensation? Apparently, debating whether to marry or not and discussing with one & all. I hope yes & then you will be free & will you come & be my girl, darling will you, will you? I miss you, I don't like having to sleep with sister but there will be no mistakes — all my love, yours A

One of Annie Davis's love letters to Sybille—her "most delicious white pig"—from 1943

Katzi and Sybille in Austria in 1949, their first encounter since the beginning of the Second World War

Bob Gottlieb, the legendary editor who launched Sybille in America

Sybille watering plants on her roof-garden in Rome

Sybille reading in the bath in Rome, with her signature visor worn to protect her eyes, 1950

Evelyn Gendel, who first met Sybille while both were living in Rome and who became her lover and devoted friend, in 1952

Katzi "clattering about" in high spirits while living with Esther Murphy in Paris, 1955

Sybille queueing at Eastbourne Magistrates' Court before the Bodkin Adams trial in 1957

Martha Gellhorn who, in Sybille's words, "radiated vitality, certainty, total courage"

Eda Lord, "a wounded bird," always equipped with coffee and cigarettes

Sybille deep in conversation with Tania Stern; Tania and her husband, Jimmy, were generous friends of Sybille's.

Sybille happily settled at Old Church Street, 1980s

While Eda remained incarcerated in Del Mar, Sybille made several expeditions further afield. One of the most memorable was to Santa Barbara, where a group of twenty friends of Aldous's assembled, meeting first for dinner, then seated in a semicircle while taking it in turn to recount their memories. Sybille, who listened intently throughout, had decided not to take notes nor use a tape recorder—"it became almost a mediumistic thing," she said later, and she "absorbed it all like a sponge." During this same period she visited Igor Stravinsky and his wife in Los Angeles, and also Christopher Isherwood, with whom she spent most of a day, time which "could not have been more agreeable and exciting." (Isherwood for his part recorded in his diary, "Sybille Bedford . . . is a hypochondriacal mess but intelligent, really perceptive.") It was Isherwood who arranged for her to meet Aldous's guru, Swami Prabhavananda, who gave her a private audience at the Vedanta Temple. "I was a bit overawed, as you can imagine."

In between these expeditions Sybille returned to Del Mar. Here, while grateful for the kindness and hospitality of Eda's aunt, her contempt for America remained undimmed. "Life here is really too crass and harsh and nothing functions and all the values are odd." She and Eda were shortly to leave California and journey east, to Denver, Chicago and New York, but shortly before their departure they were provided with a welcome interlude, several days spent visiting the wineries in the Napa Valley with Eda's old friend from her schooldays, M. F. K. Fisher.

Mary Frances had remained fondly in touch with Eda, who "has more than fulfilled all I dreamed of her in [my] boarding-school crush of 1923." Professionally Mary Frances had been successful, although her private life had been full of tragedy, with two of her three marriages ending in divorce, and her adored second husband, the writer Dillwyn Parrish, committing suicide. Now living in San Francisco, Mary Frances was revered for her highly personalised style: as one critic said of her, a large part of her appeal was that she wrote as "a whole human being, spiky with prejudice." Mary Frances had met Sybille on several occasions in France during the 1960s, both enjoying each other's company, although Mary Frances had been ambivalent in her attitude towards Sybille: while admiring her intelligence she was disturbed by what she saw as her domineering attitude towards a helplessly submissive Eda.

Since Mary Frances in her manner towards Sybille was charming one moment, caustically critical the next, it was hardly surprising that Sybille found her puzzling; after their few days together in the Napa Valley she remarked that although Mary Frances could not have been kinder, "I cannot make her out . . . [I] find her a very, very strange woman indeed." For her part Mary Frances enjoyed the expedition, particularly pleased to be able to spend time with Eda, although worried by her old friend's non-stop smoking, her hacking cough and obvious frailty—"I feel as if she is nourished on cobwebs," she wrote to a friend afterwards.

Finally, after six months in the States, Sybille and Eda sailed for Southampton in April 1969. In London they stayed at Chester Square, where Tom Matthews was now living with his new wife. Sybille was impressed by the change in atmosphere, remembering all too clearly the rows and tensions endemic during Martha's reign. "Tom seems very well and contented," she reported to Evelyn. "The servants are welcoming. So is the hostess. There is food, drink, delicious breakfast in bed; solicitude. A changed house. One only realises how peculiar it was in M's time." After a few days the two of them moved into a borrowed apartment in Chesham Place, and during the following weeks Sybille saw a number of friends, among them Rosamond Lehmann, first encountered some years earlier and whose novels she much admired. It was Rosamond who had proposed Sybille as a member of the PEN Club, to which, to her great satisfaction, she had been elected in 1962.

On this occasion Rosamond invited Sybille to dinner at her flat in Eaton Square. Although taken aback by the change in her appearance—Rosamond, once a famous beauty, was now in her late sixties and very overweight—Sybille was enchanted by her hostess's intelligence and charm, her profound interest in life and literature. "We talked and talked, about writing and Aldous and life and death and learning about human life . . . Then she walked me home, from Eaton Square where she lives to Chesham Place, less than ten minutes, then I walked her back, then she walked me home, then once more, in the May night in creamy Belgravia, the trees out with Gainsborough's vistas, all like old times and being young, walking, talking through the night. Her last words to me were, 'You ought to live in London.' I think I know that too." Soon after leaving for Provence, Sybille wrote to Evelyn, "I loved London and left it with sadness and reluctance. I love it more and more . . . Feel at home. More so than in France."

Returning to Les Bastides in May, both Sybille and Eda looked forward to a hard-working summer, Eda determined to finish her novel, Sybille writing and busily organising the material gained from her Huxley research. Despite the increase in her advance, she remained acutely anxious about the state of her finances, an anxiety she had confided to several close friends. But now, at least for a while, the problem was solved, first by the arrival of a large cheque from Tania Stern, then by an even larger sum from Martha. "I've written to my Swiss bank," Martha wrote. "After 20 August, when illicit money comes in (never never breathe about this Sibbie for it would destroy me, you must promise) you will have word from the American Express Cannes that there is $2,500 in Travellers checks for you and $2,500 for Eda—that ought to see you through the Huxley book." Sybille, long accustomed to relying on financial support from friends, was nonetheless profoundly grateful. "I think it's an extraordinary deed, and that alone is a source of joy," she wrote to her. "This will make the whole difference to the next years—doing the biography with that peace of mind which is the real need."

Over the following months, Sybille committed herself to a disciplined routine, "revising, retyping, cutting, adding to, despairing over, the 40,000 words I wrote this winter." One of the most effortful jobs was the transcription of an interview with Aldous on a series of gramophone records. "I have to begin by transcribing—less audibly—to a tape recorder. An hour gets me about two pages of transcriptions: 7 mins or so of spoken. There are ten hours of it . . . It is all fascinating and essential, but oh the mechanics of it." A rather less stressful undertaking was a meeting with Graham Greene, conducted at his "gimcrack modernissimo" apartment in Antibes. "We were alone. It was very pleasant . . . We talked about Evelyn Waugh and Aldous . . . There is a gentleness about him that may come from an immense *désabusement* . . . which is at once sad, dead-endish and a kind of facade. I think we were intimate and open in our talk—but it did not seem to match anything inside. I came home exhausted."

In October 1970, both Sybille and Eda were delighted to hear from New York that Bob Gottlieb and his new wife, the actress Maria Tucci, would shortly be arriving on the Riviera. For Eda, who had grown slack over work on her novel, the prospect of Bob's imminent appearance instantly galvanised her. "I buckled down and finished it. The last word on the day of his arrival. I handed over the manuscript that night after dinner." Fortunately Bob liked the novel, promising publication for September the following year.

The day after the Gottliebs left, Mary Frances, accompanied by her sister, Norah, arrived from California, having rented an apartment in a house almost next door to Les Bastides. The presence of Mary Frances marked the beginning for Sybille of one of the most intensely epicurean periods of her life, in the midst of a community of internationally known professionals, "a v. large section of the US Cooking Establishment," as she reported to Elizabeth David. As well as Mary Frances, also in the region were Richard Olney, for years highly regarded for his writing in the journal *Cuisine et Vins de France*; James Beard, the celebrity chef, who had founded his own cookery schools in Oregon and New York; and most famous of all, the writer and television star Julia Child, with her husband, Paul. All were living or staying in an area a few kilometres south of Grasse and within reach of Les Bastides.

Sybille had first met the Childs three years earlier, when the couple had arrived from the States on a visit to London. By then Julia had become a mass-market phenomenon in America, with her immensely influential book, *Mastering the Art of French Cooking*, selling in the hundreds of thousands, while her television show was watched by millions. Julia, an old friend of Mary Frances, had written to Sybille expressing her admiration of Sybille's article on Elizabeth David, and this had led to a meeting. "One likes them immensely," Sybille had reported. Julia "is so warm, spontaneous." Not long afterwards while in France Sybille and Eda were invited to dine at the Childs' small house at Plascassier, La Pitchoune, or "La Peetch," as Julia referred to it, where they spent several months every year.

The Childs had lived for long periods in France, Paul working as a diplomat in Paris, while Julia had enrolled in a course at the famous

Cordon Bleu cookery school. Cooking soon became her passion, but it was not until the early 1960s, when she collaborated on *Mastering the Art of French Cooking*, that she became famous. Both were fluent in French, but while Paul was scholarly and serious, Julia, over six feet tall, ungainly, with big bones and large, flat feet, was like a jolly schoolgirl, her conversation peppered with exclamations—"Yuck!," "Boo-boos!," "Wooh!," "Hooray!" Although Julia was the celebrity, it was Paul on whom his wife wholly depended, his knowledge of cuisine and wine far more profound and intellectual than hers. As Mary Frances remarked to Eda, "professionally she is Trilby to his Svengali."

Before long Sybille and Eda became regular guests at La Pitchoune, sometimes on their own, sometimes with the Childs' gentle giant of a friend, James Beard, who was currently being treated in a clinic in Grasse for life-threatening obesity. "We had a smashing evening, I must say," Julia reported to Mary Frances after one such evening. "We started with an excellent champagne (Clos des Goisses, at Sybille's recommendation), then a lovely (if I do say so) *oeuf en pistouille* (poached egg in tomato filled with eggplant mixture, cold) with a Chablis 'Fourchaume.' With the MAGNUM of H[aut] B[rion], we had a new version of the ubiquitous *Boeuf* Wellington . . . (sliced, spread with Duxelles, then baked in a very thin brioche crust) and *pommes Anna fromagées*. It was one of those evenings where everyone was happy and everything went wonderfully well including all the food."

On another occasion with the Childs, Sybille, Paul Child and Eda sat at the kitchen table while Julia, in Sybille's words, "like the dear unflappable, slightly clumsy, St. Bernard she looks . . . began whisking up things in a great copper bowl for making her own pudding, her version of baked Alaska. It is a superb chocolate ice cream (Julia made) on some cake with a cap of whipped white of egg baked for seconds in a hell-hot oven, then you sink an empty egg-shell into the mountain crust, fill it with rum, strike a match and the flames leap up, burning Vesuvius, she calls it, I call it Pelion on Ossa. That was borne flaming back into the dining room and we ate that with a bolt of Château d'Yquem (not tasted for over thirty years). Later we finished the bottle by the fire. Memorable, even more than the wines, was the generosity and spirit of our hosts. It was lovable."

Fond though she was of the Childs and much as she enjoyed the evenings at La Pitchoune, Sybille always slightly looked down on Julia's cuisine, regarding it as no more than good hotel cooking. As she told Evelyn, Julia "is competent, enamoured of French food and style, an imitator. All her home-cooked food, served with great charm and ease, tastes like first-rate mass-produced . . . Don't let it go further . . . as one has such affection for them."

When in December 1970 Mary Frances had arrived in the region, her main purpose was to see Eda as well as her old friends, the Childs, but she was eager, too, to meet Richard Olney, whose scholarly writing on food and wine she had long admired. Richard had been a close friend of Eda since the early 1950s, when after leaving the States as a very young man he had settled in Paris. Intently focused on learning to cook, he had remained in the city for nearly a decade before moving to the Midi, to Solliès-Toucas, where he had bought and restored a tiny derelict farmhouse on a hillside overlooking the ancient village. Now in his mid-forties, slender and dark-haired, Richard lived a solitary, orderly life, and apart from the occasional boyfriend saw almost no one for weeks at a time. A ruthless perfectionist, he was dedicated to his cooking, his style at once sensual and austere. Highly intelligent, Richard when in company could be both daunting and extremely charming, often relaying devastating criticism of his friends and neighbours behind their backs. "He lives so outside the world, not only world of world affairs but of private affairs. Strange boy," Sybille noted in her diary.

Soon after Mary Frances's arrival, she, Sybille and Eda were invited to dinner by Richard at Solliès-Toucas. The drive took over two hours and they arrived in mid-afternoon, escorted by their host to a vine-covered terrace overlooking the garden. Here they sat and talked over aperitifs until the early evening, when Richard led them into the small kitchen, where they sat at a table in front of a large fireplace hung with copper pots. At a leisurely pace the three women were served with course after exquisite course: artichokes *poivrade*, a roulade of fillets of sole with a mousseline of sea urchins in aspic, *daube à la provençale* with pasta *macaronade*, a rocket salad, cheese, and a raspberry sorbet. Accompanying each course was a fine vintage wine from Richard's excellent cellar. "Dinner was superb. Endless," Mary Frances reported.

"The wines were very good indeed, and also endless. The talk, which with Sybille racing a hundred words a minute, was mostly about those two subjects, wine and food, it was endless." Throughout the meal, Eda sat mostly silent, as usual smoking and drinking coffee. "Eda was gentle and comfortable to be with," Richard recalled; "her conversation was quietly ironic . . . her voice and laugh corrugated by a dedication to cigarettes . . . She loved the table and was fascinated by wine, sniffed it, but dared not taste it." It was not until the small hours that the three women finally left, tottering back to the house in the village where they were to spend the night.

The alliance between Sybille and Richard quickly grew close, each enjoying the other's artistry and expertise, with Richard in particular relishing Sybille's sharp tongue, the comedy and cruelty intrinsic to her assessment of the talents and personalities of their mutual friends. "I had a couple of evening sessions with Sybille," Richard told his brother, "critical, negative, destructive judgements about everything and everyone—the terrible thing is that we agreed about everything." Mary Frances, on the other hand, began to grow tired of these lengthy conversations, these "strange, gastronomical capers," with Richard and Sybille taking centre stage while Eda sat on the sidelines, saying little. "I almost never see Eda except through a dense Sybillian fog," she complained. Both she and Julia Child were worried, too, by Eda's fragile appearance, by her "bubbly cough," and the fact that, with Sybille working hard on her book, all the chores, all the cooking, driving, shopping, were left to Eda. "Sybille is very bad for Eda," Mary Frances warned Richard. "We must work together to separate them," a suggestion which Richard, however, firmly dismissed. Fortunately, Eda was able to take a few days off occasionally to stay on her own with Richard, away from the stresses of life at Les Bastides, where Sybille frequently burst "from her workroom to prowl and growl like a bear with a sore head."

One of the strongest bonds between Sybille and Richard was their love for and expert knowledge of wine. "A great nineteenth-century wine," Sybille said once, "is as living and romantic to me as a piece of archaic art." Like Flavia in *A Compass Error*, Sybille "had loved wine from childhood . . . [loved] the range of learning and experiment afforded by wine's infinite variety; but what she loved more than these was the taste—of peach and earth and honeysuckle and raspberries and spice and cedarwood and pebbles and truffles and tobacco leaf; and the happiness, the quiet ecstasy that spreads through heart and limbs and mind." In 1968 Sybille had written to Jimmy Stern, "I quite seriously think that if I were only ten years younger . . . I would give up writing . . . [and] get myself apprenticed in the wine trade; I should have been very happy in that." Yet while never joining the profession, she nonetheless became closely connected to it, from the early 1960s attending tastings and joining a number of societies, including the Wine & Spirit Trade Association and the Directors' Wine Club, although not the Wine Society, which she considered mainly for amateurs and on the whole "pretty mediocre."

Over the last decade or so Sybille at Les Bastides had been carefully assembling a personal cellar, buying wine on a regular basis—white wines, Riesling, Muscat and Pinot Blanc, from Alsace, while cases of red, of Médoc and Graves, were purchased from three or four chateaux, where they were stored for several years before drinking. For more immediate consumption wine was bought from a small local cooperative, and every year as well a barrel was ordered from a vintner in the Var, its contents bottled by Sybille at home. "This was a great labour, what with the hand-worked corking device . . . and my scrubbing out and washing 200 bottles under the village pump; but the wine, fresh and honest and low in alcohol . . . was a pleasure."

A more serious involvement with the wine trade began in 1967 when Sybille was lured by the "siren song" of Justerini & Brooks in St. James's. This old-established firm offered "a simple persuasive plan for financing one's drinking of fine wines. The idea was to buy young wines . . . keep them till they were ready and (almost inevitably) appreciated in value, then drink, say, one half and sell the other." The scheme turned out to be excellent value, Sybille investing in some fine clarets as well as hocks and Moselles, purchasing Châteaux Latour, Margaux and Mouton-Rothschild at under £3 a bottle. Wine for her own drinking was held in store, and "twice each year I work out my needs, study the form, consult with the merchant/guardian concerned, then draw two dozen or so." When in the company of Richard Olney or of other oenophile friends, Sybille would talk absorbedly for hours about vintages and chateaux, identifying, classifying, comparing varieties, discussing the perfect sequence and combination to accompany different ingredients and dishes. "That is what is so fascinating about wine," she said once in an interview, "one never stops discovering things. There is always more to learn."

After the departure of Mary Frances at the end of the year, Sybille and Eda remained at Les Bastides for another six months, eventually leaving for London in the middle of June 1971. Both had been worried that they had nowhere to stay, but eventually, almost at the last moment, a friend located a ground-floor apartment in Chelsea, available for a modest rent of only £10 a week. From the description, the flat, at 23 Old Church Street, sounded unappealing, with a small sitting room, a tiny windowless kitchen, a miniature bathroom, and one single-bed cubicle, with a folding cot to be opened when necessary. "We are dismayed about it," Sybille told Evelyn. "A little hole." The day they arrived it was pouring with rain and both were depressed when they saw the accommodation. "Flat pretty awful," was Sybille's view. "Inconvenient, too cramped . . . One will not take to it." Fortunately, another temporary apartment was found for Eda only five minutes' walk away, and gradually Sybille began to warm to Old Church Street. She soon discovered the small space was perfectly adequate for one, and there was a little garden, "with an acacia tree which I adore and flowering bushes," where on warm evenings she and Eda could sit and eat outside. And indeed over the following years, Old Church Street was to become Sybille's London base, and the tiny flat eventually her permanent home.

On this particular occasion, Eda, craving the hot Mediterranean summer and long hours spent in the sea, returned to France after only three weeks, while Sybille, who with her weak eyesight always found the sunlight painful, remained in London till the autumn. During the day she continued to work hard on her book, in the evenings dining with friends, among them Elizabeth David, Anne Balfour-Fraser, the Sterns, the Robson-Scotts, Rosamond Lehmann, and also Martha, who was temporarily in London. Sybille had been looking forward to seeing her old pal after such a long interval, but unfortunately the evening quickly turned sour. "She said 7.30, came at 8.20," Sybille told Eda. "She was in a disagreeable mood. Saying I bored and irritated her. 'You were much nicer and funnier years ago Sibbie, before all the *femme de lettres* stuff. You don't make me laugh any more . . .' I tried to talk open and seriously about my feelings past and present about her. Met a kind of deadness. Surely not *femme de lettres* stuff? Surely, surely? Also said I was categorical, and pompous. She may have something there."

Sybille returned to Les Bastides in October, somewhat reluctantly as she now felt far more at home in England. "Leaving England was a wrench," she told the Sterns, "and life here feels rather grim (sticking to that book) and limited. Determined to return to England and live there, DV, if & when I'll be free to think or move." Increasingly, she was coming to dislike the commercialism of the south of France, where "almost weekly: another tall building, another walk or view gone; the sea polluted," whereas London offered "peaceful parks, and peaceful walks, and some quiet streets left, a neighbourly life." Most important, there were her friends, "the physical ease of reaching them in the evening after a day of work; the libraries, the interesting life going on . . . In France one is alien if not French. Also the English are so much kinder still, more benevolent, open . . . I feel happy and at ease in London."

Meanwhile at Les Bastides there was some encouraging news for Eda: her novel *Extenuating Circumstances*, about a young English widow living in Cannes during the Occupation, had just been published in New York, and had been sold by Bob Gottlieb to Hodder & Stoughton in London. Evelyn, who had come over from the States for a short holiday, was with Sybille and Eda on the day of publication and took them both out to dinner in Cannes to celebrate. It was a cheerful evening, although Evelyn herself had experienced a difficult year, having unexpectedly been sacked in January by Knopf. "I have some ungood news," she had written to Sybille. "I've been fired. Not me alone—there's been a bloodletting: six of us in all . . . Reason is said to be that business is bad . . . [and] no, Bob did not instantly offer me safe haven . . . but he couldn't have been more sympathetic." Evelyn's next job, with a new firm, Arbor House, was short-lived, but it was not long before she found a post with Bobbs-Merrill, famous as the publisher of *The Wizard of Oz*. Here she was to settle contentedly, in charge of commissioning titles on gardening, needlework and interior decoration. "I couldn't be happier," she told Sybille, "because the atmosphere is so good. No politicking."

By now, Sybille was in the fourth year of writing her biography of Aldous. "What I am trying to do . . . is to make it flow, and continuous, to make it a clear narrative: I should like the reader to know always where he is, and when, time of years; sequence; Aldous's age . . . give a life a shape, make one see, convey emotion." Increasingly, however, she was struggling with the project, stressed by the volume of work, suffering badly from eye-strain, and then while at Les Bastides incapacitated by a long bout of ill health, described as "a sort of breakdown . . . due to overwork." Once returned to London she immediately felt better, but then fell seriously ill with a virus infection, confined to bed for nearly two months, followed by a long period of weakness, anxiety and depression. "It's very disagreeable . . . The world sways about one, and one tingles inside, above all one feels exhausted, exhausted, unable to cope, not even the next step." Eventually she began to recover, her old friend, Charlotte Wolff, helping by prescribing a daily dose of Valium to calm her nerves.

After the summer when Eda came over to join Sybille in London, she, too, was in a fragile state, "unhappy, defeatist, tired. She can't sleep; says she hasn't eaten for weeks." Although she understood Eda's strong attachment to Les Bastides, Sybille had been concerned about the effect of her isolation there: her closest friend, Richard Olney, was over two hours' drive away, while Allanah was "nice to her, niceish, but *indifferent*; and this makes Eda feel a ghost, unwanted. Something which is very bad for her." Increasingly Sybille worried about Eda's vulnerability, her endless fight against depression, the fundamental passivity in her nature which made her emotionally dependent on others, and on Sybille in particular. By now this constant need for care and protection was becoming an almost intolerable encumbrance, Sybille uncomfortably aware that the more helpless Eda became, the more she herself felt a growing resentment and irritation. "I'm becoming more worried about Eda," she told Tania. "So negative; so closed in, and, I fear, so unhappy . . . She said—today—that her instinct tells her that I do not love her now, find her a burden. The terrible thing is there is

enough truth in this to make it hard to convince her of the contrary."
Gradually the atmosphere lightened, however, after Sybille's doctor,
Patrick Woodcock, was able to treat Eda with effect, and slowly she
began to recover. "I gather it's the old old deep-seated depression on
top of a low physical state," Sybille reported to the Sterns. "Both are
very improved. The relief is immense."

Fortunately by the end of the year Sybille had returned to work.
Her publishers were insisting on delivery in March 1973, as November
was the tenth anniversary of Aldous's death. Although struggling to
cope with the pressure—writing Aldous's biography was like "wearing chains all the time"—Sybille remained as reverential as ever of
her subject. "How Aldous grows. How overwhelmed one is by what
he was; the sheer astonishing beauty of his goodness and being . . . At
times I feel very inadequate to put it across . . . What people want to
hear and believe is the malicious, the sick—not of goodness and matu-
rity and perfection. To make them see and believe. Very very hard.
One can only try." Finally, in February, shortly before her deadline,
Sybille finished the book, all 300,000 words of it, immediately sending a copy to Evelyn for comment. The achievement was tremendous,
Evelyn told her "brave, splendid beast. You can't imagine how proud
of you I am." Nonetheless in her view there were a number of flaws:
Sybille as narrator was too worshipful, throughout portraying Aldous
as a kind of saint; "and do loosen up yr tone, T—suddenly yr so mangy
& stuffy . . . Speak up, forthright & plain. Not Miss Mincy-Mouse.
Friendship brings insights, & that's fine. Make the whole thing human
& simple & yrself."

When soon afterwards a typescript was sent to Chatto, the response
on the whole was gratifying—"magnificent," as Ian Parsons described
it. He did, however, have a number of technical criticisms, most bur-
densome his insistence that she check and correct all Huxley's quotations. "Just when I thought that all was smooth with the M/S of the
biography it transpired that I had made innumerable typing mistakes
in transcribing quotations from Aldous's works . . . So I left rattled and
ashamed; and Ian Parsons was very cold. It was rather awful. So I had to
settle down to getting A's books out of the library—not my marked
copies which are in France—and try to find several hundred quotations,

sometimes half sentences hidden in the long novels and essays—a miserable job." Once these corrections had been made, proofs were printed and sent to Sybille for revision, an undertaking she found wearisome in the extreme, "the eye-strain, the boredom"; she resented the fact, too, that authors were not paid for the time spent correcting misspellings and renumbering footnotes. Eventually, by mid-August, it was done, and the book on which she had been working for nearly six years was finally out of her hands, leaving her feeling "so strange, and flat, and *désorientée*, and emptied."

In her introduction to the biography, Sybille writes, "The object of this book is to give a truthful and coherent account of the life of Aldous Huxley and of Aldous Huxley as a man . . . If the work was a labour of love, it was also a work done in a spirit of detachment." Early on she had made the decision not to read any books or articles about Aldous, nor to go in search of correspondence, preferring to rely instead on the selection of letters that had been published six years after Aldous's death,* on her own memories, and on the memories of the many still living who had known him. Throughout, her two-volume account depends heavily on lengthy quotations, which take up well over half the narrative, from correspondence and also from interviews Sybille herself conducted, interspersed with often very brief intercessions of her own. Where the book comes most vividly to life are in the substantial passages from Maria Huxley's letters, to her family and also to Sybille, and in Sybille's evocative accounts of her own association with the Huxleys, from the early years in Sanary to her last encounter with Aldous in London in 1961. Although Sybille as narrator often seems unsure, nervously changing tone, shifting tense from past to present, repeatedly bringing herself in, without explanation, as "I" or "we," it is here, when recalling her own experiences, that the text takes on a new dimension, full of character and colour, the writing instantly more fluent and relaxed.

Aware of the need for discretion, Sybille omitted a considerable amount of information regarding the sensitive subject of Aldous's voracious sexual appetite, his many adulterous liaisons, some shared

---

* *Letters of Aldous Huxley*, ed. Grover Smith (Harper & Row, 1969).

with Maria. This was to protect the reputation not only of her subject but also of the women still living who might have felt damaged by such revelations. "I never confirmed nor denied," Sybille recorded in her diary. " 'They' would not have liked it . . . Just avoided. Evaded." One whose affair with Aldous she does describe is that of the eccentric bohemian Nancy Cunard, who had died in 1965. Nancy's rackety life is told in some detail, including her acquaintance with Sybille: "To us," Sybille wrote, Nancy "was the friend one loved, whose arrival one often dreaded." Aldous's passion for Nancy in 1923 nearly ended his marriage, and the experience is movingly recounted in Sybille's narrative, based closely on what Maria had told her many years later. When Aldous's obsession eventually became intolerable, Maria had presented him with an ultimatum: "She would leave England the next morning with him or without; for him to make up his mind, but he must make up his mind <u>now</u> . . . they went straight to Italy . . . Aldous wrote *Antic Hay*. He wrote it all down* . . . it was over. He never looked back."

In the later section, covering Aldous's life from 1939 to 1963, Maria's letters, revelatory and engaging, are again quoted at length, Sybille continuing to link them with a detailed chronological account of the Huxleys' domestic circumstances, their extensive travels, their engagement with a wide circle of friends. After Maria's death in 1955, followed less than a year later by Aldous's marriage to Laura Archera, the narrative inevitably becomes more monotone, although Sybille succeeds in providing a sympathetic portrait of Maria's successor, careful to credit Laura with the kindness and support she always showed her husband. As before, Sybille makes use of long extracts from Aldous's own works, not only from his books and articles, but also from lectures, and from broadcasts on radio and television, in one instance, an interview for the BBC in 1961, including nearly ten pages of quotation. Sybille's affection and respect for Aldous, her profound love for Maria, are clearly relayed, her personal recollections, lucid, sympathetic, often witty. In the many periods of Aldous's life in which Sybille was not involved, however, her narrative is less confident as she skitters from one source to another, only infrequently taking control herself, her "Cheshire Cat

---

* In *Antic Hay*, Nancy Cunard is portrayed as Myra Viveash.

manner," as one reviewer described it, "by turns fanciful, informative and vanishing."

On account of its length *Aldous Huxley* was published in Britain in two volumes, the first in November 1973, the second in September 1974, while in the States it appeared in one volume only. The reactions of Sybille's acquaintance were on the whole appreciative, among the most encouraging Raymond Mortimer and Graham Greene. "The book enchanted me by its constant intelligence, its depth of feeling and the felicity of the style," Raymond told her, while Greene wrote, "I can't wait to shout my admiration. This surely is the big biography of our times . . . There has been nothing like it . . . You've written with such knowledge & affection & only a writer could have touched the nerve as you have done." The approval of closer friends was rather more muted: Allanah, although moved by the later years of Aldous's life, found the first volume disappointing; Jimmy Stern criticised Sybille's style, which he found less distinguished than in her previous work; while Martha admitted she had been puzzled by Sybille's adulatory attitude towards such an unsympathetic subject, "a gentle man with a steel selfishness," as Martha described Aldous. "He had a perfect right to live as he did but it is not a very interesting life in action. And in the mind, isn't there a lot of faddery and nonsense mixed with the great learning?"

Both volumes were dedicated to Aldous's son, Matthew, who himself had certain reservations about the work. "Poor Sybille," he wrote to Norah Smallwood at Chatto, "once my mother's lodestone vanishes, not merely does the territory become utterly different, but the subsequent accounts become as improbable as the *fabliaux* of the Middle Ages."

If reactions from friends were varied, the reviews on both sides of the Atlantic were even more so. Raymond Mortimer praised the book enthusiastically in the *Sunday Times*, as did Angus Wilson in the *Observer*, while V. S. Pritchett in the *New Statesman* declared the biography "the major work on a major figure in the literary and intellectual history of the twentieth century." Several critics remarked on the author's naivety about her subject, among them C. P. Snow, who found it strange that "she doesn't recognise with completely clear eyes that, for anyone so intelligent, he was also one of the most credulous men of the age." In the States, one critic described the work as "gossipy, flighty, unintellectual," another disparaged the author's "slapdash prose," while Diana Trilling in the *New York Times* complained of the work's "deficiencies of critical perceptivity . . . its wilderness of parentheses, brackets and lost antecedent nouns." Far the most damning review, however, was by Philip Toynbee in the London *Observer*, who described the biography as "not only unsatisfactory but almost, at times, repellent . . . [Huxley's] social life, so breathlessly retailed to us here, is enough to make the heart sink into the boots with its lists of names and occasions and adulations . . . [and] the trouble goes deeper. When Miss Bedford comes to deal with Huxley's many infidelities to his first wife and Maria's amused complaisance (at least on the surface), the amused complaisance of Sybille Bedford is an utterly inadequate reaction." None of this, he concludes, will "for a moment do as the first-hand description of a real, interesting and poignant human being."

Inevitably Sybille was disappointed and depressed by such reactions. "I feel curiously crushed and low," she confessed to the Sterns. "More wretched than for a long time. Set off by Toynbee, perhaps . . . This whole business of publication . . . is more shattering than I expected. One feels exposed. Also cannot imagine now ever to be able to write another word. Not even a letter. Great reluctance to buckling down to say even this much to you."

In the meantime there were further causes for anxiety. While Sybille had been correcting her proofs and preparing for publication, Eda had arrived in London from the south of France, very dejected and in a fragile state of health: an abcess had developed on the side of her jaw, requiring a course of antibiotics which made her feel weak and nauseated. Recently Eda had received a serious lecture from her doctor, who had "told her if she didn't stop smoking her toes would fall off "; but such a warning was inevitably ignored. With Sybille in her mousehole in Chelsea, separate accommodation had to be found for Eda, who stayed first at Martha's apartment in Cadogan Square, then with Anne Balfour, before a tiny flat was located only minutes away from Old Church Street. Here towards the end of her stay Eda seemed to grow less despondent: "the last ten days, she was better in some ways in spite of tears and uncertainty; because we both enjoyed having dinner together there, then watching television. She made delicious meals, and seemed to enjoy having me and making it nice . . . She was the hostess, and we were happy and easy."

Eda left again for France at the end of May 1974, where Sybille joined her for a couple of weeks before returning to London in June. In August came the wholly unexpected news that Allanah had decided to take back the little dwelling in which over the years they had stayed at Les Bastides. With the publication of the Huxley biography making it difficult for Sybille to leave London, "the monster task" of organising the departure was left to Eda, who, despite her grief at leaving her beloved Provence, efficiently packed up, arranging for most of their possessions to be placed in storage in Nice. Eda herself arrived in England in October, by which time Sybille was about to leave, due to sail to New York in order to promote her book in the States. Fortunately, Anne Balfour was able to take Eda in at her house in Sutherland Street, providing her with a couple of rooms on the top floor. Anne could hear Eda pacing back and forth, hour after hour, dense clouds of cigarette smoke drifting down the staircase. "After Eda left I had to have the whole floor fumigated," she recalled.

Sybille had been looking forward to returning to the States, delighted to be sailing in comfort on the *Queen Elizabeth 2*, "expenses paid by Alfred A. Knopf Inc. Nice of them." During her time in New York she stayed with Evelyn in the East Village, receiving invitations almost every day to lunches and dinners, "all a bit unbelieving at the belated popularity." She gave a number of interviews, appeared on television, delivered a lecture at Columbia University, and was the guest of honour at a cocktail party given by Alfred Knopf at the St. Regis Hotel, followed by dinner with Knopf and his wife, Blanche, an occasion which Sybille "did not enthuse about." She also saw a number of old friends, including Janet Flanner and Natalia Murray, Matthew Huxley and his wife, and Richard Olney, who was in New York giving a series of private cookery lessons at James Beard's apartment.

Most important was her meeting with Bob Gottlieb, who had been unfailingly supportive, if not entirely uncritical of the Huxley biography. Bob had for some while been a major figure in the publishing world; recently, as Evelyn had reported, he had been pictured in a magazine "showing editor supine on sofa editing ms, and talking Bob-nonsense . . . He is v. grand now in publishing . . . and successful as Croesus." Now, for one of the few times in his career, Bob found himself faced with taking an author out to lunch, an obligation which he had always made a point of avoiding. While his colleagues lunched daily in some midtown restaurant, Bob stayed in his office, offering no more than a sandwich to any agent or author who wished to see him. For Sybille, however, such conduct was out of the question, and she insisted that Bob take her to one of the most highly regarded French restaurants in the city. "I was terribly nervous," Bob recalled, "because what do I know about it all . . . Food is food, if it's good that's wonderful and if it isn't who cares. The menu came and they were serving rack of lamb, and I said, Sybille, would you like the rack of lamb? And she said, 'Yes, yes, but you know, my dear Bob, lamb is really nothing but the vehicle for a good claret.' Which of course she chose . . . and it <u>was</u> good."

Sybille returned to England at the beginning of December 1974, immediately immersed in the familiar state of anxiety and depression from which she had been free while in New York. "I miss you," she told Evelyn, "and the cosy life we led, and the gay one . . . London feels small, back-waterish." As the flat in Old Church Street was so tiny, her main worry now was to find somewhere with enough space for herself and Eda to live together, with separate studies and preferably with easy access to a garden. Despite all the difficulties and irritations, Sybille's devotion to Eda remained solid. "Now I shall say what is in my mind," she had written to her recently, "that you are close to me and that I love you. And need you . . . I don't want to live without you . . . I want to be with you, my Eda Bug; and I will try not to be led into superficial day to day irritation."

For some time Sybille had been searching for a suitable property, "going all over London 5 afternoons a week with 20 different estate agents with no goal in sight so far . . . I feel very discouraged." Fortunately, her financial affairs were in a better state than usual, partly due to a generous donation from Laura Huxley, to whom Sybille had confided in detail her worries about the expense of moving house, and as well a bequest of several thousand pounds from her old friend Toni

Muir, who had died the previous year. Nonetheless both she and Eda knew it would be difficult to afford the kind of accommodation they wanted, everything they viewed either too costly or too dilapidated. Then finally in January 1976 they found the ideal property, an apartment in a house in Markham Square, off the King's Road. "It is in a quiet square with trees in Chelsea . . . We shall have the maisonette on the two top floors," Sybille reported to Tania Stern. "I am very happy & hopeful, above all relieved."

The plan was to move into Markham Square in May, which would allow plenty of time for all the necessary sorting and packing. But then the renting of the flat had to be cancelled when in February Eda fell ill, developing a painful ulcer in her mouth. She made an appointment with her dentist, who immediately referred her to a specialist at Guy's Hospital. Here a biopsy revealed a cancerous tumour in her throat, requiring an immediate operation. "Eda herself is very brave," Sybille wrote to Allanah, "but it has been a great shock . . . The thing had already eaten into the throat muscles and was not cut out altogether. It now has to be killed by deep ray treatment . . . Terrifying . . . I try to be optimistic, and to SHOW optimism." Shortly afterwards Eda returned to her little flat, where Sybille visited her daily, bringing her food as well as large supplies of cigarettes which, despite her doctors' orders, Eda had refused to give up. For the next eight weeks Eda walked every morning to the Royal Marsden, the cancer hospital in the Fulham Road, undergoing treatment which left her with a painfully sore throat. "A terrible thing, of course, is trying to eat," she told Mary Frances. "Everything tastes metallic . . . and swallowing is painful." The good news, however, was that Dr. Lederman, "one of the top cancer men in England . . . told me that I was going to be quite all right."

In June Eda was feeling so much better that she was able to accept an invitation from Mary Frances to fly out to the south of France and spend a few days with her in Aix. "I feel jubilant and overwhelmed," Eda told her. "Sybille is exhilarated beyond belief. And I am made happy." Indeed, Sybille was most grateful to Mary Frances, knowing how much a return to France and time spent with her old friend would mean to Eda. "Physically and spiritually, this visit to Aix is the first light at the end of a nasty tunnel," Sybille told her. "When I first wrote to you the bad news in early spring, there was some cause for anxiety that she might not come through the treatment. Thank God, one can say now that all that fear is behind us. And the prognosis is very good."

After a week in Aix, Eda went on to stay with Richard Olney's brother James and his wife, who, with Richard away, were spending part of the summer in his little farmhouse. "Even after nine days I am still aware of this miraculous air in which one bathes," Eda reported, and "more than happy just to sit still and enjoy the garden and what I can see of the world spread out below." When James Beard, who was staying nearby, came over to see her, he was delighted to find not the usual silent, retiring Eda, but an Eda communicative and forthcoming. "I had never known Eda talk so much, or with such brilliance and ease. She talked of her childhood and youth, of her strange early womanhood and her journeyings . . . of Berlin . . . of her experiences in France during the war." The day after the James Olneys left, Richard arrived, overjoyed to find Eda waiting for him. Although shocked by how thin she had grown, he found her looking "eerily more beautiful than ever . . . She was in good spirits, but her thoughts were with eternity and the mystery of life. We were studying the world in bowls of black coffee . . . the conversation, memories and chain-smoking continued. She stayed for a week. I accompanied her to the Marseille airport and put her on a plane for London. We knew that we would never see each other again."

When at the beginning of August Eda returned to London, Sybille was delighted to see how well she looked, "charming & handsome & clear-eyed." Sybille went to visit her every day, sometimes accompanied by a friend, one of whom was Martha, who, true to form, had not hesitated to reproach Sybille for her treatment of Eda. "You MUST NOT always interrupt her when she talks," Martha reproved her. "You not only interrupt her but you also tell _her_ stories. She came back from France with _her_ stories, told you, and when she started to tell me you took them over. You have always done this . . . I notice it every time we three are together."

A rather less abrasive visitor was Evelyn, who had flown over from New York for three weeks to stay at Old Church Street, her arrival instantly buoying Sybille's spirits. During the day the two of them spent hours with Eda, cooking soup, bringing her ice cream, with Evelyn encouraging her to go out as much as possible. "Evelyn has created a festive round," Sybille told Jimmy Stern, "spoiling us with what she calls treats. She even took Eda, Anne Balfour and me to dinner at the Etoile, sending me there half an hour in advance as her wine steward, a role I enjoyed and carried out, I think, with some success." At Old Church Street she and Evelyn enjoyed sitting out-of-doors in the tiny garden, basking "in the glorious unbroken warmth . . . every night at dusk (already now) we drink our wine looking at the trees."

Sybille was so cheered by Evelyn's presence that she decided to give a party in the garden one evening in early September, "years of unreturned hospitality coming home to roost . . . Evelyn will do the donkey work, I the drinks, Eda ashtrays and introductions." Guests began arriving soon after six; just before 7:30, by which time the party was in full swing, everyone standing and talking outside, the sky suddenly darkened and it began to rain. Sybille in a panic began carrying as much as she could indoors, but then noticed that nobody followed, all happily clustered together under a tall tree, "like fowl huddling away from a shoot in progress. Everyone was shrieking with laughter and refusing to come indoors. This went on for about ten minutes; then the heavy shower was over." When eventually the guests departed, Sybille and Evelyn, in the highest spirits, elated by the success of the evening, did what they could to restore order before going out to a local pub for supper.

Shortly afterwards Evelyn returned to New York. A few days later Sybille found Eda in bed one morning having suffered a haemorrhage. Her doctor told her she must go to hospital at once to undergo a hysterectomy. "It does seem inhuman and impossible for her to face it all again," Sybille told Tania Stern. "Today, she seems less shattered, and speaks quite hopefully about a harmless outcome." The operation took place at St. Thomas's Hospital on 1 October. At first all appeared to be well, yet as the days passed Eda showed little sign of recovery, Sybille allowed in to see her for only two hours in the evening. "She seems very ill to me," she reported to Tania, while to Allanah she described how appalling it was "to see a human being disintegrating . . . The difficulty with Eda is that she is so hard to know. I feel that I do not really know her (which makes everything even sadder)." In a letter to Eda's oldest friend, Mary Frances, she wrote, "Eda is not recovering . . . What the doctors said might happen in some months is happening now . . . I cannot bear this fate for her, for her to lose life, to disappear . . . What waste & desolation it is." On 23 October, Eda died. Her funeral took place four days later in Harlow, in Essex, her ashes buried in a local churchyard, at Great Hormead in Hertfordshire.

For some while after Eda's death, Sybille was overcome by grief, distraught at the ending of a close relationship that had lasted over twenty years; she was tormented, too, by the conviction that in some way she had let Eda down. "[I] do not hold that I have been really good to her," she confessed to Allanah. "I did something, but failed her in the essentials, an emotional stability, a great need to be needed she was looking for all her life. I have been very selfish, always domineering, often putting other emotions first; bulldozing on with work . . . I also made her feel unwanted after the move to London." To Mary Frances she wrote, "I believe, when all is said, I was very very close to Eda (and I think she to me); but did I know her well? Understand her?"; while to Jimmy Stern she lamented, Eda's "absence now is almost unbearable. I had not realised how fused our lives had become . . . When people live one does not know how fortunate one is & only grumbles about the cigarette smoke. How I wish I hadn't."

TWELVE

"NOVELS AMONG OTHER THINGS ARE GALLERIES OF MIRRORS"

The impact on Sybille of Eda's death was profound and long-lasting. "Grief is something so unlike anything else—sadness, depression, unhappiness—quite different from that. Pain of absence. I miss Eda so dreadfully. I wish she knew." All Sybille's close friends were consoling and supportive, chief among them Evelyn, Martha, the Sterns, Richard Olney and Allanah. Rosamond Lehmann, too, showed great compassion, persuading Sybille to communicate with Eda through a medium. Since the death of her daughter nearly twenty years earlier, Rosamond had become deeply immersed in the spirit world, a distinguished member of the College of Psychic Studies in South Kensington, in constant contact with what she reverently referred to as the "*au delà*" ("beyond").

Desperate to believe, craving any form of communication, Sybille eagerly agreed, and Rosamond arranged a private seance for her at the college. To Sybille's joy, Eda almost immediately "came through," full of loving messages and reassurances of her own well-being. "Eda was so well," Sybille afterwards told Tania Stern, "writing again . . . and so loving and near that it made me indescribably happy . . . Rosamond telephoned afterwards, the same evening, at 11 p.m. . . . and I was able to tell her that all was transformed." However, although Sybille was convinced at the time that she had been in touch with Eda, the belief did not remain with her for long.

Anxious that Sybille should not be left on her own, Allanah invited her to stay for several months at Les Bastides, a prospect that Sybille both longed for and dreaded. "Going back to Les Bastides, to house, olive grove, every corner of our life for so many many years will not be easy. Yet I didn't think it would be right for me not to go, when Allanah has always considered her house, wherever it was, a home for me . . . We have been something like closest family for near half a century." As she expected, Sybille found herself pleased to return, enjoying the company of Allanah, of the Mimerels, the Childs, Richard Olney, while also frequently overwhelmed by sadness and regret. "Here I am in Allanah's spare room, looking down on our former home in the olive grove below, seeing the bushes we planted, and the one tree. It's all a bit overwhelming." In June 1977, to her great joy, Evelyn arrived from New York, spending a couple of days at Les Bastides before returning with Sybille for a brief stay in London.

In her will Eda had made Sybille her sole legatee, thus ensuring that she could now afford to stay permanently at Old Church Street. Despite the cramped quarters, Sybille had come to feel at home in the little flat, fearing the prospect of having to move. "The news is unexpectedly good. In fact, ever since I've been floating in a kind of disbelieving half-shocked relief," she told Allanah. The owner, Alice Binnie, "will allow me to stay without buying; and will write a letter to her trustees saying that she wishes me to stay for my natural life." Not long afterwards Allanah telephoned, "wanted to say that she has more money now . . . she wants me to have more, and to get everything I want for the flat. I was terribly touched. Really, one's friends! . . . Also oddly cheered. Money had been such a nightmare some of these last years." Not long after Evelyn returned to the States, a letter arrived enclosing a cheque for $1,000. "I love that place," Evelyn had written, "and that's why my thousand is not open to discussion . . . this way I'll be contributing extra luxuries you'd not permit yrself—a really pretty sofa; a good frig/freezer . . . Remember, it wd make me happy. So no fussing, pls."

As always, Sybille had been left desolate by Evelyn's departure, yet cheered by the fact that their period of separation would not last long, Evelyn promising to return for three weeks at the end of August.

Meanwhile in London Sybille soon became immersed in the kind of social life, "interesting, often stimulating," which, now alone, she increasingly felt she needed. "The giving and taking of affection, understanding, warmth. It gives me a sense of identity . . . It gives me a sense of still having something to offer." During the next few weeks she dined on several occasions with Richard Olney, currently in London preparing to start work as chief consultant of an eighteen-volume *World Cookery Anthology* to be published by Time/Life. Then there was an evening with Elizabeth David, "*en beauté*, as easy to talk to as ever"; dinner with Sybille's editor at Collins, Richard Ollard, almost as knowledgeable about wine as Sybille herself; time spent with Raymond Mortimer, the Sterns, Rosamond Lehmann, and "an intellectual cocktail party" given by her one-time lover, Annie Davis, and her husband, over from Spain, where they were now living. At the beginning of September Sybille attended an eightieth-birthday celebration for the president of PEN, the novelist Lettice Cooper, an occasion which rather to her surprise she enjoyed. "Too much standing of course— [but it] had a good atmosphere as everyone tried to be pleasant . . . it was very friendly—quite lacking in that superior chilly snootiness of many English intellectual parties."

By this time Sybille had expected Evelyn to be with her, but to her disappointment the visit had had to be postponed. Evelyn had not been well, it appeared, drained of energy, for several weeks obliged to work from home. "I spend the day on bed, *NY Times* & work & cups of tea & things all around me, and the days pass very slowly and peacefully, punctuated with telephone calls." She was still hoping to come to London, but first there were a number of tests to be undergone, the results revealing that she had been suffering from a severe bout of hepatitis. Once diagnosed, Evelyn felt better, glad to be able to return to work. "Only sign is that after 3 or 4 hrs in office, suddenly begin to yawn head off. So go home, fling off clothes, into nightgown and gratefully on bed for nap." Enormously relieved, Sybille suggested that she herself should come to New York in December, a plan to which Evelyn readily agreed. "Really bucked that we've agreed on Xmas visit; darling, tap wood of course, but one always does."

Over the next few weeks, Sybille received frequent reports on Evelyn's progress. After recovering from hepatitis, she was found to have an inflamed gallbladder, which would have to be removed, but once this was done everything should be all right. "I have no cancer, no ulcers, NO abnormalities of any kind . . . It may seem curious to be so pleased about an operation—but darling think of the bliss to get it over with fast?" The procedure took place at the Beth Israel Hospital on 19 September, Sybille waiting anxiously for news. "Last night, her 3rd day, she was able to telephone me herself from hospital," Sybille reported to Tania Stern. "Very reassuring." Over the next few weeks Evelyn's condition continued slowly to improve, but then at the end of October she had to undergo a second operation, followed in December by an emergency procedure, this time to cut out a large ovarian tumour. Sybille had known nothing of this until she was telephoned at midnight from New York. "They told me not to come as she was in an intensive care unit and under heavy sedation." Three days later, on 18 December, the eve of her sixtieth birthday, Evelyn died. The final operation had been too much, "her heart gave out," Sybille told Elizabeth David. Evelyn "was one of the best human beings I have ever met—sheer goodness. And no one ever had such a friend . . . It is shattering, & I'm shattered."

Inevitably, Sybille was profoundly affected by Evelyn's death, particularly following so soon after the loss of Eda. "I cannot believe it yet . . . It is very difficult to mourn two people at the same time. Yet I do; and I think the love and tenderness is greater than the grief . . . Evelyn gave me security . . . to an extraordinary extent. Indeed she often talked of transferring to a London publishing job to look after me in my old age. We both seemed to have counted on that . . . She allayed fears, made difficult or dull things seem easy or funny . . . It will be very difficult to face living without the unique things that both Eda and Evelyn in such very different ways were giving. I must try." Over the next few months Sybille corresponded with lawyers in New York over Evelyn's will, she herself named as co-beneficiary; she also spent hours answering letters of condolence from her friends, even summoning the courage to contact for the first time in many years Evelyn's ex-husband. "Write at last a handwritten note to Milton. An olive branch that does not speak its name."

Despite her grief, Sybille was determined to stay occupied, maintaining a busy social life, organising the redecoration of her flat, and regularly attending meetings at PEN. A few months before Evelyn's death Sybille one evening had dined with her old friends, Billy and Jenny Hughes, and with them a woman whom Sybille had first met in the late 1930s. Lesley Huston was the sister of Eda's then lover, Joan Black, with whom Sybille had been briefly infatuated after the war. On this occasion Sybille found herself drawn to Lesley, "a dear, sensitive, rather subtle person, with much courage and gaiety." A tall, slender beauty with a head of thick white hair, Lesley was intelligent, musical and well read; she had been married twice, her second husband the film director John Huston, from whom she had been divorced in 1945. An engaging companion, there was also an elusive quality about Lesley, a sense of privacy and self-containment. Not long after the evening with the Hugheses, Lesley invited Sybille to dinner, together with a couple of friends of hers, but the friends cancelled at the last moment so the two women spent the evening on their own. "I felt curiously shy at first," Sybille told Allanah., but "then it went very well . . . we talked till nearly 2 a.m. . . . mostly of course about past lives . . . [I] am getting to like her very much indeed."

From this time on the two women were frequently in each other's company, Sybille growing ever more infatuated while Lesley remained warm and affectionate, happy to have Sybille as a dear friend, if not attracted to her as a lover. Entranced by Lesley's beauty—she arrived one evening "looking as lovely as the queen of the night"—Sybille was delighted that she also shared many of her own intellectual interests, a love of music and art, a passion for literature. Lesley was also a good linguist, long familiar with the same European countries as Sybille. The more she came to know her, the more Sybille was impressed by Lesley's qualities, "struck as so often by that fantastic talent for seeing, reading, getting at the heart of the matter; L's response, insight . . . reminiscent of the young Aldous." She was knowledgeable, too, about food and wine, a good cook, if not on the same level of expertise as Sybille herself. It was in Lesley's flat in Ovington Gardens that in April 1978, a "surprise" birthday dinner was held for Richard Olney, the other guests Sybille, Elizabeth David, and also Jeremiah Tower, a friend of Richard's and a talented young chef from California. It was Jeremiah who undertook the cooking, while Sybille, with great care and concentration, chose the wines, bringing with her as a present six superb bottles of Lafite 1962. A few weeks later, in June, Richard, Sybille, Lesley and Jeremiah went to France, on a tour arranged by Richard, to take part in one of the wine trade's most prestigious events, the magnificent annual festival staged by the Médoc, Graves, Sauternes and Barsac wine brotherhood, the Commanderie du Bontemps.

This was not the first occasion on which Richard had travelled with Sybille, the previous experience leaving him apprehensive as to how on this occasion she would cope. Over the years Sybille had become increasingly nervous about almost any form of travel, in a frenzy that the train would be late, that no one would be on the platform to meet her, that the taxi ordered would fail to arrive; and now she was terrified by the prospect of flying. Her first flight had been the year before, when she and Richard had flown to Nice, "quite a project," as Richard had described it. By the time they boarded the plane Sybille was shaking with nerves, repeatedly crossing herself, checking her seat belt every few seconds; when they finally took off, "gasps and more crossings . . . she untwisted her hands, turned to me without looking out of the window and asked breathlessly, are we in the air? . . . [I] hugged her tightly, said yes, and that . . . everything would be all right . . . She was scarlet with terror, embarrassment and pleasure all at once, then the stewardess announced that due to catering strikes there would be no bar service . . . depression and terror struck again—one had been depending on the booze—finally got glasses of ice . . . and slipped duty-free whisky into them—S had brought along sandwiches, determined not to eat any of the poisonous airline food and ended up eating both, the trip was short and suddenly, after the drama of landing, we were in Nice and the sky was blue."

This second journey, their participation in the famous Fête de la Fleur, the flowering of the vine, later described by Sybille "as pure an enterprise for pleasure as has come my way in many a long year," proved rather less stressful. During four days the small group visited some of the greatest Bordeaux vineyards, Haut-Brion, Lafite, Ducru-Beaucaillou and Léognan, exploring the cellars, concentratedly tasting the wine, staying each night luxuriously ensconced in one of the great chateaux, where they were entertained to sumptuous luncheons and dinners. At Haut-Brion, "the steel vats gleam; the long, straight lines of barrels look as if they have been waxed . . . A cellarman appears, five large tulip glasses dangling from one well-used hand. He taps a barrel; a thin red thread curves into the glass. 'Château Haut-Brion 1977.' We look, we inhale, we draw in our mouthful: we chew, we *think*. It is a slow process . . . utterly absorbing and near an ordeal—the raw tannin puckers the inside of the cheeks, rasps the throat like claws." At Château Lafite there was a magnificent luncheon in the dining room, around an exquisitely set oval table beneath a great chandelier. "We are offered three clarets, Château Duhart-Milon '66, Château Lafite '66 and Lafite '55 . . . I am very happy."

The highlight of the Fête de la Fleur was staged at Château Ducru-Beaucaillou, a ceremony held to honour various distinguished members of the trade. "*Vignerons, négociants* . . . all are milling about the grounds . . . M. le Ministre has arrived, and the cheerful charade of citations, the enrobing . . . of the neophytes, is under way." To her delight Sybille was among those who were "enthroned"—"Do you think I'm worthy of such an honour?" she had asked Richard nervously beforehand. Afterwards there were aperitifs on the lawn followed by a banquet for all 440 guests, seated at ten tables inside a vast and uncomfortably hot marquee. Disappointingly, the "spectacular" wines "do not give their best. They are warm. Here it is the fault only of circumstances . . . but the result remains sad. Blood-warm, the Margaux 1970, a Rauzan-Ségla, is in disarray . . . the beauty of the 1967 Haut-Brion is dissipated almost within seconds in the glass." Infinitely more pleasurable was the final evening spent staying at Château Loudenne in the Médoc, a "ravishing, low-built, rose-washed chateau," where a magnificent dinner was given for twelve guests. Afterwards "we returned to the long drawing room; the French windows were open to the summer night, the vines lay still under a slim moon . . . The mood of the party was serene with that surge of optimism of spirit and physical well-being that comes after a very good wine drunk in congenial company at a leisurely pace."

Following her return to London, Sybille in a letter to the Sterns described the experience as "so perfect that it is hard to put feet back to earth. Countryside, beauty of vineyards, chateaux, cellars, ordered happy peaceful lives, charming and interesting hosts, superb hospitality, great wines drunk in perfect conditions, human and material, above all the affectionate and happy company of our own small band of friends."

This tranquil mood was not to last: shortly after arriving home Sybille received disturbing news from Nice about her sister Katzi, now in her eightieth year. The two had continued to keep in touch, Sybille dutifully visiting Katzi at least once during the months she spent staying at Les Bastides, occasions she slightly dreaded, mainly on account of her dislike for Katzi's partner, Gino Atanasio. Recently Katzi's health had started to deteriorate with alarming rapidity. "She has difficulties with her speech," Sybille reported to Allanah. "She writes '*c'est dans ma tête* [it's in my head].' I think you know what she is talking about." In January 1978, shortly after Evelyn's death, Sybille had gone to see Katzi, finding her "in a lamentable state. She must have had a kind of stroke; speech difficulties, great weakness, fear. Pitiful to watch." Then on 12 September, news came that Katzi had died, her death followed shortly afterwards by a cremation in Marseilles. Sybille was in London at the time so did not attend, but a few weeks later, while staying at Les Bastides, Allanah had driven her to Nice to visit Gino, "a heartbroken, and helpless, man."

Before the end of the year Sybille received further sad news, of the death of two old friends, Eva Herrmann in California, who had died of cancer, and Janet Flanner, who for the past few years had been living in New York, cared for by her devoted companion Natalia Murray. On the day she learned of Janet's death Sybille was on the point of leaving Les Bastides to join Lesley in Avignon, her sadness about Janet soon overcome by a feeling of intense excitement—"heart turns over"—at the prospect of seeing her adored Lesley after so many weeks apart. The two of them drove to London, where they spent a quiet Christmas together before going to Oxfordshire to celebrate the New Year with Anne Balfour at her cottage at Long Wittenham. With Anne was her partner of over a decade, Marie-Thérèse d'Arcangues, a "thin, hard-drinking, frustrated, neurotic poet figure," as Sybille described her. When Sybille and Lesley arrived they found the two women "muffled, stiff . . . playing at wood-cutters . . . M-Th, cursing like a trouper, lugs in logs . . . We thaw over tea by the fire."

Over the following years Sybille came to love Cruck Cottage, a tiny fourteenth-century cottage with a low thatched roof and a pretty garden, "minute & magical." Indoors was a low-ceilinged parlour, leading off it a miniature kitchen, and above, up a creaking wooden staircase, a couple of bedrooms and a bathroom. Celebrating the New Year at Cruck was to become a much-loved tradition for Sybille. On this occasion, she and Lesley were led into the cosy interior, Anne producing tea and scones while Marie-Thérèse, *"pipe au bec"* ("pipe in mouth"), piled logs onto the blazing fire. The following day was given over to preparations for the New Year Eve's feast, every detail of it relished by Sybille. In the evening, while birds roasted on a spit over the fire, she busied herself with "drinks, buttling, spitting, fire building, foie gras jelly chopping. During which we open and drink two bottles of champagne . . . The goose foie gras almost unbearably good . . . It was like a pain to eat the last of it. The partridges, one each, were perfectly roasted. We ate them bones in hand tearing them apart. Both Riojas had strength and fruit, the '70 quite subtle. The lovely Sauternes was just the right thing to drink on the sinking evening of the year. Which came (with telly blaring alas) and we all embraced in our various permutations with goodwill and tenderness."

Since Eda's death Sybille had been living on her own for the first time in over twenty years. Somewhat to her surprise she found she enjoyed the independence and privacy, as long as there were friends near at hand with whom she could be easily in touch. London was now the city where she felt most at home, "liking it more and more every year"; during her annual stay at Les Bastides, she would complain of homesickness, of how much she missed London, "the life, the friends, the friends at the end of a telephone, the books, a hundred and one things to do." Recently Sybille had become the owner of the little flat in Old Church Street, the money she had inherited from both Eda and Evelyn enabling her to purchase it, and also the apartment above; this she was able to let, providing a satisfying addition to what was now a more than adequate income. Since the property was hers, Sybille took pleasure in having the place repaired and redecorated, arranging everything exactly as she wanted it: her wine stored near the entrance, the tiny parlour, with its "Spartan sofa" and grey metal desk, also acting as dining room and study. Against the wall was a tall bookcase, on top of which stood ten empty bottles, souvenirs of her most revered wines. In the shady garden at the back Sybille grew lettuces and herbs in the small flower bed, always punctilious in remembering to put out food for the birds.

For some months Sybille had been hoping to return to work, planning to write a book about her travels in Europe, but somehow the project failed to materialise. Then in May 1979, she attended the trial at the Old Bailey of Jeremy Thorpe, long a distinguished Member of Parliament and until recently leader of the Liberal Party, who had been accused of conspiracy to murder. At first, like many others, Sybille believed Thorpe to be innocent, but as the hearing progressed she grew increasingly disillusioned, in her notebook recording her disgust at the sensational revelations—"whole thing sordid/tedious." Finally after a long four weeks, she decided against writing about it, dismissing the whole process as "LURID RUBBISH."

Although relieved to have the Thorpe trial behind her, Sybille still found it impossible to return to work. One barrier was the irksome burden of household chores. "I find it very hard to conserve time, peace, energy for work when there is so much to be done to keep clean and mended, let alone shopped, cooked and entertaining one's friends," she complained. "I had not realised how much Eda did . . . I miss Eda, and Evelyn, appallingly and constantly . . . yet I quite enjoy living alone (apart from the doubling of daily grind) . . . I dine out a great deal."

As indeed she did. Now approaching seventy, Sybille over the years had amassed a large number of friends, and was constantly adding to her social circle, going out most evenings, coming into contact with new worlds and sections of society. Intelligent and well read, with her novelist's fascination for the world around her, Sybille was a rewarding guest, although the quick, quiet patter of her speech often made her hard to understand. "She talks as it were to herself," as Elaine Robson-Scott remarked, she, Martha and Allanah, among others, frequently complaining to Sybille that they were unable to understand a word she said. In her diary Sybille wrote, a "great tease has sprung up [about] . . . my 'petits bruits' . . . It appears I emit little noises (squeaks? mutters) and always have. More than suspects, it's true."

One morning Sybille was woken by the telephone at 10 a.m. "Someone says Shirley and asks me to dinner. Answer sleepily but with utter readiness. Live in Regent's Park had said you do remember me? Enthusiastic yes on my part. Dawns slowly that it's someone I don't remember at all. 'Women will wear long skirts too.' What have I let myself in for." The caller turned out to be Shirley Letwin, she and her husband, William, both wealthy American academics, living in one of the beautiful Nash houses on the edge of Regent's Park. Here they entertained lavishly, their guests mainly writers, philosophers and Conservative politicians. Both Letwins had great charm, and after the inevitable anxieties over finding a suitable skirt and whether the minicab would arrive on time, Sybille found herself enjoying the occasion. She took to both her hosts, and relished talking to her fellow guests, among them Melvin Laski, editor of *Encounter*, and also the writer Peter Vansittart, who delighted her by comparing her fiction to the novels of Proust. During a subsequent evening at Kent Terrace, she met Kingsley Amis and his novelist wife, Elizabeth Jane Howard. Although slightly wary of Kingsley—"Suspect of leftish tendencies . . . Not sure I liked him"— she was enchanted by Jane, "very lovely, very Junoesque," relishing their conversation "about food, cookery . . . [and] on trying a fish suet pie."

Another friendship formed at this period was with the writer Bruce Chatwin. In 1978 Sybille had enthusiastically reviewed Chatwin's first book, *In Patagonia*, which she described as "one of the most exhilarating travel books I have read." That same month Sybille, accompanied by Lesley, met Chatwin at a dinner given by Sybille's doctor and friend, Patrick Woodcock, "a very good animated evening," she reported. Sometime later Bruce returned the compliment by writing admiringly in *Vogue* of *A Visit to Don Otavio*,[*] shortly afterwards inviting Sybille to dine at his tiny mews flat in Belgravia, her fellow guest his young lover, the fashion designer Jasper Conran. The evening was judged by Sybille to be "one of the 'weirdest' I ever had. Much enjoyment, exquisite food and drink, Bruce's incomparable conversation . . . His young friend . . . so beautiful at times, so odd at others . . . talk about clothes designing (Conran's prêt-à-porter), Ken Macpherson, Capri," then

---

[*] Later included as a foreword in the edition published by Eland Books in 2002.

with Jasper "the drive back through the night . . . in a red open classic Mercedes drown in wind and very loud DON GIOVANNI."

Rather less enjoyable was a dinner, again given by Patrick Woodcock, for Sybille and Richard Olney to meet the painter David Hockney. Patrick, a charming and exuberant host, knew little about wine, so Sybille offered to bring two bottles of the finest claret, Haut-Brion and Cos d'Estournel. When Richard arrived to collect her, he helped her decant the wine, the two of them in the taxi carefully holding the decanters between their knees to avoid disturbing the contents. On arrival Sybille asked Patrick to place the wine in a cool corner until dinner was served. When Hockney appeared, rather late, and was asked what he wanted to drink he answered, "plonk." According to Richard's account, Patrick, in a panic, "raced out and snatched the decanter of Haut-Brion, Sybille rose in horror, as if levitated, and wailed, 'OH NOooo, not that!' Patrick sheepishly returned it and came back with the Cos d'Estournel. It was hopeless. Sybille and David Hockney detested each other at sight . . . [and] the evening went from bad to worse. Without addressing Sybille, David offered to drive me home. Sybille said, 'Young man, you will drive me home first!' He decided to drop her at the corner of Old Church Street and she murmured through clenched teeth, 'You will drive me to my door.' After I had seen Sybille to her door and returned to the car, David said, 'Who the fuck is that old bitch?' "

It was during this period that Sybille formed friendships with two literary figures, Frances Partridge and Stanley Olson. Frances, now nearly eighty, was one of the last survivors of the Bloomsbury group, while Stanley, a protégé of Frances, was an American writer in his early thirties. During an occasion with Stanley at Frances's flat in Belgravia Sybille recalled not only a delicious dinner but over all "a very good evening with talk flowing . . . without the Bloomsbury cattiness/ bitchiness . . . We part, Stanley and I from Frances without kissykiss or handshake. Bloomsbury style? Probably." Yet while she was fond of Frances, it was Stanley to whom Sybille grew closer, enchanted by his intelligence and eccentricity, delighted by his dedicated epicureanism. A short, rather plump young man, with a head of glossy black hair—a "weird amalgamation of small animal and Oscar [Wilde]"— Stanley had a tiny mews flat off Montagu Square, where he lived with his spaniel, Wuzzo, while working on a life of the painter John Singer Sargent. Stanley was a generous host, almost as knowledgeable as Sybille about food and wine; he entertained her at his flat to exquisite little dinners, and enjoyed acting as barman when she gave parties at Old Church Street. Before long Sybille had grown deeply fond of Stanley; he "had extraordinary sweetness of nature; also he was quite unspoilt. The feasts and the flowers and the wines were his natural toys. If he appeared eccentric—and, my goodness, he <u>was</u> eccentric—there was no affectation in it."

Meanwhile Sybille continued to see as much of Lesley as she could. The emotional bond between them was strong, but for Lesley it remained an affectionate friendship, while Sybille found herself deeply enamoured. One evening over dinner with Lesley and Anne Balfour, Anne began talking about her lover, Marie-Thérèse d'Arcangues, who before she met Anne had apparently never been to bed with a woman. " 'How extraordinary!' S is moved to say. 'Why,' says L, 'why extraordinary? <u>I've</u> never slept with a woman.' 'Different,' says S, and Anne concurs. We don't go further." Often after an evening spent with friends, or attending a meeting at PEN, or dining together at Old Church Street, Sybille and Lesley would sit talking for hours, not parting till three or four in the morning, when Lesley would drive back to Ovington Gardens in her little blue Honda. When Lesley went abroad, as she often did, Sybille would wait impatiently for her return. "Full of tension, waiting for L to come back," she noted one evening when Lesley was due to return from a visit to Austria. "Lie on bed, drop off. Take off jeans at 10.40, half min later telephone call. Dash to Victoria. One look: Lesley's bright-eyed, well, herself. Surge of joy. We drive back here . . . Hear about Schrunz days. Take L to Honda . . . Tired but new lease. Bed midnight."

In November 1980, Sybille, to her intense delight, received a letter from the office of the prime minister, Margaret Thatcher, informing her that she was to be appointed "an Officer of the Order of the British Empire." "It's such an improbable thing to have happened to me," she told Jimmy Stern, that "I need being reminded that it's real." Founded in 1917 by George V to provide honours for the non-military, five classes of awards were established, of which the OBE is the fourth in line. The ceremony at Buckingham Palace was to be held on 10 February, and it was Anne Balfour who now took charge, determined to ensure that Sybille would be appropriately dressed, her usual garb of trousers, striped shirt, neckerchief and waistcoat exchanged for an elegant velvet jacket and silk scarf, both lent by Anne, a well-tailored flannel skirt and a pair of polished black brogues; as hats were no longer de rigueur, "I went without (the only woman in my draft who did)."

On the morning of the ceremony, Anne drove Sybille and her "best man," her Collins editor, Richard Ollard, to the Palace. Here on arrival Richard and Anne joined the rest of the audience in the ballroom while Sybille was escorted up the great gilded staircase and into a long gallery, where she waited with her fellow honorees until her name was called. Eventually, a loud voice announced "Mrs. Sybille Bedford," "and up I went; saw the Queen: tiny, in a little beigey-browny batik day dress, looking very small and plain in front of her plumed guard. I made a deep straight entirely steady curtsey . . . walked up to the Queen who muttered, fussing with the hook in my coat. 'What did you do for it?' . . . [I] said quite loud and proud, 'I am a writer, Ma'am.' The Queen: 'Oh. And how long have you been at it?' S: 'All my life, Ma'am.' The Queen: 'Oh dear! Ah, well.' She shook my hand, a very firm grip, a horse woman's grip, almost pushing one back. I managed my smart steps backwards, another deep steady curtsey . . . [then was led] to a good seat, front seat, to watch my fellow OBEs being run through . . . After which National Anthem, we stood, the Queen walked out."

Returning to Old Church Street, Sybille went "to show off the order to the neighbours," then in the evening attended a cocktail party given in her honour by Anne. Finally she was taken by Richard to dinner at a favourite restaurant of his, "to celebrate à deux. By midnight we were joined by the chef, the sommelier . . . the head waiter . . . I was being kissed by all. And the best brandy circulated till 2 a.m. by which time we all got down to the serious talk of food marketing, cooking, wine waiting and all shared a taxi home in the small hours."

During this period, Sybille's feelings for Lesley remained as intense as ever, while Lesley herself remained in emotional terms tantalisingly out of reach. "Unrequited love . . . the delirium, the hopes, the despair, the waiting. At eighteen one may believe oneself to be uniquely stricken, at thirty one may be able to say that no pain is irreversible, at seventy one knows that it is: irreversible."

Over time Sybille's frustration at what she began to regard as Lesley's deliberate evasiveness intensified, resulting in some acrimonious exchanges between them. On one occasion, after an evening spent dining with Anne Balfour, Lesley had driven Sybille back to Old Church Street. "It's two a.m. outside in the car," Sybille recorded in her diary. "I say Everything I lay on for you bores you now. Says it's tiredness. She's never bored . . . Try to say something—hesitantly—about my despair and fears. I'm brushed off. Shut out." Waking late the next morning, Sybille wrote, "feeling better physically though not in spirits. Resentments. Not good . . . L did not call . . . Unhappy afternoon trying to redirect thought and anger." Later Lesley telephoned to say that she was going away, "but fails to say when she intends to return." It was at this point that Sybille began to realise she had suffered enough, her anguish temporarily transmuting into a state almost of indifference. "Self-preservation, or the death of the heart? Honestly do not know."

With Lesley unattainable, Sybille found herself without an emotional focus, craving serious attachment as well as physical expression. Over the past few years she had occasionally gone with friends to the Gateways, a lesbian club off the King's Road, but now she began attending a much less sophisticated venue, where the girls made themselves available by the hour. When Anne Balfour heard of this she was horrified. "I kept saying, 'Sybille, I don't honestly think it's a good idea, it's dangerous.' However, she persisted and would come back after and pour it all out . . . She said to one girl, 'And where do you work?' 'In the forecourt.' So Sybille said, 'Where is that? In the Inns of Court?' 'Naah! It's a petrol station.' She did think that quite funny."

It was now that Sybille embarked on a series of relatively brief affairs, all with much younger women, the details of each liaison recorded meticulously in her diary. In every instance the initial period of excitement was soon followed by impatience and disillusion, before eventually evolving into a state of amiable friendship. The first of these encounters was with "a young and pretty painter," Laura Gethen Smith, who had recently written Sybille an admiring letter about her work. The two arranged to meet, and over the following weeks drifted into an affair, Sybille attracted by Laura and impressed by her intelligence. She took her to an event at PEN, to dinner with Anne Balfour, with Richard Ollard, and in June spent a week with her in Paris. Not long after they returned, however, Sybille began to tire of the situation, and after a number of tense evenings together, Sybille snapping irritably while Laura sat "lowering like a brooding thundercloud," she decided to bring it to an end: "some very good moments, but, but, but . . ."

Shortly afterwards, Sybille met Rosamund Williams, an aspiring writer, originally from Germany, who lived in Sussex but came regularly to London. For a time Sybille found herself much taken by "R," as she referred to her, visiting her at her house in Ditchling, although never, to Rosamund's disappointment, agreeing to stay the night. While Rosamund declared herself rapturously in love—"deliciously, happily, gladly, gratefully . . . Darling . . . Why did we have to wait so long?"—Sybille's own feelings grew ever more equivocal; after one occasion when she had taken Rosamund to meet Anne Balfour, Anne warned her, correctly, as it turned out, that she was heading for trouble. As Sybille started to retreat, Rosamund grew ever more irascible and demanding, "less and less pleasant . . . curiously un-housetrained," and after a particularly difficult evening at Old Church Street, with Rosamund, that "tiresome little woman . . . very much her mulish stubborn ingrown unseeing ungracious self," Sybille made up her mind to distance herself from the relationship.

Fortunately by this time Sybille's accord with Lesley had been restored, now achieving a harmonious balance, evolving into a close and loving friendship that was to remain unchanging and profound. After their reconciliation, Sybille wrote in her diary, "All so much more easy now for both. Happy . . . I do love her. The best of friends." At the end of 1981, Sybille went to stay with Lesley at her house at Alba in the Ardèche region of France, which she shared with a French friend of hers, Corinne Stempfer. "Magical," as Sybille described it. "Such wonderful country . . . mountains in background, wide expanse of trees, cultivated land. I loved it. And I loved Lesley's charming house, and her friends . . . it was all perfect."

After the publication of her Huxley biography, Sybille had intended to start work on a travel book. To be entitled "Euphoria," it was to be "a very personal book with a general theme," as she had described it to Bob Gottlieb. "Reminiscences rather than serious autobiography." The prospect of a life without writing seemed unthinkable, as recognising herself as a writer was crucial to her identity. "Writing does take it out of one, but there seems to be for me no peace of mind, no moral, or if you like spiritual health. I pay more for not working, than for working." Yet despite her determination, the project failed to develop, Sybille unable to find a focus, discouraged, too, by Gottlieb's apparent lack of interest. On a couple of occasions when Bob had come over to London she had lunched with him at the Ritz, but somehow the relationship was not as it had been. "The warmth all a bit *à côté* for me, a false note, aware of what small beer I am (in that US world) . . . leave sad, weighed down too by no work to offer."

With no book in progress, Sybille devoted much of her time to involvement with several societies, "literary, local residents, national and semi-international politics." In political terms, Sybille as she grew older had moved away from the leftish tendencies of her younger days and further to the right. When in 1981 the ex-Foreign Secretary David Owen left the Labour Party to launch the more centrist Social Democratic Party, Sybille at first was keen to support him—until he declared his commitment to ending racial discrimination and promoting sexual equality. "I do believe that there are marked differences in many, many ways between the two sexes," she wrote in her diary. "I believe that some races are superior or inferior to others in terms of human decency, civilisation, achievements, states of development—that some races mix less with some races; and of course there are better and worse religions. All self-evident. So—possibly no fiver from me to the SDP." Then during Margaret Thatcher's first term as prime minister, Sybille became an enthusiastic supporter of the Conservatives, to the disapproval of a number of friends, Martha among them. Yet Sybille remained unswayed. "I listened to the prime minister on *Panorama* tonight," she wrote to Tania Stern. "Many things have gone wrong, but she needs and deserves all support."

One of the societies whose meetings Sybille regularly attended was the Royal Society of Literature, of which she had been made a fellow in 1964. She served for seven years on the council and was often present for talks at the society's premises in Hyde Park Gardens, always seated in the front row, her eyes shaded by her green visor, impatiently checking her watch when the speaker droned on for too long. But it was PEN to which she became most closely attached, as a member of the committee helping organise events, acting as vice president for a number of years, and regularly attending lectures and dinners at the society's premises in Dilke Street. "PEN parties are curiously non-nightowley," she wrote approvingly in her diary. However, not every event was considered enjoyable. A "quite nice dinner," she noted after one occasion, but the talk was "dire . . . read by a pedestrian and resentful Indian writer: the MIDNIGHT'S CHILDREN man. Exasperated and coarse." In 1981 she attended PEN congresses in Paris and Lyons—"muddle, muddle all the way"—and in October that same year took part in a "state visit" held in Nice. Accompanied by Richard Olney, she found herself "in constant tow—for three days and most of the nights—of Monsieur l'Ambassadeur de la Nouvelle Zélande, M. le Deputé Maire de Menton, M. le Ministre de la Couronne Belge . . . never so many speeches . . . so many receptions . . . so many banquets . . . Infinite boredom, strain, and at times Great Fun."

It was not long after the visit to Nice that Sybille embarked on a new affair, with an attractive young woman, Jenny MacKilligin. Jenny, who had worked in publishing, lived off the King's Road, only a short distance away from Old Church Street. At first Sybille was enchanted by "my Jenny," impressed by her intelligence and love of literature; soon, she was spending whole nights at Jenny's flat, often not returning home till lunchtime the following day. There were frequent telephone calls, intense literary conversations over lengthy dinners, although Sybille was disappointed by Jenny's indifference to wine. " 'J' is worse than a gulper, a quick drinker who does not notice," she wrote disapprovingly after one occasion, going on to add, "Nevertheless, a wonderful evening, slow, tender." To Tania Stern Sybille wrote, "I feel very privileged, and a bit awed. It is very strange to be surrounded by so much gentleness and affection."

Inevitably, however, this period of enchantment came to an end. Before long Sybille was complaining of tears, jealous scenes, "so much touchiness, such a capacity for feeling hurt . . . Very weary making."

In October she and Jenny went for a few days to Vienna: "there were good moments," Sybille reported, "but they all seemed to have to be worked for." Back in London the two continued to see each other, but the relationship grew increasingly tempestuous, Sybille exasperated by the constant rows and reproaches. By the end of the year, she felt she had endured enough. "I cannot say how much J bores me, how little I look up to her opinions, or rather the way she arrives at and repeats these opinions . . . No rapport." Fortunately, however, the affair soon transmuted into a more peaceful friendship, Sybille the following year even taking Jenny with her to stay at Les Bastides.

With almost a decade having passed since the publication of Sybille's most recent book, she at last began to feel ready to return to work. In her diary for 30 April 1983, she recorded, "After the appalling initial dithering did buckle down, stuck it for hours and got something down on paper—the exertion, the relief—something flowing—the exhilaration is incredible." In fact this new work would take several years to complete, a length of time that imposed a certain strain on Sybille's relationship with Bob Gottlieb. In 1974, the year of the American publication of the Huxley biography, Sybille had signed a new contract with Knopf for two further books, neither of which had so far materialised. Eventually Bob had written an admonitory letter. "I've been embarrassed to ask you about our overdue books, and haven't known how to write <u>without</u> asking, but now our Money People are pressing me, so ask I must . . . Tell me do you think these are books you'll be delivering within the foreseeable future? Or have you turned your back on them? And if so, how do you want to handle the monies you've had for them to date—($8,000 in total, I believe) . . . The important professional thing is not to let this drag on without resolution."

Sybille was contrite. "You <u>are</u> right to ask. It is I who am horrified by my slowness, dilatoriness, the sheer passage of time. I have been, am, at work on a book. The time it's taking appals me . . . Things have been difficult in some ways in the last decade, domesticity, cookery, paperwork, entertaining, trying to sew buttons . . . However, other writers cope with these or similar impediments." The book she had in mind, she told Bob, was "not easy to describe. A kind of a novel, autobiographical, though definitely not straight autobiography; nor—God forbid—my memoirs. The working title . . . is 'Perspectives.' It is a kind of story about people and places in my time . . . Not about myself—except as a learning and blundering human creature—but with me as a narrator. Does that make any sense to you?" Richard Ollard at Collins had been shown an early section of the book, and "likes it. Says it's the best I've done so far."

As she continued to work on her book, Sybille was delighted to make a new friend, a writing friend, with whom, as before with Martha, she could talk in detail about the difficult daily struggle. Betsy Drake, American, just turned sixty, had had an earlier career as an actress in Hollywood, married for over a decade to the film star Cary Grant. After their divorce Betsy had settled in London, where she had trained as a pyschotherapist; she had also published a novel and was now at work on another. She and Sybille had met some years previously through a Chelsea neighbour, and now encountering each other again they became good friends, Betsy coming regularly to Old Church Street, Sybille dining with Betsy in her spacious flat, an easy walk away in Cheyne Gardens. The two were now in almost daily contact, reading aloud to each other from their work in progress, holding long conversations on the telephone. Although at odds over a number of subjects, politics in particular—Betsy disapproving of Sybille's conservatism, Sybille of Betsy's left-wing "Reagan antagonism"—they soon became close allies. "Odd to be really fond of someone . . . and so opposed, alienated by their notions," Sybille wrote in her diary. But "she is a good friend, as well as a dear one."

Another bond between them was the difficult relationship both had experienced with Martha, who had recently brought to an end her long friendships with both Sybille and Betsy. Her break with Betsy, in January 1983, was the more recent: "B[etsy] had a blast from Martha—a breaking off, 'poisonous,' leaving B sick and numb," Sybille recorded. Not long before, Martha in a similarly terse manner had dispensed with Sybille, telephoning her one morning to tell her, "Sybille, you are too boring . . . I'm fed up with you." Shortly afterwards, when Betsy had brought up Sybille's name, Martha had been brusquely dismissive. "Please don't involve yourself or make a thing between us. Sybille does not need me; I served her wondrously well when she did need me and have no further obligation." Sybille had been very shaken at the time, although aware that over the past few years her relationship with Martha had been deteriorating, Martha growing increasingly impatient with what she regarded as Sybille's tiresome obsession with food and wine, while Sybille was equally riled by Martha's, in her view, bleak puritanism. "She'll never understand the pleasure of giving friends something good, of giving enjoyment, well-being . . . She does hurt people, always did; never knows. Goodness, how it used to hurt me. One never quite forgets. And yet the good sides. I owe her much."

It was at this same period that Sybille embarked on another affair, with Anne Gainsford, a talented costume designer for films and theatre. After one of their first nights together, Sybille confided to Lesley that "I had again that sense of tenderness and lovingness . . . an immense feeling not only towards that woman here and now whom I have unaccountably come to love so much, but love *tout court*." Anne lived in Richmond, where Sybille on several occasions drove down to visit her, while Anne came regularly to central London, often staying overnight at Old Church Street. Sybille took her to dine in favourite restaurants, to wine tastings, and also to meetings of PEN. On one occasion Sybille accompanied Anne to the Theatre Royal in the Haymarket, where Anne was delivering some costumes, Sybille enthralled by her first sight of an auditorium from the wings, amazed by the steep rake of the stage. Not long after they met Sybille gave Anne a gold brooch which had once belonged to Esther, but when the affair ended she asked for it to be returned.

Meanwhile Sybille continued to enjoy her life at Old Church Street, one of her chief pleasures the meals, at home and with friends, recorded in detail in her diaries. One evening in 1980, for example, "made self a simple and delicious dinner of fine egg pasta with a grated zucchini in butter/fresh cream, 3 chopped prosciutto crudo, Parmesan unguent . . . Very good and pure. Opened a bottle of the STWC [Sunday Times Wine Club] Bergerac, not bad at all, if not my usual style." A few months earlier, she had attended a dinner given by Richard Olney in Conduit Street, her fellow guests the poet Kathleen Raine and T. S. Eliot's widow, Valerie. "KR enters chattering . . . I do not like her. But I do like VE . . . We start with the galantine sliver out of the stuffed suckling pig . . . The galantine and jelly not particularly good, indeed I don't like it . . . The Montrachet '75, Domaine Jacques Prieur is very very good, but overpowering on the cold gelatinous food, not truly matched." Finally, with the cheese, "the awaited 1948 Lafite. A disappointment . . . far from expectation."

During her years spent living in Chelsea, Sybille was particularly appreciative of "the neighbourliness of one's neighbours." Among those living near who had become firm friends were the actress Judy Campbell and her husband, David Birkin. Amalia Elguera, a distinguished academic originally from Peru, impressed Sybille not only by her intellect but also by her generous hospitality: a great admirer of Sybille's writing, Amalia frequently entertained Sybille at her house as well as at lavish dinners at the Connaught. Immediately next door was David Cossart, managing director of the wine merchant Ellis, Son & Vidler, of which Sybille had for some years been a customer. Delighted to have in easy reach such a knowledgeable member of the profession, she frequently asked David to accompany her to tastings in the evenings, an experience he enjoyed although at times found exhausting after a long day's work in the trade.

Another prominent figure in the same field whom Sybille came to know was Simon Loftus, who as a wine expert worked for the Adnams brewery in Suffolk, of which Sybille was a customer. Not long after they met she and Anne Gainsford drove to Southwold to visit the brewery, staying at a local hotel, the Crown, where they were entertained to a memorable dinner by Simon, the wines including a superb 1948 Latour as well as a bottle of 1978 Meursault. "I can't thank you enough," Sybille wrote to him afterwards. "One cannot thank—adequately—for being given '48 LATOUR to drink, one can only try, and one remembers for ever after."

One of the new acquaintances of whom Sybille became most fond was a young American journalist living in London, Carla Heffner, who was shortly to marry the Conservative politician Sir Kenneth Carlisle. Sybille first met Carla when she had been interviewed by her for an article about Janet Flanner. The interview had gone well, Sybille immediately taking to Carla, "quite a literary and literate girl. Loves and knows wine. Enjoyed it all immensely and liked her. Mutual, I think."

Shortly afterwards Carla invited Sybille to dinner at her flat in Putney, an occasion marking the beginning of a rewarding friendship, the evening described by Sybille as "euphoric . . . & (in my opinion) one of the most perfectly composed, cooked and served dinners I can remember ever."

In June 1983, Sybille travelled to Berlin with Carla. Her last visit to Germany, to Hamburg, had been nearly ten years earlier as one of a group of writers from PEN, an expedition Sybille described at the time as stimulating and enjoyable. But now, in Berlin for the first time in over half a century, her reactions were very different, all too aware of what, despite her "disassociation" with Nazi Germany, she described as "the horror . . . and shame of a German origin." The worst moment was at Checkpoint Charlie, while crossing the high-walled border for a day's visit to the East, when Sybille began trembling with fear as her passport was taken away for inspection. She only properly recovered after their return to West Berlin that evening, when she and Carla dined at the Café de Paris, a reassuringly French restaurant "that served impeccable *entrecôte grillé*, *pommes frites* and Fleurie served *frais*." During the rest of their visit, Carla recalled, Sybille refused to eat anywhere else.

Another, rather less stressful, expedition was made a few weeks later, a fortnight in Ireland with Anne Gainsford, with whom at this stage Sybille remained infatuated, like "a crazy, obsessed teenager." Sybille's closest confidante during the affair was Lesley, to whom she was as devoted as ever. When Lesley was away Sybille still missed her painfully. "Life is so much less joyful when you are not there," she told her. "Everything with you is on an entirely different level (height) of fun, pleasure, enjoyment." Sybille was distraught when Lesley decided to move permanently to her house in France, although the two continued to keep in touch by letter. It was Lesley to whom Sybille turned for guidance when eventually her liaison with Anne began to unravel. "[I] could easily get into mischief again," Sybille admitted, but "no, no, you can be assured that it will not be indulged . . . Let us hope that the newly acquired self-knowledge will keep one out of mischief. But I am bored. (As well as emotionally underemployed: if you knew what was good for me—I dare not speak for you—you'd never let me out of your sight.)"

Despite the time and energy consumed by her social life and love affairs, Sybille continued to work on her novel, at intervals reporting her progress to Bob Gottlieb. "How wonderful that you're well into the book," he told her. "Now that I know you're working on it, and that, DV, it will come to pass, I have no worries or complaints." In an interview Sybille described in detail the structure of her working day. "I get up late—about 11 a.m., sometimes later—having gone to bed between midnight and 1 a.m. I make tea and take it to bed . . . I try not to listen to the radio, or to look at the post which is hidden under a teatowel . . . I dress slowly, putting off the awful moment of starting work . . . Between 2 p.m. and 3 p.m. I stop for a light lunch . . . I drink nothing alcoholic, just weak black China tea. Then the real working day starts. If all goes well, I finish with about 250–300 words. Sometimes I get stuck, really stuck . . . [and] I limp around Paulton Square, trying to gather my thoughts. In the evening, I do 'cook prep' in my wretched kitchenette. If I am alone, I cook myself a good dinner and drink very good wine, my work simmering underneath. But on the whole I have a very active social life in the evening."

It was during this period that Sybille found a new writing ally, the novelist Elizabeth Jane Howard, whom she had previously met at a party given by the Letwins. Jane had recently divorced her husband, Kingsley Amis, and was now living in a pretty terraced house near Regent's Park. It was here one evening that Sybille was invited to dinner. "Liked it from the first moment," she recorded. "EJH's greeting and warmth and the presence of the VSPs [V. S. Pritchett and his wife] . . . Put next to my hostess in a charming way . . . V. animated, also friendly dinner, good, not overefficient . . . a passable white wine with a good smoked salmon mousse and hot toast . . . Jane gives, and signs, me her book just out. Very affectionate farewell. I enjoyed myself and showed it. Felt happy."

For a while after this occasion, Sybille became infatuated with Jane, although Jane herself was entirely a man's woman, uninterested in a lesbian relationship. Sybille "used to say to me, I think we could have a very lovely time, because I do know how to love (said with great conviction) . . . And I knew what she meant . . . I think she was very highly sexed and thought a lot about it, but wasn't at all offended when

I said no." Sybille for her part admired Jane's novels, while Jane had always regarded *A Legacy* as a masterpiece; before long the two women formed a close collaboration, reading passages from their work aloud to each other over the telephone, meeting regularly to discuss their progress. "The prospect—utopian!—of our future as comrades at writing is dazzling," Sybille wrote enthusiastically to Jane. "[Sybille] did make a great performance of being a writer," Jane recalled. "She saw herself in this operatic role, really. If you were a writer and she approved of you that put you into a kind of exclusive club . . . She was a good sounding-board, picking on things that were wrong or that she wanted to know more about. It was an enormous help and I was very touched."

With Jane now established as her writing partner, Sybille turned away from Betsy Drake, with whom up till then she had continued to discuss her work in minute detail. During a telephone call, described by Betsy as "breathtakingly tactless," Sybille told her, "I want my book back. Somebody else is going to read it, Elizabeth Jane Howard, because I have to have my book read by somebody I respect." Betsy, devastated, wrote Sybille a furious letter. "I really let her have it, and she called up weeping and said she apologised." But the friendship was irredeemably damaged, and from then on the two saw each other very little. Sometime later Betsy in a letter to Sybille told her, "my enthusiasm for your writing has never diminished, but eagerness to be your disrespected reader dropped as markedly as a thermometer plunged in a bucket of iced champagne."

In July 1988, four months after her seventy-seventh birthday, Sybille finally completed her book, *Jigsaw: An Unsentimental Education; a Biographical Novel.* Earlier in the year she had signed contracts with Hamish Hamilton in London and Knopf in New York, both overseen by Elaine Greene, the literary agent whom Sybille had left over thirty years ago but to whom she had now returned. Christopher Sinclair-Stevenson, the director of Hamish Hamilton, agreed to bring in Richard Ollard again as Sybille's editor, a decision with which Sybille was "overjoyed." At Knopf Bob Gottlieb, who had recently left the firm to take up the post of editor of the *New Yorker*, had been replaced by Charles ("Chuck") Elliott, who wrote enthusiastically of the book, "I enjoyed it enormously . . . I'm delighted to be publishing it." Richard

Ollard was similarly impressed, telling Sybille that he had been deeply moved by *Jigsaw*. "It is a most powerful and wholly achieved piece of writing."

In this, her fourth, and final, published work of fiction, Sybille tells the story that had long been embedded in her memory and imagination: the history of her own early years, her childhood in Germany, her life as a young girl in England and the south of France. "Novels among other things are galleries of mirrors," Sybille once stated. "I feel the past as something good and rich and not really the past." Written with an unparalleled vitality and charm, the novel's style is lucid and fluent, the characters portrayed with remarkable subtlety and conviction, as though Sybille had finally arrived at the culmination of a long journey, the destination to which in her previous novels she had been travelling all her life—from her own early childhood and her parents' history in *A Legacy*, her girlhood and arrival in France in *A Favourite of the Gods*, to her time in Sanary in *A Compass Error*. In an "Afterword" to a later edition, Sybille explained that what she had aimed to achieve with *Jigsaw* was a story narrated "in plain words, writing about myself, my feelings, my actions."

Although presented as fiction, in *Jigsaw* the difference between reality and imagination is almost impossible to discern. At every stage the story closely matches Sybille's personal experience, with people, places and events that are instantly recognisable as part of her own life. In a brief note at the front of the book, Sybille admits that all her characters are portraits of real people, some appearing under their own names, such as the Kislings and Huxleys, others thinly disguised by pseudonyms.

The book begins with Sybille's, "Billi's," early childhood in Germany, her life at Feldkirch and the time spent staying with the Herzes in Berlin. After her charismatic mother eventually walks out of her marriage, Billi is left for a while in the care of her father, and it is only after his early death that she rejoins her mother, who is never named in the book, travelling first to Italy, then France. Her mother's new young husband, "Alessandro," is a mirror image of Nori Marchesani, and the years the three of them spend living in Sanary are described in the novel with detailed actuality. The book ends early one morning, with Billi watching as Alessandro prepares to leave, knowing that from now on she will be left to cope on her own.

Jigsaw, dedicated to Allanah, was published in Britain and America in the spring of 1989, and shortly afterwards, to Sybille's delight, appeared on the shortlist for the highly regarded Booker Prize. She was photographed by Jane Bown and, for the second time, by Antony Armstrong-Jones, and she gave a number of interviews to newspapers and magazines. The reactions from friends and acquaintance were largely favourable, with praise from fellow writers, such as A. L. Barker and Victoria Glendinning, of particular satisfaction. Perhaps most unexpected was a note from Martha: "Dear Sibbie: The writing of *Jigsaw* is very beautiful. I think your best ever, and that is a real triumph. Martha." Rather more expansive was a letter from Martha's ex-husband, Tom Matthews, describing *Jigsaw* as "a beautiful book, the best of a good lot and I think the finest you have written." This was an opinion that particularly pleased Sybille as she had much respect for Matthews's own writing. "Such a stimulating letter from you this morning," she told him. "Am I a temporarily very happy writer? Yes. It would be untruthful if I said I were not. I have a certain sense of achievement with this book."

Reviews on the whole were good, Frances Partridge writing in the *Spectator* that "the stylish, casual, exhilarating ambience of the Côte d'Azur [is] marvellously described," while Paul Bailey in the *Sunday Times* remarked on "the pleasure of places vividly evoked; of human beings seen glancingly, and yet substantially realised, in arrested moments." Francis Wyndham in the *Daily Telegraph*, while favourably comparing the novel to its two predecessors, was somewhat critical of the author's style, and admitted that in his view her obsession with food and wine made him "dread those occasions in the story when mealtimes seem to be drawing near . . . However, such minor drawbacks are of little consequence, they should deter nobody from reading this book which is of absorbing interest from start to finish—a treat."

In the States, most critics agreed with the *Chicago Tribune* that *Jigsaw* was "a treasure of a book," although some were rather less complimentary. Gabriele Annan in the *New York Review of Books*, while describing the work as "compulsively readable," was irritated by Bedford's style, "lyrical, breathless, and jaunty by turns, with an occasional clipped, verbless sentence coming down like a stiff upper lip over boiling emotion." Rather more hurtful was Annan's criticism of the "bad joins between novel and biography. Bedford doesn't seem to have thought out the amalgamation of the genres." This Sybille considered unfair, although she herself admitted the near invisibility of the dividing line. "I called it biographic partly to tease, partly to be able to put a few people in with complete biographical accuracy . . . I wanted to do them justice and have them remembered as they were. Or as I thought they were."

From the time of its first publication in 1989, *Jigsaw* has never been out of print. In Britain the novel was issued in paperback by Penguin in 1990, by Eland Books in 2005, in the States by Counterpoint in 2001, and translated into French, German and Spanish. At the time of its initial appearance, Sybille was approaching her eightieth year, and although proud of her achievement she now looked forward to a life free of the demands and pressures of the deadline. With a long career behind her, she had no wish to write another book—any more than she felt at her age she was likely ever again to fall in love. As it turned out, she was to be proved wrong on both counts.

THIRTEEN

"GETTING OLD & WEAK IS HORRIBLE"

With *Jigsaw* behind her, Sybille, now approaching her eighties, was able to look forward to a life free of work—or so she believed. She had had an idea for another novel, set during the Second World War, but the project was soon abandoned. Instead her time was dedicated to an active social life, and for hours a day to reading for pleasure. As always, Sybille was a voracious reader of fiction, but whereas in the past the novels she most admired were by such writers as Edith Wharton, Hemingway, Virginia Woolf, Evelyn Waugh and Ivy Compton-Burnett, now she preferred more lightweight fiction, the historical romances of Georgette Heyer, the popular novels of Arthur Hailey—*Airport*, *Hotel*, *The Moneychangers*—and in particular thrillers, among her favourite authors Patricia Highsmith, and also Dick Francis, to whose crime novels, set in the horse-racing world, she was wholly addicted. Television and radio, too, she enjoyed, devoted to series such as *Upstairs, Downstairs*, and every evening on the BBC tuning in to *The Archers*. She never missed an episode, listening intently, her head slightly lowered, and if friends were with her, all drinking and conversation had to stop for the full fifteen minutes.

"Sybille was a gentleman, an Etonian manqué," as one of her friends astutely described her. Although her short blonde hair had now turned grey, Sybille's appearance remained largely unchanged, always dressed in the same masculine garb: loose-fitting dark trousers, a striped shirt with cufflinks, a woollen waistcoat, with round her neck a kerchief and on her wrist a heavy gold watch. Although she never cared much for cigarettes, in the evenings she occasionally smoked a cigar. When reading she wore dark-framed spectacles, and for much of the day the green visor essential to protect her eyes from the light. While lacking the energy of her younger days, she continued to engage in a busy social life, a familiar figure at literary gatherings and at the dinner parties of friends. "It's not easy to be my friend," Sybille said in an interview at this period. "I have very, very high demands on intelligence, manners, appearance . . . but on the other hand I have such kind friends."

Among the many by whom she was entertained during these later years were the writer Peter Quennell and his wife, who lived in Cheyne Row, only a short walk from Old Church Street, and also the biographer Victoria Glendinning and her novelist husband, Terence de Vere White. Sybille was in frequent contact, too, with Tom Matthews, who with his third wife had moved to a fine Regency house in Suffolk, where Sybille stayed on a number of occasions. Tom was working on a study of T. S. Eliot, and while Sybille was writing *Jigsaw* the two them had spent many hours appraising each other's work; they also indulged in lengthy exchanges on the subject of wine, about which Tom was almost as expert as Sybille. Through Sybille, Tom became a member of PEN, and when in London he often took her to dine at some of the venues she most enjoyed: the Berkeley Hotel, Buck's Club, and the Garrick. "I very much like the Garrick," she told him, "the wines, the atmosphere, the candlelight."

For years in notebooks she kept at home Sybille chronicled almost daily and in meticulous detail the food and drink she consumed. She also kept numerous wine-company catalogues, and regularly attended tastings, carefully categorising each wine in turn: "highly recommended," "borderline," "poor," with an occasional enthusiastic "YES" or a ferocious "NO" scrawled in the margin. Sybille relished talking at length to anyone in the wine trade, including restaurant sommeliers, many of whom were surprised and impressed by the depth of her knowledge; an inexperienced waiter who proved inept, however, would immediately receive an imperious scolding. For some time Sybille had been a member of the Wine Pool, a small group which met at the Reform Club in Pall Mall. Its founder was Kit van Tulleken, not only a successful businesswoman but a distinguished gourmet and oenophile, whom Sybille had first met when Kit was working with Richard Olney on his Time/Life cookery books. Sybille liked and admired Kit, and took pleasure in these occasions, although she could be critical of the food and drink set before her. In 1990, Sybille herself became a member of the Reform Club, where for a while she enjoyed taking guests to dinner, although she resigned after only four years, preferring the rather less grandiose surroundings of restaurants such as Hilaire in South Kensington and Le Colombier in Chelsea.

As she entered the new decade Sybille became increasingly aware of a diminution of energy, a reluctance to travel. "I wish I were still in travelling shape," she told Julia Child, "[but] I'm not—I dread it more and more, and do not even get to France as much as I should or would." To Mary Frances she admitted that she loved the Midi as much as ever yet found the journey too exhausting, and in London "I'm afraid I've got used to a very varied and very social social life." Nonetheless, when in 1989 Sybille to her delight was awarded a travel scholarship by the Society of Authors she spent the money on a fortnight's holiday in Menton on the Riviera, accompanied on this occasion by an attractive new friend, Penelope Bennett.

Penelope, a potter and horticulturist, lived near Sybille in Chelsea, was a member of PEN, and knew a number of Sybille's friends, Lesley Huston, Allanah and Anne Balfour among them. Sybille was charmed by Penelope and enjoyed her company, the two of them often spending evenings together at Old Church Street, Penelope nervously doing the cooking under Sybille's strict supervision. On a number of occasions, Penelope drove Sybille to wine tastings, "although all I knew about wine was the difference between red and white. It was wonderful going to those tastings, however, although Sybille used to tick me off when I exclaimed about the wine. 'Do stop making those bedroom noises!,' she would say." During their time together in Menton, Sybille remained in bed all morning while Penelope was despatched to research local restaurants, reporting back at lunchtime so that careful plans could be made for the evening.

It was in October the following year, 1990, that Sybille made what was to be her final visit to Les Bastides, staying with Allanah, and also visiting her old friends, the Mimerels in Sanary, Pierre, now in his nineties, visibly frail but as clever and charming as ever.

In Allanah, by contrast, Sybille saw worrying indications of decline. Over the past years the two had continued regularly to see each other, in France and also during Allanah's visits to London, when she stayed at the Sloane Club in Chelsea. Now in her late eighties, Allanah had grown thin and frail, her face very lined, her memory increasingly unreliable. Fortunately, for the past few years she had been devotedly cared for by Olympia Zamfirescu, a younger woman with whom Allanah had fallen deeply in love. Olympia, from a wealthy Romanian family that had been devastated by the war, had lived for some years in England, meeting Allanah only after Olympia had moved to France in the early 1980s. The effect Olympia had on Allanah was immediately apparent, Sybille delighted to find that the bossy, irritable friend of the past had been transformed. "What happiness can do," she noted. "Never has she been gentler, less possessive, a kind of miracle . . . angelic and generous . . . providing affection, comforts, food, champagne and social engagements for me beyond wildest dreams."

Sybille turned eighty on 16 March 1991, the occasion celebrated the following month by a formal dinner given by PEN, at which a speech in her honour was delivered by Elizabeth Jane Howard. Shortly afterwards Sybille was delighted by the appearance of a new edition of her first book, *The Sudden View*, since 1960 retitled *A Visit to Don Otavio*. Over the past decades the work had been reissued on both sides of the Atlantic, but it was this version, from a one-man publishing house, Eland Books, that she had found most gratifying. "I am so pleased," she wrote to Eland's founder, John Hatt. "You, unlike Folio and others, are the most punctual (and generous) publisher breathing . . . How superior your beautiful white Edition."

The previous year a collection of Sybille's articles had appeared, under the newly established imprint of Christopher Sinclair-Stevenson. Entitled *As It Was: Pleasures, Landscapes and Justice*, and dedicated "To Lesley, from her nervous passenger," the book includes accounts of Sybille's travels in Europe as well as her reporting of various trials, among them the Lady Chatterley case and the trial of the Auschwitz guards in Frankfurt. Sybille had been anxious about the book's reception, but in fact the reviews were largely appreciative, among them one by Dervla Murphy in the *Times Literary Supplement*, who described the work as subtle, shrewd and deeply moving. Another, by Jan Morris in the *Independent*, saw the collection as clarifying Bedford's "distinguished but somewhat imprecise status in the republic of letters"; Morris did add, however, that the author's enthusiasm for eating and drinking was "a little too irrepressible . . . [and] may drive readers of less urbane gourmandise all the more readily to the deep-freeze Ocean Pie."

Inevitably as the decade progressed Sybille began to lose a number of her oldest friends. In July 1992 she heard from Olympia Zamfirescu that Allanah was very ill and had been taken to hospital; after a few weeks she was allowed to return home, where she died on 3 November, three days before her eighty-eighth birthday. Sybille, devastated by the news, flew out to Nice a few days later, delivering an affectionate eulogy at Allanah's funeral at the Church of Notre Dame de Bon Voyage in Cannes. That same year in May had seen the death of Elizabeth David, and in 1993 of another old friend, Jimmy Stern, on whom for years Sybille had relied as a candid critic of her writing. In old age Jimmy had become increasingly difficult, his drunken rages, mainly aimed at Tania, often exploding dangerously out of control. Recently, however, he had changed: fragile in health, fast losing his memory, he had grown quiet and acquiescent; during the spring, after three bad falls, he had become bedridden, and in November he died, leaving Tania "very frail and distraught." Although Sybille had been frequently appalled by Jimmy's behaviour, she nonetheless mourned the loss of such an old ally, who had supported her so generously during her most penurious years.

It was during this period that Sybille, through her publisher, received a letter from an unknown correspondent in Paris. Aliette Martin, who for some years had worked as a translator, had recently come across a copy of *Jigsaw*, which had so impressed her that she had gone on to read Sybille's life of Aldous Huxley; now she was eager to translate the Huxley biography into French. In a courteous reply, Sybille agreed, on condition that she would be shown a sample chapter first. Aliette was delighted—"Thank you so much for trusting me as you do"—and sent Sybille a resumé of her professional life: her initial period as a free-lance translator, followed by seventeen years working in the theatre, as Directeur de la Coordination Artistique at the Comédie-Française, a demanding career which she loved. "Besides literature," she had writ-ten, "the other great passion of my life is the theatre."

In the event, it would be two years before Sybille and Aliette met, Aliette meanwhile spending as much time as she could on her trans-lation. "Aldous Huxley *et le projet de traduction de votre biographie ne sont pas un instant sortis de mes préoccupations. J'ai eu malheureusement un énorme surcroit de travail à la Comédie-Française*" ("Aldous Huxley and the project of translating your biography are never for a moment out of my mind. Unfortunately I have an enormous extra amount of work at the Comédie Française"). Finally in September 1993 Aliette came over to London, feeling "horribly nervous," priming herself with lunch at Harrods first before going to Old Church Street in the evening. "[I] found the bell very easily. I heard the sound of keys being shaken, and the door opened, and I saw the most extraordinary cornflower blue eyes and the very high brow. And that was it." When Sybille opened the door she saw standing before her a small, fair-haired woman in her forties, clearly very shy, whom she showed into her tiny sitting room. With a glass of white wine in hand, the two sat talking rather awk-wardly, until the taxi arrived to take them to a restaurant in South Ken-sington. Here their conversation continued in French, until towards the end of the evening Sybille insisted on reverting to English, the language with which for many years she had felt most at ease.

After Aliette returned to Paris, she wrote Sybille a long letter, to which Sybille replied by telephone: "*vous me manquez; il faut revenir*" ("I miss you; you must come back"). Over the next days and weeks, many conversations followed, during one of which Aliette spoke what Syb-ille always described as "the three fatal words." Sybille "tut-tutted . . . but somehow I knew that I had to say it, that I was not being rejected and that it would be all right." A few weeks later Aliette came again to London, dining with Sybille while en route to visit some old friends in Edinburgh. After returning to Paris, she and Sybille talked regularly on the telephone, eagerly making plans for the next visit. During one of their conversations, Aliette recalled, "Sybille told me, *'j'accepte,'* and a week later, she did say herself the fatal three words."

When Aliette next returned to London, Sybille took her to dine at the Reform Club, talking in fascinating detail, "in her breathless, passionate, sotto voce tone, so difficult to follow," about her early life in Germany, of France, Mexico, of her parents, the Huxleys, her passion for the law. From this time on, Aliette came to London frequently at weekends, Sybille at first reserving rooms for her at expensive hotels such as the Wilbraham or Claridge's, until Aliette "gently put [her] foot down," staying instead in the very cramped quarters of Sybille's flat. "23 Old Church Street, however tiny and uncomfortable, became my London home, my harbour, my anchor . . . I was too much in love to pay attention to the somewhat spartan surroundings."

Soon a pattern established itself: mornings spent with Sybille remaining in bed while Aliette read aloud to her, then a late, frugal lunch in the flat, after which Aliette went out to shop while Sybille stayed at home reading and writing letters; on Aliette's return the two would take a short walk together. In the evening they dined at home, or in a restaurant, or at the houses of friends. As Aliette recalled, "Dinner had to be a great moment of conviviality, with good food, good wine and good conversation . . . [Sybille] became most lively and dominated the scene with a flurry of interesting memories, scattered with witty anecdotes and brilliant independent views on many subjects." Sunday afternoons, by contrast, were filled with gloom and dread, as it was in the early evening that Aliette had to return to Paris. "After lunch . . . a sort of heaviness and sadness settled. Each time, when the moment came for me to leave, it was the same *arrachement* [extraction] and we parted as if we didn't know whether we would see each other again."

From then on, despite the incessant demands of her job at the theatre, Aliette came to London every other weekend, and when they were apart she and Sybille talked twice a day on the telephone. For Aliette it was an affair both intellectually stimulating and emotionally profound, she fascinated by the stories Sybille recounted in enthralling detail about her past. "She was opening a whole world to me," Aliette recalled. "I was entering unknown territories . . . another era, a very sophisticated and cosmopolitan universe, a dream land." It was not long before friends began to notice the change in Sybille, how happy she was—"suddenly radiant, a girl," as Victoria Glendinning observed. Over time Aliette was introduced to many of Sybille's circle, Elizabeth Jane Howard among them. "I met Aliette when the three of us had dinner. I liked her very much immediately, and Sybille was over the moon about her. Sybille told me fairly soon after it started that she'd fallen in love and that she never thought that would happen to her again. It changed her life."

In February 1995 it was announced that Sybille had been made a Companion of the Royal Society of Literature, her fellow honorees William Trevor and V. S. Naipaul. Shortly after receiving news of this distinguished award, Sybille while alone in the flat fell and broke her hip; she was taken to the King Edward VII Hospital to be operated on, and Aliette, in a state of frantic anxiety, flew over from Paris the following weekend to see her. As Aliette recalled, the moment she entered the room, Sybille "turned her face towards me saying, 'oh, my angel' with bright eyes and pink cheeks, [and] I knew she would be all right." For a while after leaving hospital Sybille remained comfortably ensconced in the Basil Street Hotel in Knightsbridge, before eventually returning to Old Church Street. Here she was cared for by friends and neighbours during the week, until Aliette arrived every Friday evening to stay for the weekend.

It was then that Aliette decided she must encourage Sybille to return to writing. Money was no longer a problem as Sybille was now financially secure: over the past few years she had received some generous bequests from friends, among them from Allanah, and had been able to buy and for a time let the flat above hers in Old Church Street. In 1993 she had begun negotiations with the Harry Ransom Center at the University of Texas in Austin over the purchase of her papers, which were eventually bought for the large sum of £24,975. The Center's director, Professor Tom Staley, had called on Sybille, who had found him "an immensely *simpatico* man, the first rate American academic at his finest—plus looks, charm, voice . . . I agreed to let them have the lot . . . And I feel relieved, naked, bereft, bewildered and somewhat sheepish." Most of all, however, she was proud that in Austin her archive would join those of such "august writers . . . [as] Evelyn Waugh, Graham Greene . . . Hemingway and Joyce."

After the publication of *Jigsaw*, the only commission Sybille had undertaken was from Penguin, to provide introductions for new paperback editions of her four novels. Currently she had no ideas for any future project, indeed was relieved to be able to live without the constant pressure of the deadline. Aliette, however, thought otherwise, convinced that it was too soon for Sybille to retire, determined to persuade her to begin work on another book, which would also help keep at bay the ever-present threat of depression. At first the suggestion was brushed aside—Sybille no longer had the energy, no plot or theme in mind—but slowly, as Aliette continued to coax and encourage her, she began to take the idea seriously, gradually starting to feel excited as a plan began to form, of a personal memoir, a series of reminiscences rather than a straightforward autobiography. Twenty years earlier Sybille had discussed a similar project with Bob Gottlieb, but soon afterwards had decided against it. "Although this so-called autobiographical stuff keeps pushing itself up," she had told Bob, it is "not interesting enough to put before the reader." Now, however, she felt differently, and with Aliette's support at last felt able to begin again to write.

The work was to take almost seven years to complete, as Sybille, during Aliette's absence, was able to write, or think about writing only for an hour or two a day. Wearing her green visor and a large-framed pair of spectacles, she sat at her metal desk near the tiny window, its surface piled with books and pale green paper, a tall red-shaded lamp on one side, on the other a reading stand which obscured the typewriter that, to her regret, she was no longer able to use. "[Now] the writer actually has to write. Arthritis has undone me, I can no longer tap those keys . . . Writing slow-hand is all I can do: the scrawl is back; not improved." Every day Sybille composed a few lines, occasionally a paragraph or two, went over each new sentence, every page of the chapter in progress, rewriting again and again before eventually putting it aside and beginning the next. At weekends Sybille and Aliette spent hours together struggling to decode Sybille's "insect's traces" before Aliette took "the precious sheets" back with her to Paris to copy them onto her computer. For Aliette, "it was an extraordinary discovery and a great lesson . . . seeing how her mind and memory worked, and how then she painfully assembled words, sentences, paragraphs, very slowly, step by step."

There were intervals in these periods of industry, the longest during the summer when Aliette was on holiday for the whole of August. The first two weeks, as for many years in the past, she spent with friends in Scotland, the rest of the time with Sybille. On several occasions they went together to Suffolk, at first staying at the Swan Hotel in South-wold, so that Sybille could see her old friend from the wine trade, Simon Loftus, and later with Elizabeth Jane Howard, who had recently left London and moved into Bridge House, a beautiful eighteenth-century house with a large garden in the little town of Bungay.

For their first visit to Bridge House Sybille and Aliette had been driven down from London for a weekend, followed the next year by a stay of ten days. The day's ritual was quickly established: each morning Jane took them breakfast on a tray upstairs, after which the two women remained in their bedroom until lunchtime; in the afternoon, at Aliette's insistence, Sybille took a short walk in the garden, before they again retired to their room until dinner. Night after night, as the three of them sat at table, Sybille talked obsessively about wine, and Jane began to feel anxious about the dinner she had arranged for the final evening to which several friends had been invited. "I warned them that she was very boring about wine and I was afraid would talk about it all through dinner and there was nothing they could do." In the event, however, Sybille never mentioned the subject, was charming and cheerful, genuinely interested in her fellow guests, and, to Jane's relief, "the meal turned out to be a great success."

In 1997, Sybille, accompanied by Aliette, travelled to Paris to promote French editions of both *Jigsaw* and *A Visit to Don Otavio*. The trip "half killed me," she said afterwards. "Getting old & weak is horrible . . . [but] 2 sets of publishers looked after me like angels." Richard Olney, who saw her at this period, found her physically very frail, bent like a hook with spinal arthritis, her grey hair thin and wispy; she moved cautiously with the help of a cane, "but in good spirits and working on a new book; delicate health has not cooled her passion for wine and conversation."

Back in London, Sybille gave a number of interviews, among them one in 1998 for the BBC on *Desert Island Discs*. In the course of an hour, Sybille talked mainly about her childhood and adolescence, about her parents, her life in Sanary, the kindness and protection provided by the Huxleys; at intervals chosen passages were played from the works of her favourite composers, Bach, Beethoven, Schubert and Mozart. "I'm not musical," she admitted. "I can't hold a tune, I have no ear, but I simply love great music . . . It gives me great emotional pleasure." At the end of the programme, when the key question was put to her—if on a desert island which piece of music, which book and what luxury would she choose to have with her?—she replied, Proust's *À la recherche du temps perdu*, Bach's double violin concerto, and for her luxury, "a French restaurant in full working order: not a Michelin four-star [*sic*] but a good traditional solid restaurant, and in the evening I'd go out and look at the sea with a glass in my hand, and I'd do my writing, as Ernest Hemingway said he did, and one must, in my head."

On a rather different level was an interview that appeared the same year, 1998, in *Country Life* magazine, in which Sybille talked more about the present than the past, expressing her contempt for feminism—"I do think that emancipation of women has gone far too far. It's ludicrous"— and her anxiety about the problems of overpopulation. This latter subject was one that had been causing her anxiety for many years: in an article written for *The Times* over two decades earlier, she had stated her opinion that "the overrunning of this earth by the human species is a key factor in our present universal plight." Now she returned to the theme. "The one problem that no one dares to talk about is overpopulation. You can't do it by force or by exposing children on hillsides any more . . . but you could try to make childlessness attractive—instead of giving child benefit you could reduce taxes for people who are not interrupting their working life by having brats." As to the erosion of the environment, "Great buildings and landscapes are being overrun by crowds. I don't see why one shouldn't suggest that only people who deserve to visit Chartres Cathedral should be allowed to."

While Sybille continued to work on her book, her domestic life during the week was largely enabled by the helpfulness of friends and neighbours. Although she could at times be bossy and arrogant, brusquely dismissive of those who bored or annoyed her, the fact that she retained such a large circle of friends was proof of Sybille's innate kindness and charm, her sense of humour, the fascination to others of her extraordinary memory and intellect. One of her helpers was Audrey Wood, "a Quaker saint," in Sybille's words, and for many years the lover of Sybille's old friend, Charlotte Wolff; now frail and bent almost double, Audrey nonetheless devotedly took care of Sybille, reading to her, shopping, and taking her for little walks. Another devoted assistant was Sybille's one-time girlfriend, Jenny MacKilligin, who on an almost daily basis ran errands for Sybille, cashing cheques at the bank, collecting books from the library, shopping at Waitrose for tins of corned beef, for Bovril and instant mashed potato, as Sybille when eating alone now preferred the most simple and basic of foods.

Yet as before she still enjoyed dining in restaurants, and it was in a restaurant one evening that Sybille met a woman to whom she felt instantly drawn. Some time previously Sybille had been contacted by Robin Dalton, a successful literary agent and film producer, originally from Australia, who had been interested in making a film version of *Jigsaw*. The two women met to discuss the project, and although it eventually came to nothing they quickly formed a rewarding friendship. One evening Robin invited Sybille to dinner, bringing with her a colleague, part Australian, part Italian, who had been very keen to meet Sybille. Luciana Arrighi, a dark-haired beauty in her early fifties, was a talented set and costume designer, whom Robin had hoped would work with her on the film. Sybille was immediately smitten, and when at one point Luciana briefly left the table to go to the ladies', Sybille leant over to Robin, holding out both her hands: "Look how my hands are shaking!" she said. "She is <u>so</u> beautiful!" From that moment on, Sybille and Luciana became close friends, meeting often, in constant touch by telephone, Luciana one of two acquaintances Sybille named as a contact in case of emergency.

On 16 March 2001, Sybille turned ninety, an occasion celebrated by a dinner given by a neighbour, George Naylor, a retired lawyer and notable oenophile, who had devised an exceptional sequence of wines for the evening. Before the meal there was champagne, Veuve Clicquot La Grande Dame 1990, then during dinner each course was accompanied by a different wine, Puligny Montrachet Le Clavoillon Premier Cru 1993, Château Pichon Lalande 1982, Château Ducru-Beaucaillou 1982, Château Ducru-Beaucaillou 1989, Chambertin Grand Cru 1985,

Chapelle-Chambertin Grand Cru 1990, and finally with the dessert a Sauternes, Château Rieussec Premier Cru 1986. Despite her frailty, Sybille throughout remained cheerful and alert, her eyes shining as she discussed with intense enthusiasm each wine in turn, analysing their differences and subtleties.

During the next three years Sybille continued to work on her book, enthusiastically encouraged by her agent, Sarah Lutyens, whose firm Sybille had joined after the death, in 1995, of Elaine Greene. Lutyens & Rubinstein had been founded a couple of years earlier by two young women, Sarah Lutyens and Felicity Rubinstein, highly experienced in publishing and bookselling both in London and New York. Sarah had first met Sybille when working at Macmillan, the firm which had reissued her Huxley biography, and was delighted now to have Sybille as her client. Sarah immediately proved herself not only efficient and engaged, but soon became an affectionate friend. One evening Sarah and Felicity, rather nervously, cooked dinner for Sybille, every carefully prepared dish, as it turned out, a failure, but to their relief, "Sybille was delighted and laughed so much . . . She also introduced Felicity and me to a lot of her friends," Sarah recalled, "and I often went to Old Church Street, [where] I remember being lectured on how not to open a bottle of wine." In 1999 it had been Sarah who made a significant deal with Penguin for new paperback editions of all four of Sybille's novels, and it was she who now arranged the sale of the present project, to Hamish Hamilton in London and to Counterpoint in New York.

The book, entitled *Quicksands* and dedicated to Aliette, was delivered, as agreed, by the end of July 2004, with publication planned for the following year. After reading the manuscript, Sarah reported to Simon Prosser at Hamish Hamilton that she had found it "Enchanting. Full of delights and absolutely up with the best of her inimitable prose, full too of profound comment on this last century of turmoil and war. It's going to thrill her devotees . . . There simply isn't anyone else left able to write this kind of book about this generation." Prosser, too, was impressed, writing to Sybille that *Quicksands* "is a truly beautiful book which I know will stay in my memory in that way that only certain books can . . . It is a unique journey through a life and a century—and

I feel it will endure for years to come. I am very pleased and proud to be publishing it."

Quicksands appeared in the States on 5 January 2005, and in Britain on 2 June, nearly three months after Sybille's ninety-fourth birthday. Subtitled *A Memoir*, the book is both vividly evocative and tantalisingly elusive, the story moving continuously from past to present, from one country to another. The narrative involves many of the same characters and covers much of the same ground as *A Legacy* and *Jigsaw*, Sybille again recalling her childhood in Germany, her years in Sanary, with, as before, the figure of her mother continuing to dominate her perspective on the past. "My difficulties now that I have committed myself to writing what could be called fragments of autobiography are multiple," she states near the beginning. "When I feel I must repeat myself . . . I am afraid that I shall bore . . . If on the other hand I fail to jog the unremembered memory, I may cause lack of clarity or cohesion."

Many familiar characters appear on stage, among them, as well as Lisa, who is never referred to by name, there is Sybille's sister, Katzi, the Huxleys, the Mimerels, the Mann family, the Muir sisters—some introduced only fleetingly, others in detail and at considerable length. Among the new material is the story of Sybille's meeting with the Gendels while living in Rome, in which she delicately makes reference to the subsequent "attachment" to Evelyn that ensued. She also provides a fascinating account of her marriage in 1935 to Walter (here referred to as "Terry") Bedford: the Huxleys' search for "a bugger bridegroom," the complex legal process undertaken by Sybille's lawyer friend, Sylvester Gates, and the bizarre details of the wedding day itself, culminating in the party given by the Huxleys in Albany. Once possessed of the crucial British passport Sybille is able to escape to America, although nothing is said here about the war years spent in California and New York, and there are only the occasional, vague references to later love affairs. In the final pages of the book Sybille writes tantalisingly, "I would like to have been able to say something more . . . to tell some more stories . . . Wish I could tell the half of it . . . But . . . there seems to be no time."

Oblique, laconic and elegant in style, a deft combination of artistry and recollection, *Quicksands* unfolds in layers like a complicated puzzle that is never wholly solved. As one reviewer expressed it, "To read this fascinating book is like wandering from one brilliantly illuminated patch to another in an otherwise misty landscape." While most critics praised the author's style, several were bemused by the amount of reticence and elision, and the fact that so much of the personal history previously narrated was now repeated. Joan Acocella in the *New Yorker*, described the work as "positively chaotic . . . a sort of rummage sale," while Alan Hollinghurst in the *New York Review of Books* regretted the fact that this "brilliant and original writer" should cover so much of the same ground as before, revealing almost nothing about her more recent years. Andrew Barrow in the *Observer* voiced much the same complaint—"she tells us for the third time about her first meeting with the Aldous Huxleys and then plunges into another account of her mother's drug addiction"; he nonetheless went on to praise the book, relishing the author's style as "gloriously uncondescending and pioneeringly ungrammatical."

For the rest of the year following the book's publication, Sybille remained in London, increasingly fragile, more than ever dependent on friends, always impatiently waiting for the weekend and the arrival of her adored Aliette. On Sunday 22 January 2006, while alone in her flat, she fell and broke her hip. Two friends, her neighbour George Naylor and Luciana Arrighi, were alerted by the alarm Sybille wore on her wrist; Naylor, who arrived within minutes, immediately called an ambulance. Accompanied by Luciana, Sybille was driven to the Westminster & Chelsea Hospital in the Fulham Road, from where, uncomfortable in a public ward, she was moved the next day to the private Lister Hospital. One friend who visited her soon afterwards noticed how touchingly childlike Sybille seemed, almost unaware of her situation, of the unfamiliar surroundings. "Standing beside her bed, I saw again that very young face, the pale, translucently fair skin that, as she lay on the pillow, was divested of wrinkles, the Alice blue eyes gazing up in wonder, curiosity, some confusion, and just a streak of indignation."

Aliette, telephoned by Luciana, had been horrified by news of the accident. Unusually, she had had to cancel her weekend visit to London because of a crisis at the theatre, and had been worried by her inability to contact Sybille. A few days later she arrived in London, going at once to the Lister, appalled to see the fragility and helplessness of Sybille's condition. From then on Aliette spent every Friday, Saturday and Sunday with Sybille, sitting with her, talking, reading to her, making her feel as comfortable as possible. She was furious on one occasion to find Sybille's doctor attempting to force his patient to try to walk. "She was in great pain . . . [I] told him Sybille couldn't possibly do any such thing. He said, 'If she doesn't she'll never walk again.' I said, 'You know she'll never walk again.' At this point the doctor bowed his head and left the room, and after that a much kinder doctor replaced him."

On 17 February, almost exactly a month before her ninety-fifth birthday, with Aliette by her bedside, Sybille died. It was Aliette who arranged the funeral, which took place ten days later at Mortlake Crematorium, attended by a large number of friends and admirers. Afterwards a wake was held, a generous buffet luncheon with excellent wine, provided by Kit van Tulleken and her husband at their house on Brook Green in Hammersmith. Nearly four months later, on 5 June, a memorial gathering, again organised by Aliette, was held at the Reform Club, at which a number of Sybille's friends spoke, some describing their personal memories of her, others reading from her own writing about her past. Among them was her editor, Richard Ollard, who said of his author that "her company was always refreshing, even when her circumstances were adverse . . . she recognised unpretentiousness as fully as she detected its opposite . . . sympathy rather than passing judgements was central to her understanding." That evening Aliette returned to Paris; five days later she travelled to the south of France, taking Sybille's ashes with her to Sanary, where standing on the shore in the early evening light she scattered them over the Mediterranean while quietly reciting Paul Valéry's "Le Cimetière Marin," a poem Sybille had always loved.

Since her death, Sybille's literary reputation has continued to grow. In 2015, the distinguished American writer and academic, Brenda Wineapple, wrote an article in the *New York Times* analysing the importance of Sybille's work. Brenda had first met Sybille in the 1980s, when Brenda had been working on a life of Janet Flanner. After a brief correspondence, Brenda had come over to London and called on Sybille one evening to ask for recollections of her old friend. After their conversation, which continued for several hours, Brenda found she had come away with a clear impression of Sybille's exceptional intellect and complex personality, giving her a significant insight into how it was that she had become such a fine writer. "I remember that our first talk lasted far into the night. I remember that she was then and continued to be forthright, funny, and scrupulously frank. I remember thinking . . . how remarkable it was that one of the finest stylists of the twentieth century, bar none, with a prose of incomparable precision and grace, would candidly acknowledge her daily battle against discouragement, distraction, and doubt. But that was typical . . . She understood first-hand the burdens of survival."

ACKNOWLEDGEMENTS

I am immensely grateful to the many people who have helped me during the writing of this biography. I would like to express my particular thanks to Aliette Martin, Sybille Bedford's literary executor, who allowed me free access to Sybille's diaries and correspondence, and whose memories of her friendship with Sybille were invaluable. I owe a great deal, too, to Lisa Cohen, Manfred Flügge, Sally Gordon-Mark, and to Gräfin Adelheid von der Schulenburg. I would like to give my most sincere thanks to Clara Farmer at Chatto & Windus in London, to Shelley Wanger at Knopf in New York and to my agent, Zoë Waldie. I would also like to thank Patrick Howard for his superb research, and David Milner for his remarkably perceptive copy-editing.

I would like to give grateful thanks to Julie Kavanagh and Professor R. F. Foster for their invaluable criticism and advice.

I also owe sincere thanks to the following for their contributions to this book: Elizabeth Archer, Michael Arditti, Luciana Arrighi, Paul Bailey, Anne Balfour-Fraser, Andrew Barrow, Josef Bauer, Jennifer Beattie, Penelope Bennett, Baronin Mercedes Marschall von Bieberstein, Michael Bloch, Desmond Browne QC, Peter Brugger, Elsie Burch-Donald, John Byrne, Carla Carlisle, Artemis Cooper, David Cossart, Robin Dalton, Gilpatrick Devlin, Graf Christoph Douglas, Betsy Drake, Charles Duff, Baron Wilfried von Engelhardt, Sir Anthony Evans, Antoinette Faller, Jamie Fergusson, Sue Fox, Anne Gainsford,

Elizabeth Garver, Oliver Gates, Rick Gekoski, Milton Gendel, Robert Gottlieb, Marie-Thérèse Grange, Thomas Grant QC, Thomas Gruber, Diana Halle, Nicholas Haslam, Phyllis J. Hatfield, John Hatt, Jeanne Henny, Leonhard Horowski, Elizabeth Jane Howard, Jenny Hughes, Mark Hussey, Tony Huston, John F. Jungclaussen, John Kasmin, Paul Levy, Simon Loftus, Sarah Lutyens, Jenny MacKilligin, Patricia Maguire, Philip Mansel, Alexander Matthews, Tom Miller, Julian Mitchell, Caroline Moorehead, Sir John Nutting QC, Bruce Palling, Hubert Picarda, Markie Robson-Scott, Barnaby Rogerson, John Röhl, Felicity Rubinstein, Joan Schenkar, Baron Andreas von Schoenebeck, Ian Scott, Julian Stern, Baron Berthold von Stohrer, Karl von Stohrer, Solveig and Humphrey Stone, Gina Thomas, Kit van Tulleken, Hugo Vickers, Edmund Weeger, Peter Heinrich von Wessenberg, Brenda Wineapple.

I would like to express thanks to the following libraries and archives: the British Library; the Harry Ransom Center, University of Texas at Austin; the Howard Gotlieb Archival Research Center, University of Boston; the Archive Centre, King's College, Cambridge; Bibliothèque Royale de Belgique; Special Collections, University of Oregon; the Library of Congress, Washington; the McFarlin Library, University of Tulsa; the Firestone Library, Princeton University; the M. F. K. Fisher Trust, the Schlesinger Library, Harvard University; the Julia Child Foundation for Gastronomy and the Culinary Arts; Special Collections, University of California, Los Angeles; Special Collections, University of Reading.

LIST OF ILLUSTRATIONS

All photos and images, unless otherwise stated, are used by kind permission of the Sybille Bedford Estate.

1. Sybille's parents Elisabeth ("Lisa") Bernhardt and Maximilian von Schoenebeck on their wedding day, April 1910
2. Sybille in childhood
3. Sybille with her half-sister, Katzi
4. Sybille with her mother, Lisa, Sanary, France
5. Nori Marchesani
6. Sybille and Pierre Mimerel, 1929
7. Renee Kisling
8. Sybille, Berlin, 1932
9. Sybille and Jacqueline Mimerel
10. Sybille and Sylvester Gates, Sainte-Trinide, France, 1930s
11. Sybille and Eva Herrmann, Sainte-Trinide, France, 1932
12. Sybille, Raymond Mortimer and Aldous Huxley, 1932
13. Sybille, Allanah Harper and Poodly, France
14. Sybille and Poodly, Edgartown, USA, 1941
15. Esther Murphy
16. Maria and Aldous Huxley, California, USA, 1948
17. A love letter to Sybille from Annie Davis, 1943
18. Sybille and Katzi, Austria, 1949, courtesy of Andreas von Schoenebeck
19. Robert Gottlieb © Waring Abbott
20. Sybille watering plants, Rome, 1952
21. Sybille reading in the bath, Rome, 1950

22. Evelyn Gendel, Rome, 1952
23. Katzi, Paris, 1955
24. Sybille Bedford at the Bodkin Adams trial, Eastbourne, 14 January 1957
    © TopFoto
25. Martha Gellhorn, May 1946, USA © FPG/Archive Photos/Getty Images
26. Eda Lord
27. Sybille and Tania Stern
28. Sybille at Old Church Street, London, 1980s, courtesy of Jenny MacKilligin

Every effort has been made by the publishers to trace the holders of copyright. Any inadvertent omissions of acknowledgement or permission can be rectified in future editions.

NOTES

ABBREVIATIONS

HRC: Harry Ransom Humanities Research Center, University of Texas at Austin

HGARC: Howard Gotlieb Archival Research Center, Boston University Editions of books by Sybille Bedford:

A Visit to Don Otavio: A Mexican Odyssey (Eland Books 2002)

A Legacy (Counterpoint 2001)

A Favourite of the Gods (Daunt Books 2007)

A Compass Error (Counterpoint 1968)

The Best We Can Do (Penguin 1989)

The Faces of Justice: A Traveller's Report (Simon & Schuster 1966)

Pleasures and Landscapes: A Traveller's Tales from Europe (Daunt Books 2014)

As It Was: Pleasures, Landscapes and Justice (Sinclair-Stevenson 1990)

Jigsaw: An Unsentimental Education (Eland 2005)

Aldous Huxley Vols 1 & 2 (Chatto & Windus 1973, 1974)

The Trial of Lady Chatterley's Lover (Daunt Books 2016)

Quicksands (Hamish Hamilton 2005)

PREFACE

ix "I wish I'd written more books": *In Conversation with Naim Attallah* (Quartet,, 1998) p. 11.

ix "I think as far as writing was concerned": *Desert Island Discs* BBC radio 10.7.98.

 x "My mother wanted to be a writer": ibid.

xi "a vicious cult": *Daily Mail* 1.11.24.

xi "I will not <u>choose</u> a Lesbian agent": SB to Evelyn Gendel 13.4.53 SB archive HRC.

xi "[I'm] always putting off everything": SB to Allanah Harper 9.7.58 Allanah Harper archive HRC.

xi "the English language is": *Desert Island Discs* BBC radio 10.7.98.

ONE: LISA AND "*LE BEAU MAX*"

4 "and the smell of seasons": *A Legacy* p. 33.

6 "an innocent eccentric": SB to James Stern 1.4.75 James Stern archive British Library.

8 "*Un Espion Allemande en Correctionnelle*": *La Presse* 22.12.1894.

8 "Your letter has distressed me": SB to Paul Zander 2.6.98 private collection.

8 "We leafed through": ibid.

9 "a tide of big money": *A Legacy* p. 13.

10 "had no interests, tastes or thoughts": ibid. p. 10.

13 "wrote a searing leader": *Jigsaw* p. 21.

13 "a muckraker who writes with heavy irony": *Maximilian Harden: Censor Germaniae* by Harry F. Young (Martinus Nijhoff,, 1959) p. 2.

15 "*Sie sicht so schlau aus*": Anna Bernhardt to SB 25.3.36 SB archive HRC.

TWO: BARONIN BILLI

17 "We lived inside a museum": *Jigsaw* p. 30.

17 "What was best about it": *Quicksands* p. 55.

18 "We are the only two blue-eyed blondes": Anna Bernhardt to SB 27.5.35 SB archive HRC.

18 "gave me love": *Quicksands* p. 86.

18 "I never had any maternal love": *Oldie* August 1997.

19 "My father could not stand": *Jigsaw* p. 14.

19 "cover of eccentricity": ibid. p. 54.

19 "female and north German": *Quicksands* p. 59.

20 "I was in some kind of a narrow space": *Jigsaw* p. 11.

20 "a dangerous folly": ibid. p. 13.

21 "One day": ibid.

21 "soldiers on the platforms": ibid.

22 "sunk in upholstery": ibid. p. 89.

22 "lived contentedly in a luxurious cocoon": *A Legacy* p. 10.

22 "swaddled in stuffs": ibid. p. 13.

23 "Everyone spoke freely": *Jigsaw* p. 14.

23 "he held himself aloof ": ibid. p. 29.

23 "the rather dismal public park": ibid. p. 16.

24 "I would stand before": ibid.

24 "warm, generous, pleasure-loving": ibid. p. 22.

24 "Men were attracted to them": *Quicksands* p. 88.

25 "a very small, very wrinkled": *A Visit to Don Otavio* p. 157.

25 "You cried: 'Katzi is gone' ": Anna Bernhardt to SB, 6.8.36 SB archive HRC.

26 "Here the sailors with their banners": *Quicksands* p. 153.

26 "contents undisturbed": ibid.

27 "[My mother] did not suffer": *Jigsaw* p. 22.

27 "[the] truth is that I have never grown up": SB to Evelyn Gendel 20.5.57 SB archive HRC.

27 "My father hadn't thought": *Quicksands* p. 156.

28 "gently dictatorial": ibid.

28 "[I was] entranced": ibid. p. 161.

28 "Surprise and approval": ibid. p. 158.

28 "They swarmed around me": ibid. p. 159.

28 "hard to read for me": ibid. p. 163.

28 "I can never read your writing": Martha Gellhorn to SB 19.12.63 SB archive HRC.

28 "Your handwriting is calculated": Sylvester Gates to SB 22.3.69 SB archive HRC.

28 "It just came to an end": *Quicksands* p. 162.

29 "a youngish man in a town suit": *Jigsaw* p. 32.

29 "getting on a farmhorse": ibid.

30 "a shy, stiff peasant": *Quicksands* p. 172.

30 "execrable": ibid. p. 166.

30 "treated me (affectionately)": ibid. p. 165.

30 "To her I was both an underservant": ibid. p. 172.

30 "Overnight," Sybille wrote: ibid. p. 167.

30 "The scale of its catastrophic course": ibid. p. 170.

31 "We turned ourselves": ibid. p. 168.

31 "One evening in May": *Jigsaw* p. 39.

32 "I made my first Communion": ibid. p. 45.

32 "I did not like what I was being made to hear": *Quicksands* p. 155.

32 "One could never tell": *A Legacy* p. 37.

32 "My father loved me": *Desert Island Discs* BBC radio 10.7.98.

33 "I sniff mine": *Jigsaw* p. 27.

34 "I then proceeded to walk": ibid. p. 23.

34 "My father did not reproach me": *Quicksands* p. 178.

35 "the most stimulating period": ibid.

35 "not the quality of the affection": ibid. p. 183.

36 "How could you have done this": ibid. p. 187.

36 "hard-working days": ibid.

36 "My strange, defeated, formal father": ibid. p. 193.

THREE: FROM ICY ENGLAND TO THE WARMTH OF THE MEDITERRANEAN

38 "[I] experienced a state of sheer joy": *Quicksands* p. 194.

39 "Needless to say": ibid. p. 195.

39 "Waiters, young and old": ibid.

39 "They knew perfectly well": *Sunday Times* 13.11.94.

40 "not unduly disconcerted": *Quicksands* p. 197.

40 "I was never quite clear": *Jigsaw* p. 56.

41 " 'Billi—can you understand' ": ibid. p. 58.

41 "It was as if some ice": ibid. p. 54.

41 "Our compartment door opened": *Quicksands* p. 200.

41 "we ate the food": ibid. p. 209.

42 "[I was] given a bag": ibid. p. 212.

42 "parlourmaids, icy bedrooms": *Jigsaw* p. 358.

42 "four punctual sit-down meals": ibid. p. 215.
42 "a light-hearted, self-deprecatory woman": ibid.
43 "Being taught, learning": ibid. p. 221.
43 "My attachment to England": ibid. p. 81.
44 "raised a curtain": *Quicksands* p. 223.
44 "They had not belonged": ibid. p. 241.
44 "almost from one week": ibid. p. 240.
45 "by the time we got to the station": *Desert Island Discs* BBC radio 10.7.98.
45 "a hot, ill-stuck-together bungalow": *Quicksands* p. 244.
46 "The accommodating tolerance": *Jigsaw* p. 89.
46 "The great constant was the climate": ibid. p. 149.
47 "was very well educated": *Oldie* August 1997.
47 "never relentless, quite interruptible": *Jigsaw* p. 57.
47 "gently, dearly, protectively": *Quicksands* p. 271.
48 "She would smile sweetly": ibid. p. 228.
48 "Funny kind of girl": *Jigsaw* p. 95.
48 "My mother had a knack": ibid. p. 71.
48 "and [Nori] was immensely handy": *Quicksands* p. 229.
49 "a disaster of lifelong consequences": ibid. p. 90.
49 "I carried the case": *Jigsaw* p. 69.
49 "[springing] up to offer a light": *Quicksands* p. 234.
50 "*il faut m'aider*": Lisa Marchesani to Clive Bell 17.1.28 King's/PP/CHA, King's College, Cambridge.
50 "the Don Juan of Bloomsbury": *The Diary of Virginia Woolf* (Hogarth Press) 23.7.27 Vol. 3 p. 149.
50 "beautiful Germanness": Clive Bell to Virginia Woolf 6.3.28 Virginia Woolf King's/PP/CHA, King's College, Cambridge.
50 "*Pourquoi pas de ne répondre*": Lisa Marchesani to Clive Bell 14.3.28 King's/PP/CHA, King's College, Cambridge.
51 "got hold of everything": *Jigsaw* p. 101.
51 "And so began": ibid.
52 "whose horizons embraced France": ibid. p. 168.
53 "I was hooked for life": *Quicksands* p. 238.
53 "Everything captivated": *Jigsaw* p. 101.
54 "From May to October": ibid. p. 149.
54 " 'Have I changed?' ": ibid. p. 90.
55 "salt water, rock pools": ibid. p. 92.
55 "had tried to laugh": ibid. p. 106.
55 "a mother and her daughter": ibid. p. 150.
56 "[I did have] a slight stammer": ibid. p. 116.
56 "great handsome monster": *A Compass Error* p. 36.
56 "[with] large prominent blue eyes": *Jigsaw* p. 153.
56 "[and] a smile": *Compass Error* p. 36.
56 "would go out on the dawn sea": *Jigsaw* p. 190.
57 "*Si on est ami*": ibid. p. 157.
57 "in a manner compounded": *Compass Error* p. 47.
57 "The screen was bad": *Jigsaw* p. 117.
57 "They were slim": ibid.

58 "I was car-mad": *Quicksands* p. 43.
58 "I snatched at the chance": ibid. p. 41.
58 "*je suis fier*": Pierre Mimerel to SB 2.12.58 SB archive HRC.
59 "daily life was animated": *Quicksands* p. 71.
59 "her springboard was triviality": *Jigsaw* p. 319.
59 "In the mornings I would hang about": ibid. p. 216.
59 "I knew I was being teased": ibid. p. 212.
60 "I still see him": ibid. p. 164.
60 "Without being really selfish": ibid. p. 165.
60 "serving—in different ranks": ibid.
60 "He touched my shoulder": ibid. p. 118.
61 "We all danced": ibid. p. 200.
61 "Levantine pirates": ibid.
61 "We got out of our clothes": ibid. p. 205.
61 "[He] was very sure of himself": ibid. p. 208.
62 "There ensued, at once": ibid. p. 206.
62 "ochre-washed, one-storeyed": ibid. p. 147.
62 " 'May I tell you something?' ": ibid. p. 211.
63 "jumped onto the running board": ibid. p. 231.
63 "Arrived at Les Cyprès": ibid. p. 232.
63 "As I walked back": ibid. p. 234.
63 "You are not afflicted": ibid. p. 235.
64 "*j'ai beaucoup de regrets*": Jacqueline Mimerel to SB 6.3.71 SB archive HRC.
64 "*Tu n'as, je crois*": Jacqueline Mimerel to SB 15.0.77 SB archive HRC.
64 "In terms of pain": SB diaries 16.4.81 SB archive HRC.

FOUR: THE DELIGHTS AND DANGERS OF SANARY-SUR-MER

66 "[I had] come to feel": *Jigsaw* p. 167.
67 "She was too beautiful": *Desert Island Discs* BBC radio 10.7.98.
67 "gaunt as a starving horse": *Jigsaw* p. 197.
68 "wonderful feeling": ibid. p. 272.
68 "You had better learn": ibid.
68 "I was not prepared": *Aldous Huxley* Vol. 1 p. 232.
68 "sitting on a red-tiled floor": *Quicksands* p. 249.
69 "going on with what she had been saying": *Aldous Huxley* Vol. 1 p. 234.
69 "The Huxleys took me on": *Desert Island Discs* BBC radio 10.7.98.
70 "culture-saturated purr": "With Aldous Huxley" by Robert Craft *Encounter* November 1965.
70 "seemed to stretch for miles": *Aldous Huxley: An English Intellectual* by Nicholas Murray (Abacus,, 2003) p. 92.
70 "into an inaccessible inner shell": *Quicksands* p. 288.
70 "Nature has erected": Robert Nicholls to Henry Head 28.2.30 Robert Nicholls archive HRC.
70 "offering gossip, pouring out our troubles": *Aldous Huxley* Vol. 1 p. 230.
71 "was very outspoken": ibid. p. 238.
71 "*était toujours heureuse*": "Mémoires de Suzanne Nicolas" Archives et Musée de la Littérature, Bibliothéque Royale de Bruxelles.

71   "the hilarious Huxley picnics": *Jigsaw* p. 277.

72   "We were ignorant of all": *Quicksands* p. 258.

72   "Eating your dinner with your fingers": *Aldous Huxley* Vol. 1 p. 262.

72   "He was nice to me": review by SB of *Cyril Connolly: Journal & Memoir* by David Pryce-Jones *Vogue* August 1983.

72   "spinsterish and in his little brown way": *Devoid of Shyness* by Alan Pryce-Jones (Stone Trough Books,, 2015) p. 181.

73   "I disliked this very superior": *Minding My Own Business* by Percy Muir (Chatto & Windus,, 1956) p. 53.

73   "It was bad enough": ibid. p. 54.

73   "a formidable lady": Aldous Huxley to Ottoline Morell 18.12.30, Aldous Huxley archive HRC.

73   "Never shall I forget the sight": *Aldous Huxley 1894–1963: A Memorial Volume* ed. Julian Huxley (Chatto & Windus,, 1965) p. 142.

73   "A number of disagreeable": *Aldous Huxley* Vol. 1 p. 261.

74   "Sanary," Aldous wrote: *Letters of Aldous Huxley*, ed. Grover Smith (Chatto & Windus,, 1969) p. 365.

74   "a very strange man indeed": *Aldous Huxley* Vol. 1 p. 261.

74   "A young German girl": *The Strange World of Willie Seabrook* by Marjorie Worthington (Harcourt,, 1966) p. 160.

74   "hearty, sense of humour": Margery Worthington diary University of Oregon Special Archives.

74   "Ilsa von Stembeck, a young German girl": *Come, My Coach!* by Marjorie Worthington (Knopf,, 1935) p. 18.

74   "her sun prince": *Quicksands* p. 226.

74   "the audience alight": *Jigsaw* p. 289.

75   "the staggery walk": ibid. p. 283.

76   "to find yet another pharmacy": *Quicksands* p. 265.

76   "There was no intention": ibid. p. 266.

76   "I did feel pity": ibid. p. 265.

76   "was brutal": ibid. 269.

76   "etched with a tragic": *Jigsaw* p. 192.

77   "I doubt that Aldous": Eva Herrmann to SB 21.7.56 SB archive HRC.

77   "He would have grudged the time": *Aldous Huxley* Vol. 1 p. 295.

77   "In a subtle way": ibid. p. 140.

77   "It was a measure": ibid. p. 295.

77   "her feminine appearance": *On the Way to Myself* by Charlotte Wolff (Methuen,, 1969) p. 73.

77   "I recall delicious softness": Maria Huxley to SB 15.1.45 SB archive HRC.

78   "graceful indolence": *Eyeless in Gaza* by Aldous Huxley (Flamingo,, 1994) p. 290.

78   "The first half of the flight": ibid. p. 113.

78   "with a lovely, secret Etruscan face": *A Visit to Don Otavio* (Eland, 2002) p. 84.

78   "Our friendship is for life": Chronology Aliette Martin archive.

80   "I kissed her hand": *Quicksands* p. 283.

80   "a life enhancer": *Aldous Huxley* Vol. 1 p. 258.

80   "gay and giggly": ibid.

80   "Swarmed upon by actual living Germans": *Quicksands* p. 287.

80 "Rather a dismal crew": ibid. p. 288.

80 "Swarms of literary Germans": *Aldous Huxley: An English Intellectual* by Nicholas Murray p. 260.

80 "one behaved with dignity": *Quicksands* p. 288.

81 "Maria remained distant": ibid. p. 289.

81 "One evening we went to have a look": *Aldous Huxley* Vol. 1 p. 255.

81 "It was a mixed up and foreboding time": *Quicksands* p. 274.

81 "I found bureaucracy": ibid.

82 "My German beginnings": *Jigsaw* p. 81.

82 "I never felt I had the German identity": *Oldie* August 1997 p. 28.

82 "*eine deutsche Halbjüdin*": *Mein Zwanzigstes Jahrhundert* by Ludwig Marcuse (Paul List Verlag, 1960) p. 198.

82 "much as I was inclined to admire": *Jigsaw* p. 246.

82 "So much siesta": SB diaries 26.2.77 SB archive HRC.

83 "*la journée passé vite*": SB diaries 13.7.32 SB archive HRC.

83 "a horrid house": SB to Evelyn Gendel 19.8.53 SB archive HRC.

83 "Anger that ill becomes our kind": *New Bats in Old Belfries: Some Loose Tiles* by Maurice Bowra (Robert Dugdale, 2005) p. 65.

84 "Yes. I had one very serious attachment": *Independent on Sunday* 23.5.04.

85 "a gregarious and gossipy world": *The Turning Point* by Klaus Mann (Oswald Wolff, 1984) p. 214.

85 "A galaxy indeed": *Quicksands* p. 279.

85 "*ich finde in diesem Kulturgebiet*": *Tagebücher 1933–1934* by Thomas Mann (S. Fischer, 1977) p. 81.

85 "I find everything in this cultural milieu": *Thomas Mann Diaries 1918–1939* selection by Hermann Kesten, translated by Richard and Clara Watson (Henry N. Abrams, 1982) p. 59.

85 "poor Tommy": *Paris Review* no. 126 p. 237.

86 "a sporadic camaraderie": *Quicksands* p. 291.

86 "I never knew anybody": SB to Allanah Harper 28.5.49 SB archive HRC.

87 "like M. de Charlus": *Aldous Huxley* Vol. 1 p. 277.

87 "making the round": ibid.

87 "What struck the Huxleys": ibid.

87 "*Je n'ai jamais lu*": *German Writers in French Exile 1933—1940* by Martin Mauthner (Valentine Mitchell, 2007) p. 167.

87 "long, sometimes": *Jigsaw* p. 325.

88 "not a Giorgione any longer": ibid. p. 339.

88 "with quick resource": ibid. p. 333.

88 "When [Nori] came in": ibid. p. 334.

88 "Hennaed to an impossible orange": *Eyeless in Gaza* by Aldous Huxley p. 285.

89 "I hadn't known that AH": Anna Bernhardt to SB 3.10.36 SB archive HRC.

89 "the kind of sailors' clothes I liked": *Quicksands* p. 271.

89 "*à deux* under the night sky": *Jigsaw* p. 342.

90 "with perhaps worse to follow": *Quicksands* p. 271.

90 "an exhilarating and happy time": ibid. p. 308.

90 "evenings of ease": ibid.

90 "Lisa is the hole": Anna Bernhardt to SB 26.2.34 SB archive HRC.

90 "Look after her": *Quicksands* p. 273.

91 "juvenile in concept": ibid. p. 305.

91 *"Huxley's vor ein paar Monaten"*: *Die Sammlung 1934* (Rogner und Bernhard) pp. 486, 488.

92 "I merely wanted": *Quicksands* p. 304.

92 "That money . . . the capital": ibid. p. 306.

FIVE: SAILING INTO THE UNKNOWN

94 "I prefer Berlin": Anna Bernhardt to SB 16.9.36 SB archive HRC.

94 *"Lisa n'a jamais supporté"*: Anna Bernhardt to Maria Huxley 11.11.35 SB archive HRC.

94 "I am worried and out of sorts": SB to Toni Muir 7.8.34 SB archive HRC.

95 "If this statement is agreed": Anna Bernhardt to SB 3.8.34 SB archive HRC.

95 "I thought of Lisa": SB to Evelyn Gendel 26.2.55 Aliette Martin.

96 "The last I saw of my mother": *Quicksands* 275.

96 "Don't tell lies": ibid. p. 86.

96 "My sister, ferociously disgusted": ibid. p. 275.

96 "[I] could not love her": ibid. p. 313.

96 "inner withdrawal": SB to Allanah Harper 10.11.89 Allanah Harper archive HRC.

96 "If she was against": *Quicksands* p. 313.

97 "a ruthless social butterfly": ibid. p. 312.

98 "Pierre never looked back": ibid. p. 90.

98 *"Il m'a forcé à prendre"*: SB to Evelyn Gendel 7.9.55 SB archive HRC.

98 "To my astonishment": *Jigsaw* p. 314.

99 "I became for her": *Quicksands* p. 317.

99 *"ta mère est une morphiniste"*: *Jigsaw* p. 318.

100 "He is so intelligent": SB to Toni Muir 22.8.34 SB archive HRC.

100 *"un personnage fascinant"*: "Mémoires de Suzanne Nicolas" Archives et Musée de la Littérature, Bibliothèque Royale de Bruxelles.

100 *"eine grosse Snob"*: *Mein Zwanzigstes Jahrhundert* by Ludwig Marcuse (Paul List Verlag, 1960) p. 197.

100 "We had a picnic party": SB to Toni Muir 7.8.34 SB archive HRC.

101 "Doris Grey, a pretty American girl": *Come, My Coach!* by Marjorie Worthington p. 18.

101 "I am really working at present": SB to Toni Muir 31.10.34 SB archive HRC.

102 *"Ernstlich* . . . don't you know": SB to Toni Muir 7.8.34 ibid.

102 "a nice marriage": Anna Bernhardt to SB 30.7.34 ibid.

102 "Albany was both rather wonderful": *Aldous Huxley* Vol. 1 p. 290.

103 "I sit before my hostile typewriter": SB to Allanah Harper 9.7.58 Allanah Harper archive HRC.

103 *"Auguri,* we shouted": *Aldous Huxley* Vol. 1 p. 287.

104 "Lisa looks frightfully old": Anna Bernhardt to SB 27.5.35 SB archive HRC.

104 "she is awfully fat": ibid. 30.6.35.

104 "I can't get along with her!": ibid. 30.4.35.

104 "The Court has decided against him": ibid. 30.6.35.

104 "is a white lamb": ibid. 22.7.35.

104 "the locals were prolific": *Quicksands* p. 322.

104 "We must get one of our bugger friends": ibid. p. 324.
105 "German friend": Aldous Huxley to Sebastian Sprott 22.8.35 Walter John Herbert Sprott papers GBR/0272/PP/WJHS King's College, Cambridge.
105 "on the handsome side": *Quicksands* p. 327.
105 "He was in the room within seconds": ibid. p. 329.
105 "So you have been living": ibid.
106 "It was stamped with a Deportation Order": ibid. p. 333.
106 "Some hours later": ibid. p. 335.
106 "half a dozen showgirls": ibid. p. 337.
106 "came up to me": ibid.
106 "musty brown paper": ibid. p. 306.
106 "they returned it": ibid. p. 339.
106 "national shame": SB diaries 1.6.85 SB archive HRC.
106 "I never felt I had the German identity": *Oldie* August 1997 p. 28.
107 "I felt nothing very much": *Jigsaw* p. 89.
107 "The thing about Paris for me": SB to Martha Gellhorn 4.4.53 Martha Gellhorn archive HGARC.
108 "was invariably polite": review by SB of *The Very Rich Hours of Adrienne Monnier* translated by Richard McDougall *New York Review of Books* 5.8.76.
108 "It was a bad, empty novel": *Aldous Huxley* Vol. 1 p. 326.
108 "I had read too much": *Quicksands* p. 7.
109 "rightly so but to my desolation": *Jigsaw* p. 314.
109 "quite pointless to stay": *Aldous Huxley* by Nicholas Murray p. 301.
110 "an insufferable Jew": Anna Bernhardt to SB 1.1.36 SB archive HRC.
110 "I had a row": ibid. 14.12.35.
110 "Today my room is so cold": ibid. 25.4.36.
110 "Tomorrow week is Xmas Eve": ibid. 14.12.35.
110 "it will take a <u>long</u> time": ibid. 9.6.36.
111 "Your mother is now immensely *pitoyable*": ibid. 20.12.36.
111 "immensely sorry about our poor Lisa": ibid. 7.2.37.
111 "She taught me everything": *Oldie* August 1997.
112 "When the bell rang": *Aldous Huxley* Vol. 1 p. 341.
112 "The idea was": *Quicksands* p. 314.
112 "The fee for a private lesson": ibid. p. 315.
113 "Maria Huxley once asked me": *Hindsight* by Charlotte Wolff (Quartet, 1980), p. 157.
113 "two people affected in different ways": ibid.
114 "With humble gratitude": Brian Howard to SB, and Eva Herrmann undated 1937 SB archive HRC.
114 "where one could dance": *Quicksands* p. 343.
115 "Within seconds a general fight": ibid. p. 345.
115 "We, Brian, Eddy": ibid. p. 346.
115 "German *haute culture*": ibid. p. 347.
115 "in a tight drainpipe trouser suit": ibid.
116 "anxious to show": Eva Herrmann to SB 21.7.56 SB archive HRC.
116 "It makes me rather nervous": *Brian Howard: Portrait of a Failure* ed. Marie-Jacqueline Lancaster (Anthony Blond, 1968).
116 "Brian was wrong": *The Turning Point* p. 309.

116 "[*Je veux*] *que la maison*": Maria Huxley to Jeanne Neveux 27.5.38 Nys-Huxley archive Bibliothèque Royale de Bruxelles.

116 "You probably know": Maria Huxley to Eddy Sackville-West 30.6.38 SB archive HRC.

117 "volunteer work for a group": *Quicksands* p. 350.

117 "*Je vais parler à des amis*": Maria Huxley to Jeanne Neveux 5.10.38 Nys-Huxley archive Bibliothèque Royale de Bruxelles.

117 "well read and amusing": *Cecil Beaton* by Hugo Vickers (Weidenfeld & Nicolson, 1985) p. 58.

119 "at some quiescent hour": *Quicksands* p. 260.

119 "*très grasse mais contente*": Maria Huxley to Jeanne Neveux 1.7.39 Nys-Huxley archive Bibliothèque Royale de Bruxelles.

119 "*Je suis vraiment plutôt découragée*": Maria Huxley to Jeanne Neveux 27.3.39 Nys-Huxley archive Bibliothèque Royale de Bruxelles.

120 "We had deep snow then": Eda Lord to Jimmy & Tania Stern 7.1.40 James Stern archive British Library.

120 "*aimerait venir ici*": Maria Huxley to Jeanne Neveux 30.10.39 Nys-Huxley archive Bibliothèque Royale de Bruxelles.

121 "where Allanah and I": SB to Toni Muir 9.9.49 SB archive HRC.

SIX: "A NEW EXOTIC OPULENT WORLD"

122 "the streets sunlit": *Quicksands* p. 353.

123 "on a much larger scale": *The Turning Point* p. 256.

123 "The Master was standing on the doorstep": *Quicksands* p. 291.

124 "the endless flat roads": ibid. p. 290.

124 "the sweating hot-furred": ibid.

124 "You can't appreciate the South": *Herald Tribune* 8.8.61.

124 "went straight to his master": *Quicksands* p. 290.

125 "a dentist's suburban villa": chronology by SB Aliette Martin archive.

126 "like a man with a great burden": *Aldous Huxley* Vol. 2 p. 11.

126 "It was of course": ibid.

126 "Aldous, don't you want England to win?": ibid. p. 12.

126 "*deux curieuses bonnes femmes*": *Journal: Les Années d'Exil 1937–1949* by Klaus Mann (Bernard Grasset, 1998) p. 217.

127 " 'Dear John,' said Eleanor": "What Can We Ever Do?" typescript SB archive HRC.

127 "it is so overloaded": 5.8.41 SB archive HRC.

128 "I had reached the age": *Quicksands* p. 7.

128 "Sybille is a silly little snob": Maria Huxley to Marjorie Seabrook 4.12.41 *Aldous Huxley* Vol. 2 p. 23.

128 "[She and Allanah] are not happy here": Maria Huxley to Eddy Sackville-West 9.12.40 SB archive HRC.

128 "*probablement ma meilleure amie*": Maria Huxley to Jeanne Neveux February 1942 Nys-Huxley archive Bibliothèque Royale de Bruxelles.

128 "a difficult time": SB to Katie Muir 21.6.54 SB archive HRC.

129 "In those New York years": SB to James Stern 27.12.85 James Stern archive British Library.

129 "In those American years": review by SB of *Cyril Connolly: Journal & Memoir* by David Pryce-Jones Vogue August 1983.

130 "a Yiddish bulldog": *Clement Greenberg: A Life* by Florence Rubenfeld (Scribner, 1997) p. 97.

130 "ghastly physically": Allanah Harper to SB, 28.10.43 SB archive HRC.

130 "monstrously untrained": Eda Lord to James Stern 4.9.64 James Stern archive British Library.

131 "I have got all the information": Maria Huxley to SB, 18.3.41 SB archive HRC.

131 "*Malheureusement je dois dire*": Maria Huxley to SB 13.11.42 SB archive HRC.

132 "my always dear Sybille": Maria Huxley to SB 8.3.43 SB archive HRC.

132 "very dear Sybille": Maria Huxley to SB 15.1.45 SB archive HRC.

132 "the most remarkable and adorable woman": SB to Elaine Robson-Scott 1961 SB archive HRC.

132 "the difficult facts of life": *Decision* January–February 1942 pp. 73–4.

133 "I have just read your article": Aldous Huxley to SB 10.11.42 SB archive HRC.

134 "I was, on the whole, disappointed": James Stern to SB 11.6.41 SB archive HRC.

134 "It's frightfully underfurnished": SB to Tania Stern 30.10.43 James Stern archive British Library.

134 "a full-sized kitchen": ibid.

135 "Of Hock and Fine": SB to Curtis Moffatt 11.10.44 SB archive HRC.

135 "Poor A. trying to prove": Maria Huxley to SB 23.3.41 SB archive HRC.

135 "I found myself a bit depressed": Tania Stern to James Stern 19.6.45 James Stern archive British Library.

136 "is devoted to you": Allanah Harper to SB, 28.10.43 SB archive HRC.

136 "An extremely good dinner": Anne Bakewell to Clement Greenberg 1943 SB archive HRC.

136 "Darling, wasn't it fun": Anne Bakewell to SB April 1943 SB archive HRC.

137 "a new *affaire de coeur*": SB to Toni Muir 30.10.43 SB archive HRC.

137 "her nasty old allowance-power": Anne Bakewell to SB 21.5.43 SB archive HRC.

137 "I could never have enough of you": Anne Bakewell to SB 21.5.43 SB archive HRC.

138 "If only you could be here tonight": Anne Bakewell to SB 16.5.43 SB archive HRC.

138 "I feel so worried": Anne Bakewell to SB 15.6.43 SB archive HRC.

138 "I never look at her": Anne Bakewell to Clement Greenberg 1943 SB archive HRC.

138 "too boring for words": Allanah Harper to SB 15.10.43 SB archive HRC.

138 "I must say it does bring you down": Allanah Harper to SB September 1943 SB archive HRC.

138 "delightful": SB to Toni Muir 30.10.43 SB archive HRC.

138 "Darling," Allanah wrote: Allanah Harper to SB September 1943 SB archive HRC.

139 "Remember you are a writer": Allanah Harper to SB 19.8.43 SB archive HRC.

139 "If only you were not so horrible": Allanah Harper to SB 27.7.43 SB archive HRC.

139 "quite bad": SB to Elaine Robson Scott *c*.1963 SB archive HRC.

139 "I do not know what to do": Allanah Harper to SB, 19.8.43 SB archive HRC.

140 "The news has been so exciting": SB to Toni Muir 30.10.43 SB archive HRC.

140 "in a warm place": SB to Toni Muir 30.10.43 SB archive HRC.

140 "I <u>must</u> warn you": *All We Know: Three Lives* by Lisa Cohen (Farrar, Straus & Giroux, 2012) p. 105.

141 "The past is so satisfactory": ibid. p. 31.

142 "proud, loyal": *John Strachey* by Hugh Thomas (Eyre Methuen, 1973), p. 71.

142 "You crossed my path": Esther Murphy to SB 1945 SB archive HRC.

142 "I love you and miss you": Esther Murphy to SB 1.3.45 SB archive HRC.

142 "Everything I say": Allanah Harper to SB 16.9.45 SB archive HRC.

143 "I only love you more and more": Annie Bakewell to SB 5.2.45 SB archive HRC.

143 "I will unwillingly address this letter": Annie Bakewell to SB 16.2.45 SB archive HRC.

143 "goodness of heart": *All We Know* p. 105.

144 "Supernaturally erudite": *Quicksands* p. 13.

144 "She talks constantly": *The Diaries of Dawn Powell 1931–1965* ed. Tim Page (Steerforth Press, 1995) p. 249.

144 "The only thing that matters": Allanah Harper to SB 17.5.46 SB archive HRC.

144 "everyone shrieks in America": Allanah Harper to SB 27.5.46 SB archive HRC.

144 "Oh Bull how you made me long": SB to Allanah Harper 29.6.46 Allanah Harper archive HRC.

144 "It is over five years": Joan Black to SB, 14.3.46 SB archive HRC.

145 "Poor Joan started reading": Eda Lord to SB, 23.9.46 SB archive HRC.

145 "What one also did not know": *Quicksands* p. 95.

145 "She looked very well": Allanah Harper to SB 19.9.46 SB archive HRC.

146 "Her health has suffered": SB to Allanah Harper 29.6.46 Allanah Harper archive HRC.

146 "*aversion insurmontable*": Katzi Nielsen to SB 13.11.65 Allanah Harper archive HRC.

146 "was no collaborator": *Quicksands* p. 366.

146 "I suppose I feel closer to you": SB to Allanah Harper 29.6.46 Allanah Harper archive HRC.

146 "I am very desperate in many ways": SB to Allanah Harper 29.6.46 Allanah Harper archive HRC.

146 "I had a great longing to move": *A Visit to Don Otavio* p. 20.

146 "It only costs just over a hundred dollars": SB to Allanah Harper 29.6.46 Allanah Harper archive HRC.

147 "I am delighted to be here": SB to Allanah Harper 8.8.46 Allanah Harper archive HRC.

147 "As one picks one's way": *A Visit to Don Otavio* p. 39.

148 "two spiny fishes": ibid. p. 42.

148 "I sniff before tasting": ibid. p. 50.

148 "a sun-splashed loggia": ibid. p. 123.

148 "The place belonged to the governor": SB to Allanah Harper 8.8.46 Allanah Harper archive HRC.

149 "born anti-traveller": *Quicksands* p. 13.

149 "hated to travel": *All We Know* p. 106.

149 "I am more and more enchanted": SB to Allanah Harper 25.9.46 Allanah Harper archive HRC.

149 "three or four men in fine hats": *A Visit to Don Otavio* p. 98.

150 "The actual fight sickened and depressed me": SB to Allanah Harper 16.10.46 Allanah Harper archive HRC.

150 "dirty and illiterate": SB to Allanah Harper 21.8.46 Allanah Harper archive HRC.

150 "Old Virginian ladies": SB to Allanah Harper 3.10.46 Allanah Harper archive HRC.

150 "spinsterish primadonnaism": SB to Allanah Harper 8.3.47 Allanah Harper archive HRC.

150 "if that doesn't make your flesh creep": SB to Allanah Harper 3.10.46 Allanah Harper archive HRC.

150 "rude as Yankee peddlers": *Kokio: A Novel Based on the Life of Neill James* by Stephen Preston Banks (Tellectual Press, 2016) p. 210.

151 "Mexico has made all the difference": SB to Allanah Harper 13.11.46 Allanah Harper archive HRC.

151 "everyone is too concerned": Allanah Harper to SB 7.12.46 SB archive HRC.

151 "almost frantic need": SB to Allanah Harper 8.3.47 Allanah Harper archive HRC.

152 "I got a good black suit": SB to Allanah Harper 10.5.47 Allanah Harper archive HRC.

152 "the bogus city": SB to Allanah Harper 8.3.47 Allanah Harper archive HRC.

152 "the last word in discomfort": SB to Allanah Harper 23.3.47 Allanah Harper archive HRC.

152 "I can bring a thousand cigarettes": SB to Allanah Harper 10.5.47 Allanah Harper archive HRC.

152 "After a universal cataclysm": *Quicksands* p. 100.

SEVEN: THE LOVELINESS OF ROME

153 "I cannot tell you": Allanah Harper to Cyril Connolly 23.11.46 Cyril Connolly archive McFarlin Library, Tulsa.

154 "If one has been through the bombing": Allanah Harper to SB 9.6.46 SB archive HRC.

154 "Nice as she is": Allanah Harper to SB 19.9.46 SB archive HRC.

154 "Eda as usual does not express an opinion": ibid.

154 "madly in love": Allanah Harper to SB 20.4.47 SB archive HRC.

154 "has been wonderful": Allanah Harper to SB 20.5.47 SB archive HRC.

155 "I could have Esther here": Allanah Harper to SB 13.3.47 SB archive HRC.

155 "sitting in one of the stiff armchairs": *Quicksands* p. 95.

156 "vast meals on time": SB to Toni Muir 15.11.49 SB archive HRC.

156 "She spellbound her hosts": *Quicksands* p. 99.

156 "How is it that she has lived in France so long": *The Fifties: From Notebooks and Diaries of the Period* by Edmund Wilson. Edited by Leon Edel (Farrar, Straus & Giroux, 1986) p. 376.

156 "The Mimerels were entirely out of it": *Quicksands* p. 101.

156 "I wish you would fall in love": Allanah Harper to SB 30.4.49 SB archive HRC.

156 "moral stature": SB to Toni Muir 25.6.49 SB archive HRC.

157 "I am rather sad": SB to Allanah Harper 14.2.49 SB archive HRC SB archive HRC.

157 "I know I have forfeited all claim": Esther Murphy to SB 3.6.49 SB archive HRC.

157 "how unspeakably I love you": Esther Murphy to SB 13.2.49 SB archive HRC.

157 "Some people can write love letters": *Sunday Times* 13.11.94.

157 "the sun, the sweet air": *Quicksands* p. 12.

158 "the cold is breaking me": SB to Toni Muir 9.2.49 SB archive HRC.

158 "I am not writing": SB to Toni Muir 22.1.49 SB archive HRC.

159 "made my hair stand on end": SB to Allanah Harper 10.6.49 SB archive HRC.

159 "remained the loving, generous sister": *Quicksands* p. 365.

159 "I can't tell you HOW lovely": SB to Allanah Harper 28.5.49 SB archive HRC.

159 "The streets are full": SB to Allanah Harper 10.6.49 SB archive HRC.

159 "French windows giving on to": *Quicksands* p. 49.

159 "a gentleman of the press in skirts": *Genêt: A Biography of Janet Flanner* by Brenda Wineapple (Ticknor & Fields, 1989) p. 94.

160 "the enormous moral progress": SB to Allanah Harper 8.3.49 SB archive HRC.

160 "I cannot understand": SB to Allanah Harper 19.2.49 SB archive HRC.

160 "rather nasty letter": SB to Allanah Harper 28.5.49 SB archive HRC.

160 "not an amiable quality": SB to Toni Muir 20.8.49 SB archive HRC.

160 "Klaus could no longer find himself": Golo Mann in *Escape to Life* filmed by Andrea Weiss and Wieland Speck (2000).

161 "goes on like a great heavy wheel": SB to Allanah Harper 28.5.49 SB archive HRC.

161 "romantic, German fixation": SB to Toni Muir 27.5.49 SB archive HRC.

161 "I am free of Esther": SB to Toni Muir 25.6.49 SB archive HRC.

161 "a woman of radiant vitality": *Quicksands* p. 139.

161 "Not educated in our sense": SB to Allanah Harper 28.5.49 SB archive HRC.

161 "I had what is called a good time": SB to Toni Muir 27.5.49 ibid.

162 "I never met a more self-righteous woman": review by SB of *Our Three Selves: A Life of Radclyffe Hall* by Michael Baker (William Morrow, 1985) *Guardian* 1985.

162 "How guilty one feels": SB to Toni Muir 27.5.49 SB archive HRC.

162 "Your friend Patricia Laffan": SB to Allanah Harper 10.6.49 SB archive HRC.

162 "took me aside": SB to Toni Muir 25.6.49 SB archive HRC.

163 "She was very excited about it": SB to Allanah Harper 30.4.49 SB archive HRC.

163 "Very well": SB to Allanah Harper 28.5.49 SB archive HRC.

163 "Meeting Martha": *Pleasures and Landscapes* p. 17.

164 "proud, solitary, faintly snobbish": SB to Allanah Harper 10.6.49 SB archive HRC.

164 "By full morning": *Pleasures and Landscapes* p. 15.

164 "The island is full of the old and titled": SB to Allanah Harper 1948 SB archive HRC.

165 "I left England under a cloud": Robin Maugham unpublished diaries 1949 (private archive).

165 "The talk, as I remember": *Pleasures and Landscapes* p. 20.

165 "bubbling and bawdy, and kind": SB to Toni Muir 26.8.49 SB archive HRC.

165 "I felt privileged": *Pleasures and Landscapes* p. 22.

165 "the brightest, most honourable": *Quicksands* p. 20.

166 "I owe her a good deal": ibid.

166 "By Golly!": ibid. p. 21.

166 "My God, I thought": ibid.

167 "gave me an affectionate": ibid. p. 22.

167 "though charming and comfortable": SB to Martha Gellhorn 24.7.49 Martha Gellhorn archive HGARC.

167 "set out with gleaming linen": *Quicksands* p. 43.

168 "coroneted napkins, silver dishes": SB to Allanah Harper 16.8.49 SB archive HRC.

168 "the most unsuitable topics": SB to Martha Gellhorn 24.7.49 Martha Gellhorn archive HGARC.

168 "One cannot think much": SB to Toni Muir 20.7.49 SB archive HRC.

168 "The *baronessa* tells them": SB to Martha Gellhorn 24.7.49 Martha Gellhorn archive HGARC.

168 "one warm night": *Quicksands* p. 12.

168 "an extremely subjective book": SB to Allanah Harper 28.5.49 SB archive HRC.

168 "I haven't written for much too long": SB to Toni Muir 20.7.49 ibid.

168 "I feel exhausted, discouraged": SB to Martha Gellhorn 24.7.49 Martha Gellhorn archive HGARC.

169 "July 20th No work": SB diaries SB archive HRC.

169 "now it's a bit better": SB to Martha Gellhorn 24.7.49 Martha Gellhorn archive HGARC.

169 "I've been wrestling all afternoon": SB to Allanah Harper 16.8.49 SB archive HRC.

169 "It took me three weeks": SB to Toni Muir 11.8.49 SB archive HRC.

169 "What mattered was that the book was moving": *Quicksands* p. 18.

169 "a worn-out international fairy": Esther Murphy to SB, 11.10.49 SB archive HRC.

169 "My whole feeling about her": Esther Murphy to SB, 19.10.49 SB archive HRC.

169 "madly in love": Allanah Harper to SB 27.6.49 SB archive HRC.

170 "and could not be sweeter": ibid.

170 "to me one of the most heavenly countrysides": SB to Toni Muir 21.9.49 SB archive HRC.

170 "abode of permanent peace": ibid.

171 "the Bates Sorcery Chamber": *Quicksands* p. 67.

171 "still one of the liveliest": SB to Toni Muir 15.11.49 SB archive HRC.

172 "Lord Byron of the Ladies": ibid.

172 "Quick change and off": SB to Evelyn Gendel 26.1.52 SB archive HRC.

172 "Suddenly" Sybille recalled: Joan Schenkar (unpublished) interview with SB 12.6.90.

172 "She is a monster": SB to Evelyn Gendel 13.4.53 SB archive HRC.

172 "entirely selfish": *All We Know* by Lisa Cohen p. 55.

172 "The entertaining, brittle world": SB to Evelyn Gendel 13.4.53 SB archive HRC.

172 "Allanah and I shared": *Quicksands* p. 65.

173 "an angelic, witty, suicidal imp": ibid.

173 "a horrid Dog Kennel": SB to Toni Muir 9.4.50 SB archive HRC.

173 "I have my tea there": SB to Allanah Harper 15.4.50 SB archive HRC.

173 "I have acquired a new joy": SB to Allanah Harper 21.6.50 SB archive HRC.

174 "Conversation flowed": *Quicksands* 126.

174 "I felt I'd moved to Yonkers": author's interview with Milton Gendel 8.6.12.

175 "one of those rather sarcastic": SB to Toni Muir 23.8.50 SB archive HRC.

175 "young in some ways": ibid.

175 "I didn't especially take to Sybille": author's interview with Milton Gendel 8.6.12.

175 "Yes, I did like the Gendels": *Quicksands* p. 126.

175 "I bit a nail, sat down": ibid. p. 134.

176 "tomatoes, an egg or two": ibid.

176 "The Gendels, who occasionally came": ibid. p. 136.
176 "Evelyn and I were facing each other": ibid. p. 145.
176 "I knew all the time": SB to Toni Muir 23.8.50 SB archive HRC.
176 "after that day": ibid.
176 "rather madly in love": ibid.
177 "We had to be extremely careful": ibid.
177 "the maddening, slow maid": ibid.
177 "overexalted & feeling oats": SB diaries SB archive HRC.
177 "It was a strain": SB to Toni Muir 23.8.50 SB archive HRC.
177 "that notion of For Ever": ibid.
177 "I was beside myself ": ibid.
177 "After Evelyn left me": author's interview with Milton Gendel 8.6.12.
177 "and thank God she and Evelyn": SB to Toni Muir 23.8.50 SB archive HRC.
177 "I found the first weeks": ibid.
178 "Many attachments have improbable beginnings": *Quicksands* p. 148.
178 "was very nice and very intelligent": Allanah Harper to SB 6.1.51 SB archive HRC.
178 "I love Jane as much as ever": Allanah Harper to SB 19.7.50 SB archive HRC.
178 "thank God [she] has a little more money": SB to Allanah Harper 30.12.51 SB archive HRC.
179 "the L-shaped inner facade": SB to Evelyn Gendel 20.1.52 SB archive HRC.
179 "We are going to have [a] marvel for dinner": ibid.
179 "*Je mange du cochon*": SB to Evelyn Gendel 23.1.52 SB archive HRC.
179 "*Tu peux être insupportable*": SB to Evelyn Gendel 14.2.52 SB archive HRC.
179 "Katzi well and easy": SB to Evelyn Gendel 21.1.52 SB archive HRC.
180 "Yesterday," Sybille reported: SB to Evelyn Gendel 22.1.52 SB archive HRC.
180 "This afternoon, he changed the ribbon": Evelyn Gendel to SB 19.1.52 SB archive HRC.
180 "He was ravenous": Evelyn Gendel to SB 9.2.52 SB archive HRC.
180 "They are yourself ": Evelyn Gendel to SB 24.1.52 SB archive HRC.
180 "I think of my Dear constantly": SB to Evelyn Gendel 21.1.52 SB archive HRC.
180 "I cannot really love my lovers": SB to Allanah Harper 31.12.51 SB archive HRC.
181 "I do feel": SB to Allanah Harper 27.6.52 SB archive HRC.
181 "Yes he realised that he will have to work": Evelyn Gendel to SB 12.2.52 SB archive HRC.
181 "It is gone": SB to Allanah Harper 30.6.52 SB archive HRC.
182 "Please," Evelyn begged her: Evelyn Gendel to SB 30.1.52 SB archive HRC.
182 "Don't make a nonsense": Evelyn Gendel to SB 31.1.52 SB archive HRC.
182 "even for an English publisher": SB to Evelyn Gendel 6.2.52 SB archive HRC.
182 "a tricky old bird": Leopold Loewenstein to Allanah Harper 6.1.52 SB archive HRC.
182 "I had been warned": SB to Evelyn Gendel 10.2.52 SB archive HRC.
183 "something that gives a hint": SB to Evelyn Gendel 11.2.52 SB archive HRC.
183 "has written a travel book": Martha Gellhorn to William Walton 17.11.52 *The Letters of Martha Gellhorn* selected and ed. by Caroline Moorehead (Chatto & Windus, 2006) p. 232.
183 "when the door flung open": SB to Allanah Harper 5.3.53 SB archive HRC.
184 "There doesn't seem to be any water": *A Visit to Don Otavio* p. 108.

184 " 'I have not the slightest desire' ": ibid. p. 95.

184 "weak and hysterical": SB to Allanah Harper 28.5.49 HRC SB archive.

185 "was an immediate critical success": SB interview *Paris Review* no. 126 p. 240.

185 "Great Rabbit, A thousand thanks": Allanah Harper to SB 19.2.53 SB archive HRC.

185 "Without you," Sybille told her: SB to Allanah Harper 5.3.53 SB archive HRC.

185 "his eyes were too bad": Allanah Harper to SB 19.2.53 SB archive HRC.

185 "first class": Allanah Harper to SB 26.5.55 SB archive HRC.

185 "brilliant, quite an extraordinary performance": Raymond Mortimer to Allanah Harper 18.2.53 SB archive HRC.

185 "This book can be recommended": *Sunday Times* 1.3.53.

186 "Absorbing . . . Its account of the lake": *Daily Mail*.

186 "is one of those rare books": Cass Canfield to SB 23.6.53 SB archive HRC.

186 "They did very badly indeed": SB to Toni Muir 7.7.53 SB archive HRC.

186 "A delightful, unclassifiable": *New Yorker*.

186 "one of the travel books of the year": *New York Times* 2.7.54.

186 "something new in travel": *Washington Star* 17.1.54.

186 "*Maintenant il ne reste*": SB to Allanah Harper 9.8.52 SB archive HRC.

EIGHT: "THAT OGRE, THE SNAIL NOVEL"

187 "The impulses behind writing": SB to Evelyn Gendel 29.10.61 SB archive HRC.

187 "the bad *baronessa*": *Quicksands* p. 21.

188 "her boredom with the text": ibid. p. 134.

188 "arrival showed how much": SB to Allanah Harper 9.8 52 SB archive HRC.

188 "has become my bosom companion": *The Letters of Martha Gellhorn* p. 232.

188 "This letting me in on your work": SB to Martha Gellhorn 3.1.53 Martha Gellhorn Archive HGARC.

189 "Sybille dear . . . I take everything": Martha Gellhorn to SB *The Letters of Martha Gellhorn* p. 233.

189 "There is nothing I do not know": Martha Gellhorn to William Walton ibid. p. 193.

189 "All windows closed": SB to Allanah Harper 3.11.52 SB archive HRC.

189 "Do you realise that not a chapter": Martha Gellhorn to SB 2.4.53 SB archive HRC.

189 "She has the most astounding qualities": SB to Martha Gellhorn 31.3.53 Martha Gellhorn Archive HGARC.

190 "Her heart and mind are so good": Evelyn Gendel diaries SB archive HRC.

190 "Oh his pot-roast": Evelyn Gendel to SB 23.8.53 SB archive HRC.

190 "My sister is an amoral nitwit": SB to Martha Gellhorn 31.3.53 Martha Gellhorn Archive HGARC.

191 "A soft voice called Sybille": SB to Evelyn Gendel 27.3.53 SB archive HRC.

191 "Eda was very affectionate": SB to Allanah Harper 17.4.53 SB archive HRC.

191 "They don't care for me": Evelyn Gendel diaries 13.10.53 SB archive HRC.

191 "Says: 'why don't you go out?' ": Evelyn Gendel diaries 25.11.53 SB archive HRC.

191 "I am so surprised": Evelyn Gendel diaries 2.12.53 SB archive HRC.

192 "Felt free, and also, more independent": Evelyn Gendel diaries 28.11.53 SB archive HRC.

192 "trapped in my recluse life here": SB to Toni Muir 23.5.53 SB archive HRC.

192 "I still cannot bear a Germanic country": SB to Allanah Harper 26.4.53 SB archive HRC.

192 "I am rather looking forward to it": SB to Martha Gellhorn 22.7.53 Martha Gellhorn Archive HGARC.

193 "past the vineyards": *Quicksands* p. 5.

193 "clean, honest, stolid": SB to Evelyn Gendel 9.8.53 SB archive HRC.

193 "one is automatically taken": ibid.

193 "The Germans talk about my slow descent": SB to Evelyn Gendel 10.8.53 SB archive HRC.

193 "smelling the moss, hay": SB to Evelyn Gendel 11.8.53 SB archive HRC.

193 "A resurgence of health": SB to Toni Muir 5.9.53 SB archive HRC.

193 "M said isn't it 'rather fun' ": SB to Evelyn Gendel 25.8.53 SB archive HRC.

194 "It made me feel odd": SB to Evelyn Gendel 26.8.53 SB archive HRC.

194 Sybille's "beloved," she had reported: Martha Gellhorn to William Walton 16.7.49 *The Letters of Martha Gellhorn* p. 193.

194 "and explain and be nice": SB to Evelyn Gendel 26.8.53 SB archive HRC.

194 "Let's shove": *Pleasures & Landscapes* p. 85.

194 "Oddly enough M and I ate superbly": SB to Evelyn Gendel 29.8.53 SB archive HRC.

194 "the most expensive, and I think the best": SB to Evelyn Gendel 4.9.53 SB archive HRC.

195 "It was pitch-dark": *Pleasures & Landscapes* p. 80.

195 "in black coat, silk tie": *Pleasures & Landscapes* p. 72.

195 "I don't like living in Rome any more": SB to Toni Muir 22.9.53 SB archive HRC.

196 "horrible, plebeian, ugly": SB to Evelyn Gendel 29.10.61 SB archive HRC.

196 "a monstrous agglomeration": SB to Martha Gellhorn 1.2.57 Martha Gellhorn Archive HGARC.

196 "mindless, mechanical": SB to Allanah Harper 23.9.53 SB archive HRC.

196 "philistine and difficult": *All We Know* p. 286.

196 "a murderous mood": SB to Evelyn Gendel 23.1.54 SB archive HRC.

196 "Sandy burst in at 8.45": ibid.

196 "He LOVE him-y": Evelyn Gendel to SB 25.1.54 SB archive HRC.

197 "instinctive conspirators against K": Evelyn Gendel to SB 28.1.54 SB archive HRC.

197 "[I] must say how I thank you": SB to Martha Gellhorn 7.3.54 Martha Gellhorn Archive HGARC.

197 "All is joy and ease": SB to Martha Gellhorn 8.6.54 Martha Gellhorn Archive HGARC.

197 "There was a sleekness": *Aldous Huxley* Vol. 2 p. 169.

197 "*en beauté*, animated, gay": ibid. p. 171.

198 "like a violinist's hand on his keys": ibid.

198 "the forbidding esoteric therapist": ibid. p. 172.

198 "There was a scent of honeysuckle": ibid.

198 "To me," she had told Laura: *This Timeless Moment: A Personal View of Aldous Huxley* by Laura Archera Huxley (Chatto & Windus, 1969) p. 9.

199 "Of course he knew": *Huxley in Hollywood* by David King Dunaway (Bloomsbury, 1990) p. 309.

199   "was a kind of consecration": *Aldous Huxley* Vol. 2 p. 406.

199   "Afterwards I went with them": ibid. p. 174.

199   "No orthodox analyst or doctor": SB to Martha Gellhorn 23.11.54 Martha Gellhorn Archive HGARC.

199   "tremendous experience": SB to Martha Gellhorn 11.9.54 Martha Gellhorn Archive HGARC.

200   "Bastides quite the wrong place": SB to Martha Gellhorn 9.8.54 Martha Gellhorn Archive HGARC.

200   "[I am] stuck, in writing": SB to Martha Gellhorn 11.9.54 Martha Gellhorn Archive HGARC.

200   "has always been a disaster": Martha Gellhorn to SB 27.8.55 SB archive HRC.

200   "monotonous, strenuous": SB to Allanah Harper 21.10.54 SB archive HRC.

200   "with an anti-aircraft balloon": SB to Martha Gellhorn 6.11.54 Martha Gellhorn Archive HGARC.

200   "that ogre, the snail novel": ibid.

200   "the novel seems to me": Martha Gellhorn to SB 21.1.53 SB archive HRC.

200   "sounds like Anthony Powell to me": Martha Gellhorn to SB 30.7.55 SB archive HRC.

201   "certainly established in George's mind": Martha Gellhorn to SB 30.6.56 SB archive HRC.

201   "It will not, of course, be everybody's meat": Elaine Greene to SB 7.4.55 SB archive HRC.

201   "no fait accompli has ever distressed me more": Elaine Greene to SB 9.9.57 SB archive HRC.

201   "a pretty, blowsy, reddish blonde": *Remembering My Good Friends* by George Weidenfeld (HarperCollins, 1995) p. 240.

202   "which I find delightful": SB to Martha Gellhorn 6.11.54 Martha Gellhorn Archive HGARC.

202   "he rather loves working the raffia": Evelyn Gendel to SB 15.11.55 SB archive HRC.

203   "Yes—Evelyn Gengel": Evelyn Gendel to SB 5.8.55 SB archive HRC.

203   "never went anywhere": *A Legacy* p. 11.

203   "old, landed, agreeably off": ibid. p. 31.

204   "must have stayed in me suspended in amber": *Sunday Telegraph* 7.5.89.

204   "The sources of *A Legacy*": *Quicksands* p. 29.

205   "one of the most ruthless": *A Legacy* p. 286.

205   "Much of what was allowed to happen": ibid. p. x.

206   "*admirablement écrit*": Katzi Nielsen to SB 30.12.55 SB archive HRC.

206   "You did not think?": SB to Evelyn Gendel 24.2.57 SB archive HRC.

206   "was in an awful mood": SB to Martha Gellhorn 7.3.56 Martha Gellhorn Archive HGARC.

206   "Some of Miss Bedford's creations": *The Times* 5.4.56.

207   "critics on the Third Programme": SB to Allanah Harper 25.5.56 SB archive HRC.

207   "My dear Mrs. Bedford": Nancy Mitford to SB 20.3.56 SB archive HRC.

207   "I am hugely grateful to you": Evelyn Waugh to Nancy Mitford 22.3.56 *The Letters of Nancy Mitford and Evelyn Waugh* ed. Charlotte Mosley (Hodder & Stoughton, 1996) p. 387.

207   "The real Mrs. Bedford": Nancy Mitford to Evelyn Waugh 25.3.56 *The Letters*

of *Nancy Mitford: Love from Nancy* ed. Charlotte Mosley (Hodder & Stoughton, 1993) p. 351.

207 "A novel has just appeared": *Spectator* 13.4.56.

208 "the daughter relates things": Evelyn Waugh to Nancy Mitford 22.3.56 *The Letters of Nancy Mitford and Evelyn Waugh* p. 387.

208 "Nothing that has been said": *A Legacy* p. xvii.

208 "It's the one thing I hang on to": *In Conversation with Naim Attallah* p. 7.

208 "original, witty, entertaining": *London Magazine* June 1956.

208 "a writer of extraordinary power": *Encounter* June 1956.

208 "fell madly in love": author's interview with Robert Gottlieb 13.6.11.

208 "We did everything": ibid.

209 "Cosmopolitan, ironic, penetrating": Janet Flanner *New Yorker* April 1957.

209 "a highly unlikely success": *Avid Reader: A Life* by Robert Gottlieb (Farrar, Straus & Giroux, 2016) p. 48.

209 "We are simply delighted": Robert Gottlieb to SB 25.2.57 SB archive HRC.

209 "Everything changes": SB diaries 15.1.56 SB archive HRC.

210 "A held-in day of pacing": SB diaries 16.1.56–21.3.56 SB archive HRC.

210 "a wounded bird": author's interview with Robert Gottlieb 13.6.11.

210 "makes me feel as though": Eda Lord to SB 25.2.56 SB archive HRC.

211 "I'm irritated bored and caged": SB diaries 26.3.56 SB archive HRC.

211 "Ev[elyn] for din. Irritable": SB diaries 4.4.56 SB archive HRC.

211 "First day to ourselves": SB diaries 22.3.56 SB archive HRC.

211 "I go out quickly": SB diaries 27.4.56 SB archive HRC.

211 "Dear Mrs. Bedford, Thank you so much": Ivy Compton-Burnett to SB *Secrets of a Woman's Heart: the Later Life of Ivy Compton-Burnett 1920–1969* by Hilary Spurling (Hodder & Stoughton, 1984) p. 218.

211 "struggled into a skirt": SB to Martha Gellhorn 26.8.56 Martha Gellhorn Archive HGARC.

212 "I opened manfully": SB to Evelyn Gendel 21.8.56 SB archive HRC.

212 "black kid-gloves kept on": SB to Martha Gellhorn 26.8.56 Martha Gellhorn Archive HGARC.

212 "Conversation languished": SB to Evelyn Gendel 21.8.56 SB archive HRC.

212 "stark lugubrious flat": SB's review of Hilary Spurling's two-volume biography of Ivy Compton-Burnett *Guardian* 7.6.84.

212 "I shall miss her very much indeed": SB to Allanah Harper 2.8.56 SB archive HRC.

213 "Her conduct to me": SB to Martha Gellhorn 26.8.56 Martha Gellhorn Archive HGARC.

213 "I cannot imagine London": Evelyn Gendel to SB 15.8.56 SB archive HRC.

213 "in terms of fulfilment": SB diaries 16.4.81 SB archive HRC.

NINE: "HEAVEN BLESS YOU, MRS. BEDFORD"

214 "She exuded vitality": *Stay Me, Oh Comfort Me: Journals and Stories 1933–1941* by M. F. K. Fisher (Pantheon, 1995) p. 119.

215 "veiled in smoke": *The Blue Train* by Lawrence Powell (Capra Press, 1977) p. 61.

215 "as fat as a mountain": Eda Lord to James Stern 21.10.60 Stern archive British Library.

216 "fat . . . with compact hips": *Stay Me, Oh Comfort Me* p. 114.

216 "You were so occupied": Eda Lord to SB 18.11.55 SB archive HRC.

216 "with unrelenting effort": *Quicksands* p. 358.

216 "I am so happy, on air": SB to Evelyn Gendel 9.2.57 SB archive HRC.

217 "an extravagantly painful process": SB to Martha Gellhorn 3.10.56 Martha Gellhorn Archive HGARC.

217 "The car is reparable": SB to Evelyn Gendel 16.10.56 SB archive HRC.

217 "I want you to worry about nothing": Esther Murphy to SB, 22.10.56 SB archive HRC.

217 "so beastly to Eda": SB to Evelyn Gendel 13.1.57 SB archive HRC.

217 "Things are loving now": SB to Evelyn Gendel 13.1.57 SB archive HRC.

218 "*Gino malgré son caractère extrêmement difficile*": Katzi Nielsen to SB 18.3.57 SB archive HRC.

218 "that is neither here nor there": SB to Noël Murphy 12.1.67 SB archive HRC.

218 "Eda and I never seem": SB to Evelyn Gendel 13.1.57 SB archive HRC.

218 "Paris stupefies me": SB to Martha Gellhorn 1.2.57 Martha Gellhorn Archive HGARC.

218 "Yesterday I went to see my translator": SB to Evelyn Gendel 13.1.57 SB archive HRC.

218 "new, clean, and warm": ibid.

218 "everything it was not expected to be": SB to Martha Gellhorn 23.2.57 Martha Gellhorn Archive HGARC.

219 "the oldest private bank in England": SB to Evelyn Gendel 24.2.57 SB archive HRC.

219 "I think I have that sense": ibid.

219 "so charming, so good": SB diaries 19.6.56 SB archive HRC.

219 "the German witch doctor": SB to Evelyn Gendel 9.2.52 SB archive HRC.

219 "return to London": *Hindsight* by Charlotte Wolff (Quartet, 1980) p. 208.

220 "continued, unabated racketeering": SB to Toni Muir 15.7.52 SB archive HRC.

220 "drunk and ill": SB to Evelyn Gendel 2.9.55 SB archive HRC.

220 "He was very sweet": SB to James Stern 27.12.85 Stern archive British Library.

220 "is a broken man": SB to Evelyn Gendel 20.5.57 SB archive HRC.

221 "I feel that I have made *fausse route*": ibid.

221 "The most unlikely people": ibid.

221 "Going to law courts is a good education": *Paris Review* no. 126 p. 241.

222 "the face of a very old woman": *Vogue* October 1956.

222 "Bluebeard of the time": *Quicksands* p. 357.

222 "whiny and kind": SB to Evelyn Gendel 3.5.57 SB archive HRC.

222 "George just phoned me": Elaine Greene to SB 9.9.57 SB archive HRC.

222 "He said yes how much": SB to Evelyn Gendel 19.5.57 SB archive HRC.

223 "Also they wish to buy": SB to Evelyn Gendel 13.6.57 SB archive HRC.

223 "Two muffled individuals": SB to Evelyn Gendel 20.3.57 SB archive HRC.

223 "a position which, if far from ideal": *The Best We Can Do* p. vii.

223 "It is completely fascinating": SB to Evelyn Gendel 20.3.57 SB archive HRC.

224 "the murder trial of the century": *The Times* 11.6.85.

224 "to give an accurate and detailed coverage": *The Best We Can Do* p. vi.

224 "I've not had such a feeling": SB to Evelyn Gendel 7.3.57 SB archive HRC.

224 "I had often wanted to put down a trial": SB to William J. Curran 3.9.59 SB archive HRC.

224 "police vans and press vans": *The Best We Can Do* p. 14.
224 "behind his fine hand": ibid. p. 80.
224 "rolled up sluggishly": ibid. p. 169.
225 "spherical, adipose": ibid. p. 13.
225 "You sit to answer one limited question": ibid. p. 217.
225 "settle themselves, consciously, in the box": ibid. p. 220.
225 "convincingly alive": *Daily Telegraph* 24.10.58.
225 "You have made it sound so exciting": Patrick Devlin to SB 13.11.58 SB archive HRC.
225 "jumping with joy": Evelyn Gendel to SB, 16.4.58 SB archive HRC.
226 "A brilliant account": Eugene Rostow to Robert Gottlieb Simon & Schuster publicity leaflet.
226 "is the book of my heart": Dorothy Parker *Esquire* April 1959.
226 "I had to go back some way": *Pleasures and Landscapes* p. 105.
226 "quiet, clean as whistles": SB to Evelyn Gendel 20.6.58 SB archive HRC.
226 "We've had two dips each": SB to Martha Gellhorn 31.8.58 Martha Gellhorn Archive HGARC.
227 "Eda will never decide anything": Martha Gellhorn to SB 7.7.56 SB archive HRC.
227 "deeply alien and disturbing": SB to Allanah Harper 9.7.58 SB archive HRC.
227 "I am so pleased they are here": SB diaries 7.9.58 SB archive HRC.
227 "the hog slumber of Portugal": SB to Martha Gellhorn 23.10.58 Martha Gellhorn Archive HGARC.
227 "a German and lower-middle-class": SB to Evelyn Gendel 9.10.58 SB archive HRC.
227 "All Portuguese towns are pretty": *Pleasures and Landscapes* p. 106.
227 "agreeable, fresh, plentiful": ibid. p. 110.
227 "placid, kindly, patient": ibid. p. 112.
228 "the Riviera rich": SB to Martha Gellhorn 23.10.58 Martha Gellhorn Archive HGARC.
228 "expatriate jabber": SB to Evelyn Gendel 24.6.59 SB archive HRC.
228 "You swing from her regularly": Evelyn Gendel to SB 29.6.59 SB archive HRC.
228 "when all festivities are over": SB to Evelyn Gendel 2.1.59 SB archive HRC.
228 "I'm fed up with being M's poor relation": SB to Evelyn Gendel 20.2.59 SB archive HRC.
228 "very comfortable, above all entirely quiet": SB to James Stern 28.8.59 James Stern archive British Library.
228 "twelve people": SB to Evelyn Gendel 3.4.59 SB archive HRC.
229 "I came back quivering with indignation": SB to Martha Gellhorn 24.5.59 Martha Gellhorn Archive HGARC.
229 "Tomatoes growing nicely": SB to Evelyn Gendel 13.6.59 SB archive HRC.
229 "A basket with 3 dozen young peas": SB diaries 2.7.59 SB archive HRC.
229 "I ran for a saucer of milk": SB to Evelyn Gendel 24.6.59 SB archive HRC.
230 "The material I am finding": SB to Evelyn Gendel 31.10.59 SB archive HRC.
230 "My Austrian . . . [and] Swiss court experiences": SB to Evelyn Gendel 8.11.59 SB archive HRC.
230 "by the fairness of their law courts": *In Conversation with Naim Attalah* p. 9.
230 "Bavaria is the part of Germany": SB to Evelyn Gendel 28.11.59 SB archive HRC.
230 "Paris grates more than ever": SB to Evelyn Gendel. 6.12.59 SB archive HRC.

230   "Bad atmosphere in house": SB diaries 6.12.59 SB archive HRC.

230   *"Esther boit beaucoup"*: Katzi Nielsen to SB 13.7.58 SB archive HRC.

230   *"Ivre tous les soirs"*: Katzi Nielsen to SB 15.1.59 SB archive HRC.

231   *"devient très difficile"*: Katzi Nielsen to SB 6.5.59 SB archive HRC.

231   *"Personne peut vivre"*: Katzi Nielsen to SB 24.1.58 SB archive HRC.

231   *"Je suis très déprimée"*: Katzi Nielsen to SB 20.3.59 SB archive HRC.

231   "Esther's nearly fatal illness": Janet Flanner to SB, 8.6.59 SB archive HRC.

231   *"Gino et moi"*: Katzi Nielsen to SB 1.9.59 SB archive HRC.

231   "he is cold": SB to Evelyn Gendel 29.7.60 SB archive HRC.

232   "We'd like to help": Robert Gottlieb to SB 5.2.60 SB archive HRC.

232   "I liked her very much": author's interview with Robert Gottlieb 13.6.11.

232   "an American brashness": Evelyn Gendel to SB, 23.8.59 SB archive HRC.

232   "very fond of pleasure and comfort": *Tortoise and Turtle* by Evelyn Gendel (Macdonald and Jane's, 1965).

233   *"T&T* is your book": Evelyn Gendel to SB 14.1.60 SB archive HRC.

233   "I never loved a dedication more": SB to Evelyn Gendel 23.8.60 SB archive HRC.

233   "I love it": Robert Gottlieb to SB 7.9.60 SB archive HRC.

233   "it seemed informed by moderation": *The Faces of Justice* p. 125.

234   "powerful and original intelligence": *Sunday Telegraph* 21.5.61.

234   "A new book by Sybille Bedford": *Pittsburgh Press* 2.9.61.

235   "German Jewish banker's daughter": SB to Evelyn Gendel 27.5.60 SB archive HRC.

235   "Both the M[uir]s are so uncompromisingly": SB to Evelyn Gendel 8.9.57 SB archive HRC.

235   "Toni is much the better of the two": Evelyn Gendel to SB, 1.11.55 SB archive HRC.

235   "he would become imperious": *Christopher and His Kind 1929–1939* by Christopher Isherwood (Eyre Methuen, 1977) p. 185.

235   "We had huge Scotch tea": SB to Evelyn Gendel 21.1.59 SB archive HRC.

236   "v. v. bright and well brought-up": SB to Evelyn Gendel 23.8.60 SB archive HRC.

236   "Dear Sybille," she wrote: Markie Robson-Scott to SB, 12.1.61 SB archive HRC.

236   "Instant, unalloyed, deep joy": SB to Evelyn Gendel 1.10.60 SB archive HRC.

236   "NOW LISTEN TO ME": Evelyn Gendel to SB 8.10.60 SB archive HRC.

236   "You do not often scold me": SB to Evelyn Gendel 7.10.60 SB archive HRC.

237   "seemingly a man with little taste for fiction": *The Trial of Lady Chatterley's Lover* p. 7.

237   "embarrassing to watch": ibid. p. 30.

237   "unemotional, cool, undramatic": ibid. p. 15.

237   "He had never in his life": ibid. p. 58.

237   "I felt so desperately strongly about it": SB to Evelyn Gendel 25.11.60 SB archive HRC.

238   "you are ours": Robert Gottlieb to SB 10.3.61 SB archive HRC.

238   "wet, grey, cold, dreary": SB to Solita Solano 4.2.61 Janet Flanner & Solita Solano archive, Library of Congress, Washington.

238   "Dawdle time away whining": SB diaries 24.1.61 SB archive HRC.

238   "masterpiece, tour de force": *Manchester Guardian* 23.6.61.

239   "is an amazing achievement": James Stern to SB 22.2.61 SB archive HRC.

239   "I feel so much older": SB to Allanah Harper 19.4.61 SB archive HRC.

239 "intact, incredible": SB to Evelyn Gendel 17.4.61 SB archive HRC.

239 "a grade B acquaintance": SB to Evelyn Gendel 14.5.61 SB archive HRC.

239 "She worries me": SB to Evelyn Gendel 24.4.61 SB archive HRC.

240 "You're a good friend": SB to Martha Gellhorn 25.12.60 Martha Gellhorn Archive HGARC.

240 "Well," Aldous replied: *Aldous Huxley* Vol. 2 p. 282.

240 "Only then, with no sense of urgency": ibid.

240 "It was a curious and rather moving evening": SB to Allanah Harper 26.6.61 SB archive HRC.

240 "how good it was to meet again": Aldous Huxley to SB 3.7.61 SB archive HRC.

240 "Eva writes that he did not suffer": SB to Evelyn Gendel 9.12.63 SB archive HRC.

241 "the greatest moral influence on my life": *International Herald Tribune* 17.4.89.

241 "Aldous's unfailing goodwill": *Aldous Huxley 1894–1963: A Memorial Volume* p. 143.

241 "no counter lift in the evening": SB to Solita Solano 5.11.61 Janet Flanner & Solita Solano papers, Library of Congress, Washington.

241 "I have now finished my novel": SB to James Stern 8.4.62 James Stern archive British Library.

241 "my one attempt at fiction": *A Favourite of the Gods* p. ix.

243 "down to the village": ibid. p. 257.

243 "was a New Englander with a Harvard link": ibid. p. xv.

243 "Lyre-horned oxen": ibid. p. 28.

243 "I do think you are inclined": James Stern to SB 12.1.62 SB archive HRC.

243 "technical perfection": Allanah Harper to Cyril Connolly 5.2.62 Cyril Connolly archive McFarlin Library, Tulsa.

243 "Sibbie my hero": Martha Gellhorn to SB 12.11.63 SB archive HRC.

244 "in itself the power": Evelyn Gendel to SB 2.6.62 SB archive HRC.

244 "The book is wonderful": Robert Gottlieb to SB 6.12.62 SB archive HRC.

244 "an exceedingly good novel": *Spectator* 11.1.63.

244 "while capable of subtleties": *The Times* 10.1.63.

244 "the design vanishes into a flashy stream": *New Statesman* 11.1.63.

244 "Miss Bedford is often too consciously literary": *New York Review of Books* 1.6.63.

244 "[that] drags and sags": *New York Times* 8.4.63.

244 "It has been tremendously advertised": Nancy Mitford to Evelyn Waugh 23.12.62 *The Letters of Nancy Mitford and Evelyn Waugh* p. 470.

245 "Lovely first chapter": Evelyn Waugh to Nancy Mitford ibid. p. 471.

245 "I am very sick and sunk": SB to Evelyn Gendel 5.1.63 SB archive HRC.

245 "I feel poisoned by these reviews": SB to Evelyn Gendel 28.1.63 SB archive HRC.

245 "loud-mouthed and hostile": SB to James Stern 19.1.63 James Stern archive British Library.

TEN: "THE TREMENDOUS TRIALS OF OUR TIME"

246 "I love the look of it": SB to Solita Solano 15.7.62 Janet Flanner & Solita Solano papers, Library of Congress, Washington.

246 "We buy our food at Elsinore": SB to Charlotte Wolff 20.7.62 SB archive HRC.

247 "She weighs 35 kilo": SB to Allanah Harper 15.7.62 SB archive HRC.

247 "very conscious she was": ibid.

247 "*haute literature* in a rather *vieux jeux* way": SB to Evelyn Gendel 8.7.62 SB archive HRC.

247 "horrible, plebeian, ugly": SB to Evelyn Gendel 29.10.61 SB archive HRC.

247 "I don't like it": SB to Evelyn Gendel 10.12.62 SB archive HRC.

248 "*Esther . . . toujours très distante*": Katzi Nielsen to SB, 23.10.62 SB archive HRC.

248 "*Elle m'a accusé de chose*": Katzi Nielsen to SB, 27.8.62 SB archive HRC.

248 "*ces angoisses perpétuelles*": Katzi Nielsen to SB 28.4.62 SB archive HRC.

248 "I am afraid the situation": Esther Murphy to SB, 26.8.62 SB archive HRC.

248 "a kind of monster": SB to Evelyn Gendel 28.4.62 SB archive HRC.

248 "one of the stupidest women": SB to Evelyn Gendel 4.4.62 SB archive HRC.

249 "Oh dear I shall miss her": Nancy Mitford to Evelyn Waugh 28.11.62 *The Letters of Nancy Mitford and Evelyn Waugh* p. 467.

249 "Esther was a large sandy person": Nancy Mitford to Evelyn Waugh 3.12.62 *The Letters of Nancy Mitford* p. 342.

249 "*ta grande générosité envers moi*": Katzi Nielsen to SB 5.3.63 SB archive HRC.

250 "returned in a state of collapse": Eda Lord to Tania Stern 6.12.62 James Stern archive British Library.

250 "What's the use of being brilliant": *All We Know* p. 134.

250 "The view from every window": Eda Lord to Tania Stern 27.5.63 James Stern archive British Library.

250 "ravishing and no noise": SB to Laura Huxley 21.2.63 Aldous & Laura Huxley archive University of California, Los Angeles.

250 "thirty-five miles from Venice": SB to James Stern 23.2.63 James Stern archive British Library.

250 "the inside of a meat grinder": SB to Solita Solano 5.6.63 Janet Flanner & Solita Solano papers, Library of Congress, Washington.

251 "large motor coaches": SB to Elaine Robson-Scott 8.5.63 SB archive HRC.

251 "Below our bedroom windows": SB to Solita Solano 26.5.63 Janet Flanner & Solita Solano papers, Library of Congress, Washington.

251 "we find ourselves again making beds": Eda Lord to Tania Stern 27.5.63 James Stern archive British Library.

251 "She's a kitten": SB to Elaine Robson-Scott ?.6.63 SB archive HRC.

251 "no possibility of coming and going": Eda Lord to Barbara Gamow 23.10.63 George & Barbara Gamow archive Library of Congress, Washington.

251 "Allanah is being so very very sweet": SB to Evelyn Gendel 7.7.63 SB archive HRC.

252 "terribly. I love her more than anyone": Evelyn Gendel to SB, 11.7.73 ibid.

252 "shutters closed from dawn to sinking sun": *A Compass Error* introduction.

252 "a true cave": SB *Harper's & Queen* October 1982.

252 "This place is bliss": SB to Martha Gellhorn 15.8.63 Martha Gellhorn archive HGARC.

252 "bare, clean and spacious": SB to James & Tania Stern 15.10.63 James Stern archive British Library.

252 "No noise except cicadas": SB to Martha Gellhorn 15.8.63 Martha Gellhorn archive HGARC.

253 "devastatingly sexually attractive": unpublished typescript SB archive HRC.

253 "Not only the mean little voice": ibid.

253 "festively decked out": ibid.

253 "His presence came as a shock": ibid.

253 "a kind of flat gloom": ibid.

254 "what that sentence would have been": ibid.

254 "a case of judicial murder": *Observer* 30.4.89.

254 "strange, doomed business": SB to Evelyn Gendel 31.7.63 SB archive HRC.

254 "Tortiss Tortiss Tortiss": Evelyn Gendel to SB 14.12.63 SB archive HRC.

254 "Darling listen": Evelyn Gendel to SB 27.12.63 SB archive HRC.

255 "rushed off feet": SB to Allanah Harper 7.2.64 SB archive HRC.

255 "the most hideous town I have ever seen": SB to Allanah Harper 15.2.64 SB archive HRC.

255 "2 TV sets & 4 telephones": SB to Charlotte Wolff 23.2.64 SB archive HRC.

255 "Last night at dinner": SB to Allanah Harper 15.2.64 SB archive HRC.

255 "I had five mortal weeks at Dallas": SB to Tom Matthews 14.4.64 T.S. Matthews archive Princeton University Library.

255 "lying back in his chair": "The Trial of Jack Ruby for the Murder of Lee Harvey Oswald" *As It Was: Pleasures, Landscapes and Justice* p. 200.

255 "bumbles about the scene": ibid. p. 172.

255 "with a kind of dead-chicken stare": ibid. p. 199.

256 "overflowing with humanity": ibid. p. 211.

256 "the long-discarded forensic art": ibid. p. 214.

256 "I did sixteen thousand words": SB to Allanah Harper 5.4.64 SB archive HRC.

256 "The summary of the testimony": *Salt Lake Telegram* 25.3.64.

256 "feted everywhere": SB to the Sterns 2.5.64 James Stern archive British Library.

256 "has put on some weight": SB to Robson-Scotts 14.4.64 SB archive HRC.

256 "I only know there's red wine": author's interview with Robert Gottlieb 13.6.11.

257 "with the help of Manhattan's finest butcher": *Avid Reader: A Life* by Robert Gottlieb p. 48.

257 "We had a good time together": author's interview with Robert Gottlieb 13.6.11.

257 "I miss you so much": Evelyn Gendel to SB, 15.4.64 SB archive HRC.

257 "I'm deeply, intrinsically attached": *Paris Review* no. 126 p. 246.

257 "I admired her so": SB to Evelyn Gendel 3.7.65 SB archive HRC.

258 "absolute, pure, nameless": *Martha Gellhorn: A Life* by Caroline Moorehead (Chatto & Windus, 2003) p. 393.

258 "the plain fact is I should never have married": Martha Gellhorn to SB 30.7.55 SB archive HRC.

258 "One was very sad for M": SB to Evelyn Gendel 28.9.63 SB archive HRC.

259 "The bliss of no housework": SB to Evelyn Gendel 14.4.63 SB archive HRC.

259 "I love Billy Hughes": SB to Evelyn Gendel 19.8.61 SB archive HRC.

259 "Sybille was obsessed with legal process": author's interview with Jenny Hughes 15.4.15.

259 "she was a very difficult person": ibid.

260 "Sybille was furious": author's interview with Anne Balfour-Fraser 3.6.10.

260 "I am devoted to Anne": SB to Evelyn Gendel 31.10.63 SB archive HRC.

260 "it was so beautiful . . . so magical": SB to Evelyn Gendel 10.12.64 SB archive HRC.

261 "like living with a caged tiger": Eda Lord to Barbara Gamow 15.10.64 Gamow archive, Library of Congress, Washington.

261 "One could not ask": *A Compass Error* Introduction.

262 "Katzi can work": SB to Noël Murphy 12.1.67 SB archive HRC.

262 "sorting, packing, rearranging": Eda Lord to Barbara Gamow 11.12.64 Gamow archive, Library of Congress, Washington.

262 "Yugoslavia was very exhausting": SB to Martha Gellhorn 11.6.65 Martha Gellhorn archive HGARC.

262 "anything more would have been unendurable": *As It Was* p. 230.

262 "It filled me with a sick loathing": SB to Robert Gottlieb 5.3.65 SB archive HRC.

263 "the first large-scale case of its kind": *As It Was* p. 218.

263 "Some killed by injecting disinfectant": ibid. p. 225.

263 "What did you think these camps were for?": ibid. p. 221.

263 "Each one was asked": ibid. p. 225.

263 "a hot, grey, leaden morning": ibid. p. 257.

263 "he said in a voice no longer quite audible": ibid. p. 259.

263 "In my entire writing life": SB to David Lyle 6.9.66 SB archive HRC.

264 "Relieved," Sybille told Evelyn: SB to Evelyn Gendel 6.9.66 SB archive HRC.

264 "a story about people and events": *A Compass Error* Introduction.

264 "Bedford is of course a brilliant writer": Cass Canfield to Ian Parsons 20.12.63 Chatto & Windus archive University of Reading, Special Collections.

265 "Bob hit the ceiling": Evelyn Gendel to SB, 20.5.64 SB archive HRC.

265 "don't think up to it": SB to Evelyn Gendel 30.5.64 SB archive HRC.

265 "Aldous's influence on myself": SB to Ian Parsons 12.8.64 Chatto & Windus archive University of Reading, Special Collections.

265 "something of the first importance": SB to Evelyn Gendel 30.5.64 SB archive HRC.

265 "Do you realise": SB to Robert Gottlieb 5.3.65 SB archive HRC.

265 "the use and organisation and writing": SB to Evelyn Gendel 14.11.64 SB archive HRC.

265 "I am not going to be a tame biographer": SB to Robert Gottlieb 5.3.65 SB archive HRC.

266 "something commensurate with the kind of book": SB to Robert Gottlieb 5.3.65 SB archive HRC.

266 "an appropriate living wage": SB to Robert Gottlieb 18.4.65 SB archive HRC.

266 "This really does distress me": ibid.

266 "You say there must be something odd": Robert Gottlieb to SB, 19.9.65 SB archive HRC.

267 "it doesn't really matter very much": *A Compass Error* p. 49.

267 "the great handsome monster": ibid. p. 36.

268 "peacefully lying asleep": ibid. p. 106.

268 "Let me say at once": SB to Evelyn Gendel 12.4.68 SB archive HRC.

268 "don't let us argue about it": SB to Robert Gottlieb 12.4.68 SB archive HRC.

268 "I found that early monologue": James Stern to SB, 10.12.68 SB archive HRC.

268 "one colossal error in the construction": Allanah Harper to SB, 12.1.69 SB archive HRC.

268 "I was making an experiment": SB to Alexander Wilson 22.6.92 SB archive HRC.

268 "beautiful, civilised, clear-eyed": *Daily Mail* 14.10.68.

268 "a work of distinction": *Observer* 11.10.68.

268 "slightly maniacal about explanation": *Sunday Times* 13.10.68.

268 "curiously irrelevant, dated, and mannered": *Times Literary Supplement* 24.10.68.

268 "scholarly (in a modest way)": SB to Robert Gottlieb 12.4.68 SB archive HRC.

ELEVEN: "FOOD IS PART OF THE LOVE OF LIFE"

269 "I love food, good food": *Paris Review* no. 126 p. 248.

269 "Dear Mrs. David . . . I read 'Point de Venise' ": SB to Elizabeth David 9.7.63 Elizabeth David archive Schlesinger Library, Harvard University.

270 "Dear Mrs. Bedford, It isn't every day": Elizabeth David to SB 10.7.63 SB archive HRC.

270 "books, and books and books": SB to Allanah Harper 2.9.77 SB archive HRC.

271 "without whose friendly help": Preface to *Venus in the Kitchen* by Norman Douglas (Heinemann, 1952).

271 "v. v. tipsy": SB to Evelyn Gendel 21.3.65 SB archive HRC.

271 "oddly enough": Eda Lord to Barbara Gamow 11.10.66 Gamow archive Library of Congress, Washington.

271 "If one had to sum up in a few words": *Sunday Times* 1.1.67.

271 "I enjoy talking to you so much": Elizabeth David to SB 5.10.68 SB archive HRC.

271 "I was an innocent in those days": *Writing at the Kitchen Table: The Authorized Biography of Elizabeth David* by Artemis Cooper (Faber, 2011) p. 229.

272 "which—even if she began next week": Ian Parsons to Jan van Loewen 26.10.67 Chatto & Windus archive University of Reading, Special Collections.

272 "for the biography of one of the world's": SB to Robert Gottlieb 25.4.67 SB archive HRC.

272 "If you had serious objections": Evelyn Gendel to SB, 23.4.67 SB archive HRC.

272 "PUBLISHERS ARE PEOPLE TOO!" Robert Gottlieb to SB, 20.4.67 SB archive HRC.

272 "When I have, DV, ordinary books": SB to Evelyn Gendel 27.4.67 SB archive HRC.

273 "if a delivery date were inserted": Jan van Loewen to Ian Parsons 1.12.67 Chatto & Windus archive University of Reading, Special Collections.

273 "S&S rather generously let one choose": SB to Martha Gellhorn 26.8.68 Martha Gellhorn archive HGARC.

273 "Eda the general handyman": *Provence 1970: M. F. K. Fisher, Julia Child, James Beard and the Reinvention of American Taste* by Luke Barr (Clarkson Potter, 2013) p. 105.

273 "Last year's depression": SB to James Stern 16.3.68 James Stern archive, British Library.

273 "as well and strong this summer": SB to Martha Gellhorn 26.8.68 Martha Gellhorn archive HGARC.

274 "unprivate": SB to Evelyn Gendel 19.10.67 SB archive HRC.

274 "the sheer drudgery . . . of sifting, noting": SB to Martha Gellhorn 26.8.68 Martha Gellhorn archive HGARC.

274 "The Huxleys most kind and hospitable": SB to Allanah Harper 16.12.68 SB archive HRC.

274 "[I] did enjoy Washington": SB to Martha Gellhorn 0.12.68 Martha Gellhorn archive HGARC.

274 "is kindness herself ": SB to James Stern 31.12.68 James Stern archive British Library.

274 "Eda tells me every morning": SB to Martha Gellhorn 24.1.69 Martha Gellhorn archive HGARC.

274 "shrivelled with boredom": SB to James Stern 31.12 68 James Stern archive British Library.

274 "Smoking is the very devil": Eda Lord to James Stern 31.12.68 James Stern archive British Library.

274 "miles and miles of broad sand": Eda Lord to James Stern 31.12.68 James Stern archive British Library.

275 "it became almost a mediumistic thing": SB article *Publisher's Weekly* 7.4.69.

275 "could not have been more agreeable and exciting": SB to Allanah Harper 6.2.69 SB archive HRC.

275 "Sybille Bedford . . . is a hypochondriacal mess": *Christopher Isherwood The Sixties Diaries Vol. Two: 1960–1969* ed. Katherine Bucknell (Chatto & Windus, 2010) p. 541.

275 "I was a bit overawed": SB to Allanah Harper 6.2.69 SB archive HRC.

275 "Life here is really too crass": SB to Tania Stern 17.2.69 James Stern archive British Library.

275 "has more than fulfilled all I dreamed": M. F. K. Fisher to Donald & Eleanor Friede 18.6.60 *A Life in Letters: Correspondence, 1929–1991* by M. F. K. Fisher selected and compiled by Norah K. Barr, Marsha Moran, Patrick Moran (Counterpoint, 1998) p. 169.

275 "a whole human being": Clifton Fadiman Foreword by Bee Wilson to *The Gastronomical Me* by M. F. K. Fisher (Daunt Books, 2017), p. x.

276 "I cannot make her out": SB to Barbara Gamow 13.3.69 George & Barbara Gamow archive Library of Congress, Washington.

276 "I feel as if she is nourished on cobwebs": M. F. K. Fisher to Paul & Julia Child 13.7.69 Julia Child archive Schlesinger Library, Harvard University.

276 "Tom seems very well and contented": SB to Evelyn Gendel 0.5.69 SB archive HRC.

276 "We talked and talked": SB to Evelyn Gendel 18.5.69 SB archive HRC.

277 "I've written to my Swiss bank": Martha Gellhorn to SB 27.7.69 SB archive HRC.

277 "This will make the whole difference": SB to Martha Gellhorn 2.8.70 Martha Gellhorn archive HGARC.

277 "revising, retyping, cutting": SB to Martha Gellhorn 2.8.70 Martha Gellhorn archive HGARC.

277 "I have to begin by transcribing": SB to Martha Gellhorn 2.8.70 Martha Gellhorn archive HGARC.

277 "gimcrack modernissimo": SB to Evelyn Gendel 25.9.70 SB archive HRC.

278 "I buckled down and finished it": Eda Lord to Barbara Gamow 20.11.70 George & Barbara Gamow archive Library of Congress, Washington.

278 "a v. large section of the US Cooking Establishment": SB to Elizabeth David 23.12.70 Elizabeth David archive Schlesinger Library, Harvard University.

278 "One likes them immensely": SB to Evelyn Gendel 27.11.67 SB archive HRC.

279 "professionally she is Trilby to his Svengali": M. F. K. Fisher to Eda Lord 19.2.75 M. F. K. Fisher archive Schlesinger Library, Harvard University.

279 "We had a smashing evening": Julia Child to M. F. K. Fisher 2.6.69 Julia Child Additional Papers, 1890–2004, Schlesinger Library, Radcliffe Institute, Harvard University.

279 "like the dear unflappable, slightly clumsy, St. Bernard": SB to Evelyn Gendel 3.2.68 SB archive HRC.

280 "competent, enamoured of French food": SB to Evelyn Gendel 27.11.67 SB archive HRC.

280 "He lives <u>so</u> outside the world": SB diaries 19.1.80 SB archive HRC.

280 "Dinner was superb": M. F. K. Fisher to James Beard 10.10.70 *Epicurean Delight: the Life and Times of James Beard* by Evan Jones (Knopf, 1990) p. 285.

281 "Eda was gentle and comfortable": *Reflexions* by Richard Olney Introduction by Alice Waters (Brick Tower Press, 1999) p. 38.

281 "I had a couple of evening sessions": Richard Olney to James Olney ibid. p. 127.

281 "strange, gastronomical capers": M. F. K. Fisher to Paul & Julia Child 13.7.69 Julia Child archive Schlesinger Library, Harvard University.

281 "I almost never see Eda": M. F. K. Fisher to Arnold Gingrich 22.11.70 M. F. K. Fisher archive Schlesinger Library, Harvard University.

281 "bubbly cough": Julia Child to M. F. K. Fisher 2.6.69 M. F. K. Fisher archive Schlesinger Library, Harvard University.

281 "Sybille is very bad for Eda": *Reflexions* by Richard Olney p. 127.

281 "from her workroom": Eda Lord to Richard Olney ibid. p. 133.

281 "A great nineteenth-century wine": SB to Raymond Mortimer 9.9.78 Raymond Mortimer archive Princeton University Library.

281 "had loved wine from childhood": *A Compass Error* p. 32.

282 "I quite seriously think": SB to James Stern 16.3.68 James Stern archive British Library.

282 "pretty mediocre": SB to Martha Gellhorn 5.5.71 Martha Gellhorn archive HGARC.

282 "This was a great labour": *Harper's & Queen* October 1982.

282 "siren song": ibid.

282 "a simple persuasive plan": ibid.

282 "twice each year I work out my needs": ibid.

283 "That is what is so fascinating about wine": *Harper's & Queen* 1975.

283 "We are dismayed about it": SB to Evelyn Gendel 23.5.71 SB archive HRC.

283 "Flat pretty awful": SB to Evelyn Grendel 22.6.71 SB archive HRC.

283 "with an acacia tree which I adore": SB to Allanah Harper 11.7.71 SB archive HRC.

284 "She said 7.30, came at 8.20": SB to Eda Lord 21.8.71 SB archive HRC.

284 "Leaving England was a wrench": SB to James & Tania Stern 12.10.71 James Stern archive British Library.

284 "almost weekly: another tall building": SB to Laura Huxley 9.12.72 Laura Huxley archive University of California, Los Angeles.

284 "the physical ease of reaching them": ibid.

284 "I have some ungood news": Evelyn Gendel to SB, 5.1.71 SB archive HRC.

285 "I couldn't be happier": Evelyn Gendel to SB 27.4.73 ibid.

285 "What I am trying to do": SB to James Stern 16.11.71 James Stern archive British Library.

285 "a sort of breakdown": SB to Solita Solano 15.11.72 Janet Flanner & Solita Solano archive, Library of Congress, Washington.

285 "It's very disagreeable": SB to Evelyn Gendel 19.12.72 SB archive HRC.

285 "unhappy, defeatist, tired": SB to James & Tania Stern 1.10.72 James Stern archive British Library.

285 "nice to her, niceish": SB to Tania Stern 2.5.73 James Stern archive British Library.

285 "I'm becoming more worried about Eda": SB to Tania Stern 12.1.76 James Stern archive British Library.

286 "I gather it's the old old deep-seated depression": SB to James & Tania Stern 3.10.72 James Stern archive British Library.

286 "wearing chains all the time": *The Times* 17.2.84.

286 "How Aldous grows": SB to Laura Huxley 19.12.72 Laura Huxley archive University of California, Los Angeles.

286 "brave, splendid beast": Evelyn Gendel to SB 23.2.73 SB archive HRC.

286 "Just when I thought that all was smooth": SB to Tania Stern 22.5.73 James Stern archive British Library.

287 "the eye-strain, the boredom": SB to James & Tania Stern 9.6.73 James Stern archive British Library.

287 "so strange, and flat": SB to Allanah Harper 12.8.73 SB archive HRC.

287 "The object of this book": *Aldous Huxley* Vol. 1 p. xi.

288 "I never confirmed nor denied": SB diaries 10.7.85 SB archive HRC.

288 "To us," Sybille wrote: *Aldous Huxley* Vol. 1 p. 132.

288 "She would leave England the next morning": ibid. p. 137.

288 "Cheshire Cat manner": *The Times* 1.11.73.

289 "The book enchanted me": Raymond Mortimer to SB 18.10.74 SB archive HRC.

289 "I can't wait to shout my admiration": Graham Greene to SB 5.12.73 SB archive HRC.

289 "a gentle man with steel selfishness": Martha Gellhorn to SB 1.12.73 SB archive HRC.

289 "Poor Sybille," he wrote: Matthew Huxley to Norah Smallwood 9.11.73 Chatto & Windus archive, University of Reading, Special Collections.

289 "the major work on a major figure": *New Statesman* 20.9.74.

289 "she doesn't recognise with completely clear eyes": *Financial Times* 19.9.74.

290 "gossipy, flighty, unintellectual": *Nation*.

290 "slapdash prose": *World*.

290 "deficiencies of critical perceptivity": *New York Times Book Review* 24.11.74.

290 "not only unsatisfactory": Philip Toynbee *Observer* 26.10.73.

290 "I feel curiously crushed": SB to James & Tania Stern 4.11.73 James Stern archive British Library.

290 "told her if she didn't stop smoking": *Reflexions* by Richard Olney p. 174.

290 "the last ten days, she was better": SB to Tania Stern 2.5.73 James Stern archive British Library.

291 "the monster task": SB to Tania Stern 4.9.74 ibid.

291 "After Eda left": author's interview with Anne Balfour-Fraser 3.6.10.

291 "expenses paid by Alfred A. Knopf Inc.": SB to Tania Stern 4.9.74 James Stern archive British Library.

291 "all a bit unbelieving": SB to Allanah Harper 14.12.74 Allanah Harper archive HRC.

291 "did not enthuse about": Eda Lord to James & Tania Stern 24.11.74 James Stern archive British Library.

292 "showing editor supine": Evelyn Gendel to SB 8.5.74 SB archive HRC.

292 "I was terribly nervous": author's interview with Robert Gottlieb 13.6.11.

292 "and it <u>was</u> good": *Avid Reader: A Life* by Robert Gottlieb p. 48.

292 "I miss you": SB to Evelyn Gendel 8.12.74 SB archive HRC.

292   "Now I shall say": SB to Eda Lord 8.5.74 SB archive HRC.

292   "going all over London": SB to James & Tania Stern 19.5.74 James Stern archive British Library.

293   "It is in a quiet square": SB to Laura Huxley 12.1.76 Aldous & Laura Huxley archive University of California, Los Angeles.

293   "We shall have the maisonette": SB to Tania Stern 21.1.76 James Stern archive British Library.

293   "Eda herself is very brave": SB to Allanah Harper 20.4.76 Allanah Harper archive HRC.

293   "A terrible thing, of course": Eda Lord to M. F. K. Fisher 19.5.76 M. F. K. Fisher archive Schlesinger Library, Harvard University.

293   "I feel jubilant": Eda Lord to M. F. K. Fisher M. F. K. Fisher archive Schlesinger Library, Harvard University.

293   "Physically and spiritually": SB to M. F. K. Fisher 13.6.76 M. F. K. Fisher archive Schlesinger Library, Harvard University.

294   "Even after nine days": Eda Lord to M. F. K. Fisher 15.7.76 M. F. K. Fisher archive Schlesinger Library, Harvard University.

294   "I had never known Eda": James Beard to SB, 23.11.76 SB archive HRC.

294   "eerily more beautiful": *Reflexions* by Richard Olney p. 205.

294   "charming & handsome": SB to Tania Stern 5.8.76 James Stern archive British Library.

294   "You MUST NOT always interrupt her": Martha Gellhorn to SB 10.8.76 SB archive HRC.

295   "Evelyn has created a festive round": SB to James Stern 26.8.76 James Stern archive British Library.

295   "in the glorious unbroken warmth": ibid.

295   "years of unreturned hospitality": ibid.

295   "like fowl huddling away": SB to James Stern 3.9.76 James Stern archive British Library.

295   "It does seem inhuman": SB to Tania Stern 14.9.76 James Stern archive British Library.

295   "She seems very ill": SB to Tania Stern 17.10.76 James Stern archive British Library.

295   "to see a human being disintegrating": SB to Allanah Harper 12.10.76 Allanah Harper archive HRC.

296   "Eda is not recovering": SB to M. F. K. Fisher 19.10.76 M. F. K. Fisher archive Schlesinger Library, Harvard University.

296   "[I] do not hold": SB to Allanah Harper 17.10.76 Allanah Harper archive HRC.

296   "I believe, when all is said": SB to M. F. K. Fisher 22.11.89 M. F. K. Fisher archive Schlesinger Library, Harvard University.

296   "absence now is almost": SB to James Stern 5.11.76 James Stern archive British Library.

TWELVE: "NOVELS AMONG OTHER THINGS ARE GALLERIES OF MIRRORS"

297   "Grief is something so unlike": SB to Tania Stern 5.1.77 James Stern archive British Library.

297   "Eda was so well": SB to Tania Stern 7.1.78 James Stern archive British Library.

298 "Going back to Les Bastides": SB to M. F. K. Fisher 10.3.77 M. F. K. Fisher archive Schlesinger Library, Harvard University.

298 "Here I am in Allanah's spare room": SB to James & Tania Stern 9.4.77 James Stern archive British Library.

298 "The news is unexpectedly good": SB to Allanah Harper 17.7.77 Allanah Harper archive HRC.

298 "wanted to say that she has more money": SB to Evelyn Gendel 21.9.77 SB archive HRC.

298 "I love that place": Evelyn Gendel to SB 13.8.77 SB archive HRC.

299 "interesting, often stimulating": SB to Allanah Harper 6.7.77 Allanah Harper archive HRC.

299 "The giving and taking of affection": ibid.

299 *"en beauté,* as easy to talk to as ever": SB to Alannah Harper 2.9.77 Allanah Harper archive HRC.

299 "an intellectual cocktail party": SB to Allanah Harper 17.10.77 Allanah Harper archive HRC.

299 "Too much standing of course": SB to Allanah Harper 2.9.77 Allanah Harper archive HRC.

299 "I spend the day on bed": Evelyn Gendel to SB 19.7.77 SB archive HRC.

299 "Only sign is": Evelyn Gendel to SB 20.8.77 SB archive HRC.

299 "Really bucked that we've agreed": ibid.

300 "I have no cancer": Evelyn Gendel to SB 15.9.77 SB archive HRC.

300 "Last night, her 3rd day": SB to Tania Stern 22.9.77 James Stern archive British Library.

300 "They told me not to come": SB to Tania Stern 7.1.78 James Stern archive British Library.

300 "her heart gave out": SB to Elizabeth David 31.12.77 Elizabeth David archive Schlesinger Library, Harvard University.

300 "I cannot believe it yet": SB to Tania Stern 7.1.78 James Stern archive British Library.

300 "Write at last a handwritten note": SB diaries SB archive HRC.

301 "a dear, sensitive, rather subtle person": SB to Allanah Harper 31.8.77 SB archive HRC.

301 "I felt curiously shy at first": ibid.

301 "looking as lovely": SB diaries 8.7.83 SB archive HRC.

301 "struck as so often": SB diaries 4.10.78 SB archive HRC.

302 "quite a project": *Reflexions* by Richard Olney p. 227.

302 "gasps and more crossings": ibid.

302 "as pure an enterprise for pleasure": *Pleasures and Landscapes* p. 147.

303 "the steel vats gleam": ibid. p. 149.

303 "We are offered three clarets": ibid. p. 151.

303 *"Vignerons, négociants"*: ibid. p. 152.

303 "Do you think I'm worthy": *Reflexions* by Richard Olney p. 232.

303 "do not give their best": *Pleasures and Landscapes* p. 152.

303 "ravishing, low-built": ibid. p. 153.

303 "we returned to the long drawing room": ibid. p. 155.

303 "so perfect that it is hard": SB to James & Tania Stern 20.6.78 James Stern archive British Library.

304 "She has difficulties with her speech": SB to Allanah Harper 26.11.77 Allanah Harper archive HRC.

304 "in a lamentable state": SB to Tania Stern 7.1.76 James Stern archive British Library.

304 "a heartbroken, and helpless, man": SB to Julia Child 15.10.78 Julia Child archive Schlesinger Library, Harvard.

304 "heart turns over": SB diaries 10.12.78 SB archive HRC.

304 "thin, hard-drinking": SB to Evelyn Gendel 16.7.65 SB archive HRC.

304 "muffled, stiff . . . playing at wood-cutters": SB diaries 30.12.78 SB archive HRC.

305 "minute & magical": SB to Tania Stern 5.1.77 James Stern archive British Library.

305 "*pipe au bec*": SB diaries 29.12.79 SB archive HRC.

305 "drinks, buttling, spitting": SB diaries 31.12.79 SB archive HRC.

305 "liking it more and more": SB to M. F. K. Fisher 25.12.78 M. F. K. Fisher archive Schlesinger Library, Harvard University.

305 "the life, the friends": SB to Tania Stern 3.11.80 James Stern archive British Library.

306 "whole thing sordid/tedious": notes for an unpublished article, SB archive HRC.

306 "I find it very hard": SB to M. F. K. Fisher 3.2.81 M. F. K. Fisher archive Schlesinger Library, Harvard University.

306 "She talks as it were to herself ": Elaine Robson-Scott to Tania Stern 17.6.85 James Stern archive British Library.

306 "great tease has sprung up": SB diaries 22.10.79 SB archive HRC.

306 "Someone says Shirley": SB diaries 12.1.79 SB archive HRC.

307 "Suspect of leftish tendencies": SB diaries 2.2.80 SB archive HRC.

307 "very lovely, very Junoesque": SB diaries 6.4.83 SB archive HRC.

307 "about food, cookery": SB diaries 2.2.80 SB archive HRC.

307 "one of the most exhilarating travel books": *New York Review of Books* November 1978.

307 "a very good animated evening": SB diaries 19.11.78 SB archive HRC.

307 "one of the 'weirdest' I ever had": SB diaries 14.7.83 SB archive HRC.

308 "raced out and snatched the decanter": *Reflexions* by Richard Olney p. 236.

308 "a very good evening": SB diaries 31.8.78 SB archive HRC.

308 "weird amalgamation": SB diaries 12.4.79 SB archive HRC.

309 "had extraordinary sweetness": SB to Allanah Harper 21.12.89 SB archive HRC.

309 " 'How extraordinary!' S is moved to say": SB diaries 5.4.79 SB archive HRC.

309 "Full of tension, waiting for L": SB diaries 18.5.79 SB archive HRC.

309 "It's such an improbable thing": SB to James Stern 3.2.81 James Stern archive British Library.

310 "I went without": SB to Robert Hertzberg 5.6.81 SB archive HRC.

310 "and up I went": ibid.

310 "to show off the order": ibid.

310 "to celebrate *à deux*": ibid.

310 "Unrequited love": *Jigsaw* p. 218.

311 "It's two a.m. outside in the car": SB diaries 8.1.81 SB archive HRC.

311 "feeling better physically": SB diaries 9.1.81 SB archive HRC.

311 "Unhappy afternoon": SB diaries 10.1.81 SB archive HRC.

311 "but fails to say when": SB diaries 19.2.81 SB archive HRC.

311 "Self-preservation, or the death of the heart": ibid.

311 "I kept saying": author's interview with Anne Balfour-Fraser 3.6.10.

311 "a young and pretty painter": SB to Tom Matthews 14.4.81.

312 "lowering like a brooding thundercloud": SB diaries 7.6.81 SB archive HRC.

312 "some very good moments": SB diaries 5.4.81 SB archive HRC.

312 "deliciously, happily, gladly": Rosamund Williams to SB 22.9.81 SB archive HRC.

312 "less and less pleasant": SB diaries 8.10.81 SB archive HRC.

312 "tiresome little woman": SB diaries 25.2.82 SB archive HRC.

312 "All so much more easy": SB diaries 4.4.81 SB archive HRC.

312 "I do love her": SB diaries 27.4.81 SB archive HRC.

312 "Such wonderful country": SB to James Stern 3.11.81 James Stern archive British Library.

313 "a very personal book": SB to Robert Gottlieb 17.1.74 SB archive HRC.

313 "Writing does take it out of one": SB to Evelyn Gendel 17.1.74 SB archive HRC.

313 "The warmth all a bit *à côté*": SB diaries 18.5.82 SB archive HRC.

313 "leave sad, weighed down": SB diaries 19.4.83 SB archive HRC.

313 "literary, local residents": SB to M. F. K. Fisher 31.5.81 M. F. K. Fisher archive Schlesinger Library, Harvard University.

313 "I do believe that there are marked differences": SB diaries 20.2.81 SB archive HRC.

313 "I listened to the prime minister": SB to Tania Stern 25.2.80 James Stern archive British Library.

314 "PEN parties are curiously non-nightowley": SB diaries 4.8.85 SB archive HRC.

314 "quite nice dinner": SB diaries 16.6.82 SB archive HRC.

314 "muddle, muddle all the way": SB to James & Tania Stern 30.9.81 James Stern archive British Library.

314 "in constant tow": SB to James & Tania Stern 23.10.81 James Stern archive British Library.

314 " 'J' is worse than a gulper": SB diaries 13.7.82 SB archive HRC.

314 "I feel very privileged": SB to Tania Stern 9.9.82 James Stern archive British Library.

314 "so much touchiness": SB to Lesley Houston 3.11.82 SB archive HRC.

314 "Very weary making": SB diaries 23.10.82 SB archive HRC.

315 "there were good moments": SB to Lesley Huston 3.11.82 SB archive HRC.

315 "I cannot say how much J bores me": SB diaries 21.12.82 SB archive HRC.

315 "After the appalling initial dithering": SB diaries 30.4.83 SB archive HRC.

315 "I've been embarrassed to ask you": Robert Gottlieb to SB 21.2.86 SB archive HRC.

315 "You are right to ask": SB to Robert Gottlieb 17.3.86 SB archive HRC.

316 "Reagan antagonism": SB diaries 21.4.83 SB archive HRC.

316 "Odd to be really fond of someone": SB diaries 11.9.83 SB archive HRC.

316 "she is a good friend": SB diaries 4.9.83 SB archive HRC.

316 "B[etsy] had a blast from Martha": SB diaries 21.1.83 SB archive HRC.

316 "Sybille, you are too boring": *Martha Gellhorn: A Life* by Caroline Moorehead p. 484.

316 "Please don't involve yourself": Martha Gellhorn to Betsy Drake 13.9.83 *The Letters of Martha Gellhorn* p. 456.

317 "She'll never understand the pleasure": SB diaries 18.12.78 SB archive HRC.

317 "she does hurt people; always did": SB diaries 25.9.83 SB archive HRC.

317 "I had again that sense of tenderness": SB to Lesley Huston 21.9.83 SB archive HRC.

317 "made self a simple": SB diaries 24.11.80 SB archive HRC.

317 "KR enters chattering": SB diaries 4.7.80 SB archive HRC.

318 "the neighbourliness of one's neighbours": SB diaries 6.5.85 SB archive HRC.

318 "I can't thank you enough": SB to Simon Loftus 25.3.85 SB archive HRC.

318 "quite a literary and literate girl": SB diaries 22.11.82 SB archive HRC.

319 "the horror . . . and shame of a German origin": SB diaries 1.6.85 SB archive HRC.

319 "that served impeccable *entrecôte grillé*": *A Thousand Acres: Writings from "Country Life"* by Carla Cooper Carlisle (Snakeshead Press, 2014) p. 156.

319 "a crazy, obsessed teenager": Carla Carlisle to author 7.9.18.

319 "Life is so much less joyful": SB to Lesley Huston 6.12.84 SB archive HRC.

319 "[I] could easily get into mischief": SB to Lesley Huston 16.12.84 SB archive HRC.

320 "How wonderful that you're well into the book": Robert Gottlieb to SB 24.3.86 SB archive HRC.

320 "I get up late—about 11 a.m.": *Royal Society of Literature Magazine* Summer 1995.

320 "Liked it from the first moment": SB diaries 5.10.83 SB archive HRC.

320 "used to say to me": author's interview with Elizabeth Jane Howard 1.3.08.

321 "breathtakingly tactless": author's interview with Betsy Drake 18.4.08.

321 "I really let her": ibid.

321 "my enthusiasm for your writing": Betsy Drake to SB 28.6.88 SB archive HRC.

321 "I enjoyed it enormously": Charles Elliott to SB 1.7.88 SB archive HRC.

322 "It is a most powerful": Richard Ollard to SB 17.8.88 SB archive HRC.

322 "Novels among other things": SB to M. F. K. Fisher 22.11.89 M. F. K. Fisher archive Schlesinger Library, Harvard University.

322 "in plain words": *Jigsaw* p. 354.

322 "I wanted to do them justice": SB to M. F. K. Fisher 22.11.89 M. F. K. Fisher archive Schlesinger Library, Harvard University.

323 "Dear Sibbie: The writing of *Jigsaw*": Martha Gellhorn to SB 22.7.89 SB archive HRC.

323 "a beautiful book, the best of a good lot": Tom Matthews to SB 30.5.89 SB archive HRC.

323 "Such a stimulating letter from you": SB to Tom Matthews 31.5.89 T. S. Matthews archive Princeton University Library.

323 "stylish, casual, exhilarating": *Spectator* 20.5.89.

323 "the pleasure of places": *Sunday Times* 7.5.89.

323 "dread those occasions in the story": *Daily Telegraph* 6.5.89.

323 "a treasure of a book": *Chicago Tribune*.

324 "compulsively readable": *New York Review of Books* 27.4.89.

324 "I called it biographic": SB to M. F. K. Fisher 22.11.89 M. F. K. Fisher archive Schlesinger Library, Harvard University.

THIRTEEN: "GETTING OLD & WEAK IS HORRIBLE"

325 "Sybille was a gentleman": "Sybille" by Jenny MacKilligin 14.8.18 unpublished article.

326 "It's not easy to be my friend": *Telegraph Magazine* 11.8.05.
326 "I very much like the Garrick": SB to Tom Matthews 1.11.79 T.S. Matthews archive Princeton University Library.
327 "I wish I were still in travelling shape": SB to Julia Child 10.3.89 Julia Child archive Schlesinger Library, Harvard University.
327 "I'm afraid I've got used": SB to M. F. K. Fisher 22.11.89 M. F. K. Fisher archive Schlesinger Library, Harvard University.
327 "although all I knew about wine": author's interview with Penelope Bennett 3.11.18.
328 "What happiness can do": SB to Lesley Huston 7.6.84 SB archive HRC.
328 "angelic and generous": SB to Tania Stern 11.1.87 James Stern archive British Library.
328 "I am so pleased": SB to John Hatt 1.8.91 Eland Books archive.
329 "distinguished but somewhat imprecise status": *Independent* 8.9.90.
329 "very frail and distraught": SB to Bush Maier-Graefe 6.12.93 SB archive HRC.
330 "Thank you so much for trusting me": Aliette Martin to SB 11.9.91 SB archive HRC.
330 "Aldous Huxley *et le projet de traduction*": Aliette Martin to SB 10.9.92 SB archive HRC.
330 "horribly nervous": Aliette Martin unpublished memoir.
330 "*vous me manquez*": ibid.
330 "the three fatal words": *Jigsaw* p. 211.
330 "tut-tutted . . . but somehow": ibid.
331 "Sybille told me, '*j'accepte*' ": ibid.
331 "in her breathless, passionate, sotto voce": ibid.
331 "gently put [her] foot down": ibid.
331 "Dinner had to be a great moment": ibid.
331 "After lunch . . . a sort of heaviness": ibid.
331 "She was opening a whole world": ibid.
332 "suddenly radiant, a girl": *Observer* 13.3.11.
332 "I met Aliette when the three of us had dinner": author's interview with Elizabeth Jane Howard 1.3.08.
332 "turned her face towards me": Aliette Martin unpublished memoir.
332 "an immensely *simpatico* man": SB to Robert Hertzberg 14.5.93 SB archive HRC.
332 "august writers . . . [as] Evelyn Waugh": ibid.
333 "Although this so-called autobiographical stuff": SB to Robert Gottlieb 17.1.74 SB archive HRC.
333 "[Now] the writer actually has to write": *Quicksands* p. 163.
333 "insect's traces": ibid.
333 "the precious sheets": Aliette Martin unpublished memoir.
333 "it was an extraordinary discovery": ibid.
334 "I warned them that she was very boring": author's interview with Elizabeth Jane Howard 1.3.08.
334 "the meal turned out": ibid.
334 "half killed me": SB to Robert Hertzberg 22.12.97 SB archive HRC.
334 "but in good spirits": *Reflexions* by Richard Olney p. 376.
335 "I'm not musical": *Desert Island Discs* BBC radio 10.7.98.
335 "I do think that emancipation of women": *Country Life* 17.12.98.

335 "the overrunning of this earth": *Times* 20.12.75.

335 "The one problem that no one dares": *Country Life* 17.12.98.

336 "a Quaker saint": Aliette Martin unpublished memoir.

336 "Look how my hands are shaking!": author's interview with Robin Dalton.

337 "Sybille was delighted": author's interview with Sarah Lutyens 15.1.19.

337 "Enchanting. Full of delights": Sarah Lutyens to Simon Prosser 19.8.04 email.

337 "is a truly beautiful book": Simon Prosser to SB 1.9.04 SB archive HRC.

338 "My difficulties now that I have committed myself ": *Quicksands* p. 56.

338 "I would like to have been able": ibid. p. 36.

338 "To read this fascinating book": *Criterion* May 2005.

339 "positively chaotic": *New Yorker* 18.4.05.

339 "brilliant and original writer": *New York Review of Books* 11.8.05.

339 "she tells us for the third time": *Observer* 18.6.05.

339 "Standing beside her bed": *Sybille Bedford: In Memory* by Elsie Burch Donald (Eland Books, 2007) p. 37.

340 "She was in great pain": author's interview with Aliette Martin 15.3.13.

340 "her company was always refreshing": *Sybille Bedford: In Memory* by Elsie Burch Donald p. 54.

341 "I remember that our first talk": Brenda Wineapple's introduction to *The New York Review of Books*'s edition of *A Legacy* was first published in the *NYRB* journal on 5.3.15.

INDEX

A NOTE ON THE TYPE

Pierre Simon Fournier *le jeune* (1712–1768), who designed the type used in this book, was both an originator and a collector of types. His services to the art of printing were his design of letters, his creation of ornaments and initials, and his standardization of type sizes. His types are old style in character and sharply cut. In 1764 and 1766 he published his *Manuel typographique*, a treatise on the history of French types and printing, on typefounding in all its details, and on what many consider his most important contribution to typography—the measurement of type by the point system.

Composed by North Market Street Graphics,
Lancaster, Pennsylvania

Printed and bound by Berryville Graphics,
Berryville, Virginia

Designed by Cassandra J. Pappas